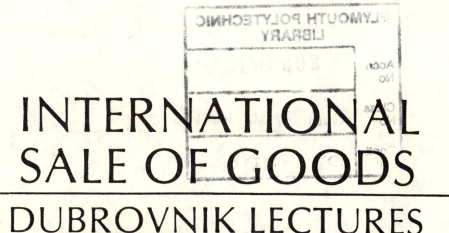
INTERNATIONAL SALE OF GOODS

DUBROVNIK LECTURES

Edited by

PETAR ŠARČEVIĆ
Rijeka/Lausanne

PAUL VOLKEN
Berne/Fribourg

OCEANA PUBLICATIONS, INC. NEW YORK • LONDON • ROME

Library of Congress Cataloging-in-Publication Data

Main entry under title:

International sale of goods.

   "Based on the lectures presented at a postgraduate
course on the international sale of goods, held 11-23
March 1985 at the Inter-university Centre (IUC) of
Postgraduate Studies at Dubrovnik, Yugoslavia"—
Foreword.
   Includes index.
   1. United Nations Convention on Contracts for the
International Sale of Goods (1980)—Congresses.
2. Export sales—Congresses.   I. Šarčević, Petar.
II. Volken, Paul.   III. Inter-university Centre of
Post-graduate Studies.   IV. Title: Dubrovnik lectures.
K1028.3198.157   1985   341.7'54   85-26028
ISBN 0-379-20835-0

© Copyright 1986 by Oceana Publications, Inc.

Manufactured in the United States of America

CONTENTS

FOREWORD v
ABBREVIATIONS vii
CONTRIBUTORS ix

CHAPTER ONE:
The Vienna Sales Convention: History and Perspective
(Kazuaki Sono) 1

CHAPTER TWO:
The Vienna Convention: Scope, Interpretation, and
Gap-Filling (Paul Volken) 19

CHAPTER THREE:
Usages of Trade and Other Autonomous Rules of Inter-
national Trade According to the UN (1980) Sales Convention
(Aleksandar Goldštajn) 55

CHAPTER FOUR:
Formation of International Contracts under the Vienna
Convention: A Shift above the Comparative Law
(Kazuaki Sono) 111

CHAPTER FIVE:
Rights and Obligations of the Seller under the UN
Convention on Contracts for the International Sale of
Goods (Fritz Enderlein) 133

CHAPTER SIX:
Obligations of the Buyer under the UN Convention on
Contracts for the International Sale of Goods (Leif Sevón) 203

CHAPTER SEVEN:
Provisions Common to the Obligations of the Seller and the
Buyer (Jelena Vilus) 239

CHAPTER EIGHT:
Passing of Risk in International Sales of Goods
(Bernd von Hoffmann) 265

CHAPTER NINE:
General Principles of European Contract Law
(Ulrich Drobnig) 305

CHAPTER TEN:
The Vienna Convention and Standard Form Contracts
(Jan Hellner) 335

CHAPTER ELEVEN:
The International Sales Price as Basis for Customs Valuation
(Hans van Houtte) 365

CHAPTER TWELVE:
Uniform Substantive and Conflicts Rules on the International
Sale of Goods and their Interaction (Giorgio Conetti) 385

CHAPTER THIRTEEN:
International Sales and Security Interests with an Outline
of Conflicts Laws (Hans Hoyer) 401

CHAPTER FOURTEEN:
The Geneva Convention on Agency in the International
Sale of Goods (Petar Šarčević) 443

INDEX 485

FOREWORD

The law on the international sale of goods is enjoying a period of revival. In the wake of the unsuccessful Hague Uniform Laws of 1964, UNCITRAL has succeeded in giving new life to an old hope: worldwide unification of the law of trade.

In promoting the Vienna Sales Convention of 1980, UNCITRAL has not only reactivated old dreams. The influence of the Vienna Convention should speed up unification in other fields of international trade law as well. Efforts to establish uniform rules of law on important matters such as agency, arbitration, prescription, payments on transportation, leasing, factoring, and others have already been or are about to be completed.

The finalization of these legal instruments marks the completion of only the first phase of interplay between legal theory and commercial reality. In the next stage the new legal texts must be made an integral part of international trade practice. This is where legal academia— research and teaching—comes into play.

The fourteen articles of this book are based on the lectures presented at a postgraduate course on the International Sale of Goods, held 11 - 23 March 1985 at the Inter-University Centre (IUC) of Postgraduate Studies at Dubrovnik, Yugoslavia. The IUC is an international, interuniversity organization devoted to the purpose of furthering teaching and research cooperation between academic institutions throughout the world. At present, 140 universities and other institutions of higher learning are members of the IUC, thus enabling them to take part in course planning, recruit resource persons, support student participation, etc.

Although this was the first time that the Dubrovnik Centre sponsored a course on international trade law, the almost astonishing international response has encouraged the Direction of IUC and the course directors to organize courses on topics related to international trade law on a regular basis.

The core of the articles in this volume forms a systematic commentary on the 1980 Vienna Convention on the International Sale of Goods. The main topic has been broadened to include related subject matters such as Agency, Sales price and Customs Valuation, Usages, and Standard Forms in International Contract Law.

The organization of the Dubrovnik seminar and publication of the lectures would not have been possible without the generous personal and financial support of many persons and institutions. The course directors—editors—would like to express their gratitude to all those who have contributed to the realization of the course and this book. In particular we owe our gratitutde to the Direction and Staff of the Inter-University Centre in Dubrovnik for making the course possible; to the Law Faculties at Rijeka and Trieste, Fribourg and Louvain, Trier and Vienna, Hamburg and Berlin-Potsdam, Stockholm and Helsinki, Zagreb and Novi Sad as well as to UNCITRAL and the Swiss Institute of

Comparative Law at Lausanne for supporting the participation of their professors and other specialists who lectured at the course.

Our thanks also goes to the University of Zagreb, the IUC in Dubrovnik, the Swiss National Fund, the German Akademischer Austauschdienst and the Industrie- und Handelstag for providing financial assistance and scholarships. Finally, we are deeply grateful to Dr. Susan Šarčević whose assistance has been instrumental in realizing this book. With her skill and endless patience she made the English language revisions and word-processed the entire manuscript.

Lausanne   Petar Šarčević
July 1985   Paul Volken

ABBREVIATIONS

Am.J.Comp.L.	American Journal of Compartive Law
Am.J.Int.Law	American Journal of International Law
Annuaire	Annuaire de l'Institut de Droit International
AWID	Zeitschrift "DDR-Aussenwirtschaft," Informationen — Dokumente
Brit.Yb.Int.L.	British Yearbook of International Law
D.P.C.I.	Droit et pratique du commerce international
ECR	European Court Reports
GA J.Int'l & Comp.L.	Georgia Journal of International and Comparative Law
Harv.Int'l L.J.	Harvard International Law Journal
I.E.C.L.	International Encyclopedia of Comparative Law
I.L.R.	International Law Reports
J.Bus.L.	Journal of Business Law
JWTL	Journal of World Trade Law
Law & Pol'y Int'l Bus.	Law & Policy in International Business
Lloyd's Mar. Comm.L.Q.	Lloyd's Maritime and Commercial Law Quarterly
NILR	Netherlands International Law Review formerly:
NTIR	Nederlands Tijdschrift voor International Recht
O.J. or O.J.E.C.	Offical Journal of the European Communities
RabelsZ	Rabels Zeitschrift für ausländisches und internationales Privatrecht
Recueil des Cours	Collected Courses, Hague Academy of International Law
Rev. belge dr.int.	Revue belge de droit international
Rev.crit.	Revue critique de droit international privé
Rev.dr.unif.	Revue de droit uniform
Rev.int.dr.comp.	Revue internationale de droit comparé
Rev.trim.dr.eur.	Revue trimestrielle de droit européen
Riv.dir.int.priv.proc.	Rivista di diritto internazionale privato e processuale
RIW/AWD	Recht der Internationalen Wirtschaft/Aussenwirtschaftsdienst des Betriebs-Beraters

U.N.T.S.	United Nations Treaty Series
Vand.L.Rev.	Vanderbilt Law Review
WM	Wertpapier-Mitteilungen
YaleLJ	Yale Law Journal
ZHR	Zeitschrift für das Gesamte Handelsrecht und Konkursrecht
ZSR	Zeitschrift für Schweizerisches Recht

CONTRIBUTORS

GIORGIO CONETTI, Professor of Law, University of Trieste, Italy; Director of the Institute of International Law, Trieste.

ULRICH DROBNIG, Professor of Law, University of Hamburg, FRG; Director of the Max Planck Institute for Foreign and Private International Law, Hamburg.

FRITZ ENDERLEIN, Professor of Law, Academy for Political and Legal Science of the GDR, Potsdam; Director of the Institute for Foreign and Comparative Law, Potsdam.

ALEKSANDAR GOLDŠTAJN, Professor of Law, University of Zagreb, Yugoslavia.

JAN HELLNER, Professor of Law, University of Stockholm, Sweden.

BERND von HOFFMAN, Professor of Law, University of Trier, FRG.

HANS van HOUTTE, Professor of Law, University of Louvain (K.U. Leuven), Belgium.

HANS HOYER, Professor of Law, University of Vienna, Austria; Director of the Institute of Comparative Law, Vienna.

LEIF SEVÓN, Director of Legislation, Ministry of Justice, Helsinki, Finland.

KAZUAKI SONO, Professor of Law, Hokkaido University, Sapporo, Japan; former Secretary of the United Nations Commission on International Trade Law, 1980-1985.

PETAR ŠARČEVIĆ, Professor of Law, University of Rijeka, Yugoslavia; Swiss Institute of Comparative Law, Lausanne, Switzerland.

JELENA VILUS, Professor of Law, University of Novi Sad, Yugoslavia; Scientific Advisor at the Institute of Comparative Law, Belgrade.

PAUL VOLKEN, Head of Section, Federal Office of Justice, Berne, Switzerland; Lecturer at the Law Faculty of the University of Fribourg.

INTERNATIONAL
SALE OF GOODS

DUBROVNIK LECTURES

CHAPTER ONE

THE VIENNA SALES CONVENTION: HISTORY AND PERSPECTIVE

KAZUAKI SONO
Secretary of UNCITRAL, Vienna

1. Introduction

With bright prospects for the entry into force of the United Nations Convention on Contracts for the International Sale of Goods of 1980, now popularly known as the Vienna Sales Convention,[1] unification at a global scale is finally in sight in this field after over half a century of efforts. The Vienna Sales Convention now enjoys praise throughout the world as a workmanlike attempt to devise legal rules and practical procedures for international sales transactions. Once the Vienna Sales Convention enters into force, it will assist to smooth the process of international sales.

The Convention will be made applicable to the sales contract concluded between parties having places of business in different Contracting States. Nationality of parties has no relevance to the application of the Convention. Freedom of contract has been retained. Most of the provisions of the Convention are supplementary to

agreements between parties. Detailed practical
and basic rules are provided to assist parties in
cases where their agreements do not otherwise
provide.

2. Predecessors: the 1964 Hague Conventions

The attempt to unify the law of international
sale of goods is not new in the international
arena. Indeed, the work of the United Nations
Commission on International Trade Law (UNCITRAL)
which resulted in the adoption of the Vienna
Sales Convention was the culmination of a long
process of unification in this area, whose origins go back to a decision of the International
Institute for the Unification of Private Law
(UNIDROIT) in 1930 to proceed with the preparation of a uniform law on the international sale
of goods under the auspices of the League of
Nations. As is well known, Professor Ernst Rabel's report submitted to UNIDROIT suggesting
both the feasibility and the desirability for the
unification was instrumental to this move. This
unification effort, with an interruption between
1939 and 1951 due to the Second World War, carried on into the early 1960's, and resulted in
the convening of a diplomatic conference at the
Hague in 1964. The conference adopted the two
uniform laws, one on the international sale of
goods (ULIS) and the other on the formation of
contracts for international sales, annexing them
to two international conventions.[2] These conventions are presently in force but the number of
Contracting States is limited and they are mostly
from Western Europe.[3]

3. Interaction of UNCITRAL with the 1964 Hague Conventions

When UNCITRAL, which was created by the United Nations General Assembly in 1966 to promote "the progressive harmonization and unification of the law of international trade,"[4] held its first session in 1968, it of course considered if there was any way to promote wider acceptance of the two Hague Conventions which were, after all, precious products of international endeavours since 1930. By that time, three States had ratified the Hague Conventions, and the Conventions had thus not yet come into force. The Commission therefore considered it desirable first to inquire about the intentions of States to adhere to the Hague Conventions and the reasons thereagainst in case of a negative attitude.

The received replies, together with an analysis thereof, were considered by the Commission at its second (1969) and third (1970) sessions. At the second session, some representatives expressed the view that the Hague Conventions were suitable and practical instruments, and that an effort should not be undertaken at that time to revise them. Other representatives, however, believed that the Conventions were not suitable for worldwide acceptance. Above all, the responses to the questionnaire were mostly too pessimistic to promote the Hague Conventions. The reasons were diverse: The Hague Conventions were too dogmatic, complex, predominatly of the European civil law tradition and lacked clarity even for ordinary lawyers. Moreover, the Hague Conventions had no global representation in the rule-making. In fact, at the 1964 Hague Conference, Latin America was only represented by Colombia, Asia by Japan and Africa by Egypt.

4. UNCITRAL work toward a new convention

The Commission accordingly decided to create a Working Group on the Internatinal Sale of Goods, consisting of 14 (later increased to 15) States chosen from its members, and instructed it to ascertain whether the Hague uniform laws might be modified so as to render them capable of wider acceptance by countries of different legal, social and economic systems, or whether it would be necessary to elaborate a new text. The Working Group was also instructed to consider ways and means by which a more widely acceptable text might best be prepared and promoted.

The Working Group devoted its first seven sessions to the consideration of the Hague Uniform Law on the International Sale of Goods (ULIS), and by 1974 had considered and prepared a number of revisions of articles of that uniform law. At its sixth session (1975), the Working Group decided to draft the revised text of ULIS in the form of an "integrated" convention rather than in the form of a uniform law annexed to a convention (as was the case with ULIS) in order to make the substantive provisions of the uniform law applicable even without resort to a further domestic legislation whenever feasible (i.e., self-executory), and, at its seventh session (1976), the Working Group adopted its draft text as well as a commentary thereon prepared by the Secretariat. The Commmission, on the basis of the draft text prepared by the Working Group, subsequently approved a draft convention on the international sale of goods in 1977.

Thereafter the Working Group devoted its final two sessions to a consideration of the formation and validity of contracts for the international sale of goods. It based its deliberations on the

1964 Hague Uniform Law on the Formation of Contracts for the International Sale of Goods and a
draft prepared by UNIDROIT of a law for the
unification of certain rules relating to the
validity of contracts of international sale of
goods. In 1977, the Working Group adopted the
text of a draft convention on the formation of
contracts for the International Sale of Goods and
upon its request a commentary thereon was subsequently prepared by the Secretariat.

In 1978, the Commission decided to integrate
the draft convention on the formation of contracts and the draft convention on the international sale of goods into a simple text and
adopted the UNCITRAL Draft Convention on Contracts for the Interational Sale of Goods. At the
same time, it recommended to the General Assembly
that a conference of plenipotentiaries be convened for adoption of the Convention. It is noteworthy that, throughout the above process, at
each stage of the adoption of a draft text of a
convention either at the level of the Working
Group or of the Commission, the text was sent
with the accompanying commentary to Governments
and interested international organizations for
their comments and proposals, and that they were
carefully analysed and considered in improving
the text.

5. Adoption of the Vienna Sales Convention; a tribute to the Hague Uniform Laws

Careful preparation for the holding of a diplomatic conference ensued thereafter including
the preparation of a commentary, draft provisions
for the Convention concerning implementation,
reservations and other final clauses, as well as

solicitation of comments on the draft Convention from Governments and interested international organizations and the analysis thereof. At the United Nations Conference on Contracts for the International Sale of Goods, held from 10 March to 11 April 1980 at the Hofburg in Vienna, the Vienna Sales Convention was adopted unanimously on 10 April with 62 States participating. There were relatively few amendments to the UNCITRAL draft text, which attested the soundness of the preparatory work.

Retrospectively observed, it was indeed bad luck for the Hague Conventions to have been a-dopted in 1964, which was the wrong time. Although the legislative process was open to all States, the newly emerging developing countries were not yet necessarily at the forefront of the international scene. Socialist countries were almost about to join or even to initiate the global unification effort of the law of trade perhaps partly based on the then new trend for the strengthening of the East-West economic relations, but the timing was still a few years short. The United States decided to join in the unification movement in 1964 for the first time, but was not well-prepared for the Hague Conference although it participated. While definitely not fair at all to the authors of the Hague Uniform Laws, particularly in light of the fact that many of their substantive approaches have indeed been retained in the Vienna Sales Convention in a simplified and practical fashion, the adoption of the Hague Conventions setting forth the uniform laws for the "international" sale of goods predominantly by Western European countries was politically an unintended act of intellectual imperialism for those who did not participate in the legislative process.[5]

6. Essential characteristics of the Vienna Sales Convention

Besides retention of the principle of the freedom of contract in international sales, the essential characteristics of the Vienna Sales Convention are simplicity, practicality and clarity. It is free of legal short-hand, free of complicated legal theory and easy for businessmen to understand.

The use of any legal short-hand expression, such as force majeure, tends to produce different meanings depending upon which legal system applies. Therefore, the Convention avoids the use of any short-hand terms which might be susceptible to receiving different interpretations. In cases in which a short-hand expression had to be used, such as the word "delivery," the drafters of the Convention provided a clear definition. That the Convention is free from dogma is important because it is, after all, businessmen who must understand the meaning of the provisions. The Convention is written in businessmen's language with practical details. In a dogma-oriented jurisprudence, a rule tends to be drafted in an abstract way so as to cover all possible situations. This was the approach of the 1964 Hague Conventions. However, the Vienna Sales Convention is modest in this respect. It even admits that some matters are not covered and are left to be resolved by the law applicable under the traditional rules of private international law. Paragraph (1) of article 7 of the Vienna Sales Convention reads in part: "In the interpretation of this Convention, regard is to be had to its international character and to the need to promote uniformity in its application..." This provision discourages any resort to domestic

legal concepts and tries to free judges, particularly in countries of the common law tradition,
from the iron chains of precedents, thus permitting them to examine foreign cases as well in
order to attain uniformity in the application of
the Convention.

7. Prospects for global implementation

The Vienna Sales Convention will enter into
force on the first day of the month following the
expiration of twelve months after the date of the
deposit of the tenth instrument of ratification
or accession. Twenty-one States[6] signed the Convention while the Convention was open for signature until 30 September 1981, and at present
there are seven ratifications or accessions from
the following States: Argentina, Egypt, France,
Hungary, Lesotho, Syrian Arab Republic and Yugoslavia. Of course, much time is often needed in
many countries for internal processing for ratification or accession even after a substantive
decision has been made. However, we have been
informed that official steps toward ratification
were already being taken in several States and
there are clear indications that the Convention
will obtain many ratifications or accessions at a
truly global scale in the near future.

The following are some indications which at-
test this prediction: The Attorney-General of
Australia announced on 22 November 1984 at the
Asian-Pacific Regional Trade Law Seminar the
decision of his Government to commence process
for accession. Bulgaria and Venezuela announced
at the 1983 United Nations General Assembly (Legal Committee) that ratification and accession
were favourably being considered. The Convention
is before the Parliament of Czechoslovakia. Aus-

tria and China are reported to be in the process
for ratification. The favourable attitude of
Canada, Iceland and Sierra Leone is also known.
The Scandinavian counries (Denmark, Finland,
Norway and Sweden) which signed the Convention on
the same day are proceeding for ratification
again in a concerted manner, together with their
effort to establish a common text relating to
domestic sales in line with the rules contained
in the Convention. In the United States, after
the American Bar Association indicated its support for the Convention, the President recommended its ratification and the Convention is now
before the Senate. It is also noteworthy that
other European countries, including those which
are members of the 1964 Hague Conventions, are
strongly in favour of the Vienna Sales Convention. Once the exact date of the entry into force
of the Vienna Sales Convention becomes definite,
it is expected that these States, particularly
those Contracting States of the Hague Conventions, will proceed to ratification jointly by
denouncing the Hague Conventions in accordance
with the formula as provided in the Vienna Sales
Convention dealing with the transition.

On a more general scene, the following move-
ments may also be noted. At the international
trade law seminar of the Council of Mutual Economic Assitance (CMEA) held in Moscow in March
1983, where senior officials of ministries of
foreign trade of CMEA countries assembled, general approval was given to the Convention as well
as to the Prescription Convention. The Asian-
African Legal Consultative Committee has recommended that its member States favourably consider
ratifying the Vienna Sales Convention. The
LAWASIA at the Manila Conference held in September 1983 also adopted a resolution urging govern-

ments in the region to ratify the Convention
within the shortest possible time. The German-
speaking States -- Austria, Federal Republic of
Germany, German Democratic Republic and Switzerland -- have already established a common German
text of the Convention. Many other international
meetings, including the Asian-Pacific Regional
Trade Law Seminar (Canberra, November 1984), the
First International Trade Law Seminar (Ottawa,
October 1983) and the Andean Regional Trade Law
Seminar (Bogota, April 1985), focus on the Vienna
Sales Convention because of its importance. The
International Chamber of Commerce has urged its
national committees to approach their respective
governments for ratification within the shortest
possible time.

8. Its sister convention: Prescription Conven-
   tion

Because of the popularity of the Vienna Sales
Convention and due to the increasing reputation
of the work of the commission in general, its
sister convention, i.e., the Convention on the
Limitation Period in the International Sale of
Goods (New York, 1974) (often referred to as
Prescription Convention),[7] is also attracting
favourable attention as a useful convention to
supplement the Vienna Sales Convention on important aspects of limitation on the assertion of
rights and claims arising from international
sales. A protocol to this Prescription Convention
was adopted in 1980 at the same diplomatic conference which prepared the Vienna Sales Convention in order to align the contents of the Prescription Convention with those of the Vienna
Sales Convention particularly in respect of the
sphere of application.[8] The Prescription Conven-

tion will enter into force on the first day of the month following the expiration of six months after the date of the deposit of the tenth instrument of ratification or accession. Fourteen States[9] signed the Convention while the Convention was open for signature until 31 December 1975, and at present there are eight ratifications or accessions from the following States: Argentina, Czechoslovakia, Dominican Republic, Egypt, Ghana, Hungary, Norway and Yugoslavia. It is expected that this Convention will also enter into force in the near future at almost the same time as the Vienna Sales Convention.

The Prescription Convention establishes unified rules for the operation of the limitation or prescription period in the international sale of goods. The Convention attempts to avoid the sharp contrast in approaches between common law countries and civil law countries, i.e., between the common law "statute of limitation" approach at the procedural law level and the civil law "prescription" approach at the substantive law level. Besides regulating the limitation period (which is four years as a general rule) for rights and claims arising from international sales contracts, the Convention touches upon the interesting question of international res judicata or the international effect of prescription, a legal aspect on which solution can be found only through a convention.

9. A prologue: toward a global restoration of the rule of reasons

However, why are we undertaking such an exercise? About two years ago I wrote a commentary on the Vienna Sales Convention in Japanese. I asked my wife to help me in straightening the

manuscript. Since she would read the paper in
that case, I was expecting that she would understand what an important work I was doing. She did
the work but kept silent, but I was curious to
hear her reaction to the work. She said, "What
you wrote is very easy to understand and makes
sense." I smiled at her. "But, she continued,
"it's all common sense. Do you really have to
spell out all those details as to the rights and
duties of the seller and buyer, including the
seller's obligation to deliver the goods in conformity with the contract and the buyer's obligation to pay the price, which are so obvious?" I
told her that it took fifty years to reach this
legal text. Her response was, "It's unbelieva-
ble." I felt sorry for her because her message
was apparent that she thought I had been doing
something more intelligent. However, this is
unfortunately the reality of international life.

In the medieval age in the Mediterranean area,
there existed a lex mercatoria which knew no
boundary in its application. However, as the
modern notion of sovereignty became crystallized,
the localizatin of the law of trade commenced
through the intervention of national legislatures. The trend was further intensified particularly after the Industrial Revolution as each
sovereign State endeavoured to strengthen its own
national legal system to appear as a modern industrial nation. The commercial law of each State
became sophisticated as legal theories refined
it. The complexity was further aggravated as
lawyers, sometimes for the pure sake of logic
whether based on the reality of life or not,
assisted in the expansion of the jungle of technicalities within each State to the exclusion of
laymen. The lawyers, as specialization and division of work within the law developed, sometimes

even neglected the need to reflect upon the <u>rai-son</u> <u>d'être</u> of the law.   Geldart wrote on the first page of his famous book, <u>Elements</u> <u>of</u> <u>English</u> <u>Law</u>, that lawyers speak of the law while laymen speak of laws. However, we might have often been indeed such laymen.

The last fifty years which were necessary to come up with the present text of the Vienna Sales Convention represented a series of precious efforts to unwind such sophisticated localization of the law in favour of delocalization and the restoration of the rule of reasons in order to eliminate unnecessary legal obstacles to the flow of trade. When delegates participate in the elaboration of international legal texts, it is understandable for them first to compare a proposed rule with their domestic counterpart. However internationally minded they may be, their basic commitment is after all to their sovereign, particularly when they represent their governments. Those who concentrate on nothing but how the reasonable global rule should be must learn the need for patience when they hear such statements as "My delegation fully supports the proposed rule because it corresponds to our law." At the same time, however, the "compromise in the constructive spirit" has been one of the important driving forces for delocalization.

Many developing countries neither have sophisticated legal systems nor extremely refined legal theories which are beyond the reach of laymen. At the unification forum, they often keep silent when subtle technical points are discussed which can only be comprehended by those who have traditionally been exposed to such arguments by long training, and look at the laws of developed nations with suspicion. They insist on the establishment of a new legal order which would ensure their participation on a fair and equal basis. This is quite understandable. Businessmen are also at a loss when they are told of inscrutable legal logic beyond their comprehension. The jungle of technicalities has well developed to strengthen the lawyers' monopoly of "laws." However, let us forget for a moment that we are lawyers, and read articles 25 to 88 of the Vienna Sales Convention as a businessman who has no legal education. It will be rediscovered that the Convention is clear and easy to understand and, most importantly, it will be realized that the rules are after all full of common sense and spelled out in businessmen's language. If "mutual trust," the need of which is often emphasized by the Chinese delegation in UNCITRAL, prevailed in business, many of the provisions may not even be necessary. What the Vienna Sales Convention has done is therefore in a sense the restoration of the rule of reasons through the delocalization of laws, or the restoration of "the law" in Geldart's sense. This is, however, just the beginning of the global process for the unification of the law relating to international trade. Moreover, practically speaking, the Vienna Sales Convention was rather an easy one to begin with because the parties' autonomy is most respected in the sales area throughout the world and the rules contained in the Convention are only supplementary for those cases where parties did not provide otherwise in their contracts.

When it comes to the question of ratification or accession, however, we are still faced with the cool reality: Politicians would straightforwardly ask about the "benefit" which they can expect out of the ratification before acting in its favour. In such a field as the sale of goods and particularly where the rules contained in a

convention are voluntary in nature as compared to
a mandatory character, we cannot expect the emergence of strong lobbying groups. Only when
statesmen can foresee the implication in a long-
range global perspective of the accession as a
vitally important step for the creation of a
better international order, the positive step can
be expected. Fortunately, however, favourable
attitudes prevail all over the world and no seriously critical comments on the Vienna Sales
Convention have been heard, and many individuals
are now working hard to persuade their governments to move forward. It also seems to be becoming clearer to national legislatures that, to say
the least, States will not lose anything by acceding to the Convention because of the very
supplementary nature of the rules in the Convention to the parties' autonomy. Whatever motive it
may be, by getting on board we can further ac-
celerate the speed of the bandwagon which has
already started rolling. Above all, we know that
it is much easier to understand one convention
than to understand a great number of foreign
laws, the miscomprehension of which has often
been the source of unnecessary disputes.

NOTES

The views expressed in this article are those of
the author in his personal capacity.

1. Official Records of the United Nations Conference on Contracts for the International Sale
of Goods (United Nations Document A/CONF.97/19;
United Nations Sales Publication No. E.81.IV.3)
(Text of the Convention also reprinted in

UNCITRAL <u>Yearbook</u> (1980), Vol. XI, Part three, I
(United Nations Sales Publication No. E.81.V.8)).
2. Convention relating to a Uniform Law on the
International Sale of Goods, The Hague, 1 July
1964, and Convention relating to a Uniform Law on
the Formation of Contracts for the International
Sale of Goods (Both texts are reprinted in <u>Regis-</u>
<u>ter</u> <u>of</u> <u>Texts</u> <u>of</u> <u>Conventions</u> <u>and</u> <u>Other</u> <u>Instruments</u>
<u>Concerning</u> <u>International</u> <u>Trade</u> <u>Law</u>, Vol. I, Chap-
ter I (United Nations Sales Publication No.
E.71.V.3)). For the historical detail of the
process which led to the adoption of the Hague
Uniform Laws, see P. Winship, "The Scope of the
Vienna Convention on International Sales Con-
tract," in N.M. Galston and H. Smit, eds., <u>Inter-</u>
<u>national</u> <u>Sales:</u> <u>the</u> <u>United</u> <u>Nations</u> <u>Convention</u> <u>on</u>
<u>Contracts</u> <u>for</u> <u>the</u> <u>International</u> <u>Sale</u> <u>of</u> <u>Goods</u>
(New York 1984) pp. 1-1, 1-4 to 1-13.
3. Belgium, Federal Republic of Germany, Israel,
Italy, Netherlands, San Marino, The Gambia and
United Kingdom. Israel ratified only ULIS.
4. General Assembly Resolution 2205 (XXI) of 17
December 1966 (reprinted in <u>UNCITRAL</u> <u>Yearbook</u>
(1968-70), Vol. I, Part one, II (United Nations
Sales Publication No. E.71.V.1)). The Commission
annually publishes a <u>Yearbook</u> relating to the
work carried out by the Commission during the
year covered. The <u>Yearbook</u> reproduces nearly all
of the documents prepared by the Secretariat over
the course of the year for the commission and its
Working Groups, and reports of the Commission and
its Working Groups. Detailed information at each
stage of the development as described below toward the formulation of the Vienna Sales Convention may therefore be found in the <u>UNCITRAL</u> <u>Year-</u>
<u>book</u> of a particular year.
5. E. Bergsten, "Basic Concepts of the UN Convention on the International Sale of Goods," in

P. Doralt, ed., <u>Das</u> <u>UNCITRAL-Kaufrecht</u> <u>im</u> <u>Ver-</u>
<u>gleich</u> <u>zum</u> <u>österreichischen</u> <u>Recht</u> (Vienna 1985),
pp. 15 and 16.

6. Austria, Chile, China, Czechoslovakia, Denmark, Finland, France, Federal Republic of Germany, German Democratic Republic, Ghana, Hungary,
Italy, Lesotho, Netherlands, Norway, Poland,
Sinapore, Sweden, United States of America, Venezuela and Yugoslavia.

7. <u>Official</u> <u>Records</u> <u>of</u> <u>the</u> <u>United</u> <u>Nations</u> <u>Con-</u>
<u>ference</u> <u>on</u> <u>Prescription</u> <u>(Limitation)</u> <u>in</u> <u>the</u> <u>In-</u>
<u>ternational</u> <u>Sale</u> <u>of</u> <u>Goods</u> (United Nations Docu-
ment A/CONF.63/16; United Nations Sales Publica-
tion No. E.74.V.8); for commentary of this Convention, see United Nations Document A/CONF.63/17
(reprinted in <u>UNCITRAL</u> <u>Yearbook</u> (1979), Vol. X,
Part three, I).

8. See note 1, above.

9. Brazil, Bulgaria, Byelorussian SSR, Costa
Rica, Czechoslovakia, German Democratic Republic,
Ghana, Hungary, Mongolia, Nicaragua, Norway,
Poland, Ukranian SSR and the Soviet Union.

CHAPTER TWO

THE VIENNA CONVENTION: SCOPE, INTERPRETATION, AND GAP-FILLING

PAUL VOLKEN
Lecturer, University of Fribourg

I. INTRODUCTION

1. This year the Vienna Convention celebrated its fifth anniversary on April 11. Although the Convention has not yet entered into force, the five-year period has been long enough to make it an "adult" in the international world of treaties. In fact, no other international legal instrument has, in such a short time, served so often as a topic of lively discussion among businessmen[1]. Thus the time has come for the Convention to enter into the ordinary academic curriculum for lawyers.

2. The present paper will deal with three aspects of the Vienna Convention. First it will analyze the Convention's sphere of application, then turn to the rules governing its interpretation, and finally come to the procedure that should take place in cases where a legal question is governed by the Convention but, as a matter of fact, does not find a clear answer in it.

Before concentrating on these three main
topics, however, we should first take a brief
look at the legal nature of the Convention and
its legal rules.

II. LEGAL NATURE OF THE CONVENTION

3.   The Vienna Convention consists of statutory
rules on the international sale of goods which,
as a formal source of law, are contained in an
international treaty. Thus, two different types
of legal rules are at stake at the same time,
i.e., the traditional rules on contract law and
the public international rules on the law of
treaties.

4.   Turning first to the public international
law side, we note that the modern theory on the
law of treaties recognizes different groups of
international treaties. One of the most generally
accepted of these classifications distinguishes
between contractual and law-making treaties
(traités-lois, traits-contrats)[2].
      The Vienna Convention belongs to the cate-
gory of law-making treaties; however, even this
group contains several subdivisions, one of the
most generally accepted being the distinction
between **self-executing** and **non-self-executing**
treaties[3].

5.   Treaties which are **not** self-executing create
rights and obligations for the Contracting States
only. Individuals living in the Contracting
States cannot assert any rights arising directly
from the treaty itself. In order to become effective towards individuals, a non-self-executing
treaty needs to be transformed into domestic
statutory law. By ratifying or acceding to a non-

self-executing treaty, a Contracting State accepts the international duty to provide for the
appropriate domestic legislation. As long as such
implementory legislation is missing, there is no
possibility for a national court to render the
treaty obligations effective[4].

6. The situation is very different if a treaty
obligation is deemed to be self-executing. In
such a case the legal rules arising from the
treaty are open for immediate application by the
national judge. And all persons living in a Contracting State are entitled to assert their
rights or demand the fulfillment of another person's duty by referring directly to the legal
rules of the treaty itself.[5]

7. Both self-executing and non-self-executing
treaties are to be found in the fields of private
international law and international commercial
law. Very often, legal rules arising from treaties may be partly self-executing and partly non-
self-executing.
     The various ILO Conventions dealing with
labor law or questions of social security are
classical examples of non-self-executing treaties.[6] The GATT of October 1947, the EFTA Agreement of January 1960, and various regional or
bilateral agreements with the EC are examples of
treaties with a mixture of self-executing and
non-self-executing rules.[7]

8. The rules of the Vienna Convention are
clearly self-executing. In this respect they
differ from the Hague Conventions of 1 July 1964
which, in fact, did not contain any rules on
contracts. All they did was to oblige the Contracting States to incorporate the **Uniform Law on**

the **International Sale of Goods** (ULIS) or the **Uniform Law on the Formation of Contracts for the International Sale of Goods** (ULF) into their own domestic legislation[8]. Thus, although ULIS and ULF were in substance of an international character, as far as their form is concerned, they had to be transformed into national statutory law by each Contracting State. A similar technique has been applied by the drafters of the Geneva Conventions on bills of exchange (1930) and on checks (1931).[9]

9. However, an important caveat has to be added to all that has been said thus far about the immediate applicability of the self-executing rules of a treaty.

   According to the generally accepted principles of public international law, all States are free to decide how they wish to comply with their international legal duties. Whereas some States expressly permit treaty-made rules to be immediately enforceable before their national courts, other States provide that all international texts -- whether self-executing or not -- must first be transformed into national statutory law. This often seems to be the case in Great Britain and the same is true in the Scandinavian countries.[10] The national courts of such countries will never apply treaty rules as such, but only in the form of a national statute.[11]

10. Such a difference might be of particular importance when it comes to questions concerning interpretation or gap-filling[12]. In States where the immediate applicability of self-executing, treaty-made rules is accepted, the courts will be fully aware that they are applying the legal rules of a multilateral convention, since in each

individual case of application they must refer to
the Convention itself. It is not sure whether the
same can be said of the court of a State where
transformation is required, for in such States
the national judges will only refer to the national statute and national case law[13]. As a
result, differences are likely to occur in the
application and interpretation of the same rules.

III. SPHERE OF APPLICATION, IN GENERAL

11. As indicated in its title, the Vienna Convention deals with contracts for the international sale of goods. It does not, however, apply to
all types of international contracts of sale; the
Convention restricts its sphere of application to
a certain group of sales: First, the Convention
covers only those contracts which have been concluded between a given group of persons; second,
the rules of the Convention are limited to contracts which, on the one hand, fall within a
particular territorial sphere, and, on the other
hand, are concluded within a given period of
time; and third, application of the rules of the
Convention is limited to a specific category of
sales.

The Convention's field of application is
restricted by several rules, the most important
of which are found in Articles 1 to 6. Four
aspects have to be taken into account when defining the Convention's sphere of application, i.e.,
a **personal**, a **territorial**, a **temporal**, and a
material aspect.

IV. PERSONAL ASPECT OF APPLICABILITY

12. The Convention refers to a positive and a
negative criterion for determining the parties

whose contracts of sale fall under the Vienna
rules. According to Art. 1 para. 1, the Convention applies to sales contracts between parties
whose places of business are situated in different States (positive criterion)[15]. Para. 3 of the
same article states that the nationality of the
parties to a contract is of no importance and
that the Convention applies irrespective of the
fact whether these parties are engaged in commerce or are ordinary private individuals.[16]

13. Some of the terms contained in Art. 1 need
further explanation. As to the notion "State,"
Art. 1 para. 1 distinguishes between two possible
variations: The States in which the parties'
places of business are located must either both
be Contracting States (lit. (a)) or at least the
State whose substantive laws have to be applied
under the national conflict-of-laws rules
(lit.(b)). In the first case, we have a substantive definition of the Convention's sphere of
application whereas the second subparagraph is
known as the so-called conflictual way of defining the Convention's scope. We will return to
this definition. [17]

14. In regard to the term "place of business,"
Art. 1 para. 2 provides that both parties, before
or at the conclusion of the contract, must have
been aware of the fact that their business places
are situated in different States. In other words,
the parties must consciously have entered into an
international contract. If there is no such a-
wareness, the Convention does not apply, and
national rules, including the rules on private
international law, will govern the contract.[18]

15.   In international trade, parties often
create business places in different States since
a locally based office tends to help promote
business in the particular country.

If a party has more than one place of business, the place which has the closest relationship to the contract and its performance is to be
taken into consideration. Sometimes the representative of a local business place is only entitled
to prepare the conclusion of a contract, while
the contract itself is accepted and signed by a
member of the headquarters abroad. Such proceedings make the contract international only in
cases where the other party knew or ought to have
known of the real partner to the contract[19].

The fact that one party has no business
place at all is no reason to refuse application
of the Convention. Art. 10 subpara. (b) refers to
the habitual residence of such a party.[20]

V.   TERRITORIAL ASPECT OF APPLICABILITY

16. The personal and territorial aspects of applicability are closely related to each other,
both aspects being dealt with mainly in Art. 1
para. 1. As a basic rule, the Convention applies
to sales contracts if both parties have their
places of business in different States. The Convention adds two alternative restrictions to this
basic criterion. The first restriction requires
that both (or all) the States in which the business places are located be Contracting States
(Art. 1 (1)(a)), and the second stipulates that
the Convention applies only if a rule of private
international law, i.e., a conflicts rule, leads
to the law of a Contracting State.

17. The way in which the Vienna Convention defines its territorial sphere of application gives rise to a series of questions related to both the basic criterion and the two restrictions.

1. The basic criterion

18. The basic criterion, according to which a sale is considered international if the parties to the contract have their places of business in different States, is too broad, yet at the same time, too restrictive.

The criterion is too **broad** in the sense that it considers even those sales as international in which the goods, from their fabrication to consumption, have never left the original country. Let us assume that a New York company owns prefabricated construction elements stored in Geneva. The New York owner sells these elements to a French company that plans to build a Hotel in Geneva. Since the parties have their places of business in different States, the Convention applies, even though the construction materials have never left Switzerland and, moreover, not even Geneva.

Why should such a sale be exempted from the rules of the Swiss Code of Obligations? Do we really need to take recourse to Art. 6 of the Convention (opting-out clause) in order to preserve the national character of a purely local transaction?

19. On the other hand, the basic criterion is also too **restrictive** in that it excludes all sales from the Convention between two parties which import or export goods but have their places of business in the same State.

Let us illustrate this with another example. If a Baltimore firm that owns furniture stocked in Italy sells the furniture to a Boston firm, which, on its part, needs that type of furniture for a new sales office in Paris, the Convention will not apply. In fact, a sales contract concluded between the two US companies will not fall under the scope of the Convention even if the sales transaction includes an international shipment because the parties' places of business are located in the same country.

20. For the sake of clarity it should be emphasized that a choice between subparagraphs (a) and (b) of Art. 1 will not modify the outcome of the above cases in any way. In fact, even before the option between subparagraphs (a) and (b) can produce its effects, the Convention presupposes in both situations that the parties to the sales transaction have their places of business in different States.

However, even though the Vienna Convention does not apply to our second example, most businessmen will agree that selling goods which are stored in Italy and have to be shipped to France cannot be considered a purely domestic transaction. Thus, the case would be solved by referring to the traditional conflict-of-laws rules.[21]

21. In international transactions in nine out of ten cases the transnational character of a contract is determined by the place where either the parties to the transaction or the goods themselves are located. Nevertheless, in defining the international character of a sales transaction, the Vienna Convention refers only to the contracting parties without any reference whatsoever to the goods to be purchased.

22. The solution provided by the Vienna Convention can be understood only if it is regarded as an overreaction provoked by Article 1 of ULIS. In fact, under ULIS -- in addition to the location of the parties' places of business (Art. 1 (1)) -- the sales contracts had to comply with one of the following international elements: Either they had to provide for international shipment of the goods (subpara. (a)), or offer and acceptance had to be effected in different States (subpara. (b)); or the conclusion and the fulfillment of the contract had to take place in different States (subpara. (c)).[22]

If ULIS might have been too ambitious on this point, the Vienna Convention's definition is clearly too one-sided. In addition to the requirement that the parties' places of business be located in different States, the Convention should have at least added, either as a variation or cumulative element, that the goods be shipped across a national border.

2.   The two restrictions

23. The Vienna Convention applies only if and in so far as, in addition to the basic criterion (Art. 1 (1)), one of the two requirements provided by subpara. (a) or (b) is met.

Subpara. (a) cumulates the conditions of applicability in the sense that the States in which the contracting parties' places of business are located, must, at the same time, both be Member States of the Convention. Accordingly, a sales contract between a German company and a New York-based company will not fall under the Convention unless both States, the FGR and the US, have ratified. And it goes without saying that, in case of litigation, the forum must also be situated in a Contracting State; otherwise, the Court would not be bound to apply the rules of the Convention. Thus, in States that ratify, it appears that under such restrictive conditions the Vienna Convention will have but a very poor chance of being applied for a long time.

24. Under the criterion of **subpara. (b)**, the Convention has a far better chance of being applied. In fact, the State of the Forum need not be a Contracting State nor do both places of business need to be situated in such States. It will be sufficient if the sales transaction is international in character (places of business in different States, Art. 1 (1)), and the conflicts rules of the forum lead to the substantive law of a Member State to the Convention.[23]

Under the generally acknowledged principles of private international law, this might, in the first instance, be the law which has been expressly chosen by the parties themselves or, in the absence of such a choice, the law which has the most significant relationship to the transaction and the parties. In sales contracts this will usually be the law of the State in which the seller has his place of business, for he is the one who carries out the most characteristic performance of the transaction.[24]

Unfortunately, it seems that government officials and contract lawyers are often not very familiar with the principles of private international law. For this reason the Vienna diplomatic Conference of 1980 accepted a reservation under Art. 95 of the Convention providing for the exclusion of subpara. (b) of Art. 1.[25]

3.   Federal clause and regional cooperation

25.   Two final remarks, one on federal States and the other on regional cooperation, should serve to close this section on the territorial sphere of application.

26.   There are two groups of **federal States** to be distinguished. In the first group, the law of contracts is unified on the federal level. This is the case, e.g., in the Federal Republic of Germany, Switzerland or Yugoslavia. In the second group, the law of contracts falls within the legislative power of each federal unit. The United States,[26] Great Britain, Canada and Australia belong to this group. In this second group, ratification of the Vienna Convention presupposes implementory legislation not only on the federal level but also in each state, province or territory of the federation.

Since such a procedure is rather time-consuming, **Art. 93** gives federal States the opportunity to declare, at ratification or accession, that for the time being the Convention shall apply only to some of its territorial units. This enables the Convention to be applied in those units sooner.[27]

27. The Vienna Conventions aims at worldwide unification of the sales law. Such an undertaking cannot be realized without accepting numerous compromises. On the other hand, economic and legal cooperation often find a more favorable climate if they take place merely on a regional level.

Since the Vienna Convention intends to strengthen, not to paralyze closer legal cooperation, **Art. 94** expressly grants each Contracting

State the freedom to participate in a more elaborated regional unification.

VI.   TEMPORAL ASPECT OF APPLICABILITY

28.   Two questions are of particular interest in regard to the time factor: **First,** at which moment does the Convention become binding and when does it cease to be effective? This is the side of the problem dealing with public international law. The **second** question is connected much closer with the law of contracts: Which contracts and which legal questions of contract law are governed by the rules of the Convention and from what moment on do the rules apply?

29.   Contrary to the other three aspects of applicability, the rules governing the application ratione temporis are not contained in the first chapter but in the final clauses of the Convention.

Art. **99** deals with the international entry into force of the Convention itself; **Art. 100** specifies from which moment on the Convention's rules apply to a given sales transaction; and **Art. 101** relates to the denunciation procedure.

30.   As to its international entry into force, the Convention draws a distinction between the time it initially enters into force and the time it enters into force for States whose adherence follows this date.

According to Art. 99 para. 1, the initial international entry into force presupposes ten ratifications, acceptances, approvals or accessions, and the Convention will enter into force twelve months after the deposit of the tenth such document.

For States which ratify or adhere after that magic date, the Convention becomes binding twelve months after the deposit of the appropriate instrument.

An exception exists, however, in regard to States which are parties to ULIS or ULF. Even after the twelve-month period, the Convention shall not become binding for these States until the effects of ULIS or ULF have ceased (Art. 99 (6)).[29]

31. The international entry into force is to be distinguished from the date when the Convention becomes applicable to an individual sales transaction. **Art. 100** deals with this aspect.

The general rule can be stated as follows: There is no retroactivity. In particular, the Convention distinguishes between the formation and the execution of a given sales contract.

32. As to the formation of contracts, the rules of the Convention (Art. 14-24) shall apply only when the proposal for concluding the contract is made **on or after** the date of the Convention's international entry into force (Art. 100 (1)). International entry means the date when the Convention enters into force with respect to the Contracting States where the parties to the sales transaction have their places of business.

The same rule applies to the execution of a sales contract (Art. 100 (2)).

33. The effects of a denunciation of the Convention are subject to the same twelve-month period as its entry into force (Art. 101 (2)).

The Convention does not differentiate between the denunciation effects under public international law[30] and those with repsect to a

particular sales contract. Will contracts which
have been concluded under the auspices of the
Convention continue to be governed by the Convention or do the individual and the international
effects cease on the same date? And what about a
contract under litigation? Does the judge have to
continue the lawsuit as if the Convention were
still in force, or does he have to change the
applicable rules of law?

These questions constitute part of the general problems of intertemporal law. But a legal
text that consists of more than a hundred articles and, in view of its international bearing,
needs uniform application, could easily have
dedicated a small paragraph to this problem as
well. In the absence of such a rule, the courts
will probably take recourse to their national
principles of intertemporal law.

VII. MATERIAL ASPECTS OF APPLICABILITY

1.   In general

34. As to the material scope of application, the
Vienna Convention is to apply to sales contracts
as far as goods are concerned. In this respect
the Convention follows the system of ULIS. The
terms "sales contract" and "goods" were not defined in ULIS, and there is no explicit definition under the Vienna Convention either.

In regard to the term "contract," implicit
reference can be made to Articles 30 and 53 of
the Convention. According to Art. 30, the **seller**
must deliver the goods, hand over the documents
and transfer the property in the goods. And under
Art. 53 the **buyer** must pay the price and take
delivery of the goods.

As to the goods, the Convention applies to the sale of many different types of goods: to the sale of food, wheat, corn, coffee, to the sale of machines, cars, manufactured tools, to the sale of steel, books, records. As a rule, the Convention is not restricted to so-called commercial sales. On the other hand, in Art. 2 subpara. (a) it expressly excludes the sale of goods bought for personal, family or household use (**consumer sale**).[31]

2. Restrictions

35. The exclusion of consumer sales is not the only restriction provided by the Convention. In order to systematically cover all the types of restrictions, five different groups have to be singled out: There are restrictions relating to the **type of sale**, others to the **category of goods** falling under the Convention, and still others to the **category of transactions**; a fourth group relates to **the binding effect** of the Convention itself and a fifth concerns **the extent** to which legal questions are covered by the Convention.

After making some general remarks on groups three to five, we shall focus our comments on the restrictions relating to the type of sales and the category of goods.

36. Articles 3 and 5 contain restrictions or limitations relating to a series of transactions that are excluded from the Convention.

According to **Art. 3**, contracts for the supply of goods to be manufactured or produced are to be considered sales and not labor or service contracts, and as such are governed by the rules of the Convention. The situation differs, however, when the party ordering the goods furnishes a substantial part of the work materials himself. In the latter case, the manufacturer reduces his activity to the mere lending of his personal skills or labor, and thus the element of a labor or service contract prevails (Art. 3 (2))[32].

Art. 5 excludes all questions concerning (contractual or non-contractual) product liability from the scope of the Convention.

37. Art. 4 indicates to what extent legal questions on contract law fall under the Convention. Accordingly, the Convention applies to all aspects of the formation of contracts (Art. 14-24) as well as to the rights and obligations of the seller (Art. 30) and those of the buyer (Art. 53). On the other hand, Art. 4 expressly excludes **validity** problems and all questions relating to the **transfer of property.**[33]

38. In regard to the binding effect of the Vienna Convention and its limits, we refer to Art. 6. Under this article, which makes the Convention optional, the parties can agree that the rules of the Convention shall be excluded. The exclusion may concern the Convention as a whole or be restricted to some parts or even to only certain articles.[34] The opting-out clause is available, however, under one restriction. Under Articles 12 and 96 any Contracting State may declare that a given international sales contract must be in writing. If a State has made such a declaration, then the parties' agreement on total or partial exclusion or modification of the Convention must necessarily be in writing as well.

3.   Types of restricted Sales

39. As was already mentioned, so-called **consumer** sales (Art. 2 (a)), sales by **auction** (Art. 2 (b)), sales on **execution** and sales by **authority** (Art. 2 (c)) are excluded from the Convention's scope.

Sales on execution and by authority were already excluded under Art. 5 of ULIS.[35] The Vienna Convention excludes them as well along with two new items, consumer and auction sales.

40. The exclusion of consumer sales seems to be appropriate. In view of the fact that the national legislation of many countries has developed special rules to protect consumers, the Vienna Convention did not want to interfere with this body of specialized rules, most of which are mandatory in character.

The reasoning for the exclusion of auction sales was similar to that which caused the drafters of ULIS to exclude sales on execution and those by authority. In all three cases, special local regulations apply.[36]

4.   Categories of restricted Goods

41. Most of the items mentioned in Art. 2 subparas. (d), (e), and (f) have already been excluded under Art. 5 of ULIS. The drafters of the Vienna Convention have made one change in regard to ships, vessels or aircraft. Whereas under Art. 5 subpara. (b) of ULIS the exclusion was restricted to **registered** ships, vessels or aircraft[37], Art. 2 subpara. (e) of the Vienna Convention leaves aside any registration requirement.

42. The debate that took place in Vienna shows that, in the end, lack of equal treatment by different States led to this deletion. Since the registration requirements vary substantially from State to State, it can occur that the very same type of aircraft or watercraft needs to be registered in one State but not in another.[38]

As a result, the same ship or aircraft would fall under the Convention in one State, but be excluded from the Convention in another. It goes without saying that such a divergency would hardly be in line with the goals of international unification of the sales law. And it is understandable that the idea of deleting any reference to the registration procedure was a rather tempting proposal for the Vienna drafters. However, in doing so, they tremendously broadened the exception of Art. 2 subpara. (e).

43. In fact, if we take it literally, under the existing text any aircraft, ship or vessel would be excluded from the Convention, not just big seagoing vessels or intercontinental aircraft.

At this point some difficulties may arise. What about a private pleasure yacht, a sailboat, a rowboat or a surfboard? All these are types of watercraft, but are they to be considered ships or vessels, or should they be regarded as sports articles?

44. P. Schlechtriem[39] favors a functional approach, i.e., a solution that would take into account the special requirements of a ship or aircraft register that serve as a basis for corresponding mortgages.

J. Honnold[40], on the other hand, indicates that UNCITRAL was unable to find a workable distinction between large, mortgaged and small private craft, and he fears that the courts might encounter the same difficulties. Accordingly, he insists that Art. 2 subpara. (e) be read without any qualifications. At least in this respect, the premises for divergency in the interpretations of civil law and common law judges seem to be inevitable.

VIII. INTERPRETATION

1. General remarks

45. As was already mentioned[41], the legal nature of the Convention's rules is twofold. We are dealing, on the one hand, with provisions on traditional contract law, and on the other hand, with rules contained in an international treaty.

Thus, the question arises as to whether public international law rules on interpretation or those of the law of contract are to be applied. The answer to this question depends on the legal nature of the rule to be interpreted.

46. Public international law creates rights and duties among the Contracting States themselves. The Vienna Convention provides for such obligations in Part IV in the final clauses (Art. 89-101) dealing with ratification or accession, with reservation or denunciation. These rules of the Convention are without a doubt to be interpreted according to the principles of public international law, i.e., according to Articles 31-33 of the Vienna Convention on the Law of Treaties of 1969[42].

47. All other provisions of the Vienna Sales Convention have to do with the rights and duties of the individual parties to a sales transaction.

With respect to these rules, the Convention contains its own rules on interpretation: Articles 7
and 8.

Here the Convention distinguishes between
two levels of interpretation: Art. 7 concerns the
interpretation of the rules of contract law contained in the Convention itself, and Art. 8 the
interpretation of specific statements or the
conduct of the individual parties to a transaction.

2.   Interpretation procedure

48. Art. 7 para. 1 states that, in interpreting
the Convention, regard shall be had 1) to the
international character of the Convention and its
texts, 2) to the need to promote uniform application of its rules and 3) to the observance of
good faith in international trade. Para. 2 deals
with the principles which are to serve as guidelines for gap-filling.

49. Although Art. 7 para. 1 mentions the elements of interpretation and the general goal to
be achieved -- i.e., promotion of uniformity in
the application of the Convention -- it does not
say anything about the ways and means to achieve
that end.

Do national courts have to adhere to the
text of the Convention, to the literal meaning of
its words, or are they entitled to go a step
further, to consult the preparatory work and take
a look at the Convention's history and the genesis of a particular rule?

50. It is common knowledge that common law
judges seem traditionally less willing to take
recourse to preparatory materials or to refer to

the genesis of a statute and its rules[43]. J.
Guttenridge once put it this way: "The meaning of
legislation must be deduced **solely** from the word
of the statute."

Even though, due, e.g., to the influence of
the American Uniform Commerical Code, the plain-
meaning rule has been softened in modern contract
law of the common law countries, the rule still
exists and is observed.[44]

51. European legal scholars are traditionally
more accustomed to work with different elements
of interpretation. The plain meaning of a text
and its grammatical structure are also of great
importance on the Continent; nevertheless, it
seems that civil law judges are more willing to
refer to the preparatory work or legal history of
a text than their common law colleagues would be.
And if the real meaning of a legal text still
remains doubtful in spite of various interpretation theories, Continental European judges are
far less scrupulous about taking a functional
approach than their English or American counter-
parts. Thus, it appears to be inevitable that, in
both civil law and common law countries, interpretations will be influenced to a certain extent
by national theory. As long as the ultimate goal,
i.e., uniform application of the Convention's
rules remains unchallenged, such recourse does
not disturb anyone. Things may change, however,
if such differences lead to ambiguity or even to
contradiction.

52. Differences in interpretation theories are
an important threat to the uniform application of
international instruments, however, not the only
one. Another considerable danger arises, e.g.,
from inaccurate translations of texts[45].

An example based on personal experience may
illustrate this point. After the international
adoption of a new multilateral convention, the
German-speaking countries usually meet in order
to prepare a common German-language version of
the new instrument. Since the French version
always serves as the official text in Switzerland, Swiss delegates to the translation meetings
must be especially careful to avoid unacceptable
discrepancies between the French and the German
versions.

55. With respect to the Vienna Sales Convention,
the translation meeting was held in January 1982
in Bonn, and the preparatory draft of the translation was drawn up on the basis of the official
English text. At the meeting, three out of four
Swiss interventions were raised against deviations from the French version that were considered too far-reaching. The meeting made it
clear that in most instances the deficiencies
were not due to the basic German draft, but to
the fact that the original English and French
texts contained discrepancies. In many cases
consultation of the Spanish and Russian versions
was inevitable. Thus, sincere efforts towards
achieving uniform application of the Vienna Convention may require consulting its texts not only
in one but in several official languages.

54. In order to achieve uniform application of
the Convention, in addition to applying basically
similar interpretation theories and taking other
linguistic versions of the same provision into
account, the courts of one country should be able
to consult the judicial decisions and doctrine of
another country. Achieving this aim will require
considerable effort either on the part of Unci-

tral or another appropriate international entity[46].

Undertakings of this kind already exist. The
Unidroit in Rome publishes a periodical survey of
the cases related to the conventions on international shipment of goods; the Asser Institute in
the Hague does the same in regard to the conventions of the Hague Conference; and the EEC publish a loose-leaf digest on the decisions of the
Luxembourg EEC-Court.

55. Finally, according to Art. 7 para. 1 of the
Convention, the interpretation should promote
good faith in international trade.

This element is from the chapter on formation of contracts. The original idea was that in
the course of dealings leading to the formation
of a contract, the parties should observe the
principles of fair dealing and acting in good
faith. This idea was finally accepted as a general interpretation rule to be applied to the Convention as a whole. Similar rules are to be found
in national legislations.[47]

As soon as the Convention enters into force,
Art. 7 para. 1 will be of paramount importance,
and rather soon thereafter, an ample judicial
practice will be engaged in handling this rule.

3. Gap-filling

56. According to Art. 7 para. 2, a question that
is governed by the Convention but does not find
an express solution in it shall be settled in
conformity with the general principles on which
the Convention is based or, in the absence of
such principles, in conformity with the law applicable by virtue of the conflict-of-laws rules.

Depending on one's legal education, these general statements can imply rather different things as is illustrated by the following two examples.

57. In an early comment on the Uncitral Draft the German scholar **Ulrich Huber**[48] stated:

> The question of what has to be considered as a gap under the Convention, cannot be answered on a mere rational basis. Someone who has a positive stand towards the Convention will discover but few gaps. On the other hand, if a person is sceptical about the international unification of the sales law, he will every now and then run into unsettled questions. In addition, a common law jurist, because of his legal tradition, will probably tend towards a more restrictive intrepretation of the Convention and its provisions. Thus, he might more often be confronted with a gap, than would be a civil law jurist. Civil law jurists are more frequently used to work with generally framed, systematically conceived legal codes. Out of this experience, they are more readily prepared to solve unsettled questions or to fill gaps by referring to the general principles contained in the code itself.

58. On the other hand, **John Honnold** wrote in his book on the Vienna Sales Convention[49]:

> The invitation to seek and apply general principles of the Convention calls for **caution** and **restraint**. Before deciding a case on the basis of an un-

> stated "general principle" a tribunal
> should answer two questions: **First,** is
> the case at hand clearly analogous to
> those that fall within the Convention's
> specific provisions? **And second,** would
> the extension of a provision by analogy
> conflict with another policy embodied
> in the Convention?

And he continues: Like the inductive approach
employed in case law development, different steps
have to be taken: The first step is the examination of instances and cases expressly regulated
by specific provisions of the Convention. The
second step is to choose between the following
conclusions: a) Did the Convention deliberately
reject the extension of a specific provision?,
or, b) Does the lack of a specific provision to
govern a given case result from the failure of
the Convention's drafters to foresee this case
and resolve it? Only in this second hypothesis
can the gap-filling procedure take place.

59. As the two different statements indicate,
personal legal education will be of extreme importance in influencing not only the interpretation of the Convention but also the filling of
gaps.

This is all the more true in view of the
fact that Art. 7 para. 1 invites one, in the
final instance, to resort to the principles of
the national law applicable by virtue of conflicts rules.

In this respect, ULIS and the Vienna Convention follow a basically different philosophy.
Whereas Art. 17 of ULIS was self-contained in the
sense that all interpretation and gap-filling
problems had to be solved within the uniform text
itself, the Vienna Convention is more open and

remains accessible to solutions which allow recourse to the principles of the national law of
sales.

4. Statements and Conduct of the Parties

60. Whereas Art. 7 deals with the intrepretation
of the **Convention** and its rules, Art. 8 applies
to the interpretation of the statements and conduct of the **parties**.

   In this sense, the rules of Art. 8 specify,
e.g., whether the communications between two
parties have been sufficient in form and substance so as to be considered a firm offer or
create a contract. This rule initially comes from
the part on formation (Art. 4 ULF).

61. The eternal conflict between the subjective
intent of the speaker and the real understanding
of the addresee continues in connection with the
interpretation of the statements or conduct of
the contracting parties.

   Art. 8, which had to face the conflicting
interests in this field, commences with a rule on
the subjective intent of the declaring party
(para. 1); however, the rule requires a qualified
addressee, for it presupposes that the latter
knew or could not have been unaware of the speaker's intent.

   In most cases it cannot be proved that one
is dealing with a qualified addressee. Therefore,
Art. 8 refers, in the second instance, to the
standards of a reasonable person (para. 2).

62. Whether subjective intent or standards of a
reasonable person, in both cases Art. 8 para. 3
indicates the elements of interpretation: Due
consideration is to be given to all relevant

circumstances, to the negotiations, to the practices between the parties and to their subsequent
conduct. These elements are fully in line with
the traditional rules of interpretation of modern
contract law.

***

63. In spite of certain similarities between
national law and the new Vienna rules or even
because of these very similarities, it should be
emphasized that, when it comes to the application
of internationally unified law, even the best
legal education in a national system remains
patchwork if it is not complemented by elaborate
training in comparative law. A worldwide unification of the sales law cannot be realized by the
mere drafting and entry into force of a multilateral Conventon. What has been done thus far by
Unidroit, Uncitral or the Vienna diplomatic Conference is a necessary precondition to such unification. If, however, the unification is to come
to life, then important additional work will have
to be done by legal scholars through their writing and teaching. In fact, the uniform law of
sales will not be and -- this is even more important -- will not remain uniform unless we can
count on a young generation of lawyers with an
adequate international legal education.

NOTES

1. Several books and numerous articles have
already been written on the Convention. (Cf. list
in P. Doralt, ed., <u>Das</u> <u>UNCITRAL-Kaufrecht</u> <u>im</u>
<u>Vergleich</u> <u>zum</u> <u>österreichischen</u> <u>Recht.</u> <u>Referate</u>
<u>und</u> <u>Diskussionen</u> <u>des</u> <u>Symposiums</u> <u>in</u> <u>Baden</u> <u>bei</u>

Wien, 17. -19. April 1983, Bd. 1 (Wien 1985) pp.
11-14. In addition, several symposia on the
International Sale of Goods have taken place in
recent years, e.g.: a) Symposium of Baden bei
Wien, 17.-19. April 1983 (cf. P. Doralt, supra n.
1; b) Annual International Law Seminar of the
Organization of American States (OAS), Rio de
Janeiro, Brazil, 18-19 August 1983; c) International Conference on the Techniques of International Commerce, Abidjan, Ivory Coast, 21-23
November 1983; d) Institut suisse de droit com-
paré, Colloque relatif à la Convention des Nations Unies sur les contrats de vente internationale de marchandises, Lausanne, 19-20 novembre
1984 (publication en préparation); e) Asian
Pacific Trade Law Seminar, Canberra, Australia,
22-27 November 1984.
2. Ch. Rousseau, Droit international public, t.
I (Paris 1970), p. 68; A. Verdross/B. Simma,
Universelles Völkerrecht. Theorie und Praxis
(Berlin 1981), p. 271.
3. J.P. Müller/L. Wildhaber, Praxis des Völker-
rechts, 2nd ed. (Bern 1982), p. 116. A. McNair,
The Law of Treaties (Oxford 1961), p. 79 et seq.
4. Müller/Wildhaber, supra n. 3, at p. 97 et
seq.; Verdross/Simma, supra n. 2, at pp. 436,
440.
5. Müller/Wildhaber, supra n. 3, at p. 116;
Verdross/Simma, supra n. 2, at p. 441.
6. Cf. Convention no. 111 of the ILO on discri-
mination in the field of employment and profession of 25 June 1958.
7. Cf. J.P. Müller/L. Wildhaber, supra n. 3, at
pp. 118-122, and cases mentioned.
8. R. Herber, "Vorbemerkung zum Verhältnis der
einheitlichen Kaufgesetze zu den Haager Ueberein-
kommen," in H. Dölle ed., Kommentar zum Einheitlichen Kaufrecht (München 1976) p. XXXIX. ULIS

and ULF had different official dates in some Contracting States because they were signified by the date on which they became nationally effective.

9. Geneva Convention of 7 June 1930 providing a Uniform Law for Bills of Exchange and Promissory Notes, League of Nations Treaty Series 143, 259; Geneva Convention of 19 March 1931 providing a Uniform Law for Cheques, League of Nations Treaty Series 143, 357.

10. Müller/Wildhaber, _supra_ n. 3 at p. 97; Verdross/Simma, _supra_ n. 2 at pp. 436, 440.

11. As to **Great Britain** see, e.g., the House of Lords in Buchanan & Co. vs. Babco Forwarding and Shipping, (1978) A.C. 141; (1977) I All E.R. 518. The case involved an Act of Parliament that implemented the Geneva CMR Convention of 1956 on the liability of carriers transporting goods by road. The House of Lords refused to take into account the case law of courts in Continental Europe, for the British implementary legislation did not contain a provision on interpretation and consideration of case law of other Contracting States.
However, the outcome was different in Fothergill vs. Monarch Airlines (1980) 2 All E.R. 696, (1980) 3 W.L.R. 209. In this case the Act of Parliament, which implemented the Warsaw Convention of 1929 (amended at the Hague in 1955) on the Liability for Carriage of Goods by Air, provided for a rule of interpretation and the consideration of the text in a foreign (French) language.

12. Cf. _infra_, N. 57-59; J. Honnold, _Uniform Law for International Sales under the 1980 United Nations Convention_ (Deventer 1982), pp. 125-128.

13. Cf. cases mentioned in n. 11.

14. P. Volken, _Konventionskonflikte im interna-_

tionalen Privatrecht (Zürich 1977), pp. 238-242.
15. Art. 1 para. 1: "This Convention applies to contracts of sale of goods between parties whose places of business are in different States."
16. The same rule can already be found in ULIS. Its Art. 1 para. 3 provides: "The application of the present Law shall not depend on the nationality of the parties." And Art. 7 of ULIS adds: "The present Law shall apply to sales regardless of the commercial or civil character of the parties or of the contracts."
17. Cf. infra n. 23, 24.
18. R. Herber, "Anwendungsbereich des UNCITRAL-Kaufrechtsübereinkommens," in P. Doralt, ed. supra n. 1, at p. 34; J. Honnold, supra n. 12, at N. 12-14, 40. P. Schlechtriem, Einheitliches UN-Kaufrecht, Beiträge zum ausländischen und internationalen Privatrecht, Bd. 46 (Tübingen 1981) pp. 9-10.
19. Same opinion J. Honnold, supra n. 12, at N. 41; P. Schlechtriem, supra n. 18, at p. 12.
20. Cf. "Commentary on the Draft Convention," prepared by the Secretariat (Doc. A/Conf. 97/5), in UN-Conference on Contracts for the International Sale of Goods; Vienna, (1984) p. 295; P. Schlechtriem, supra n. 18, at pp. 9-10. 1980; Official Records (New York 1981), p. 14 et. seq. Commentary on Art. 9, para. 7-9.
21. As to the relationship between substantive sales law and conflict-of-laws rules see H. Dölle, "Einheitliches Kaufgesetz und internationales Privatrecht," RabelsZ (1968) p. 438, with English summary at pp. 448-449; J. Kropholler, "Der 'Ausschluss' des internationalen Privatrechts im einheitlichen Kaufgesetz," RabelsZ (1974) p. 372 with English summary at pp. 386-387. Are in favor of the **exclusion** of conflicts rules: R. Herber, supra n. 18, at pp. 36-37; J.

Honnold, _supra_ n. 12, at N. 47. Are in favor of retaining the reference to conflicts rules: The Commentary of the Secretariat, _supra_ n. 20, at p. 15; Th. Krapp, 1 _ZSR_ (1984) p. 295; P. Schlecht-riem, _supra_ n. 18 at pp. 9-10.

22. Art. 1 para. 1 of ULIS reads as follows:

> 1. The present Law shall apply to con-tracts of sale of goods entered into by parties whose places of business are in the territories of different States, in each of the following cases:
>
> (a) where the contract involves the sale of goods which are at the time of the conclusion of the contract in the course of carriage or will be carried from the territory of one State to the territory of another;
>
> (b) where the acts constituting the offer and the acceptance have been effected in the territories of differ-ent States;
>
> (c) where delivery of the goods is to be made in the territory of a State other than that within whose territory the acts constituting the offer and the acceptance have been effected.

Art. II and III of the Hague Convention of 1964 relating to ULIS offer different reservations to this article.

23. In this sense the original Draft of UNCITRAL, see Commentary, _supra_ n. 20, at p. 15.

24. The Hague Conference on Private International Law is about to renew and revise the rules on the Law Applicable to Contracts for the International Sale of Goods. An extraordinary session of the Conference is to take place at The Hague from 14 October - 2 November 1985.

According to Art. 7 para. 1 of the new Draft

Convention of the Hague Conference: "A contract of sale is governed by the law chosen by the parties." And Art. 8 para. 1 adds: "To the extent that the law applicable to a contract of sale has not been chosen in accordance with Article 7, the contract is governed by the law of the state where the seller has his place of business at the time of conclusion of the contract." See Hague Conference on Private International Law -- Sales Preliminary Document No. 4 of August 1984, at pp. 13, 15; and report by A.T. von Mehren, p. 28 et seq. pp. 48-58.

25. Art. 95 was adopted on 10 April 1980 at the last plenary meeting of the Vienna Conference; the proposal was put forward by the Czechoslovakian delegation, Official Records, supra, n. 20, at p. 229. An earlier proposal of M.R. Herber (FRG) which suggested deleting Art. 1 (1)(b) was fortunately rejected altogether, see Official Records, supra n. 20, at pp. 236-238.

26. See, however, the Uniform Commercial Code, which has been adopted by 51 jurisdictions.

27. See Official Records, supra n. 20, at pp. 165, 434, 435. On the other hand, such a State will appear on the list of ratifications or accessions although the Convention applies only to some of its units.

28. See Official Records, supra n. 20, at p. 436. Art. 94 was not only adopted with respect to the General Conditions of Delivery of Goods that are applicble to transactions between organizations of CMEA-Member states (in this sense J. Honnold, supra n. 12, at N. 460); Art. 94 applies also to the Benelux, the Scandinavian countries or to Australia and New Zealand.

29. Are Member States of ULIS and ULF: Belgium, Gambia, the Federal Republic of Germany, Israel,

Italy, Luxembourg, the Netherlands, San Marino, the United Kingdom.

30. A former Contracting State ceases to be bound by the Convention.

31. Cf. J. Honnold, supra n. 12, at. N. 50; P. Schlechtriem, supra n. 19, at p. 13.

32. R. Herber, supra, n. 18, at p. 39; J. Honnold, supra n. 12, at N. 59-60.

33. R. Herber, supra, n. 18, at pp. 40-41.

34. The exclusion may also take place by an express reference to general conditions. On the other hand, the choice of a forum does not necessarily include the choice or exclusion of the Convention; J. Honnold, supra n. 12, at N. 74-84; P. Schlechtriem, supra n. 19, at pp. 21-22.

35. Art. 5 para. 2 ULIS:
    The present Law shall not apply to sales:
    ...
    (b) by authority of law or on execution
    or distress.

36. See U. Huber, "Der UNCITRAL-Entwurf eines Uebereinkommens über internationale Warenkaufverträge," RabelsZ (1979) p. 422. Official Records, supra n. 20, at p. 16, para. 6.

37. Art. 5 para. 1 ULIS:
    The present Law shall not apply to
    sales: ...
    (d) of any ship, vessel or aircraft,
    which is or will be subject to regis-
    tration;

38. See Official Records, supra n. 20, at pp. 16, 240.

39. Supra n. 19. at p. 16.

40. Supra n. 12, at N. 54.

41. Cf. N. 3.

42. The Vienna Convention on the Law of Treaties of 1969 is reprinted in Am.J.Int.Law (1970) p. 875.

43. See supra n. 11.

44. J. Honnold, supra n. 12, at. N. 90-92.

45. See also J. Honnold, supra n. 12, at N. 90 et seq.

46. The same postulate was formulated by P. Schlechtriem, in P. Doralt, ed. supra n. 1, at p. 46.

47. See, e.g., § 1-203 UCC; § 242 BGB; Art. 2 ZGB.

48. Supra n. 36, at pp. 432-433.

49. Supra n. 12, at N. 102.

50. Art. 17 ULIS:

> Questions concerning matters governed by the present Law which are not expressly settled therein shall be settled in conformity with the general principles on which the present law is based.

51. See Official Records, supra n. 20, at p. 18.

52. See F. Bydlinski, "Das allgemeine Vertragsrecht," in P. Doralt, ed. supra n. 1, at pp. 74-75.

CHAPTER THREE

USAGES OF TRADE AND OTHER AUTONOMOUS RULES OF INTERNATIONAL TRADE ACCORDING TO THE UN (1980) SALES CONVENTION

ALEKSANDAR GOLDŠTAJN
Professor of Law, Zagreb

I. INTRODUCTORY REMARKS

The United Nations Convention on the International Sale of Goods (1980), although formally confined to contracts for the international sale of goods, contains provisions which could be applied to all kinds of international commercial transactions. There are two reasons for this view. The first is that this Convention, which deals with international commercial contracts, includes some general provisions that in domestic legislation belong to the general part of the law of contract. This approach was necessary in order to provide the convention with a minimum of general rules and to enable it to function in a special field. This was achieved by the inclusion of two solutions in the "General Provisions" of the Convention--one concerning the interpretation of the Convention (Art. 7(1)), and the other dealing with the substantial problems of the applicable law and the interpretation of contracts (Art. 7(2), Art. 8, and Art. 9). These solutions exceed the framework of contracts of international sale of goods.

The second reason is that this way of introducting rules of general significance for all international commercial contracts will, in my opinion, be necessary until a general code of the lawof contract pertaining to international trade transactions has been adopted.

If we compare changes in the regulation of trade usages or the definitions of what is considered to be an international sale under the Hague Sale Conventions (1964) and the 1980 UN Convention, it can be noted that a step-by-step approach has been used to achieve solutions of general significance in recent developments.

My second remark concerns the title of my contribution: "Usages and Other Autonomous Rules of International Trade." Usages of trade constitute an essential part of the autonomous rules of international trade. The reason for their being emphasized in the text of the Convention and regulated separately lies in the fact that usages of trade are interpreted differently in domestic laws, even though the actual business practice is identical. In the preparatory stages preceding adoption of the Hague Conventions and the 1980 UN Convention, special attention was devoted to trade usages. The formulation accepted in the Convention will need theoretical explanations, and practice will show to what extent consensus has been achieved internationally. This is due to differences in the legal traditions of individual legal systems and recently also to the doubts that the developing countries have displayed in usages of trade. There is, therefore, nothing unusual in the statement made by Professor Honnold:

...One of the most important features
of the Convention is the legal effect
it gives to commercial usages and practices.[1]

The Convention will give legal writers, especially those concerned with arbitral case law,
an opportunity to clarify and do away with some
of the doubts the developing countries have in
regard to usages of trade applicable to international commercial contracts.

My third remark relates to the significance of
the Convention in the sense that it constitutes
the first step towards global unification of the
law of international trade to the extent to which
this can be achieved by conventions. The role of
the Convention will be to serve as a "background"
law for international contracts of sale, instead
of various national systems.[2]

The fact that the Convention was adopted indicates implicitly that UNCITRAL succeeded in
achieving world-wide cooperation in the field of
the international law of commercial contract. Its
adoption justifies the conclusion that in global
terms the political, ideological and juridical
impediments that acted as doctrinal and political
obstacles to international cooperation in the
creation of a world legal order in the field of
commercial transactions have been removed. As
Professor Schmitthoff stated:

The ideological and economic division
of the world would not provide an
obstacle. The successful co-operation
of countries of different social ideol-
ogy and in a different stage of economic and industrial development within
the framework of UNCITRAL proves this.
Faithful to its original brief,
UNCITRAL has restricted itself to the

technical task of removing legal barri-
ers to the flow of international trade
and has been little affected by the di-
visive effect of politics.[3]

During preparation of the Draft Convention, in
connection with a few points, it was suggested
that the interests of industrial and developing
countries called for different rules. These
rules--as Professor Honnold stated--arose in sur-
prisingly technical settings. Happily, the delegates finally found acceptable solutions even to
these problems.[4]

The adoption of the Convention has not fully
removed different viewpoints on the suitability
of uniform legal methods for all societies. It
will therefore be necessary to examine the justi-
fiability of the reservations made in regard to
usages of trade and the method applied during
preparation of the Convention, i.e. whether a
convention which only contains optional rules is
a satisfactory way of establishing a global system of international law of contract for commercial transactions. This question implies that
the issue of freedom of contract, or the autonomy
of the parties' will, was a crucial problem which
the Convention solved by making all its provisions optional. This problem is important because
the view was expressed that the Convention should
also contain mandatory rules. These issues were
taken into consideration during discussions on
the possibility of establishing a uniform legal
system for international commercial transactions.
As a result, extensive agreement has been reached
between Eastern and Western legal scholars regarding the prospects of the law of international
trade. This interplay of legal schools has made
it possible for UNCITRAL to achieve cooperation
in all regions of the world.

Finally, the modern _lex_ _mercatoria_ has not yet found a satisfactory place in legal writing. Contrary to developed business practice, classical textbooks are rather late in this respect, sticking mainly to the traditional doctrine about the sources of commercial law and law in general. Many textbooks have still not gone beyond the framework set by municipal rules, thus ignoring the fact that practice has developed innominate contracts, i.e. types of contracts that do not exist in any national law, although quantitatively such contracts by far exceed the number of nominate contracts regulated by national laws, and, in terms of economic significance, play an exceptional role in domestic trade, especially international commerce. This was noted more than half a century ago by Rabel[5], who drew attention to the now well-known fact that not infrequently domestic laws exist only on paper. The practice has bypassed them as the result of usages of trade and commercial practices thanks to freedom of contracting.

Significant contracts, such as leasing, factoring and franchising, and numerous types of contracts in the spheres of banking, insurance, maritime affairs, oil and gas, and film making show a great degree of similarity. In the practice they have spread far beyond their countries of origin (frequently the U.S.A.). These contracts are economically much more significant than many types of contracts regulated by national laws, e.g., leasing contracts or contracts of goods inspection,[6] and thereby contribute to the security of the contracting parties in international sales.

This flaw in legal writing is being gradually eliminated by leading writers in the field of the law of international trade. "Novelty is always a

painful experience to the lawyer who traditionally has a conservative outlook. But the international lawyer can fulfil his function of assist-
ing international business only if he is fully
aware of the developing tendencies of the modern
world" (Schmitthoff).[7] The general theory of law
formed during the period of "nationalization" of
the medieval lex mercatoria takes modern developments into account. This, in turn, raises
the question of the limits of national
legislations in regulating the law of international trade. Indeed, if we have a look at textbooks, we cannot but notice that most of them
ignore international trade practice, which leads
to discrepancies between living law and the law
found in statutes and books. Antiquated municipal laws, on the one hand, and legal doctrine,
on the other, confine themselves to legal problems concerning the so-called special part of the
law of contract in the continental system, to nominate contracts, i.e. to those which were and
still are regulated by actual laws of contract.
These laws do not include the varied and numerous
contracts established by modern business practice, which have not been incorporated into municipal laws for reasons we shall discuss below.
Therefore, the obsolete provisions of municipal
laws, with rare exceptions, such as the United
States Uniform Commercial Code and the writings
based on such provisions, cannot satisfy the
needs of modern international business transactions. What is more, judicial case law has
contributed but little to the development of
municipal laws due to the fact that business circles prefer arbitration as a method of solving
commercial disputes. Arbitral case law, however,
has only recently become accessible to the public

and is gradually attracting the interest of legal writers.[8]

II. PREREQUISITES OF THE MODERN LEX MERCATORIA

1. Economic Background

Regardless of the economic order of individual countries and differences in social systems, the view has generally been accepted that international trade functions within the framework of market economies. The world market is based on market business methods. Countries with centrally-planned economies have resigned themselves to the fact that international commercial relations remain subject to the rules of market economies. Big enterprises specialized in individual branches have a monopoly on foreign trade.

On the other hand, developing countries do not have a uniform economic and legal system, as do countries with centrally-planned economies.

For the purposes of foreign trade, all countries have accepted the legal concept of freedom of contracting and use enterprises as the legal form of contracting parties. The concept of corporation and enterprise, as the forms in which parties enter into individual commercial transactions, includes the notion of legal person, separate from and independent of its incorporators. The concept of legal person is known world-wide and is the "universally accepted heritage of mankind" (Schmitthoff). In market-economy countries this concept is based on the economic and philosophical concepts of their social order, and in planned economies state-owned enterprises are separate from their incorporators.

2. Legal Factors

Almost 25 years ago I wrote in an article "The New Law Merchant":

> Notwithstanding the differences in the political, economic and legal systems of the world, a new law merchant is rapidly developing in the world of international trade. It is time that recognition be given to the existence of an <u>autonomous</u> commercial law that has grown <u>independent</u> <u>of</u> <u>the</u> <u>national</u> <u>systems</u> <u>of</u> <u>law</u>.

I further stated:

> Two legal factors have made this development possible: the optional character of the law relating to the purchase and sale of goods, and the ever-growing use of arbitration in commercial disputes. The optional nature of commercial law is due to the fact that that branch is founded on the autonomy of parties' will--freedom of contracting enables those engaged in international trade to overcome the historical peculiarities of the various national systems of law.[9]

In my report at the Colloquium of Experts on the New Sources of the Law of International Trade held in London (1962) within the framework of the International Association of Legal Science under the auspices of UNESCO, I stated as follows:

> The law governing trade transactions is neither capitalist nor socialist; it is a means to an end, and, therefore, the fact that the beneficiaries of such transactions are different in this or

that country is no obstacle to the development of international trade.[10]

This statement was made at a time when international legal experts were preoccupied with
East-West relations. As a result of the London
Colloquium, at which basic questions concerning
the genesis, content and development of the law
of international trade were discussed, extensive
agreement was reached between Eastern and Western
scholars regarding the prospects of the law of
international trade. Professor Schmitthoff was
right in saying:

> In the 1950s and 1960s, when lawyers
> from countries of different economic
> structure and in different stages of
> economic development met at interna-
> tional conferences an important **dis-
> covery** (emphasis added) was made: the
> legal techniques of carrying on inter-
> national trade are the same everywhere,
> irrespective of the political, ideolo-
> gical or economic orientation of the
> countries in question.[11]

Professor Schmithoff's General Report "The Law
of International Trade, Its Growth, Formulation
and Operation,"[12] which he presented at the
London Colloquium, marked the beginning of a new
era that can be characterized as the "rediscovery
of the international character of commercial law"
(Schmitthoff).

The optional character of municipal laws, with
exceptional state interference by invocation of
ordre public, is the legal expression of market
economies. For this reason, the UN Sales Convention (1980) has only non-mandatory rules. As the
result of economic competition on the free international market, new types of contracts are being
created, either completely original or in combi-

nation with the existing types of nominate and/or
innominate contracts, one of whose significant
features is complexity.[13]

In view of the nature of international commercial contracts, it follows that this kind of
transaction belongs to the sphere of private law.
As was stated in the Report of the Secretary
General of the United Nations on the Progressive
Development of the Law of International Trade,
the expression "the law of International Trade"
may be defined as the body of rules governing
commercial relationships of a private law nature
involving different countries.[14]

The reasons for the universal similarity of
the law of international trade lies in the fact
that this branch of law is based on three fundamental propositions:

    (i)   The principle of autonomy of the par-
        ties' will;

    (ii)   That contracts must be faithfully ful-
        filled (pacta sunt servanda);

    (iii) The use of arbitration.

In the microsphere of international trade, including commercial transactions between independent enterprises, commodity-money relations are
known to have existed under different social systems long before the emergence of capitalist and
subsequently socialist societies. There is no
need to insist on this statement after agreement
on the acceptability of legal techniques has been
reached with the CMEA socialist countries, whose
planned economies, are, with respect to freedom
of contracting, based on different economic foun-
dations. Nevertheless, it is useful to mention
this here because only developing countries found
it necessary to make certain corrections in the
UN Sales Convention, especially in regard to
usages of trade. Similar reservations had been

previously expressed by planned-economy countries.

Some characteristics of codification are common to all legal systems and are conditioned by
the possibilities of each codification, be it national or international. One should take into account the fact that there is something in business practice that differs from written municipal
laws; there is something that takes no account of
municipal laws, something that ignores or even
negates them. Commercial law is not created in
parliaments alone; its makers also include those
engaged in business. It should be added that the
increasing significance of commercial arbitration, which sanctions this law and its awards,
transcend the legal conceptions of municipal law.

Several factors have contributed to this development, as I stated earlier:[15]

(i) The non-mandatory character of municipal rules;

(ii) The inadequacy of municipal rules;

(iii) A certain similarity of municipal
rules pertaining to commercial transactions;

(iv) The positive climate of municipal law
in respect of commercial arbitration;

(v) The limited effect of ordre public;

(vi) Economic and sociological factors.

Each of these factors deserves some explanation. However, a general remark should be made
with respect to the law of international trade.

All legal systems agree, subject to some limitations, that the parties are at liberty to stipulate expressly the proper law of the contract.
Commercial practice has made maximum use of the
possibilities arising from the optional character
of municipal rules. This destiny has been shared
by international legislation in the field, as in-

dicated by business practice in the application
of the Hague Uniform Laws on the International
Sale of Goods.

Of the most important reasons for departing
from municipal rules, the following can be mentioned:

a) Municipal rules are too generalized and
traditionally rely on historical concepts, both
with regard to general principles and the regulation of individual kinds of transactions;

b) International business practice is developing within the framework of individual
branches, thus specialization is one of its basic
features;

c) Domestic legislation does not take international elements into account, whereas the
law of international trade must respect the recognized principles of international law created
by business practice;

d) Statutes are more difficult to change
and accordingly more difficult to adjust to the
needs of international trade.

In regard to the needs of international trade,
we should further add that international trade
has created new forms of transactions; moreover,
it has created complex types of contracts, which,
due to their complexity, cannot be easily classified under standard transactions governed by national laws, especially in view of the fact that
in international commercial transactions partners
are involved who are outside the influence of national laws.

Since muncipal laws cannot give an answer to
everyday questions that arise in international
commercial practice, the law-making monopoly has
disappeared to a considerable extent in the field
of commercial law, the law-creating role being
shared by law-makers and parties representing

other interests. Modern commercial law embodies
concepts and institutions which have come about
as the result of international practice.

What was said under a) and b) also holds true
for international codification concerning commercial contracts.

It should be added that the law of international trade is to be applied and interpreted
uniformly. Imposing a national framework upon
them would hinder uniform interpretation, which
is a precondition for legal security.

III. THE CONTENT OF THE LAW OF INTERNATIONAL
TRADE--LEX MERCATORIA

1. Denomination

There are various nuances among legal writers
regarding both the name and substance of lex
mercatoria.

Professor Schmitthoff defined the law of international trade as follows:

> The autonomous law of international
> trade is derived from two sources, viz.
> international legislation and interna-
> tional commercial custom.
> The term "international legislation" is
> a misnomer, since the power to create
> legal rules in a particular territory
> can only be exercised by, or by author-
> ity of, the national sovereign.
>
> International commercial custom con-
> sists of commercial practices, usages
> or standards which are so widely used
> that businessmen engaged in interna-
> tional trade expect their contracting

parties to conform with them and which are formulated by international agencies, such as the International Chamber of Commerce, the United Nations Ecnomic Commission of Europe, or international trade associations. The term "international commercial custom" is used solely to denote custom formulated by international agencies; the commercial custom which is not so formulated is referred to as commercial usage or practice (usances).[16]

In his well-known theoretical work Commercial Law in a Changing Economic Climate, Schmitthoff states that the autonomy of the parties' will in the law of contract is the foundation on which an autonomous law of international trade is developed by the parties. It is, as he says,

therefore wrong to attribute the character of international or supranational law to international trade law... The best way to describe the peculiar character of international trade law is to refer to it as transnational law.[17]

Later, Professor Schmitthoff specified that the "transnational law of international trade is a new lex mercatoria."[18]

The term "transnational law" for the new lex mercatoria is also used by other authors to denote the law of international trade as "the Transnational Law of International Commerce."[19] Professor Goldman was guided by the same thought when he said:

Nous n'avons pas besoin de dire que cet ordre juridique est supérieur aux ordres juridiques nationaux... Il est différent, il est transnational, mais non pas supranational; il est à tra-

vers les frontières, mais pas aux-
dessus des frontières.[20]

Most learned authors have accepted the term
lex mercatoria. Among those who use it are
Bonell[21], Coing[22], Fouchard[23], Loussouarn[24],
Klein[25], Lalive[26], Vischer[27], Lando[28], Delaume[29],
while some use both terms, namely "transnational
law" and lex mercatoria, as for example Schmitthoff[30], Goldman[31], David[32] and Berman[33].

Therefore, we shall alternately use the terms
"international commercial law," "the law of
international trade," "the transnational law of
international trade" and lex mercatoria, although the latter is suitable for legal experts
but not for businessmen. It should be noted that
multilateral conventions and current literature
still prefer the term "international commercial
law" or "the law of international trade." The
latter has been accepted as a conventional expression, regardless of the doctrinal distinctions which make it possible to differentiate
between truly international law in the sense of
public international law and private international law.

2. The Content of Lex Mercatoria

Lex mercatoria is the autonomous law of international trade. Thus, I wrote in the 1960s that
it is time that recognition be given to the
existence of an autonomous commercial law that
has grown independently of national systems of
law.[34]

Schmitthoff sees a separate body of legal
rules in the law of international trade. Thus, it
is necessary to take into account the division of
traditional commercial law into two branches, the

law applying to home transactions and that applying to international business.[35] The law of
international trade is a separate branch of law.
The autonomous law of international trade is derived from two sources--as Schmitthoff puts it--
from international legislation and international
commercial custom.

According to Fouchard, usages of trade make up
the hard kernel (le noyau dur) of the lex mercatoria:

> Règles de droit nées d'une pratique ré-
> pétée dans un milieu déterminé et ap-
> plicables sauf convention contraire des
> parties... avaient connaissance ou au-
> raient dû en avoir connaissance.[36]

According to one view, the international law
of commercial transactions--lex mercatoria--is an
international body of rules based on an understanding among merchants and the contractual
practice of the international community consisting predominantly of merchants, shipowners, in-
surers and bankers from all countries of the
world. The source of universality is not only
comparative law, i.e. the similarity of merchants' concepts and institutions in various legal systems, but primarily the contemporary process of interaction on the part of those involved
in the international commercial community. Custom
is the primary source, while the law of international trade is a special type of international
law.[37]

Horn maintains that the relevant alternative
to international legislation is not so much customary law as international commercial custom in
the broadest sense, i.e. commercial usages, standard clauses, contracts or contractual rules.[38]
The approach of the supporters of lex mercatoria
and "transnational law" is based on the recog-

nition of the great influence which the will of
the parties engaged in international transactions
has had on the sources of international trade
law. This influence has been exercised directly
by means of the drafting of contract clauses, ad-
hesion contracts, standard contract forms and
general conditions, and the gradual formation of
usages and customs employed in contractual dispositions or in dealings between merchants.[39]

Professor Goldman noted:

> International economic relationships
> may perfectly well be governed by a
> body of specific rules including trans-
> national custom, general principles of
> law, and arbitral case law. Within this
> body of rules, the general principles
> of law are not only those referred to
> in Article 38(c) of the Statute of the
> International Court of Justice; there
> may be added to it principles progres-
> sively established by general and con-
> stant usages of international trade.

In one of his more recent works Professor
Schmitthoff says that "the concept of trade usages is known to most legal systems." Furthermore, he classifies usages of trade as codified
trade usages (which, in his opinion, include formulated international trade usages) and unformu-
lated international trade usages of general application.[41]

As for myself, I stated that a new autonomous
law was being developed in practice, embodied in
standard contract forms, standard clauses, general conditions of trade, commercial customs and
trade usages.[42]

Usages of trade constitute the most important
part of lex mercatoria. National laws and multilateral conventions explicitly emphasize usages

of trade. This, however, does not exhaust the content of lex mercatoria. Along with usages of trade, all other phenomenal forms of business practice must be taken into account, together with all the implications arising from their legal qualification, although it differs from the legal qualification of usages of trade. Here we have in mind commercial practices in international trade in general, and, in particular, general conditions, standard clauses, standard contracts as well as general principles of law and codes of conduct which have recently been drafted with the intention of contributing to the formation of fair-play rules. These forms of business practice will be discussed in the part of this paper dealing with the lex mercatoria as a form of positive law.

Numerous authors classify only usages of trade and other forms of international business practices under the modern lex mercatoria. The fact alone that a considerable number of international trade contracts are governed nowadays by international conventions and uniform laws "cannot be considered as proof of the existence of an autonomous lex mercatoria, because these conventions become relevant only to the extent that they have been ratified by States, and therefore have become positive law within the various national systems."[43]

Another dilemma involves the qualification of practices which have not or not yet become usages of trade. Schmitthoff rightly draws attention to the lack of clarity regarding the transition from practice, custom and customary law, which, until recently, has made it difficult to determine usages of trade,[44] adding:

> In practice, the distinction between
> statutory, recognized, acknowledged and

adopted trade usages is sometimes not
strictly drawn and the transition is
gradual.[45]
In judicial and international arbitration
practice these distinctions are sometimes referred to as questio facti and sometimes as a
"fruitful area of research." The "transition from
what practice is doing to usages and to custom
and eventually to law is a very slow one, and
even in the formulating agencies expressions of
the lex mercatoria are not generally accepted...
If we disregard the form and look at the substance, more indications show themselves on the
horizon."[46]
It has been necessary to present all these
opinions and differences among authors in order
to determine the content of the lex mercatoria
more easily. It is not suprising that some important questions are still being researched in academic circles in order to be able to take a stand
on the status of lex mercatoria in the legal
system. As Goldman stated, "The commentators in
the early 1960s began to take note of this evolution. Clive Schmitthoff was the first in England to salute the 'New Law Merchant.'" Professor
Goldman concluded in 1964 that the lex mercatoria
could be acknowledged a place.
In a lecture held at the Hague Académie de
droit international[48], Professor Kegel confirmed,
under the marginal title "Doctrine (Clive M.
Schmitthoff and others)," the existence of the
    most modern doctrine, namely the doc-
    trine of a New Law Merchant. This trend
    is represented mainly by Clive M.
    Schmitthoff, Philippe Kahn, Berthold
    Goldman and Eugen Langen, and in the
    East Block by Laszlo Réczei and
    Aleksander Goldstajn.

Article 9(2) of the UN Sales Convention (1980) gives legal effect to commercial usages by stating that the usage must be one which "in international trade is widely known to, and regularly observed by, parties to contracts of the type involved in the particular trade concerned."

The lex mercatoria obtained international recognition in the Vienna Convention (1980), and prior to that in the Hague Sales Conventions-- ULFIS and ULIS. In addition, it has been recognized by legislation changes at the national level, all of which have resulted in the emergence of the new lex mercatoria. Nevertheless, some categories such as general principles of law, codes of conduct, non-legal arrangements and non-legal sanctions still attract attention in the legal theory of international trade, and thus also in the general theory of law. Professor Schmitthoff warns that modern law teaching aims at teaching law in its social, political and academic context. The living law cannot be distilled in a pure and isolated form; it is a part of the social life of the community.[49]

II. THE NEW INTERNATIONAL ECONOMIC ORDER AND LEX MERCATORIA

As far as international commercial transactions are concerned, East-West economic relations have found a satisfactory solution. Countries with centrally-planned economies as well as those with free-market economies have held the law of international trade to be acceptable for both economic and social systems due to the fact that the external commercial law of the CMEA countries transcends the division based on different economic concepts for home transactions. Coopera-

tion with representatives of the CMEA countries
has been achieved within the framework of
UNCITRAL and other formulating agencies.

The developing countries are faced with the
extremely difficult task of linking their own
less developed economies with the complicated
mechanism of international trade that has been
developed over the centuries without their active contribution and without regard to the needs
of the new independent developing States.[50]

In view of this problem, the UN Sales Convention sought to satisy the needs of the developing
countries within the framework of UNCITRAL by
developing a system that is private law in nature
and that, in the eyes of the developing countries, would serve their needs in the same measure as those of their partners abroad.

This question had already emerged at the Hague
Diplomatic Conference on the International Sale
of Goods in connection with the provisions of the
two sales conventions regarding the duties of the
parties to communicate information needed by the
other party "promply," i.e. within as short a
period of time as possible under the circumstances, and in connection with the meaning of
the wording of the Draft Convention that communications shall be made by the usual means consid-
ering the circumstances.

At the UN Conference on the Limitation Period
in International Sales (New York 1974), the representatives of some developing African countries pleaded for the longest possible limitation periods for claims, stating that due to lack
of funds, they might be subjected to sanctions if
they failed to meet their obligations on time.

During preparation of the UN Sales Convention,
the developing countries suggested different
rules in a few instances, e.g., the time for

giving notice of defective goods and the circumstances under which a party may suspend performance due to the possible failure of counterperformance. The position of several industrial
States that the strict notice requirements contained in their domestic rules should be retained
was also opposed by the representatives of developing countries.

The next issue concerned the excuse for failure to notify the lack of conformity of the
goods. Efforts to relax the notice requirements
(Article 39) had failed by narrow margins. Infor-
mal discussions revealed--as Professor Honnold
stated--that some developing countries were
seriously dissatisfied with this result and that
the representatives of industrial countries had
strongly resisted relaxation of the notice requirements proposed. The issue was reopened and a
compromise solution worked out. (This led to the
inclusion of Article 44 in the Convention).[51]

Despite some objections of a political nature,
the discussion during preparation of the Draft
Convention was focused primarily on legal techniques rather than on economic and political
issues.[52] As a result, in some fields it was difficult to distinguish the views of the representatives of socialist countries from those of
others. Political overtones were felt in positions on usages of trade insisted upon by the
developing countries.[53] This ended in a compromise, which, however, resulted in much more complex solutions for some issues, but such was the
"price of unification."[54]

The problems that had to be solved by the
drafters of the Convention will emerge again in
practice in connection with the interpretation of
the Convention's provisions.

The most serious objection made by the developing countries concerned usages of trade, the
result being that a provision proposal similar to
that contained in Article 9(2) of ULIS was eliminated from the Draft "as unnecessary." More
specifically, the ULIS provision that in the
event of conflict between the applicable usage
and the Uniform Law, the usages prevail unless
otherwise agreed by the parties, was regarded to
be in conflict with the constitutional principles
of some States and against public policy in
others.[55] A compromise solution was reached, resulting in the following formulation of Article
9(2) of the Convention:

> The parties are considered, unless
> otherwise agreed, to have impliedly
> made applicable to their contract or
> its formation a usage of which the
> parties knew or ought to have known and
> which in international trade is widely
> known to, and regularly observed by,
> parties of the contracts of the type
> involved in the particular trade con-
> cerned.

Regarding the inapplicable concept of "usage,"
Honnold said:

> "Usage" and similar legal ideas have
> been used in settings that are funda-
> mentally different from trade usages to
> which Article 9 refers... Even more re-
> mote from the current problem is
> "custom" as a source of public interna-
> tional law that binds States. Govern-
> ments have sometimes viewed such
> "custom" as inconsistent with their
> sovereignty... Echoes of these fears
> were heard in UNCITRAL in early discus-
> sions of trade usages, but it became

evident that construing sales of contracts in the light of expectations
current in international trade does not
impair the sovereignty of States.[56]

I believe that this stand on usages of trade
is the result of a misunderstanding. Let us first
take a look at the terminology "usage," "usage of
trade," "custom." Even in some continental systems it frequently occurs that no distinction is
made in legal writings between "usages" and "usages of trade." Without going into these problems
outside the framework of commercial laws, especially the law of international trade, a distinction should be made between "custom" in
public international law and "usages of trade"
("usances"). "Modern legal systems generally accord a significant role to customs--or usages as
they have come to be called--and give a similar
role to courses of dealing between parties." As
for the American Uniform Commercial Code, the
term "usage of trade" is "relatively new and
favoured by the Code over the more traditional
and narrower term 'custom'."[57]

As I once noted:

It should be borne in mind that in
international trade the contracting
parties' rights and duties are rarely
determined solely by their own stipu-
lations. This self-regulation is normally supplemented above all by rules
derived from practice, i.e. commercial
usages... Commercial usages are created
within a specialized branch, their applicability being self-understood
therefore. Commercial usages are opera-
tive in relation to those who know them
or who were in the position to know
them. What is customary should be ef-

fective _ipso_ _facto_; it is not necessary
to decree it, and still less to have
explicit agreement.
I further stated:
If the contract lacks more detailed
clauses, it is executable in the customary way. In doubtful cases it is to
be taken that the meaning of the contract agrees with the meaning attaching
thereto in commercial traffic... The
parties must be supposed, while appre-
ciating the general practice, to have
chosen the application of trade usages.
Generally speaking, the parties reduce
what they are expressly agreeing about
to special details, omitting to cite
expressly the usages which they
consider to be implicit in their contract. Such a method of forming contracts is practised for economic reasons, as a time and money saving expe-
dient, while the inclusion of usages
instead of detailed formulation in each
individual case makes for uniform application. A conscientious party pre-
sumes the application of usages and
expects the other party to do likewise.
Failing this, the party observing the
usages would be put in an unequal position in relation to the partner who
either does not know the usages or
disregards them.
Therefore, usages of trade will always be applied unless they are excluded in a way which
discloses a contrary intention. Commercial usages
applicable in international trade do not exist to
satisfy the needs of individual countries but the
higher interests of the international community.

Commercial usages constitute one of the sources of the law of international trade.[58] Professor Eörsi has also obsearved that "the law regulating the international flow of commodities might in principle be uniform for all types of countries."[59]

As I myself have pointed out, the two Hague Conventions (1964) on international sales do not adequately take into account the interests of new States.[60] However, on the basis of the improved formulation of the UN Sales Convention on usages of trade, there is no reason to oppose the generally accepted views on the indispensability of usages of trade and the conditions for their application to international commercial contracts. There are two arguments supporting this.

One is based on the economic position of the contracting parties in international trade, and the other on the legal technique that will inevitably be used in modern trade, especially international trade. These two arguments deserve a brief explanation. As already noted in connection with the economic prerequisities, international trade takes place under the market conditions on the world market. International commercial transactions are concluded between independent enterprises having the status of legal persons all over the world. These participants in international commercial transactions are free to conclude business transactions and determine their content. Under these conditions, the legal prerequisite of international trade transactions is that they should take place within the framework of private law, which is characterized by optional rules, the application of mandatory rules in a narrow field being the exception. Any deviation from this rule would substantially hinder the flow of international business transactions and

partly make them impossible. For this reason, the
Vienna Convention does not contain any mandatory
rules.

It is, therefore, not possible to give an af-
firmative answer to the question whether the request of the developing countries for the establishment of a new international economic order
could be satisfied by departing from the general
stand on usages of trade in international trade.
Even under this unthinkable presumption, the ob-
jectives of the new international economic order
would not be attained. As the representative of a
developing country, Date-Bach pointed out:

> It is important to recall that the
> Draft Convention on Contracts for the
> International Sale of Goods regulates
> only a legal form. It is within UNCTAD
> that the issues relating to the sub-
> stance of international trade have
> usually been debated, studied and solu-
> tions sought for such issues. Most of
> the work done in UNCITRAL is unlikely
> to lead to really significant changes
> in the economic relations between de-
> veloped and developing countries. Of
> course, form can never be totally iso-
> lated from substance...
> ...In the case of international sales,
> there are both international buyers and
> sellers in all countries...
> ...An important reason why ULIS and
> ULFIS did not find acceptance in most
> developing countries is the political
> fact of the non-representation of most
> developing countries at the diplomatic
> conference. In political terms, this
> attitude is quite understandable...

However, the distinguished UNCITRAL representative from Ghana rightly observed:
> It is understandable for organized com-
> munities to refuse to submit to legis-
> lation produced by a legislative pro-
> cess in which they have not partici-
> pated... In some developing countries,
> some large-scale traders whose business
> may include international trade are il-
> literate.

In regard to usages of trade, Date-Bach said:
> The Draft gives no overriding effect to
> customs and usages. They are to bind
> the parties only if they have agreed
> to them, expressly or impliedly. Ac-
> cordingly, it follows that no such
> custom or usage can be implied if it is
> in conflict with any term expressly
> agreed upon by the parties. Trade prac-
> tices and usages evolved in interna-
> tional trade can thus be excluded by
> the parties to international sales con-
> tracts if they agree on terms inconsis-
> tent with practices and usages.[61]

Macroeconomic relations are regulated by public law, and thus international macroeconomic
relations are a part of international economic
law. Macroeconomic relations influence the sphere
of microeconomic relations, which includes the
law of international trade, in that they
determine the position of the parties engaged in
microeconomic relations. Therefore, changes in
international trade law in favour of the economic weaker can be achieved by altering the economic prerequisites for individual situations in
contractual relations, but not by optional rules
of the law of contract. As participants in international business transactions, individual firms

cannot change the economic positions of weaker partners from developing countries. Economic laws of the world market are in force here.[62]

The second argument is of a legal nature. There is no doubt that something can be achieved within the framework of the law of contract, as shown by the work of the UN Economic Commission for Europe, and this will also be the case with the UN Sales Convention. On the other hand, it should be emphasized that usages of trade are optional rules and that the Convention does not cover issues concerning the validity of "any usage" (Article 4(a)).

Municipal laws are generalized and therefore cannot meet the needs of individual branches. This holds true for any codification; even international conventions cannot avoid this trap. Special rules, the most important being primarily usages of trade, are those factors which are continuously being developed to satisfy the specific needs of international trade. Usages of trade and practices are legal tools and a kind of legal technique, just as municipal law provisions or international conventions are. This does not exclude the possibility that in individual situations the economically stronger partners can create a more favourable position for themselves within general associations if they act as centres of trade in their respective branches. However, they do so by the strength of their economic position, not because of weaknesses of legal solutions. This economic position adapts itself to the economic situation on the market.

"The dominant theme of the Convention is the role of the contract made by the parties--a theme of deeper significance than may be evident at first glance." To avoid the area of uncertainty posed by the vague contours of "mandatory rules,"

"such controls over contracts are out of place in
the international market and are excluded by the
Convention. The Convention's rules play a supporting role, supplying answers to problems that
the parties have failed to solve by contract"
(Honnold).[63] Uniform law is "the last link in a
hierarchical chain and recourse to it will be had
only when from the sources preceding it the mutual rights and obligations of the parties cannot
be established" (Réczei).[64] Therefore, as a part
of the lex contractus, usages of trade have been
recognized as a source of commercial law and
international trade law.

   As Schmitthoff notes:
      The motives for entering into a con-
      tract, for making use of legal tech-
      nique, may be very different in the
      various national economies. The dis-
      tinction between the legal technique of
      contracting and the motivation for con-
      tracting enables us to depoliticise the
      law of international trade.[65]
   And, as I stated:
      The fact that the beneficiaries of
      transactions are different in this or
      that country is no obstacle to the de-
      velopment of international trade.[66]
Just as the developing countries did not take
part in the creation of usages of trade, this
also holds true for many other countries not at
the level of the developed countries. It took a
long time to establish usages of trade and practices which, like legal techniques, have been
accepted universally as a result of their rational content. This is confirmed, for example, by
the ICC Uniform Customs and Practice for Documentary Credits and INCOTERMS, which have world-wide
acceptance, and the FIDIC contract, which has

been accepted by organizations in 73 countries. Moreover, the legislators of some developing countries have incorporated it into some provisions of their law.[67]

The weaker position of the less developed countries is a fact. The economic reasons for this have already been pointed out; however, in addition, the lack of a workable infrastructure and education should also be mentioned. In many countries the legal infrastructure lags behind that of the industrial countries. As a result, the enterprises in countries with an advanced economy and considerable share of foreign trade are in a better position. Furthermore, their market economies[68] and national systems are better suited to international sales. The experience with the Hague (1964) Sales Convention shows that some large firms excluded ULIS in their standard contracts.[69]

V.   LEX MERCATORIA AS POSITIVE LAW

1.   Lex Mercatoria--Transnational Law of Commercial Transactions

The term lex mercatoria is the common denominator of all the sources of the autonomous law of international trade. The law merchant arose in the Middle Ages as a body of international customary rules. The international character of the old law merchant is the result of four factors: the unifying effect of the law of fairs, the universality of customs of the sea, the activity of notary publics, and the use of arbitration as special courts. The second period was characterized by the incorporation of this international law merchant into national laws;

however, even during this period commercial law
did not entirely lose its international character. At this time the law-creating custom of the
international business community was also active,
as it had been in the Middle Ages. The third,
contemporary, stage is characterized by the fact
that the law of international trade has reverted
to the concept of internationalism (Schmitthoff).[70]

If we compare the medieval lex mercatoria with
the modern law merchant, we see that the same
factors that led to the creation of the medieval
law also played an important role in the formation of the modern law. These include the universal practice of international trade (standard
contracts and general conditions produced by
formulating agencies and various associations)
and the use of arbitral tribunals as special
courts for international commercial disputes. In
contrast to the spontaneous creation of the law
merchant in the Middle Ages, the modern lex mercatoria is contained, to a great extent but not
exclusively, in the acts of formulating agencies
and business associations.

The modern lex mercatoria comprises standard
contract forms, general conditions of business,
commercial customs, trade usages, and guide
texts as well as general standards such as good
faith, pacta sunt servanda, duty to cooperate,
duty to inform, responsibility, and general principles.

The body of the modern lex mercatoria consists of sources which vary in origin (the actual
practice as rendered in written as well as
unwritten usages; the work of various formulating
agencies), in content (codified and non-codified
practices, recommendations, guides, codes of conduct) and in legal qualifications (usages of

trade as implied contract terms, general conditions if invoked, recommendations, codes of conduct and guide texts, if and to the extent they
reflect the current practice). In my opinion,
Professor Schmitthoff has best characterized the
present situation by saying:

> We have to face the fact that the new
> law merchant which is emerging before
> our eyes is an entirely new phenomenon.
> When trying to understand it and take
> it as what it was in the Middle Ages
> and what it will be again: unsystema-
> tic, complex and multiform, but of be-
> wildering vigour, realism and origina-
> lity.[71]

Just as the sources of lex mercatoria are
fluid, there are also nuances in the docrtine regarding the position of lex mercatoria in the
legal system. According to Schmitthoff, transnational law is the uniform law developed by
parallelism of action in various national systems
in an area of optional law." As a result, lex
mercatoria is found in "various formulations of
the appropriate international institutions,"[72]
such as the International Chamber of Commerce,
UNCITRAL and UNIDROIT.

Goldman maintains that

> the criterion for determining the ambit
> of lex mercatoria does not solely re-
> side in the **object** of its constituent
> elements, but also in its **origin** and
> its **customary,** and thus spontaneous,
> nature... Lex mercatoria today ful-
> fills in an effective manner the fun-
> ction of positive law, and national
> courts of the highest level recognized
> it as such. Lex mercatoria and **positive
> law;** lex mercatoria and the **general**

theory of law--these are two aspects of the accomplishment of the newly reborn lex mercatoria.[73]

On the other hand, according to Bonell[74], lex mercatoria is not an independent legal system, whereas Coing[75] notes that in the case law of West Germany it is in principle held that spontaneous norms, such as lex mercatoria, are rules of law (Rechtsnormen). Opponents who underrate lex mercatoria, which is not a fully closed system, overrate at the same time the level of perfection of state legislation.

2. Lex Mercatoria and Positive Law

There is agreement in doctrine that the new lex mercatoria is not and cannot be separated from national law. Schmitthoff notes that the autonomy of the parties' will in the law of contract is the foundation on which an autonomous law of international trade can be built, because

the national sovereign has no objection that in that area an autonomous law is developed by the parties, provided always that that law respects in every national jurisdiction the limitations imposed by public policy. International trade law acquires its autonomous character by leave and licence of all national sovereigns. Ultimately it is founded on national law but has been developed by international business in an area in which all national sovereigns are in principle desinterested.[76]

However, Professor Schmitthoff goes on to say that the transnational law of international trade is:

essentially founded on a parallelism of
action in the various national legal
systems. The aim of this parallelism of
action is to facilitate the conduct of
international trade by establishing
uniform rules for it.[77]

Delaume also emhasized the links between lex mercatoria and national legislation by saying:

La lex mercatoria c'est quelque chose
de supplémentaire qu'on peut incorporer
dans le mesure ou les lois impératives
ne s'y opposent pas.[78]

The law of international trade is derived from
the various systems of national law and is fully
reconcilable with the concept of national sovereignty.[79]

Thus one can refer to the coexistence of the
state order and the lex mercatoria. This co-
existence is not the same as coexistence between
state orders.[80] Therefore, it is necessary to
present the position of lex mercatoria in the
general theory of law. It is a fact "that we are
living in a world of national laws and we cannot
get away from it." For this reason it would be
quite wrong to assume that lex mercatoria provides an answer to everything... "We cannot have
such a legal system and the ideal of the lex mercatoria is not to provide a complete separation
of legal transactions from national laws. Essentially we must have a national localization of
laws... One of the characteristics of our time is
a separation of domestic commercial law and the
law of international trade."[81]

With respect to the relations between lex mercatoria and national laws, the law of international trade is entering a phase of development
which could be characterized as a transition from
tolerance to action. Lex mercatoria was "na-

tionalized" as a result of "nationalism which has
been introduced in the field of law as the unfortunate result of the French codification"
(Tunc).[82]

Another distinguished French author, Professor
R. David, stressed this situation by saying that

> the unity of civil and commercial law
> is, frequently, no more than a sham.
> The law governing trade relations is in
> theory only to be found therefore in
> the provisions of the codes and sta-
> tutes compiled by jurists. More impor-
> tant in the practice of business are
> the standard forms and the general con-
> ditions emanating from commercial or-
> ganizations.[83]

The reasons for codification should be sought
rather in the economic sphere:

> The national legislations were symptoms
> of a world political development to-
> wards national economic imperialism:
> they followed the course of the great
> economic powers away from cooperation
> and towards the power struggle for a
> dominant position...

In France, England or Germany, national legal
unification is attributed to other causes. Consequently, depending on their models and the needs
of the individual country, the "nationalization"
of lex mercatoria became and still is a symbol
of sovereignty and, moreover, "a triumph for the
isolation of the national private legal systems
towards each other."[84]

The economic interdependence of national economies, the abandonment of autarky, and the wish
for international cooperation have become a driving power in the unification of the law applicable to international commercial transactions.

Reciprocity in the law of international trade contributes to harmonization of the law and paves the way for a law of coordination.[85] There are numerous examples of international cooperation in the field of international trade law. In modern economic development it can be noted that those engaged in international commercial transactions tend to sever traditional ties in order to be governed by a rational law which is less bound to a particular milieu. A strong economic position is certainly a significant factor in the acceptance of a commercial practice; nevertheless, it is a fact that standard contracts and general conditions have often been corrected as the result of competition and therefore contain rational solutions.[86]

Inter-state cooperation is also evidenced in international cooperation at the level of the UN Economic Commission of Europe, UNIDROIT, the International Chamber of Commerce, and especially within the framework of UNCITRAL. In addition, national legislators and judicial case law have recently demonstrated that national legal systems are being adapted to meet the needs of international trade, e.g., the Code of International Trade (Czechoslovakia, 1963) and the Law on International Economic Contracts (German Democratic Republic, 1976), both of which contain special provisions pertaining to the application of trade usages and were enacted for application in international trade relations outside the CMEA group.

The United Kingdom Arbitration Act (1979) makes a distinction between domestic and non-domestic arbitration. According to the special case procedure that is a specific English form of judicial review, in non-domestic arbitration, judicial review may be excluded before the commencement of arbitration.[87] Furthermore, English

law has in fact abandoned the specific common law
institute--the doctrine of consideration--in international commercial transactions in connection with documentary credits.[88]

The French law applicable to international
commercial contracts is "d'origine essentielle-
ment jurisprudentielle." French authors find "a
remarkable law-maker's acceptance of lex mercatoria" in the new French Code of Civil Procedure. Article 1496(1) provides that in international arbitration the arbitrator shall settle
the dispute in accordance with the **rules of law**
which the parties have chosen, and in the absence
of such choice, in accordance with those rules
of law which he considers to be appropriate. The
Code's expression "rules of law" is meant to
refer to customary rules as well as to legislative ones. The second paragraph of Article 1496
provides that in "all cases the arbitrator shall
take account of trade usages." This repeats the
wording of Art. VII of the 1961 Geneva Convention, Art. 42(1) of the 1965 Washington ICSID
Convention, Art. 13(5) of the ICC Arbitration
Rules, and Art. 33(3) of the UNCITRAL Arbitration
Rules, as well as that of the rules of many in-
stitutional arbitrations.[89]

In view of the contemporary development of
international economic relations, we are of the
opinion that States are no longer passive as far
as international economic cooperation is concerned and that they are no longer satisfied with
the mere fact that freedom of contract has been
legislated as a basic rule for commercial contracts. Instead, they have become interested in
removing obstacles posed by national law in order
to facilitate their participation in the international division of labour. There are two ways to
obtain this goal: the first, by participation in

the creation of international conventions and adjustment of domestic legislation, and the second,
and more effective, by autonomous formation of
rules within this framework on the part of the
international business community. Thus we can
speak of the phenomenon of law being created outside legislation by "public and private rule
making,"[90] selbstgeschaffenes Recht,"[91] "transnational commercial law,"[92] "private legislation,"[93] and "non-authoritative sources of
law,"[94] all of which are synonyms for autonomous
law, autonomous in relation to legislation.

The pluralism of the sources of the law of
contract and the need for an autonomous law of
international trade are based on the tacit agreement of all national law-makers who have made
creative commercial practices possible through
optional rules. This was the first phase in the
development of the modern lex mercatoria. The
second phrase, which is still underway, began
when national law-makers abandoned their passive
roles and agreed to cooperate in drawing up international legislation. This eventually led to a
parallelism between domestic commercial law and
the international law of trade. It has become
evident that the rules applicable in international commercial transactions cannot be fixed unilaterally by the will of the rulers of a single
country.

Regarding the methods and techniques of unification, "legislation is one of the methods by
which it is conceivable that the unification of
private law will be attained, but it is not the
only one."[95] In addition, even in principle,
legislation cannot be considered the sole source
of law in this field.

VI.   THE STRUCTURE OF THE UN SALES CONVENTION

1.   The Contract

As I stated earlier, contracts are based on the fundamental proposition of this branch of law, i.e. on freedom of contract. Therefore, the Convention provides that the parties may exclude the application of the Convention as a whole or derogate from or vary the effect of any of its provisions (Art. 6).

The need to create in this branch of law, except to a minor extent in the sphere of public law, is evident. This is illustrated, for example, by the types of nominate contracts, i.e. those regulated by national codification. The number of nominated contracts in national laws is small, e.g., the Swiss Law of Contract (OR) provides 19 types of contracts, five of which do not pertain to commercial transactions; the German Civil Code (BGB) 11, and the German Commercial Law (HGB) seven. Five types of contracts contained in the BGB will rarely be considered for use in commercial transactions. This shows that domestic legislation lags behind business needs.

2.   Basic Legal Characteristics of the Convention

a) Provisions of the Convention are of a non-mandatory character;

b) The Convention does not contain any provisions falling within the so-called general part of the law of contract;

c) The Convention is not the only source of law for international sales contracts. Trade terms, like the ICC INCOTERMS, and the Convention are complementary, each performing a different

function. Therefore, a reference to trade terms
in a contract should not be taken as an exclusion
or modification of the Convention.[96]

The parties may entirely exclude application
of the Convention by choosing a law other than
the Convention (a national law as the proper law
of the contract). If the parties agree that the
Convention does not apply without designating the
national law to be applied, the rules of private
international law determine the applicable national law.

The Convention does not contain a provision
(similar to that found in Art. 3 of ULIS)
specifying that exclusion may be express or implied. The working of ULIS has been eliminated
because special reference to implied exclusion
"might encourage courts to conclude, on insuffi-
cient grounds, that the Convention had been whol-
ly excluded."[97] This legal-political motivation
for deleting explicit provisions on ways of excluding application of the Convention does not
influence the general rules pertaining to the
formation of contracts.

3. Usages of Trade and Trade Practices

The Convention has taken into account international practice and modern legal systems, both of
which accord significance to the rule of usages.
"Where the contract is silent, current practices
and usages may apply."[98] Usages of trade constitute the core of the lex mercatoria.

In regard to the way of determining the intent
of the parties, the Convention specifies in Art.
8(3):

> In determining the intent of a party or
> the understanding a reasonable person
> would have had, due consideration is to

be given to all relevant circumstances
of the case including the negotiations,
any practices which the parties have
established between themselves, usages
and any subsequent conduct of the parties.

The general provision on trade usages is contained in Art. 9:

(1) The parties are bound by any usage
to which they have agreed...

(2) The parties are considered, unless
otherwise agreed, to have impliedly
made applicable to their contract or
its formation a usage of which the
parties knew or ought to have known and
which in international trade is widely
known to, and regularly observed by,
parties to contracts of the type involved in the particular trade concerned.

The Convention, like national laws, does not
define usages of trade. An exception is the American Uniform Commercial Code (UCC, section 1-
205):

A usage of trade is any practice or
method of dealing having such regulari-
ty of observance in a place, vocation
or trade as to justify an expectation
that it will be observed with respect
to the transaction in question. The
existence and scope of such usage are
to be proved as facts.

Réczei commented on the role of usages briefly
and clearly by saying that the application of
the uniform law begins where that of usages
ends.[99]

First of all, it should be emphasized that
usages of trade are optional rules. They cannot

abrogate a mandatory rule of the proper law of a contract that concerns the validity of either the contract or that of any usage (Art. 4(a)) of the Convention).

The function of usages is to give particular meaning to and supplement or qualify terms of agreement (American UCC, Section 2 - 205(3)). Farnsworth explains that although the Convention text is much less detailed than the UCC, there are obvious parallels.[100] Usages "give particular meaning, supplement or qualify terms of contract."[101] Thus it follows that usages have the same role as optional provisions of national codes. As stated in the US UCC Commentary (1 - 205, Comment 4), usages "are the framework of common understanding controlling any general rules of law which hold only when there is no such understanding."

Another question is that of proving the existence of usages. The US UCC provides that the existence and scope of usages are to be proved as facts.

As optional rules, usages have the same function as the optional provisions of national laws of contract; nevertheless, they differ from the latter as follows:

a) Usages are applied because of the presumed agreement of the parties on usages (Art. 8(2) and Art. 9(2)). It is reasonable to expect that the other party will observe the usages of their trade. Usages are lex contractus as an expression of the impossibility to provide for everything in a contract. Therefore, the Convention gives contractual effect to usages (Honnold).[102]

b) Contrary to the general provisions of the Convention, usages are special rules and thus have priority over the provisions of the Convention and the applicable national law.

c) The rule *iura novit curia* does not apply to usages. They must be proved, which is usually possible by means of expert witnesses. It must be proved that the usage has been "regularly observed" over a period of time, thus justifying the conclusion that the parties "knew or ought to have known" of it. Therefore, it is not necessary that the usage be ancient or longstanding, which is a prerequisite in English law for proof of "custom" that requires that the custom be not only notorious but also ancient or immemorial, universal or the like.[103] It is sufficient to establish actual practice; *opinio iuris sive necessitatis* is not required.

d) In view of Articles 6 and 9, the Convention has the character of a contract model that gives the parties a general framework which they can supplement or modify by mutual agreement through standard contract forms, general conditions of business and usages of trade.[104] An applicable usage has the same effect as a contract.

e) The validity of a usage is determined according to the applicable national law (Art. 4).

f) The applicable usage should be widely known in international trade. It is not necessary for it to be international, it should only be a usage which is applied in international trade. This can be a national or local custom which meets the requirements of the Convention.[105]

As for the question when a usage can be considered to be international, it is held that a usage is international when it is so widely known in international trade that the parties can be expected to know or ought to have known it, as provided by the Convention. It is not necessary that a usage be universally practiced (this cannot be expected), nor is a quantitative test decisive, i.e. that a usage is applied in most countries, but only if it is applied in trade centres in a particular branch and accepted by those of that branch.[106]

4. Hierachical Ranking of the Sources of Lex Mercatoria

The hierarchical ranks of the applicable rules of law are derived from their legal nature, their legal classification.

The hierarchical ranks of the sources of lex mercatoria can be determined in the following order:

   (i)   The contract;
   (ii)   The practice established between the contracting parties;
   (iii) General conditions or standard contract forms (if expressly or impliedly accepted by the contracting parties):
   (iv)   Usages of trade (international and national;
   (v)   The Convention (unless excluded by the contract;
   (vi)   The general principles underlying the Convention;
   (vii) The national law applicable to the contract (if so provided by the contract, or failing an agreement of the parties, by virtue of the rules of private international law);
   (viii) In all cases of the mandatory provisions of the applicable domestic law;
   (ix)   Judicial and international arbitration case law;
   (x)   Scholarly writing (indirectly).

In order to avoid uncritical application, the
"General Principles" of the Convention should be
considered before turning to domestic law.[107]
Since the Convention, as a whole, is optional in
character, the question arises as to whether
this provision of the Convention (Art. 7(2)) can
be abrogated. There is no unanimity on this
point. In view of the fact that this provision
relates to the interpretation of the Convention
and not to the interpretation of contracts, its
exclusion by contract could be an obstacle to
promoting uniformity of application of the Convention.[108]

In connection with usages of trade, codes of
conduct and guide texts should also be mentioned
as they have recently been attracting increasing
attention. Whereas guide texts have an education-
al significance and consist of a compilation of
actual practices and possible recommendations,
codes of conduct pretend to be internal norms of
conduct for a specific circle of those concerned,
or recommendations for the formation of a specific type of contract. Codes of conduct are not,
nor are they expected to be, legally binding, and
as such can be qualified as soft law.[109] In spite
of this, some of the provisions of the codes may
form part of the body of lex mercatoria under
given circumstances. Codes of conduct may inter-
vene where there are no usages, as is the case
when new products or services are introduced.[110]

VII. LEX MERCATORIA AND THE GENERAL THEORY OF LAW

What is lex mercatoria? Is it an independent,
a true legal system? Can lex mercatoria function
independently of a national legal order and how

is it related to national legal systems? All of
these questions should be answered. The basic objection raised against the lex mercatoria is that
it is multiform, incomplete, unsystematic and exclusively optional, thus lacking the attributes
of a true legal system.

On the other hand, national legal orders only
formally meet the traditional criteria regarding
the characteristics of a legal system. In regard
to commercial law--and this is the subject matter
with which we are concerned--national legal
orders cannot be considered to be closed systems,
because they too are not complete; they open the
door to multiformity and the system of national
legal orders makes it necessary to take into account the variety of sources to be applied. To a
great extent, national legislation on commercial
law consists of blanket norms in its general
parts in that they refer to usages of trade and
the principle of good faith. The example of the
German Civil Code is more explicit in this respect (§ 242 BGB), especially if the provisions
of the German Commercial Law (§ 346 HGB) are also
taken into consideration. The most modern
national codification, the American Uniform
Commercial Code, provides that "every contract or
duty within this Act imposes an obligation of
good faith in its performance or enforcement"
(Sec. 1 - 203). It is the only national law which
contains a definition of usages of trade (Sec. 1
- 205(2)). According to the UCC, the "underlying
purposes and policies" of usages are:

    a) to simplify, clarify and modernize
    the law governing commercial transac-
    tions;
    b) to permit the continued expansion of
    commercial practices through custom,

usage and agreement of the parties.
(Sec. 1 - 102(2))

National legislations have necessarily taken into account the need for specialization in commercial life, a need which cannot be satisfied by the codification of general rules, especially as far as the individual requirements of individual types of contracts or trade branches are concerned.

In international trade there is no confrontation between domestic legislation and lex mercatoria as the law of international trade. These are two systems which complement each other. We cannot, however, disregard the fact that lex mercatoria also contains standards of conduct specified for international trade relations, which, as general norms, meet the needs of practice. Their significant feature lies in the fact that they take the specificities of international commercial transactions into account.

In addition to this legal argument, we should also comment on the sociological aspect. Lex mercatoria operates in a specific economic and social climate. The economic background has already been discussed here. International business is also characterized by professional discipline and the authority of the milieu. Professional discipline is not only an expression of the conviction of the usefulness of a specific conduct, the rationality of individual solutions and standards, but also the result of pressure exercised by power centres concentrated in international trade centres. This development is enhanced by specialization in the international economy and frequent monopolistic positions. As a result, self-discipline is achieved without judicial intervention, including arbitration, as is especially the case in banking, the film industry and in large-scale specialized industries having a monopolistic position in a particular market.

National systems and <u>lex mercatoria</u> complement each other. National legal orders complement <u>lex mercatoria</u> particularly in matters falling under the general rules of the law of contract. "<u>Lex mercatoria</u> indeed constitutes a legal order--imperfect or incomplete though it may be, like international order itself" (Goldman).[111] "The ideal for <u>lex mercatoria</u> of our time is not to provide a complete separation of legal transactions from national laws... One of the characteristics is a scission, a separation of domestic commercial law and the law of international trade" (Schmitthoff).[112]

In such a dynamic field as <u>lex mercatoria</u>, international case law and scholarly writing will surely be helpful when it comes to application of the Convention.

NOTES

1. J. Honnold, <u>Uniform Law for International Sales under the 1980 United Nations Convention</u> (Boston 1982) p. 144.
2. J. Hellner, <u>The UN Convention on International Sale of Goods -- an Outsider's View</u>, Jayme, Kegel and Lutter, eds. <u>Ius Inter Nationes</u> (Heidelberg 1983) p. 71.
3. C.M. Schmitthoff, "The Codification of the Law of International Trade," <u>J.Bus.L.</u> (1985) p. 37.
4. J. Honnold, <u>supra</u> n. 1, pp. 51, 54.
5. E. Rabel, <u>Das Recht des Warenkaufs</u>, vol.1 (Berlin 1957) pp. 19-20.
6. A. Goldštajn, "The Contract of Goods

Inspection," 14 Am.J.Comp.L. (1965) p. 383.

7. C.M. Schmitthoff, "Nature and Evolution of the Transnational Law of Commercial Transactions," N. Horn and C.M. Schmitthoff, eds. The Transnational Law of International Commercial Transactions (Deventer 1982) p. 31.

8. A. Goldštajn, "International Conventions and Standard Contracts as Means of Escaping from the Application of Municipal Law," C.M. Schmitthoff, ed. The Sources of the Law of International Trade (London 1964) p. 111.

9. A. Goldštajn, "The New Law Merchant," J.Bus.L. (1961) pp. 12-13 and 17.

10. A. Goldštajn, supra n. 8 at p. 110.

11. C.M. Schmitthoff, Commercial Law in a Changing Economic Climate 2nd ed. (London 1981) pp. 18-20.

12. C.M. Schmitthoff, supra n. 8.

13. A. Goldštajn, "Tipologija trgovačkih ugovora" [Classification of Commercial Contracts], A. Goldštajn, ed. Ugovori autonomnog privrednog prava [Autonomous Commercial Law Contracts] (Zagreb 1974) p. 11.

14. United Nations Doc. No. A/6396,23 September 1966, para.1.

15. A. Goldštajn, "The New Law Merchant Reconsidered," F. Fabricius, ed. Law and International Trade, Festschrift für Clive M. Schmitthoff (Frankfurt 1973) pp. 176-178.

16. C.M. Schmitthoff, supra n. 8, p. 16.

17. C.M. Schmitthoff, supra n. 11, pp. 11, 22.

18. C.M. Schmitthoff, supra n. 7, p. 19.

19. N. Horn, "Uniformity and Diversity in the Law of International Contracts," N. Horn and C.M. Schmitthoff, eds. supra n. 7, p. 11.

20. B. Goldman, in F. Klein and F. Vischer, eds. Basle Symposium on the Law Governing Contractual

Obligations (Proceedings), (Basle/Frankfurt 1983) p. 194.

21. M.J. Bonell, "The Law Applicable to International Commercial Contracts: The Standpoint of Italian Doctrine and Case-Law," Basle Symposium, supra n. 20, p. 16.

22. H. Coing, "La détermination de la loi contractuelle en droit privé allemand," Basle Symposium, supra n. 20, p. 29.

23. Ph. Fouchard, "La loi régissant les obligations contractuelles en droit international privé français," Basle Symposium, supra n. 20, p. 105 and "Les usages, l'arbitre et le juge," Ph. Fouchard, Ph. Kahn and A. Lyon-Caen, eds. Le droit des relations économiques internationales, Etudes offertes à B. Goldman (Paris) p. 67.

24. Y. Loussouarn, Basle Symposium, supra n. 20, p. 130.

25. F.E. Klein, Basle Symposium, supra n. 20, p. 134.

26. P. Lalive, Basle Symposium, supra n. 20, p. 135.

27. F. Vischer, Basle Symposium, supra n. 20, p. 137.

28. O. Lando, Basle Symposium, supra n. 20, p. 141.

29. G.R. Delaume, Basle Symposium, supra n. 20, p. 178.

30. C.M. Schmitthoff, Basle Symposium, supra n. 20, pp. 120-121.

31. G. Goldman, Basle Symposium, supra n. p. 127; B. Goldman, "Lex Mercatoria," 3 Forum internationale 1983.

32. R. David, Arbitration in International Trade (Deventer/London 1985) para. 367.

33. H. Berman and C. Kaufman, "The Law of International Commercial Transactions (Lex Mercatoria)," 19 Harv.Int'l.L.J. (1978) pp. 222-225.

34. A. Goldštajn, <u>supra</u> n. 9, p. 12.

35. C.M. Schmitthoff, <u>supra</u> n. 11, p. 18.

36. Ph. Fouchard, Fouchard, Kahn and Lyon-Caen, eds. <u>supra</u> n. 23, p. 67.

37. H. Berman and C. Kaufman, <u>supra</u> n. 33, p. 274; J.D.M.Lew, <u>Applicable Law in International Commercial Arbitration</u> (Dobbs Ferry, N.Y. 1978) p. 274.

38. N. Horn, <u>supra</u> n. 19, p. 15.

39. H.A. Grigera Naon, "The UN Convention on Contracts for the Sale of Goods," Horn and Schmitthoff, eds. <u>supra</u> n. 7, p. 90.

40. B. Goldman, "Lex Mercatoria," <u>supra</u> n. 31, p. 21.

41. C.M. Schmitthoff, <u>Interpretation and Application of International Trade Usages</u> (ICC Publication No. 374 Paris) pp. 25, 31-34.

42. A. Goldštajn, <u>supra</u> n. 9, p. 12.

43. M.J. Bonell, <u>supra</u> n. 21, p. 161.

44. C.M. Schmitthoff, "Das neue Recht des Welthandels," <u>RabelsZ</u> (1964) p. 75.

45. C.M. Schmitthoff, <u>supra</u> n. 41, p. 36.

46. C.M. Schmitthoff, <u>Basle Symposium</u>, <u>supra</u> n. 20, p. 189.

47. B. Goldman, "Lex Mercatoria," <u>supra</u> n. 31, p. 5.

48. G. Kegel, "The Crisis of Conflict of Laws," 112 <u>Recueil des Cours</u> (The Hague 1964) vol.II, p. 17.

49. C.M. Schmitthoff, "The Effects of the Accession of the United Kingdom to the European Communities on Law Teaching in England," <u>The Law Teacher</u> vol.7 (London 1973) p. 70.

50. E. Boka, "The Sources of Law of International Trade in the Developing Countries of Africa," C.M. Schmitthoff, ed. <u>supra</u> n. 8, p. 227.

51. J. Honnold, <u>supra</u> n. 1, pp. 144, 278 and 283.

52. Gy. Eörsi, "Problems of Unifying Law on the

Formation of Contracts for the International Sale of Goods," Am.J.Comp.L. (1979) p. 315.

53. J. Honnold, "UNCITRAL: Mission and Methods," Am.J.Comp.L. (1979) p. 208; S.K. Date-Bach, "Problems of Unification of International Sales Law from the Standpoint of Developing Countries," Problems of Unification of International Sales Law (London/Rome/New York 1980) p. 46.

54. Gy. Eörsi, supra n. 52, p. 323.

55. Commentary to the Text of Draft Convention prepared by the Secretariat of UNCITRAL UN A/CONF./97/5 14 March 1979, para. 5.

56. J. Honnold, supra n. 1, pp. 146-147.

57. E.A. Farnsworth, "Unification of Sales Law: Usages and Course of Dealing," UNIFICATION Liber Amicorum Sauverplanne (Deventer 1984) pp. 81, 83-84.

58. A. Goldštajn, "Commercial Usages as the Source of the Law of the Law of International Trade," Mélanges Fragistas (Thessalonikki 1967) pp. 400-402.

59. Gy. Eörsy, "Regional and Universal Unification of the Law of International Trade," J.Bus.L. (1967) p. 147.

60. A. Goldštajn, "Uniform Laws of International Purchase, Sale and Autonomous Mercantile Law," Collection of Studies on Foreign and Comparative Law (Beograd 1966), p. 181.

61. S.K. Date-Bach, supra n. 53, pp. 40, 43-44 and 47.

62. A. Goldštajn, "Prolegomena Zakonu o obveznim odnosima [Prolegomenon to the Obligation Act], A. Goldštajn, ed. Obvezno pravo [The Law of Obligations] vol.I (Zagreb 1979) pp. 31-32.

63. J. Honnold, supra n. 1, pp. 47-48.

64. L. Réczei, "The Rules of the Convention Relating to its Field of Application and to its Interpretation", Problems of Unification of In-

ternational Sales Law (London/Rome/New York 1980)
p. 81.
65. C.M. Schmitthoff, supra n. 7, p. 21.
66. A. Goldštajn, supra n. 8, p. 110.
67. N. Horn, supra n. 19, p. 9.
68. O. Lando, "Unification of Commercial Law
between Societies at Equal and at Different
Levels of Industrial and Social Development,"
Legal Organization of Commerce (Aarhus 1979)
pp.28-29.
69. J. Hellner, supra n. 2, p. 75.
70. C.M. Schmitthoff, "The Unification of the Law
of International Trade," J.Bus.L. (1968) p. 108;
Schmitthoff, supra n. 44, p.49; Y. Loussouarn and
J.Bredin, Droit du Commerce International (Paris
1969) p. 14.
71. C.M. Schmitthoff, supra n. 70, p. 112; A.
Goldštajn, Medjunarodna trgovačka arbitraža i lex
mercatoria [International Commercial Arbitration
and Lex Mercatoria] (Zagreb 1984) p. 56.
72. C.M. Schmitthoff, Basle Symposium, supra n.
20, p. 189.
73. B. Goldman, "Lex Mercatoria," supra n. 31,
pp. 6-7.
74. M.J. Bonell, supra n. 21, p. 160.
75. H. Coing, supra n. 20, p. 50 footnote 70 and
p. 52.
76. C.M. Schmitthoff, supra n. 11, p. 76.
77. C.M. Schmitthoff, supra n. 7, pp. 21-23.
78. G.R. Delaume, supra n. 29, p. 178.
79. C.M. Schmitthoff, "The Legal Organisation of
Commerce and its Relation to Social Conditions,"
Legal Organization of Commerce (Aarhus 1979) p.
17.
80. Ph. Fouchard, "Les usages, l'arbitre et le
juge," supra n. 23, pp. 67, 139, 145.
81. C.M. Schmitthoff, Basle Symposium, supra n.
20, pp. 121, 123.

82. A. Tunc, "English and Continental Commercial Law," J.Bus.L. (1961) p. 237.

83. R. David, supra n. 32, p. 15.

84. F. Wieacker, "On the History of Supranational Legal Systems of Commerce," Legal Organization of Commerce (Aarhus 1979) pp. 13-14.

85. G. Schwarzenberger, Power Politics (London 1964) p. 203.

86. A. Goldštajn, "The Formation of Contracts," J. Honnold, ed. Unification of Law Governing International Sales of Goods (Paris 1966) pp. 41, 366.

87. C.M. Schmitthoff, "The United Kingdom Arbitration Act 1979," Yearbook Commercial Arbitration, vol. V (1980) p. 231.

88. C.M. Schmitthoff, supra n. 20, p. 125.

89. Fouchard, Basle Symposium, supra n. 20, p. 81; J.D. Bredin, "Le loi du juge," Fouchard, Kahn and Lyon-Caen, eds. supra n. 23, p. 27; Goldman, supra n. 31, p. 13.

90. S. Strömholm, "'Public' Rule Making and 'Private'," Scandinavian Studies in Law (Stockholm 1971).

91. Grossmann-Doerth, "Selbstgeschaffenes Recht der Wirtschaft und staatliches Recht" cited at Langen, Transnational Commercial Law (Leiden 1973) pp. 11.

92. E. Langen, Transnational Commercial Law (Leiden 1973) pp. 8, 12.

93. Macaulay, "Private Legislation and the Duty to Read," 19 Vand.L.Rev. (1966) p. 1051.

94. D. Karlen, Judicial Administration, the American Experience (London 1970) p. 68.

95. A. Goldštajn, supra n. 58, p. 392; R. David, "The International Unification of Private Law," International Encyclopedia of Comparative Law, vol.II Ch.5, pp. 55-56.

96. J. Honnold, supra n. 1, pp. 47-48.

97. UNCITRAL Commentary, supra n. 55, p. 44 para. 2.

98. J. Honnold, supra n. 1, pp. 61, 106.

99. L. Réczei, "The Field of Application and the Rules of Interpretation of ULIS and UNCITRAL Conventions," 24 Acta Juridica Academiae Scientiarum Hungaricae (Budapest 1982) p. 179.

100. E.A. Farnsworth, supra n. 57, p. 82.

101. Ibid. p. 84; H.J. Mertens and E. Rehbinder, Internationales Kaufrecht (Frankfurt 1975) p. 144, No. 27.

102. J. Honnold, supra n. 1, p. 146; E.A. Farnsworth, supra n. 57, p. 85; H.J. Mertens and E. Rehbinder, supra n. 101, pp. 121-122; L. Réczei, supra n. 99, p. 181.

103. J. Honnold, supra n. 1, p. 147; E.A. Farnsworth, supra n. 57, p. 85; H.J. Mertens and E. Rehbinder, supra n. 101, p. 118 No. 6.

104. H.J. Mertens and E. Rehbinder, supra n. 101, pp. 119-120.

105. J. Honnold, supra n. 1, p. 148; H.J. Mertens and E. Rehbinder, supra n. 101, p. 121; L. Réczei, supra n. 99, p. 181.

106. A. Goldštajn, supra n. 71, p. 35.

107. J. Honnold, supra n. 1, p. 133.

108. H.J. Mertens and E. Rehbinder, supra n. 101 pp. 139 No. 5, 142 No. 18, 144.

109. G. Farjat, "Réflexions sur les codes de conduite provés," Fouchard, Kahn and Lyon-Caen, eds. supra n. 23, p. 281.

110. P. Sanders, "Codes of Conduct and Sources of Law," Fouchard, Kahn and Lyon-Caen, supra n. 23, pp. 281, 298; F. Farjat, supra n. 109, p. 54.

111. B. Goldman, supra n. 31, p. 22.

112. C.M. Schmitthoff, Basle Symposium, supra n. 20, p. 189.

CHAPTER FOUR

FORMATION OF INTERNATIONAL CONTRACTS UNDER THE VIENNA CONVENTION: A SHIFT ABOVE THE COMPARATIVE LAW

KAZUAKI SONO
Professor of Law, Hokkaido University

1. A PRELUDE

We have been told that the meeting of minds in the exchange of an offer and its acceptance creates a contract and that the freedom of contract which guarantees the prevalence of the parties' will is the basis of modern society. This historical reasoning seems to have constantly influenced lawyers in dealing with legal rules surrounding the formation and enforceability of contracts. However, let us set aside this historical aspect for the moment and commence our discussion by accepting the reality of life that a contract is a powerful legal device to maintain order in a business relationship through its binding nature upon the parties.

An offer is then a unilateral authorization to the offeree to create such a powerful device -- it is a gift of power to the offeree. Such an empowerment is often unsolicited, usually not given in exchange for some value from the other party (hence unilateral), and is sometimes given even to a stranger. The rules which regulate certain communication of private messages as an offer and regulate these communications should therefore be carefully tailored so as to take fully into account this unilateral aspect of the empowerment. For example, should the revocation of such an empowerment be permitted before the offeree exercises the power? The answer may be assimilated to the solutions for the revocability of a unilateral authorization to act on behalf of the authorizer or the cancellation of a promise of gift which, particularly when made orally, is treated by most legal systems as revocable until acted or relied upon. Until then, no harm is done to the other party. The other party has not lost anything which he should not have. The revocation will create no confusion in the social order and the status quo may be maintained.

Once an offer has been made, the offeree has the power to create a contract by accepting the offer. Once he exercises this power by so-called acceptance, he becomes bound by the contract to the same extent as the offeror. However, to be sure, the offeree has no obligation to accept the offer. In ordinary situations he even has no duty to respond. Therefore, the rules which regard certain communication of private messages as an acceptance and regulate these communications should also reflect this voluntary and non-obligatory aspect of the acceptance. For example, should the withdrawal of an acceptance be permitted before it reaches the offeror? Perhaps. This is because the offeror will not lose anything which he should not have by permitting such withdrawal. It is possible to test the soundness of most of the rules of the Vienna Sales Convention relating to the formation of the contract in the light of the simple perspectives described above.

The law relating to the formation of contracts has long been a popular area for comparative law analyses because of apparent differences in highly particularized technical rules on offer and acceptance existing between the common law and civil law systems. It is not striking, therefore, that most commentators on the Vienna Sales Convention also refer to the differences between the two legal systems and examine Part II of the Convention with critical lawyers' eyes to see which system has prevailed in each of the rules. They conclude that the Vienna Sales Convention has accomplished an equitable and workable compromise between the two legal systems. However, the Vienna Sales Convention is, after all, for the business community and seeks to establish a sound ground upon which international trade can be promoted without undue problems arising from complications due to legal rules which until today have been diverse even among countries belonging to one of the two main systems. Therefore, the soundness of the rules in the Convention should also be examined from this practical aspect to see whether ordinary businessmen who do not have the legal sophistication of lawyers would also feel comfortable. This paper intends to focus on this latter aspect.

Before proceeding further, however, perhaps one "scholarly" comment may be permitted. Despite the often referred to differences between the common law and civil law systems in their approaches to the formation of contracts, the differences may appear to have become marginal because of many modifications introduced in regard to the basic principles of each system. This may

be illustrated by taking the popular question of
the revocability of an offer as an example.

The basic principle under the common law is
that an offer is revocable until accepted even if
it states that it is irrevocable. However, if the
offer is supported by consideration coming from
the offeree, the offeror cannot revoke the offer
without the offeree's consent. In essence, in
this case the power to create a contract (i.e.,
option) has already been purchased by the offeree
in exchange for some value and the offeror is
therefore bound by his authorization. The basic
principle that an offer is revocable has also
been modified to a great extent whenever adherence to the principle would have produced unfair
results. For example, the inducement created by
an offer upon the offeree to act on reasonable
reliance thereon has often been regarded sufficient to constitute "consideration," thus making
the offer no longer revocable (see also Uniform
Commercial Code § 2-205 of the United States).
The general approach of the civil law, on the
other hand, is that, unless an offer is stated
revocable, the offer is irrevocable during the
period of time fixed in the offer or, if no such
period is stated, for the duration of a reasonable period. It can, however, be easily anticipated that this principle would not be adhered to
by courts in situations such as follows: X, a
manufacturer of powerful engines, is aware of Y's
interest in his engines. X writes to Y offering
to sell a certain quantity of the engines for a
stated value and gives Y 45 days to consider. The
next day X changes his mind and writes to Y
instructing him to ignore the offer. Y receives
the first letter but does not yet do anything
about the offer, including serious thinking.
Because of the second letter, Y ignores the first

letter. However, 20 days later Y learns from a third source that the first letter indeed contained a very attractive offer. Thereafter, upon examination of the offer for the first time, he also finds it so and therefore accepts.

2. BASIC APPROACH OF THE CONVENTION

(1) Certain points to be clarified at the outset

(a) Withdrawal of offer or acceptance: The withdrawal of an offer should be clearly distinguished from the revocation of an offer which might take place after the offer has become effective. An offer, which is the authorization to the offeree to create a contract by acceptance, becomes effective when it reaches the offeree (Articles 15(1) and 24). The offer may therefore be withdrawn if the withdrawal reaches the offeree before or at the same time as the offer. This is the same regardless whether or not an offer is stated to be irrevocable (Article 15(2)). Such a withdrawal will not inconvenience the offeree in any manner.

The same principle applies to the withdrawal of an acceptance. An acceptance may be withdrawn provided that the withdrawal reaches the offeror before or at the same time the acceptance reaches the offeror (Article 22).

(b) Revocability of offer: After an offer reaches the offeree, he might not act upon it immediately. During this period, the offeror may change his mind and might wish to cancel the offer he has made. This constitutes the revocation of an offer. Unless the offeror himself indicated that the offer shall remain irrevocable or the offeree has already acted in reliance on the offer, the offeror, who unilaterally gave the power to create a contract to the offeree, should be able to revoke the offer provided that the revocation reaches the offeree at least before he dispatches acceptance (Article 16). Although the contract has not yet been created, i.e., not until the acceptance reaches the offeror (Article 18(2), but cf. Article 18(3)), once the acceptance has been dispatched, it is reasonable that the offeree be protected for his expection of the contract and that revocation should no longer be permitted.

By nature, there is no room to conceive of revocating an acceptance because an acceptance becomes effective when it reaches the offeror and thereby a contract will be created. Therefore, with regard to acceptance, only its withdrawal is conceivable (see (a) above).

As has already been stated, an offer may not be revoked if it indicates that it is irrevocable. In this regard, Article 16(2)(a) states that an offer cannot be revoked "if it indicates, whether by stating a fixed time for acceptance or otherwise, that it is irrevocable." However, it should be noted that the crucial test of the irrevocability of an offer is whether it "indicates" expressly or by implication that it is irrevocable under the circumstances. The indication of "the fixed time for acceptance" in an offer would in itself not necessarily always make the offer irrevocable. This point may be clarified by the following example. An offer dated 1 September states, "If I do not receive your reply of acceptance by 15 September, this offer expires." It is clear from this statement that the period for acceptance of the offer lapses on 16 September, but it is unascertainable from this statement alone whether the offeror meant the

offer is irrevocable during this period. Civil
law lawyers may consider this statement to indicate that the offer is irrevocable until 15 September and lapses thereafter. However, common law
lawyers may maintain that the offer lapses after
15 September but that the offer does not indicate
that it is irrevocable. Therefore, whether the
offeror intended the offer to be irrevocable
would still have to be assessed in the light of
all the circumstances of the offer being made,
including the trade usages and the practices
which the parties have established between themselves (Articles 8 and 9).

At most, Article 16(2)(a) might be read as a
presumption that an offer with a fixed time for
acceptance is also intended to be irrevocable,
but this presumption is rebuttable. The difficulty associated with the determination of irrevocability of an offer is, however, only conceptual
under the Convention. This is because the Convention in any event affords the necessary protection to the offeree by providing in Article
16(2)(b) that an offer cannot be revoked "if it
was reasonable for the offeree to rely on the
offer as being irrevocable and the offeree has
acted in reliance on the offer." The difference
between the civil law and common law approaches
to this point has been submerged beautifully.

**(c) How long the offer remains valid (period
for acceptance of offer):** As indicated above, an
offer becomes effective when it reaches the offeree. An offer usually remains effective thereafter for a certain period of time unless terminated earlier by a rejection of the offer by the
offeree (Article 17) or validly revoked. After
the lapse of this period, the empowerment to the
offeree to create a contract by its acceptance

ceases to exist. The offer must therefore be
accepted during this period (see also Article
20).

An acceptance will not be effective if the
indication of assent does not reach the offeror
within the time he has fixed or, if no time is
fixed, within a reasonable time, due account
being taken of the circumstances of the transaction, including the rapidity of the means of
communication employed by the offeror. An oral
offer must be accepted immediately unless the
circumstances indicate otherwise (Article 18(2)).

(2) Offer (Article 14)

An offer is an empowerment to the offeree to
create a contract in accordance with the terms of
the offer by accepting it. Being such a serious
authorization, it must be sufficiently definite
and must indicate the intention of the offeror to
be bound in case of acceptance.

Since there are no particular words which must
be used to indicate such an intention, sometimes
a careful examination of the "offer" may be required in order to determine whether such an
intention existed. This is particularly true if
one party claims that a contract was concluded
during negotiations which were carried out over
an extended period of time, and no single communication was labelled by the parties as an "offer" or an "acceptance." In determining the existence of the requisite intention to be bound in
case of acceptance, due consideration must be
given to all relevant circumstances of the case,
including any practices which the parties have
established between themselves, trade usages and
any subsequent conduct of the parties (Article
8(3)).

It is not ordinarily conceivable that such an authorization would be made other than to one or more specific persons. Therefore, a proposal other than one addressed to one or more specific persons will be considered merely as an invitation to make offers, unless the contrary is clearly indicated by the person making the proposal. For example, widespread distribution of a catalogue of merchandise will usually be regarded as a solicitation for the recipients to place an order irrespective whether or not it states that the contents are subject to change without notice. However, a catalogue sent to specific dealers on a restricted mailing list may sometimes be construed as an offer to each dealer.

If the contents of a proposal for concluding a contract are not sufficiently definite, this fact alone may manifest that the person making the proposal is still engaged in negotiations and has not yet seriously indicated his intention to be bound by acceptance. In this connection, Article 14(1) of the Convention provides in part that a proposal is sufficiently definite if it indicates the goods and expressly or implicitly fixes or makes provision for determining the quantity and the price. This provision is helpful in ordinary situations by establishing the presumption that a proposal which lacks one of these elements would not be regarded as sufficiently definite. However, it should be noted at the same time that, even if these elements are present in a proposal, the decisive test to make the proposal as an offer is whether the intention to be bound by acceptance can be found in the proposal under the circumstances. For example, where a seller offered to sell a million dollars worth of equipment to be manufactured with the only specifications being the type and quantity of the goods,

it would normally be the case that a seller would
not contract for such a large sale without specifications such as delivery dates and quality
standards. Therefore, the lack of any indication
in respect of these matters would suggest that
there has not yet been an intention to be bound
by acceptance.

However, once the offeror's intention to be
bound in case of acceptance can be found, the
missing terms of the contract will be supplied by
trade usages or by the provisions of the Convention (e.g., Article 31 concerning how and where
the goods are to be delivered; Article 33 concerning the time of delivery; Article 57 concerning place of payment; Article 58 concerning time
of payment; and Article 65 concerning detailed
specifications of the goods).

With regard to the price, it is not necessary
that the price be calculable at the time of the
contract. For example, the offer and the resulting contract might call for the price to be that
prevailing in a given market on the date of
delivery, which might be months or even years in
the future. In such a case, the offer expressly
makes provision for determining the price. Where
the buyer sends an order for goods listed in the
seller's catalogue or where he orders spare
parts, he may have decided to make no specification of price at the time of placing the order.
This may occur because he does not have the
seller's price list or he may not know whether
the price list he has is current. Nevertheless,
it may be implicit in his action of sending the
order that he is offering to pay the price cur-
rently being charged by the seller for such
goods. If such is the case, the buyer has implicitly made provision for the determination of the
price.

It should further be noted that many national sales laws provide a mechanism for fixing the price for cases where a validly concluded contract does not include any provision therefor either expressly or implicitly. The Vienna Sales Convention itself also provides such a mechanism (Article 55). The time may eventually come, after wide popular adherence to the Convention, that the awareness of its contents would make it difficult to assert that the price had not been indicated even implicitly as long as the offeror's intent to be bound by acceptance could otherwise be proved.

That an offer becomes effective when it reaches the offeree has already been discussed (see (1)(a) above).

(3) Acceptance (Article 18)

A statement made by or other conduct of the offeree indicating assent to an offer is an acceptance. The acceptance of an offer becomes effective at the moment the indication of assent reaches the offeror (Articles 18(1) and 24). Therefore, if the offeree receives no response to his acceptance from the offeror, it may be prudent to enquire whether the offeror in fact received the communication. However, where so permitted by virtue of the offer or as a result of practices which the parties have established between themselves or of trade usages, the offeree may indicate assent by performing an act, such as one relating to the dispatch of the goods or payment of the price, without notice to the offeror. In such cases, the acceptance becomes effective at the moment the act is peformed, provided that the act is performed within the period for acceptance of the offer.

Acceptance by means of "an assent by performing an act" described above calls for some analysis. The Convention refers by way of illustration
to such acts as one relating to the dispatch of
the goods or payment of the price. Dispatch and
payment are clear examples of decisive steps
taken by the offeree to enter into the invited
contractual relationship with the offeror. However, the Convention refers to an act such as
"one relating to the dispatch." Thus the question
arises whether commencement of the preparation to
perform, e.g., by assembling parts for equipment
ordered without notice to the offeror would be
sufficient? Should room for speculation be permitted to the offeree? In this connection, it may
be noted that "an assent by performing an act"
without notice to the offeror, if it can be
regarded as an acceptance, will become effective
at the moment the act is performed, and no more
room for withdrawal of the acceptance which is
otherwise ordinarily possible is anticipated (see
(2)(a) above). It may also be noted that, since
assent by an act requires no notice to the offer-
or, the only means for the offeror to become
aware of the acceptance is through the act of the
offeree. These factors seem to dictate that, in
order for an act to sufficiently constitute "an
assent by performing an act," the act must be
such a decisive step that little room will be
left for its retraction due to the very nature of
the act. This also seems to suggest that, unless
an offer uses such a phrase as "Ship immediately," it would be prudent for the offeree to give
notice of assent to the offeror in any event (see
also Article 16(2)(b)).

Silence or inactivity with respect to an offer
will not in itself amount to either acceptance or
rejection. The Convention is neutral on this

point. However, if the silence is coupled with other factors which under the circumstances give sufficient assurance that the silence of the offeree is an indication of assent, the silence can constitute acceptance. In particular, silence can constitute an acceptance if the parties have previously so agreed. Such an agreement may be explicit or it may be established by an interpretation of the intent of the parties as a result of the negotiations, any practices which the parties have established between themselves, trade usages and any subsequent conduct of the parties (Articles 8(3) and 9).

In this connection, it may also be worth noting that the assimilation of the offeree's silence to an acceptance may be associated with the underlying consideration of the need to protect the offeror against being misled by the offeree's silence. In such cases, this assimilation may be invoked only in favour of the offeror and not the offeree. This may be illustrated by the following example. In accordance with a basic agreement between the parties relating to a long-term supply of merchandise, the seller is required to respond to any orders placed by the buyer within two weeks of receipt. Each of several orders received subsequently for the first six months were acknowledged by the seller within two weeks and complied with promptly. Orders placed during the following three months were not acknowledged, but the buyer received the merchandise shortly after two weeks of each order. However, for a similar order placed during the tenth month, no response came and no merchandise was received. Since the buyer had not received any negative communication from the seller within two weeks of the order, the buyer had thought that, as before, he would obtain the merchandise as ordered and

made arrangements accordingly. The seller admits
that he received the order, but asserts that he
did not accept the order. In this example, the
buyer would probably prevail. On the other hand,
if, in the above example, the buyer had purchased
the merchandise from a third person or acted
otherwise in disregard of the order because the
merchandise had not been received for a substantial period of time after the order, the
seller would not be able to assert acceptance
based on his own silence.

The above observation may suggest that the
ultimate issue in regard to silence may often be
the question of the observance of good faith
under particular business circumstances, the
breach of which will be sanctioned by assimilat-
ing the silence to acceptance or rejection (see
Article 7(1)).

(4) Assent with additions or modifications (Article 19)

Since offer is an authorization to the offeree
to create a contract in accordance with the terms
contained in the offer by accepting it if he so
wishes, the acceptance must conform to the offer.
Otherwise, a contract cannot be created. A reply
to an offer which purports to be an acceptance
but contains additions, limitations or other
modifications is a rejection of the offer and
constitutes a counter-offer. Before accepting or
rejecting an offer, the offeree may request clar-
ification of the offer or enquire about the possibility of the offeror modifying the terms of
the offer. This is, of course, distinct from acceptance or rejection.

However, in assenting to the offer, the offeree may often add new terms. If the additions

or modifications materially alter the original terms of the offer, it is a rejection of the offer and constitutes a counter-offer. However, additions or modifications may occasionally be of such a nature that they do not materially alter the terms of the offer, and it may be reasonable for the offeree to think that those additions or modifications have been accepted by the offeror unless the offeror objects to such modifications without delay. Therefore, in such a case, the offeree should give notice if he does not agree even with minor modifications, and only when he objects orally to the descrepancy or dispatches a notice to that effect without undue delay, the offeree's purported acceptance can be treated as a rejection of the original offer (cf. article 18(1) concerning silence). If he does not so object, the assent by the offeree with immaterial modifications will be treated as an acceptance, and the terms of the offer with the modifications contained in the acceptance become the terms of the contract.

In assessing whether a modification of the terms of an offer is material or not, it should be noted that under Article 19(3) additional or different terms relating, among other things, to the price, payment, quality of the goods, place and time of delivery, the extent of one party's liability to the other or the settlement of disputes will be considered to alter the terms of the offer materially. Besides these examples, there are certainly many more instances where modifications will be regarded as material, and instances of modifications which will not be regarded as immaterial would, in fact, be rare. It has been suggested that the following situations may fall under this rare category: variation by the seller of the vessel designated for

shipment under a CIF contract and slight variation in the packaging of the goods. However, even
in such cases, it would depend upon the circumstances of the transaction in question. Modifications considered to be unimportant to the offeree
may be important to the offeror, and vice-versa.
Therefore, as further illustrated below, prudence
seems to call for a notice or enquiry in case of
any doubt in order to prevent serious disputes
which might otherwise arise later.

However, it is often the case that parties do
not pay attention to fine print appearing on the
contract forms. In this context, it is of particular importance that Article 19(3) regards modifications of the terms of the offer relating to
the settlement of disputes as material. This is
because the dispute settlement mechanism could
vitally affect the substantive interests of the
parties. Disputes often arose in the past where a
party insisted on arbitration in accordance with
an arbitration clause which he added while the
other party declined, and the cases were divided
as to whether the arbitration should take place.
Under the Convention the addition of an arbitration clause to the terms of the offer is a material alteration of the terms of the offer. This
point, however, is subject to an important clari-
fication. The Convention provides that the parties are considered, unless otherwise agreed, to
have impliedly made applicable to their contract
or its formation a usage of which the parties
knew or ought to have known and which in international trade is widely known to, and regularly
observed by, parties to contracts of the type
involved in the particular trade concerned (Article 9(2)). Where, therefore, according to the
usages or practices relevant to a particular
transaction resort is to be had to arbitration in

cases of disputes, a lack of reference in the
contract to arbitration would not alter the situation unless the offeror specifically excluded
arbitration in the offer. Thus, in such a case,
even if the offeree, in accordance with usages or
practices, has added an arbitration clause to
the terms of an offer, to which the offeror was
silent in regard to arbitration, that addition
would not have to be considered a material alteration of the terms of the offer.

To highlight some of the possible problems
relating to the so-called "battle of forms" which
might arise regardless of the applicable law, the
following example may be given. The offeror (X)
sends a purchase order to the offeree (Y) for
certain items listed in Y's special discount-sale
catalogue. The purchase order indicates that the
goods would be purchased only if a warranty be
given for the goods and if delivered within two
weeks. It further states that the order is
strictly under the terms stated thereunder and
that no addition to or modifications of the terms
will be permitted without written approval of the
purchaser. Y acknowledges the receipt of the
order, indicates his pleasure to comply with the
order, and sends his acknowledgement form duly
filled out and signed. The form, however, states
that only those terms stated thereunder become
the terms of the contract unless objected to
immediately, and it contains a clause in bold
print disclaiming warranty. Since a material
alteration has been made by Y to the terms of X's
purchase order, this is a rejection of the original offer and constitutes only a counter-offer.
A week later, however, X receives the goods from
Y and he utilizes them. X could have duly rejected the delivery, but he did not. He thought
that the goods were with warranty. In the example

given above, Y's terms would prevail. Disputes
often arise after a party has acted on a capri-
cious belief that there is a contract according
to his own terms.

(5) Late acceptance (Article 21)

In principle, the assent to an offer which
reaches the offeror after the expiration of the
period during which the offer remains open will
not create a contract because the authorization
to the offeree to create a contract has already
expired.

However, even if the assent reaches the offer-
or after the expiry of the period for acceptance
of the offer, the offeror may nevertheless be
willing to treat it as an acceptance and there is
no reason to preclude this. Therefore, the offer-
or, if he so wishes, may treat a late acceptance
as effective by, without delay, informing the offeree orally or dispatching a notice to that
effect. If he does not choose to do so, there
will, of course, be no contract.

Occasionally, there may also be situations
where a letter or other writing containing a late
acceptance shows that it has been sent in such
circumstances that if its transmission had been
normal it would have reached the offeror in due
time. Even in such cases, the fact remains that
the assent did not arrive in time during the
effective period of the offer. Accordingly, the
offeror need not in principle be bound by the
late acceptance. However, if the offeror keeps
silent after the receipt of the late acceptance,
the offeree will often be misled into believing
that the acceptance reached the offeror in time
and there is a contract. Therefore, in such a
case, the offeror should give notice to the of-

feree if he no longer wishes to enter into a contract, and unless, without delay, the offeror orally informs the offeree that he considers his offer as having lapsed or dispatches a notice to that effect, the late acceptance will be treated effective as an acceptance (cf. Article 18(1) concerning silence).

The above observation would suggest that it would always be advisable for the offeror to notify the offeree of his intention without delay whenever he receives a late acceptance. This point is important particularly because it may often be difficult to determine whether or not an assent has been sent in such circumstances that it would have reached the offeror in due time if the transmission had been normal.

3. FORM OF CONTRACT (ARTICLES 11, 12, 13 AND 96)

A contract need not be concluded in or evidenced by writing and is not subject to any other requirement as to form. It may be proved by any means, including by witnesses (Article 11). Many contracts for the international sale of goods are concluded by modern means of communication which do not always involve a written form of contract. Where States require that such contracts be in writing for purposes of administrative control, such as foreign exchange or import and export regulations, a writing might nevertheless be required. Even in such cases, however, the contract itself would be enforceable between the parties without such formalities. On the other hand, some States consider the requirement that contracts for the international sale of goods be in writing to be a matter of important public policy even in the context of the relation between the parties. Therefore, Articles 12 and 96 provide a certain mechanism for a State to make reservation in this regard when it ratifies or accedes to the Convention. However, since Article 13 provides that "writing" includes telegram and telex, the possibility of such reservation would in most cases not result in much practical difference.

4. MODIFICATION OR TERMINATION OF CONTRACT (ARTICLE 29)

A contract may be modified or terminated by the mere agreement of the parties. After a contract has been concluded, the need may arise in the course of its performance with regard to technical modifications of certain provisions, such as those concerning specifications or delivery dates. Even if such modifications of the contract may increase the costs of one party or decrease the value of the contract to the other, the parties may agree that there will be no change in the price. Such agreements are effective.

A contract in writing which contains a provision requiring any modification or termination by agreement to be in writing may not be modified or terminated by any means other than in writing. However, in some cases a party might act in such a way that it would not be appropriate to allow him to later invoke such a provision against the other party. Therefore, to the extent the other party has relied on such conduct, the first party cannot invoke the provision. This may be illustrated by the following example: A written contract for the sale of goods to Y to be manufactured by X over a two-year period of time provided that all modifications or termination of the contract had to be in writing. Soon after X

delivers the first shipment of goods to Y, Y's
contracting officer tells X to make a modification in the design of the goods for the subsequent shipments. Even though X does not receive
written confirmation of the request, he modifies
the design as requested and the next five monthly
deliveries are accepted without objection by Y.
However, the sixth delivery is rejected as not
conforming to the contract. In this example, Y
cannot reject the sixth delivery. It was certainly not a prudent act for X not to have requested
a written confirmation of the modification requested at the time of the first delivery. However, each time the buyer receives the goods in
the modified design without objection, the more
the buyer loses his justification to object to
the change in design without a written confirmation. In the above example, whether X must rein-
state the original design for the future deliveries under the remainder of the contract would
depend upon the extent of the modification of the
design which has already been made and the expenses and inconveniences which the seller would
bear if the original design were to be restored.
It is clear that this is a matter which should be
discussed by the parties in advance of the seventh delivery.

CHAPTER FIVE

RIGHTS AND OBLIGATIONS OF THE SELLER UNDER THE UN CONVENTION ON CONTRACTS FOR THE INTERNATIONAL SALE OF GOODS

FRITZ ENDERLEIN
Professor of Law, Potsdam

Introduction

This paper deals with the rights and obligations of the seller under the UN Convention on Contracts for the International Sale of Goods[1] (referred to hereinafter as the Sales Convention or merely the Convention).

Sales laws do not usually **expressly** define the rights and obligations of both parties because the rights of the buyer are at the same time the obligations of the seller and vice versa. Under a sales contract the seller has the obligation to deliver the goods and transfer the property in the goods. And these are exactly the rights of the buyer: demanding delivery and transferring property. Whereas the buyer is obliged to take delivery and pay the price, it is the seller's right to demand that delivery be taken by the buyer and that the price be paid.

Therefore, sales laws usually deal only with the **obligations** of the parties, which is the case

in the Sales Convention. It contains chapters on
the obligations of the seller and those of the
buyer, but not on their rights. These are implied
in the obligations of the other party. Thus, one
finds the rights of the buyer implied in the
obligations of the seller in Articles 30-44 and
the rights of the seller implied in the obligations of the buyer in Articles 53-60.

But these are only what I call the original
rights and obligations under a sales contract. In
case of breach of contract, additional rights and
obligations arise which may be referred to as
secondary rights and obligations. In the Sales
Convention they appear under the heading "Remedies for breach of contract." Here again, the
remedies for breach of contract by the seller
found in Articles 45-52 contain the secondary
rights of the buyer and the secondary obligations
of the seller. In the same token, the remedies
for breach of contract by the buyer found in
Articles 61-65 contain his additional obligations
and the secondary rights of the seller.

The rights and obligtions of both seller and
buyer appear in the Sales Convention in a very
balanced manner which is already and, on the
part of the drafters, wisely indicated in the
overall order of the various chapters of the
Convention. Accordingly, Part III of the Convention consists of the following five chapters:

Chapter I: General Provisions
Chapter II: Obligations of the Seller
Chapter III: Obligations of the Buyer
Chapter IV: Passing of Risk
Chapter V: Provisions Common to the Obliga-
              tions of the Seller and of the
              Buyer.

Under the rules of the final provisions of the
Sales Convention, States becoming parties to the

Convention may exclude Part II on Formation of
the Contract or Part III on the Sale of Goods.
Art. 92 provides that a Contracting State may
declare at the time of signature, ratification,
acceptance, approval or accession that it will
not be bound by Part II of the Convention or that
it will not be bound by Part III of the Convention.

During preparation of the Sales Convention and
at the discussions of the diplomatic conference,
there were some indications that several States,
e.g., the Scandinavian States, would like to
exclude Part II of the Convention. On the other
hand, I could not imagine that a State would
accede to the Convention only for Part II and
exclude Part III.

Looking at the provisions in Part III, one
finds in general not only that the solutions in
regard to the rights and obligations of both
parties are very balanced but also that these
provisions are in accordance with commercial
practice and the requirements of contemporary
international trade relations.

Part III cannot be separated from Part I; it
cannot be understood or applied without Part I.
This concerns not only the scope of the Convention, and, for instance, the exclusion of sales
for personal, family and household use (Art. 2)
or the exclusion of the liability of the seller
for death or personal injury caused by the goods
to any person (Art. 5) but also in particular the
nearly absolute party autonomy in Art. 6. According to Art. 6 the parties may derogate from or
vary the effect of any of the provisions of the
Convention. Since the only exception to this
freedom of the parties is referred to in Art. 12,
the whole of Part III does not contain any mandatory provisions. In regard to their rights and

obligations, the parties may agree to whatever
they like in their contract as long as it does
not contradict the general principles of good
faith and fair dealing. There were long discussions about including a provision to this effect
during preparation of the Convention in UNCITRAL.
In both the Working Group and the plenary of the
Commission Professor Eörsi from Hungary proposed
the inclusion of a provision that would oblige
both parties to observe the principles of good
faith and fair dealing. However, a very small
majority of delegations, mainly from common law
countries rejected the proposed provision as
being too vague. What remains of the proposal can
now be found in Art. 7, which provides that in
the interpretation of the Convention,

> regard is to be had to its internation-
> al character and to the need to promote
> uniformity in its application and the
> observance of good faith in interna-
> tional trade.

If the judges applying the Convention are to
develop good will, they will have to regard the
observance of good faith not only when interpreting the Convention but even more so when interpreting the contract and activities of the parties.

The rules of the Convention will come into
play only if the parties did not stipulate the
necessary provisions themselves. The basis for
the relations between the parties is their contract. In practice there are very different types
of sales contracts. Here I am not referring to
the different types of goods to be sold but to
very short contracts, which merely state the kind
of goods, their quantity and price or, on the
other hand, very long contracts, which are very
detailed with elaborate descriptions of the qual-

ity of the goods, the manner of inspecting the goods, the various dates and time-limits for single steps to be taken by the parties in performing the contract etc.

When I speak of the contract, I include, of course, the General Business Conditions of the parties, provided they have become part of the contract, or standard forms or general conditions for specific goods referred to by the parties. This means that there are sales contracts which hardly need to be complemented by the law and, on the other hand, others which have to be complemented to a varying degree by the provisions of the Convention.

(Whether the Convention itself will be sufficient in all cases is a different question, as is which gaps of the Convention will have to be filled by national law. Sometimes it may be difficult to decide whether there is a gap or whether the question could be answered by the principles of the Convention according to para. 2 of Art. 7. In any case, Art. 4 makes it clear that the Convention is not concerned with the validity of the contract or of any of its provisions, i.e., if any provisions of the contract are inconsistent with the mandatory rules of the national laws of the parties. Furthermore, the Convention is not concerned with the effect of the contract on the property in the goods sold.)

One more point has to be kept in mind regarding the connection between Part III and Part I of the Convention. According to Art. 9, the parties are bound by any usage to which they have agreed and by any practices which they have established between themselves. Furthermore, the parties are considered to have impliedly made applicable to their contract usages of international trade. Since this is the subject matter of Professor

Goldstajn's paper, I need not go into detail here. Instead, I would like to stress that the contract of the parties will not be complemented immediately by the provisions of Part III of the Convention. It will first be complemented by usages and established practices, and thereafter, only those questions which remain open will be answered by the rules of the Convention.

This order -- contract, usage, Convention -- is sometimes made clear in the text of the Convention. Some articles refer expressly to the contract and provide solutions if there is no agreement between the parties. Other articles refer to the contract and stipulate the consequence **if** there is a certain agreement. But whenever there is a reference to the provisions of the Convention, this is automatically -- via Art. 9 -- also a reference to usages and practices.

Another common feature of Part III to which I would like to refer in my introduction is the frequent use of language such as "reasonable," "usual," "adequate," "appropriate." These are likewise references to international usages and permit the court or arbitration -- if necessary -- to construe the agreement between the parties according to the specific circumstances of each individual case.

The Sales Convention is not the only uniform law on the international level. There was its predecessor, the Hague Convention or ULIS. Usually, in commentaries to the UN Sales Convention, there are frequent references to ULIS and to the history of its drafting.[3] I do not deny the usefulness of comparing the two documents. Some of the provisions of ULIS are identical to those of the Sales Convention, while others are only slightly modified. Therefore, many ideas, comments and decisions concerning ULIS could also be helpful in applying and interpreting the Sales Convention. This is especially true for countries that were members to ULIS and have now become members to the Sales Convention. I do not come from such a country. The German Democratic Republic (GDR) was not a member to the Hague Conventions; however, it is a member to the Council for Mutual Economic Assistance (CMEA, in Western publications sometimes referred to as Comecon) and participated actively in the elaboration and development of the General Conditions of Delivery of Goods between Organizations of the Member Countries of the Council for Mutual Economic Assistance, which are at present in force as GCD CMEA 1968/1975, version of 1979.[4]

In spite of their somewhat misleading name, these General Conditions are also an internationally unified sales law and contain, contrary to the Sales Convention, mandatory rules to a large extent. The GCD, which entered into force as a multilaterally agreed legal regulation as early as 1958, and were preceded by bilaterally agreed GCD since 1951, were in fact the first successful international unification of sales law. These GCD are now applied to all sales between the CMEA member countries on three continents. I stress "on three continents" since the GCD are often referred to as the uniform sales law of the Eastern European countries. However, there are also members of the CMEA in America and Asia, i.e., Cuba, Mongolia, and Vietnam. In regard to Vietnam it should be pointed out that Vietnam does not apply the GCD version of 1979 but rather a version signed by Vietnam with each of the other CMEA member countries on a bilateral basis.

I already mentioned that the GCD have a some-

what misleading name. It is true that in internal
relations socialist countries also distinguish
between sales contracts and contracts of delivery
because in the former there is a transfer of
property but in contracts of delivery there is
none. (Of course, in a contract of delivery there
is also transfer of possession, the transfer of
quasi-property rights which we call operational
administration.) But this distinction between
sales and deliveries was certainly not the reason
for naming the GCD as such, for there is also
transfer of property in international trade between socialist countries (I shall come back to
this later).

What I consider misleading is not the Deliveries but rather the notion "General Conditions"
instead of "Uniform Law."

The reason for the name GCD is simple and can
be found in the history of the document. The GCD
began as GC in the proper sense of general conditions which, elaborated by other national or
international bodies, became part of the contract
only by agreement if the parties so wished. In
the course of time the GCD were prescribed by the
socialist States for all transactions between
their foreign trade organizations, first on a
bilateral and later on a multilateral basis.
Thus, they changed their nature from GC proper
into law, but the old name remained.

There are, of course, many differences between
sales among CMEA countries, which we refer to as
intrasystemic relations, and sales between socialist and non-socialist countries, which are
usually designated as **inter**systemic relations.
Trade between CMEA member countries is conducted
on the basis of intergovernmental trade agreements creating rights and obligations between the
States themselves. This trade is performed on the

basis of State planning and joint State measures concerning the specialization and co-operation of production and the development of the socialist economic integration.

Therefore, some of the provisions of the GCD are quite unique and cannot be found in the Sales Convention. On the other hand, there are also certain common features in intrasystemary and intersystemary sales, and -- as a result -- some provisions of the GCD correspond with those of the Sales Convention.

When UNCITRAL started to work on the Sales Convention, the GCD were even mentioned as one of the preparatory documents.[5] For this reason, it might be appropriate to compare the Sales Convention not only with ULIS, as has been done many times, but also with the GCD[6].

Besides the GCD/CMEA, there is another document which should be of interest to us. This is, I shall give you the full title: the General Conditions of Delivery of Goods from the Member Countries of the Council for Mutual Economic Assistance to the Republic of Finland and from the Republic of Finland to the Member Countries of the Council for Mutual Economic Assistance."[7] These GCD CMEA-Finland were approved by the Commission on Cooperation between CMEA and the Republic Finland in November 1978, that is, before the Sales Convention was adopted at the Vienna Conference.

It is especially interesting to note that it was agreed that these GCD apply to the mutual sales between non-socialist and socialist countries. In contrast to the other GCD/CMEA, however, they have to be agreed in the commercial contracts; otherwise, they are not law. Nevertheless, I shall refer to them as well.

In addition, it is quite common to draw comparisons between the Sales Convention and one's own national law. Such comparisons are, of course, useful for governments that are preparing ratification of or accession to the Sales Convention. Moreover, they are useful for business circles of a given country that have to adapt their contracts and general business conditions to the new law. And, finally, they are of interest to students and scholars of comparative law.

In a recently published commentary (in German) to the Sales Convention which was written by my colleagues Professor Dietrich Maskow, Associate Professor Monika Stargardt and myself,[8] we compared the Sales Convention to our national law quite extensively, finding a lot of similarities and even identities.[9] I attribute this to the fact that whereas in most countries there is only one civil law or even if there is a special commercial law, there is only one legal regulation governing commercial contracts of sale, in my country we have three different laws of sale: one for internal relations between socialist enterprises which we call Vertragsgesetz or Contract Act, one for relations where citizens are parties (mainly consumer sales) which is our Civil Code and a third one for international relations which is the Code on International Commercial Contracts of 5 February 1976 (referred to as GIW, according to the German abbreviation).[10]

As far as I know, there are only two countries having comprehensive special codes for international trade contracts: the GDR and Czechoslovakia, which as early as 1963 enacted its Act Number 101/1963 on legal relations in international trade.[11]

Therefore, a comparison between the Sales Convention and these two special codes of the GDR and Czechoslovakia may be justified especially because both the codes and the Sales Convention took into account international business practices, international usages and, in general, the requirements of the economic relations on the basis of the peaceful co-existence of States having different political, economic and legal systems.

Part III: Sale of Goods, Chapter II: Obligations of the Seller

Chapter II of Part III, Obligations of the Seller, is divided into three sections:

Section I   Delivery of the goods and handing over of documents

Section II   Conformity of the goods and third party claims, and

Section III Remedies for breach of contract by the seller.

Article 30

The three sections are preceded by Art. 30 which states the obligations of the seller in a general manner as follows:

The seller must deliver the goods, hand over any documents relating to them and transfer the property in the goods, as required by the contract and this Convention.

Emphasis is placed on the requirements of the contract, while those of the Convention are only supplementary.

The main obligations of the seller, i.e., delivering the goods and transfering the property in the goods, are essential in all legal systems,

whereas what is done to "deliver" the goods and
how the transfer of property occurs may be different. But there is no sale without delivery and
transfer of property.

The obligations of the seller referred to in
Art. 30 are dealt with in greater detail in the
following articles. Art. 31 defines delivery, and
Art. 34 deals with the documents. The Convention
does not go into detail, however, in regard to
the transfer of the property. Whereas in the GCD
several articles deal with the problem when the
right of property passes from the seller to the
buyer (Articles 5-9), the Sales Convention keeps
silent. It does not designate when the property
passes, nor what has to be done in order to let
the property pass. The effect of the contract in
relation to the property in the sold goods is,
according to Art. 4, outside the scope of the
Convention. This is left to national law.

Article 31

Art. 31 of Section I deals with the place of
delivery and specifies what the seller has to do
to "deliver" the goods. Of course, the place of
delivery is usually agreed between the parties
and therefore Art. 31 begins by stating:

> If the seller is not bound to deliver
> the goods at any other particular
> place...

Parties quite seldom fail to agree on the place
of delivery because this place is decisive for
several other topics, e.g., usually the passing
of risk.

Often parties agree on the place of delivery
by referring to clauses of the Incoterms[12].

If the parties did not agree on the place of
delivery, the obligation of the seller

to deliver consists

(a) if the contract of sale involves carriage of the goods -- in handing the goods over to the first carrier for transmission to the buyer;...

International sales regularly involve carriage of the goods. This does not necessarily mean that the **contract** also involves carriage. There is no carriage involved if the goods are already with the buyer -- for instance, a machine which was originally leased -- or if the buyer himself goes to the seller and takes the goods -- for instance, if he buys "ex works." In other cases the seller organizes the transport of the goods to the buyer and hands over the goods to a carrier. Art. 31 speaks of the **first** carrier because there are usually several carriers involved. (At this point it is not necessary to consider the possibility of a multimodal transport operator. A single carrier is also the first carrier even if there is no second one.)

If the seller has handed over the goods to the first carrier, he has fulfilled his obligation to deliver. (His obligation to deliver also includes an element of time. He has performed the delivery only if he has delivered the goods to a certain place **and** at a certain time. The time of delivery is specified in Art. 33).

The seller has already effected delivery in handing over the goods to the **first** carrier, for instance, the railway taking the goods to the harbour for the next carrier. Delivery is not effected at a later time, for instance, when the goods pass the frontier. In the GCD, there is a difference when the carriage is by rail, the place of delivery then being the border station where the goods are transferred from the railway of the seller's country to the railway receiving the goods (e.g., buyer's country or transit country).

In any case, handing the goods over to a carrier means handing them over to an **independent** organization. If the seller himself operates trucks, he is not the carrier. This also has significance for possible exemptions from liability on the part of the seller.

The place of delivery should not be mistaken for the place of destination. The seller has already delivered the goods after having handed them over to the first carrier, not at a later date when the goods have been transported by the carrier or carriers to the place of destination where the buyer is to take delivery (see Art. 60). (Thus, if a carriage is involved that the seller has to arrange, the place of delivery by the seller and the place of taking delivery by the buyer are different places. However, as we shall see later, the place of delivery might also be identical with the place of taking delivery.)

The place of destination is significant in view of the buyer's obligation to examine the goods (see Art. 38 para. 2).

Sometimes, the place of delivery and the place of destination are identical, as in the case of an "ex ship" delivery clause.

If the contract of sale does not involve carriage of the goods, the seller's obligation to deliver consists

> (b) if... the contract relates to specific goods, or unidentified goods to be drawn from a specific stock or to be manufactured or produced, and at the time of the conlcusion of the contract the parties knew that the goods were at, or were to be manufactured or produced at, a particular place -- in

placing the goods at the buyer's disposal at that place;...

The place where the goods have to be placed at
the buyer's disposal could be, for instance, a
factory, a mill, a plantation, a warehouse etc.
This is exactly the ex works clause of Incoterms.

Finally, if both situations do not apply, the
seller's obligation to deliver consists

(c) ... -- in placing the goods at the
buyer's disposal at the place where the
seller had his place of business at the
time of the conclusion of the contract.

Turning to our national law, we see that the
whole of Art. 31 is in principle the same as Art.
43 GIW, but in a reversed order. In addition, the
GIW defines the obligation of the seller to deliver as performing all acts that are required to
give the other party the right of disposition of
the goods to be delivered (Art. 51 para. 1).

Art. 31 of the Sales Convention differs sig-
nificantly from ULIS. Under Art. 19 para. 1 ULIS,
delivery meant the "handing over of goods which
conform with the contract." Defective goods,
therefore, could not be delivered. This connection with the quality of the goods has been
omitted in the Sales Convention. The delivery of
non-conforming goods is nevertheless a delivery,
but, of course, the buyer has recourse to several
remedies.

On the other hand, the GCD contain very detailed provisions on the place of delivery which
deal with the basis of delivery differently when
carriage is effected by rail (Art. 5), by road
(Art. 6; here the GCD distinguishes whether the
seller or the buyer is responsible to provide the
trucks), by water (Art. 7, which is further divided into "fob" or "cif" and "C & F"), by air
(Art. 8), and finally by postal dispatch.

A similar detailed provision is also found in
the GCD CMEA-Finland where, moreover,

> it is recommended to the parties to
> provide in the contract... for the
> application of the Rules for the Inter-
> pretation of Trade Terms prepared by
> the International Chamber of Commerce
> -- Incoterms 1953, as amended in 1967
> and 1976 [the 1980 amendment could not
> yet be mentioned in 1978, F.E.] when
> interpreting individual provisions on
> the basic terms of delivery.

Article 32

Art. 32 deals with several aspects of the
transport of the goods. The basic rule contained
in para. 2 reads as follows:

> If the seller is bound to arrange for
> carriage of the goods, he must make
> such contracts as are necessary for
> carriage to the place fixed by means of
> transportation appropriate in the cir-
> cumstances and according to the usual
> terms for such transportation.

Here again, the contract is important. The seller
is not obliged to arrange carriage in all cases.
Such an obligation will therefore follow from the
contract or from usage. However, if the seller is
bound to arrange carriage, para. 2 of Art. 32
applies. If such an agreement exists, it should
also include the place of destination, "the place
fixed" by the contract.

The means of transportation to be chosen by
the seller have to be "appropriate in the circumstances." The circumstances which have to be
taken into account include the kind and quantity
of the goods, their packing as well as the dis-

tance between seller and buyer, the season, the available means of transport, existing transport relations etc. In the case of perishable goods, refrigerated wagons would be appropriate or, depending on the nature of the goods, a fast means of transport such as airplane or express railway.

Para. 1 of Art. 32 concerns the obligation of the seller to give notice of the consignment to the buyer:

> If the seller, in accordance with the contract or this Convention, hands the goods over to a carrier and if the goods are not clearly identified to the contract by markings on the goods, by shipping documents or otherwise, the seller must give the buyer notice of the consignment specifying the goods.

In commercial practice the seller usually gives the buyer notice of the consignment in any case. Also, according to Articles 43 and 44 GCD or Art. 52 lit.a GIW, the seller always has to give notice in time. Since notice is an important item in commercial practice, the GCD CMEA-Finland deal with this question very extensively. Chapter 10 contains four articles consisting of 10 paragraphs with detailed instructions on notices of the seller to the buyer pertaining not only to the handing over or shipping of goods but also to certain situations when the goods will be ready for shipment a given period in advance.

The obligation of the seller to give the buyer notice of having loaded or delivered the goods into the custody of the railway or on board the vessel is also contained in several clauses of the Incoterms, e.g., FOR/FOT, or FOB.

Under the Convention, a buyer should not forget to ask the seller to give notice of the

consignment if this is necessary to make the
required arrangements for taking over the goods
in view of their nature and the means of transport. In this respect, Art. 23 of GCD contains
very detailed provisions on the markings of the
goods.

Another problem connected with the transport
of the goods is their insurance during shipment.
In general, the seller is not obliged to insure
the goods during carriage. Such an obligation can
follow from the contract or from the chosen delivery clause, e.g., Incoterms CIF.

The Convention also proceeds from this general
practice, as specified in para. 3 of Art. 32:

> If the seller is not bound to effect
> insurance in respect of the carriage of
> the goods, he must, at the buyer's
> request, provide him with all available
> information necessary to enable him to
> effect such insurance.

We find a similar provision in Art. 52 lit. d GIW
which, in addition, requires the seller to also
send the buyer those documents or particulars
that are required for the buyer to bring a claim
against the carrier.

Article 33

Art. 33 deals with the time of delivery; it
starts with the obvious:

> The seller must deliver the goods:
> (a) if a date is fixed by or determina-
> ble from the contract, on that date;...

Usually the parties will agree on the time of
delivery in their contract; however, the delivery
can also be determinable from the contract if it
follows from established practices or usages
impliedly made applicable.

The seller must deliver the goods
  (b) if a period of time is fixed by or
  determinable from the contract, at **any**
  time within that period unless circumstances indicate that the buyer is to
  choose a date;...
If the parties, for example, agree on June as the
time of delivery, the seller may deliver on the
first of June as well as on the thirtieth.
Agreement on a period of time often gives him the
necessary flexibility to prepare the goods for
delivery and arrange the transport.

On the other hand, if the buyer himself has to
arrange the carriage of the goods, if he has, as
in the FOB clause, to charter a vessel or reserve
the necessary space on board a vessel, this
should be taken as an indication that the buyer
may choose a date of delivery within the agreed
period.

If, for other reasons, e.g., the capacity of
his warehouse, the buyer is interested in fixing
an exact date for receipt of the goods, he should
reserve the right to choose the date of delivery.
In this case, the buyer has to send the seller
the necessary shipping instructions in due time.

The GCD provide shipping instructions and
notices of delivery in a very detailed manner
(Art. 39-48).

If there is no agreement between the parties
and no date or period is determinable from the
contract or from practices or usages, the seller
must deliver the goods
  (c) ... within a reasonable time after
  the conclusion of the contract.
As far as early or partial delivery is concerned, the Convention contains a provision to
that regard later under the remedies of the buyer. In all cases early or partial delivery are

regarded as breach of contract (see Articles 51 and 52). However, as far as partial delivery at an early date is concerned, an answer can be found in Art. 37.

Under some laws, consent of the buyer is required, as is provided, e.g., by Art. 12 GCD. According to Art. 44 GIW, if the buyer consents to early delivery, he has the corresponding duty to perform his obligations earlier. If the seller delivers early without the consent of the buyer, the buyer may reject the goods; however, if he does not do so forthwith, he must keep them.

A topic not covered by the Convention is the agreement to deliver at a fixed time. Provisions on fixed-time contracts can be found in the GCD (Art. 11 A) as well as in the GCD CMEA-Finland (Art. 8.3.1.).

Article 34

Art. 34 which deals with documents relating to the goods provides:

> If the seller is bound to hand over documents relating to the goods, he must hand them over at the time and place and in the form required by the contract.

Here again, the contract is dominant. The seller is not bound to hand over documents in all cases; the Convention does not oblige the seller to hand over documents at all. But **if** the seller is bound by the contract directly, by the chosen clause of Incoterms, or by usages, then, again, he must do what the contract, the clause, the usage etc. says in regard to the kind of documents, their form, the time and the place.

Which are those documents relating to the goods? In the first place, these could be docu-

ments of title, i.e. documents that control delivery of the goods such as bills of lading,
warehouse receipts etc.

Other relevant documents could include the
insurance policy, invoice, certificate of origin,
certificate of control or quality etc. In addition, there can also be technical documentation
related to the goods. Especially in the case of
plants and machinery, the seller usually provides
the buyer with documents concerning maintenance
and repair of the goods. Provisions on the handing over of technical documents are contained in
Art. 24 et seq. GCD, where reference is made to
drawings, specifications, instructions for maintenance, operation, assemblage etc. as well as
the existing practice in the corresponding branch
of industry in the seller's country. Under this
provision, the seller shall make the technical
documentation available to the buyer within time
limits that ensure normal use of the machinery
and effecting operation of the equipment as well
as its maintenance and repair. The required form
of the documents will include the number of
copies, the language, and, as the case may be,
the manner of multiplication (printed, typed,
photocopied).

In contrast to the Convention, which keeps
silent on the question of confidentiality or
trade secrecy, the GCD specifies in Art. 25 the
extent to which the technical documentation may
be used by the buyer, or by the seller if he
manufactures the goods according to the technical
documentation of the buyer. Technical documentation transferred in accordance with the contract
shall in no case be published. And Art. 5.2.1 of
the GCD CMEA-Finland provides in this respect:

    The party who received technical docu-
    mentation... shall have no right to use

> it without the written consent of the
> other party, for purposes other than
> those provided for in the contract, to
> copy or multiply it, to transfer or
> otherwise give information of its con-
> tent to third persons.

The second and third sentences of Art. 34 deal
with a separate problem, the cure of non-conforming documents:

> If the seller has handed over documents
> before that time [the time agreed be-
> tween the parties], he may, up to that
> time, cure any lack of conformity in
> the documents, if the exercise of this
> right does not cause the buyer unrea-
> sonable inconvenience or unreasonable
> expense. However, the buyer retains any
> right to claim damages as provided for
> in this Convention.

It appears to be self-evident that the seller
could cure any lack of conformity before the
agreed date for handing over the documents. For
instance, he could supplement the documents if
copies were missing, exchange documents if they
were delivered in the wrong language etc. It is
up to the seller to choose the method for curing
the non-conformity.

This provision was not contained in the draft
prepared by UNCITRAL but was proposed by the
Canadian delegation during the diplomatic conference. In content it is similar to the curing of
defects in the goods themselves as specified in
Art. 37.

Article 35

The next section of this part of the Convention is entitled "Conformity of the goods and

third party claims." Articles 35 and 36 define
the seller's obligations with respect to the
quality of the goods; Articles 41 and 42 contain
the seller's obligations with respect to delivering goods which are free from rights of third
parties. This section also contains obligations
of the buyer such as his obligation to examine
the goods (Art. 38) and to notify the seller of a
non-conformity (Art. 39) or a third party claim
(Art. 43).

Again, Art. 35 stresses the importance of the
contract:

> (1) The seller must deliver goods which
> are of the quantity, quality and de-
> scription **required by the contract** and
> which are contained or packaged in the
> manner **required by the contract.**

It is quite obvious that also under national
law the seller must deliver goods in accordance
with the contract. Art. 35 differs from some
national laws in its combination of quantity,
quality, and description with respect to non-
conformity. The obligation of the buyer to give
notice of any non-conformity relates therefore
not only to quality but to quantity and description as well.

Under GDR law, if only part of the goods are
delivered, the missing part is treated as delay
(Articles 278, 280) and not as non-conformity.
This also holds true for the delivery of wrong
goods, i.e., goods which do not conform to the
description, goods which we call "an aliud."

Art. 35 continues to define the requirements
in regard to the quality of the goods if the
parties did not agree otherwise:

> (2) Except where the parties have
> agreed otherwise, the goods do not
> conform with the contract unless they:

(a) are fit for the purposes for
which goods of the same description
would ordinarily be used;

(b) are fit for any particular purpose expressly or impliedly made
known to the seller at the time of
the conclusion of the contract, except where the circumstances show
that the buyer did not rely, or that
it was unreasonable for him to rely,
on the seller's skill and judgement;

(c) possess the qualities of goods
which the seller has held out to the
buyer as a sample or model;

(d) are contained or packaged in the
manner usual for such goods or, where
there is no such manner, in a manner
adequate to preserve and protect the
goods.

Litera (b) on any particular purpose made
known to the seller and (c) on samples or models
could already be included under para. 1, the
agreement of the parties. Nevertheless, it is
useful to clarify the issue. The particular purpose must not be an express part of the contract;
it is sufficient that this purpose has been made
known to the seller. If the goods are not suitable for the particular purpose which the buyer
has in mind, the seller should advise him accordingly. Thus it follows that it does not suffice
for the buyer to indicate his intentions at the
time of delivery. The seller should be aware of
the particular purpose at the time of the conclusion of the contract, instead of being informed
of it later. Otherwise the seller is not in a
position to react, to give advice or to refuse
conclusion of the contract.

It may be more difficult to detect when a

particular purpose is **impliedly** made known to the seller. In any case, the buyer will not and may not always rely on the seller's skill and judgement. If the buyer uses the goods himself in his factory, he may well be better informed than a seller who is a trader and not a producer.

If the buyer did not rely on the seller's judgement, then it is irrelevant whether the seller **did** give judgement or not. It could well be that the buyer informed the seller about a particular purpose and at the same time ordered goods with clear and detailed technical specifications. As was already mentioned, the seller will be obliged to counsel the buyer, but the seller will not be responsible if the buyer insists on his order and shows that he does not rely on the seller's judgement.

In the case of a sample or model, a problem might arise if the contract described the quality of the goods in a different manner than is shown by the sample or model. Only if there is not a different description in the contract will the sample or model prevail. Otherwise, I do not think that the sample should prevail in any case if the description in the contract was clear and unambiguous.

The most common requirement for the quality of the goods is given under (a): The goods should be "fit for the purposes for which goods of the same description would ordinarily be used."

In regard to the quality of the goods, the GIW of the GDR also uses the purpose as its starting point and continues as follows:

> Where the purpose is neither agreed nor
> ascertainable by the [seller], he must
> render performance in such a manner as
> is usual in his country. (Art. 45)

The Act 101/1963 of Czechoslovakia also requires that the goods be fit for their customary use (Art. 297).

Art. 15 of GCD speaks of "goods of usual average quality existing in the seller's country for the delivery of the given type of goods" and of "goods of usual average quality corresponding to the usual purpose of these goods in the seller's country." Compared with the Convention, the GCD clarifies matters in two important aspects. Firstly, there may be several degrees of different quality which all could and would ordinarily be used for a certain purpose; here the GCD ask for **average** quality. Secondly, the **usual** purpose for which the goods would be used might not be the same in all countries. Therefore, proceeding on the basis of his experience in his country, the seller would be obliged to deliver goods of a quality fitting the usual purpose in the seller's country.

Included in the definition of the quality of the goods in Art. 35 is their packaging. Indeed, it is sometimes difficult to decide whether the packaging is part of the goods or whether it is separate, as, e.g., in the case of a nice box for a bottle of perfume.

It is therefore justified to treat packaging as an aspect of the quality of the goods. Another reason is the function of the packaging to preserve and protect the goods. Defects and shortcomings of the packaging will result in defects of the goods themselves.

The manner of packaging required by the Convention, i.e., adequate to preserve and protect the goods, has to be decided on the basis of the kind of goods concerned and their quantity, and foremost on the type and duration of the carriage, the course of the transport, the climate

in the country of destination (whether hot or
cold, dry or humid).

Finally, para. 3 of Art. 35 contains an
exception to the seller's liability.

> (3) The seller is not liable under
> subparagraphs (a) to (d) of the preced-
> ing paragraph for any lack of conform-
> ity of the goods if at the time of the
> conclusion of the contract the buyer
> knew or could not have been unaware of
> such lack of conformity.

It seems to be a general rule of law in many
legal systems that the buyer's knowledge of any
defects of the goods excludes the liability of
the seller, except when the buyer requested and
the seller promised to cure the defects before
delivery.

Para. 3 refers only to para. 2. It does not
refer to para. 1, which besides quality also
refers to quantity and description. Indeed, it is
hardly imaginable that, at the time of the formation of the contract, the buyer knew of any later
non-conformity in regard to differences of quantity or false deliveries with respect to the
description of the goods. Should such a case
nevertheless occur, quantity and description
could be incorporated into para. 3 by way of
analogy.

Whereas in Art. 285 of GIW the buyer's knowledge of a defect of the goods also excludes the
liability of the seller, it is real knowledge,
definitive knowledge that is required. It is not
sufficient that the buyer ought to have known or
that he "could not have been unaware." The Convention does not specify the criteria by which
the buyer's supposed knowledge is to be determined. Mere negligence, in my opinion, would not
suffice. There is certainly no obligation on the

part of the buyer to inspect the goods before placing an order with the seller or accepting an offer.

Article 36

As we have just seen in Art. 35, lack of conformity comprises quality as well as quantity and description. But what time is decisive for determining whether conformity exists or not? The answer is given in Art. 36:

(1) The seller is liable in accordance with the contract and this Convention for any lack of conformity which exists at the time **when the risk passes to the buyer,** even though the lack of conformity becomes apparent only after that time.

The time for determining whether conformity exists or not is traditionally the time of passing of the risk. The same provision is found in many national laws. The Convention deals with the passing of risk in Articles 66 to 70. In the practice of international trade there is considerable difficulty regarding evidence connected with the time of passing of the risk.

Risk usually passes when the seller hands over the goods to the first carrier (Art. 67). Under the FOB clause, the risk passes when the goods have effectively passed the ship's rail. Who is going to inspect the goods at that very moment? Only in rare cases does the carrier detect irregularities or defects of the packaging or discover, when counting the consignments, that items are missing. Thus he is seldom able to make an entry into the documents accompanying or representing the goods.

In most cases the buyer will detect apparent

defects only at the time of taking over the
goods. And he will detect latent defects only
after a thorough examination of the goods or not
until after the goods have been used.

The situation in which the lack of conformity
becomes apparent only after the risk has passed
to the buyer is covered by Art. 36. Nevertheless,
even in these cases the buyer must prove that the
lack of conformity already existed at the time of
passing of the risk.

Under para. 2 of Art. 36 there is no such
requirement:

> (2) The seller is also liable for any
> lack of conformity which **occurs after
> the time** indicated in the preceding
> paragraph and which is due to a breach
> of any of his obligations, including a
> breach of any guarantee that for a
> period of time the goods will remain
> fit for their ordinary purpose or for
> some particular purpose or will retain
> specified qualities or characteristics.

This paragraph contains two different cases. In
case (i), the seller has given a guarantee. This
could be part of the contract or a promise made
by the seller. In any case, there is no automatic
guarantee and the Convention does not oblige the
seller to grant a guarantee. If there is a guarantee, the seller remains liable for the quality
of the goods for the specified period of guarantee. In no case, however, is the seller liable
for **all** later defects. If the buyer does not
observe maintanance instructions, if he uses
incorrect feedstuffs, if he operates a machine
incorrectly etc., the seller will not be liable.
The defects, even if they occur at a later time,
must be caused by a fault of the seller. In
guarantee clauses sellers usually restrict their

liability to defects in material, poor workman-
ship or construction.

In case (ii), without having issued a guarantee, the seller has committed a breach of one of
his obligations, for instance, failure to package
the goods in a manner which preserves and protects them. If the packaging is defective, the
goods may well have been damaged during transport
but also after the passing of the risk. Whereas
it did not rain before, bad weather conditions
thereafter may have caused the poorly protected
goods to spoil.

Article 37

Art. 37 does not contain an obligation of the
seller but one of his rights. It concerns the
cure of defects before the date for delivery and
is similar in substance to Art. 34 concerning
documents. Art. 37 reads as follows:

> If the seller has delivered goods be-
> fore the date for delivery, he may, up
> to that date, deliver any missing part
> or make up any deficiency in the quan-
> tity of the goods delivered, or deliver
> goods in replacement of any non-
> conforming goods delivered or remedy
> any lack of conformity in the goods
> delivered, provided that the exercise
> of this right does not cause the buyer
> unreasonable inconvenience or unreason-
> able expense. However, the buyer re-
> tains any right to claim damages as
> provided for in this Convention.

As we have seen in discussing Art. 33, the
date for delivery may be at the very beginning or
within a period of time. If the seller has chosen
a date for delivery at the beginning of the

period, he may cure any non-conformity up to the end of the period. It seems that the seller has the same right even if the buyer has chosen a date within the agreed period. The buyer's choice of a specific date does not change the originally agreed period of time for delivery by the seller.

If the buyer has chosen a date because the ship he ordered under a FOB clause will call at the port at that date, it may be difficult for him to provide another ship at a later date. This is an example of the inconvenience mentioned in Art. 37. The seller's right to cure defects does not mean that expenses connected therewith will be borne by the buyer.

Of course, the seller may cure non-conformities not only up to the date of delivery. Under certain circumstances, as we will discuss in connection with Art. 48, he also has such a right after the date for delivery (and under Art. 46 an obligation as well).

The right of the seller to cure the non-conformity of the goods presupposes his knowledge of the non-conformity. In cases involving missing parts or short deliveries, the seller may be aware of this himself or he will be made aware of it through information of the carrier. In other cases he should be notified by the buyer. The buyer is responsible for examining the goods (Art. 38) and giving notice to the seller (Art. 39). This obligation of the buyer arises immediately after receipt of the goods. It does not depend on the date for delivery in the contract. On the other hand, the rights of the buyer under Art. 45 et seq. of the Convention will arise only **after** the date for delivery, as agreed between the parties, because the premature delivery will not change the date for delivery.

Another question, which will be discussed

later in connection with Art. 52, concerns whether the buyer, in case of a premature delivery,
also has to pay for the goods earlier than originally agreed. This question may be answered differently in different situations. The right to
cure non-conformity under Art. 37 comprises four
different possibilities which could appear singly
as well as combined.

The seller may deliver any missing part, for
instance, of a machine. He may also make up any
deficiency in the quantity of the goods delivered, for instance, if he originally delivered
only 80 of 100 contracted bottles of a certain
liquid. Art. 37 also applies in this regard to
the case of delivery in parts. In other words,
whereas some national laws require agreement
between the parties or permission by the buyer
for delivery in parts or installments, under the
Convention the seller who did not ship the complete consignment in the first case may supplement his delivery up to the date for delivery
even without such permission, provided, however,
it does not cause the buyer unreasonable inconvenience or unreasonable expenses, a topic that
will be discussed shortly.

A third method of the seller's curing of non-
conformities is for him to deliver goods in replacement of the non-conforming goods delivered
earlier. Whether the goods conform or not has to
be judged in accordance with Art. 35.

Does Art. 37 also apply in regard to Articles
41 and 42? I would say yes. I admit, Articles 41
and 42 do not use the term "conform" or "conformity" and the heading of Section II speaks of
conformity of the goods **and** third party claims,
which could give the impression that these are
different things. Nevertheless, goods with defects in title can also be replaced. The only

difference is that third party claims will usually not arise during the time period between the
early delivery and the date of delivery as envisaged in the contract. But if the buyer himself
detects the defect, he should inform the seller
and the seller should be able to replace the non-
conforming goods.

If the seller replaces goods, he, of course,
has to bear all connected expenses.

The fourth method of curing non-conformities
is to remedy any lack of conformity in the goods
delivered. To remedy means to repair the defective goods or part of the goods either at the
seller's place or at the place of the buyer,
whichever is more convenient, more effective and
less expensive.

In any case, we have to keep in mind that
curing non-conformities should never cause the
buyer inconveniences or expenses that are unreasonable. It is questionable what the seller can
demand from the buyer. As for the reasonability,
in general each case is different and can be
decided only in the light of the individual circumstances. There is, however, a difference between inconvenience and expense. Whereas the
Convention does not permit unreasonable inconvenience and unreasonable expense for the buyer,
consistently using the notion "unreasonable" in
both cases, the inconvenience rests with the
buyer but the expenses, even the reasonable ones,
may be claimed from the seller as damages.

Article 38

Upon receipt of the goods the buyer wants to
know whether they conform with the contract, and,
therefore, he examines the goods. The seller, on
the other hand, is also interested in knowing

whether the buyer is satisfied or whether there
will be claims. Therefore, he obliges the buyer
to examine the goods.

Art. 38 of the Convention also obliges the
buyer to examine the goods and even provides for
the time to do so:

> The buyer must examine the goods, or
> cause them to be examined, within as
> short a period as is practicable in the
> circumstances.

As mentioned earlier, this obligation of the
buyer could also have been placed in another
section of the Convention that deals with the
remedies of the buyer. If the buyer does not
examine the goods, he may lose his rights under
Art. 45 et seq.

However, it is not the examination itself that
determines whether he keeps his rights arising
from non-conformity of the goods or whether he
loses them, but rather the notice to the seller
(Art. 39). The examination is carried out only in
preparation of the notice. If the buyer discovers
a non-conformity without examining the goods, he
may and has to notify the seller.

The goods need not be examined personally by
the buyer or his own staff. The buyer may also
order third persons, for instance, specialized
and impartial control organizations, to examine
the goods. The purpose of the examination is to
decide whether the goods conform with the contract or not. In any case, it has to be carried
out with due care.

The manner and extent of the examination will
often be agreed upon by the parties, especially
in the case of machines and equipment (for instance, the parties will agree on a cold run or a
mathematical performance test or both). The methods of examination depend largely on the type of

goods. The parties may also agree on a mathemati-
cal-statistical control of quality or on the
application of specific control or analytical
procedures. It is possible that established practices have already been developed between the
parties (Art. 9). Furthermore, in certain
branches usages may have been developed regarding
methods of control which have to be taken into
account, e.g., the examination of each single
item or spot-checks.

In general, the examination will show only
patent defects. Admittedly, the Convention does
not use the terms "patent" and "latent," or "apparent" and "hidden" defects. Nevertheless, the
distinction is present, as is shown by the provision of Art. 39.

The length of the period for examination depends on the circumstances, and therefore, no
fixed period has been designated. As was mentioned in connection with Art. 37, the period for
examination commences after receipt of the goods.
There may be cases where this is not practicable
and where the buyer may be justified in waiting
till the end of the period or the original date
for delivery.

The circumstances which have to be taken into
account include the place where the goods are
situated at the time of passing of the risk (cf.
Art. 36 para. 1 and Art. 66 et seq.); the type of
goods, for instance, a single piece, bulk goods,
perishable goods, consumer goods; how the goods
are packaged or the type of container; whether
there is a package which, for example, will not
be opened till the goods reach the final consumer; whether the buyer uses the goods himself
or resells them; the technical prerequisites
at the buyer's disposal; and, as mentioned earlier, whether usages and practices apply.

As was shown in connection with Articles 31
and 32, the carriage of the goods from the seller
to the buyer can be considered as part of the
normal transaction. For this reason para. 2 of
Art. 38 provides:

> (2) If the contract involves carriage
> of the goods, examination may be de-
> ferred until after the goods have ar-
> rived at their destination.

An examination of the goods at the frontier or
when passing the rail of a ship is hardly imaginable, and, in general, is neither possible nor
necessary. Therefore, it seems to be natural to
defer the examination until after the goods have
arrived at their destination.

In case, however, there are frequent disputes
as to whether defects detected after arrival have
been caused during carriage and thus before or
after passing of the risk, it is to be recommended that a control organization examine the
goods at the place and time of passing of the
risk.

The last possibility is dealt with in Art. 38,
i.e., the buyer does not keep the goods.

> (3) If the goods are redirected in
> transit or redispatched by the buyer
> without a reasonable opportunity for
> examination by him and at the time of
> the conclusion of the contract the
> seller knew or ought to have known of
> the possibility of such redirection or
> redispatch, examination may be deferred
> until after the goods have arrived at
> the new destination.

This provision covers two different cases:
A) The buyer himself is competent for further
carriage of the goods from the place of delivery
to the place of destination and;

(B) The buyer resells the goods without taking them over in the first place.

But even if the buyer takes over the goods, for instance, 1000 television sets, and resells them from his warehouse, he is not obliged to open each and every box to examine the set. In such cases it is quite normal to make spot-checks.

It is necessary that the seller knew of the possibility of redispatch or "ought to have known" since, by deferring the examination, he has to expect notices at a much later date. On the other hand, in international trade, whenever the buyer is a trader, the seller must take into account the possibility of redirection or redispatch.

Was it at all necessary to oblige the buyer to examine the goods? Would the necessity of the notice as stipulated by Art. 39 not have been sufficient? Obviously, some legal systems can do without the duty to examine the goods; at any event, the duty to give notice **implies** that the goods must first be examined.

Article 39

Art. 39 reads:

(1) The buyer loses the right to rely on a lack of conformity of the goods if he does not give notice to the seller specifying the nature of the lack of conformity within a reasonable time after he has discovered it or ought to have discovered it.

The Convention not only mentions the time when the buyer **has** discovered the lack of conformity but also the time when he **ought to have** discovered it. This is the time, at least as far as

apparent defects are concerned, when the buyer
was obliged to examine the goods in accordance
with Art. 38.

The right of a buyer to rely on a lack of
conformity of the goods lapses if he does not
give notice within reasonable time. Here lack of
conformity relates to quality, quantity and description, as provided by Art. 35. Notification
of third party rights and claims has been dealt
with separately in Art. 43.

The rights which the buyer loses in case of
omission of notice include the right
  (i)   to claim damages (Art. 45 para. 1 (b),
  (ii)   to require delivery of substitute goods
         (Art. 46 para.2),
  (iii) to require repair (Art. 46 para. 3),
  (iv)   to fix an additional period of time for
         performance (Art. 47),
  (v)   to declare the contract avoided (Art.
         49),
  (vi)   to reduce the price (Art. 50).

After having lost his above-mentioned rights,
the buyer has to retain the non-conforming goods
and pay the price in spite of the non-conformity,
provided Art. 40 or Art.44 does not apply.

At the diplomatic conference, many delegations
from developing countries spoke against the content of Art. 39 and the loss of the buyer's
rights. According to their views, such a consequence would be unknown in many countries; moreover, it would be much too harsh and would un-
justifiably favour the seller.

However, other delegations asked why a buyer
should not be interested in discovering non-
conformities and if he detected them, why he
should not notify the seller. The sooner the
better for him because otherwise the seller would
not be able to remedy the defect. As long as the

seller is not aware of the defect, he is not able
to discover its cause. This discussion resulted
in a new Article 44 which was not contained in
the draft.

The reasonable time mentioned in Art. 39 is in
any case a short period. It is in the interest of
the buyer himself to inform the seller if he is
interested in having the goods replaced or re-
paired. Reasonable, in many cases, will mean
giving notice immediately.

The reasonable time commences at the time of
discovery of the non-conformity. In the case of
apparent defects this will usually be the time of
the taking over and examination of the goods. In
regard to latent defects, the time of discovery
of the non-conformity will be the time of commencement of the use of the goods, the time of
putting them into operation or even later.

If the buyer already discovers defects before
taking over the goods, the reasonable time also
commences at the time of the discovery, i.e.,
before taking delivery (Art. 60).

The buyer's notice should enable the seller to
take the necessary steps to remedy the non-conformity. For this reason, an exact description of
the non-conformity is required. The notice should
relate the essential result of the examination of
the goods.

The parties may agree on the means of evidence
which have to be attached to the notice.

It is recommended that the buyer specify his
claims at the time of giving notice. Whether he
requests substitute goods or repair, he has to do
so in conjunction with his notice or within a
reasonable time thereafter (Art. 46 paras. 2 and
3).

Even latent defects will become visible some-
day. The later they are discovered the more dif-

ficult it is to decide whether they were caused
by a breach of an obligation of the seller or by
outside influences after passing of the risk or
by normal wear and tear. Therefore, a maximum
period is laid down in para. 2 of Art. 39:

> (2) In any event, the buyer loses the
> right to rely on a lack of conformity
> of the goods if he does not give the
> seller notice thereof at the latest
> within a period of two years from the
> date on which the goods were actually
> handed over to the buyer, unless this
> time-limit is inconsistent with a con-
> tractual period of guarantee.

The maximum period is two years. This period does
not cease to run when the seller is repairing the
goods, as is the case in a period of prescription. Nor does the period commence anew after the
non-conformity has been cured by substituting a
defective part.

This exclusive period was greatly disputed
during preparation of the Convention since it is
shorter in many national laws. However, in the
light of and under the conditions of **international** trade, the length of the two-year period has
been considered justifiable. Moreover, it may be
modified by the parties.

The GIW prescribes different periods for different kinds of non-conformity, as do the GCD.
Notices in regard to non-conformity of quality
have to be given within six months, notices in
regard to quantity within three months (Art. 285
para. 3 GIW, resp. Art. 72 para. 1 GCD). Indeed,
non-conformity in regard to quantity should be
discovered by the buyer in a relatively short
time. In addition, non-conformity in regard to
quantity may be caused by the carrier and the

difficulties of settling matters increase as time
passes.

The two-year period commences when the goods
are actually handed over to the buyer, not at the
time when the risk passes or when the goods are
handed over to the first carrier. According to
the GIW, the period commences when the goods
arrive at the place of destination (Art. 285
para. 3), and that is often but not always identical with the handing over of the goods to the
buyer. In contrast, according to Art. 72 para. 1
GCD, the maximum period already commences with
the date of delivery.

Art. 39 refers to a contractual period of
guarantee. If the time-limit of two years is
inconsistent with a contractual period of guarantee, the latter prevails. In any case, the buyer
may give notice during the period of guarantee.
If the period of guarantee is three years, notice
can be given within these three years. (According
to Art. 285 para. 4 GIW even up to one month
after the expiration of such guarantee period.)

Of course, if a contractual guarantee has been
granted by the seller, the buyer is still obliged
to examine the goods within a reasonable period
of time and to give notice of any discovered non-
conformity within reasonable time. He may not
wait till the very end of the period of guarantee
to give notice of apparent defects.

What happens if the period of guarantee is
shorter than two years? Here it has to be decided
whether the contractual guarantee is given in
addition to the remedies of the Convention or
whether the guarantee shall replace the Convention's remedies. In the first case -- guarantee
in addition -- the period of two years remains
valid. In the second case -- guarantee replacing
the remedial rights under the Convention -- the

period for giving notice will be shortened.

A last point should be mentioned. If the buyer's notice does not reach the seller in time or if the notice does not reach the seller at all, this does not deprive the buyer of his rights. This brings us to Art. 27 which reads as follows:

> Unless otherwise expressly provided in this Part of the Convention, if any notice, request or other communication is given or made by a party in accordance with this Part and by means appropriate in the circumstances, a delay or error in the transmission of the communication or its failure to arrive does not deprive that party of the right to rely on the communication.

The risk of transmission is carried by the seller. The GIW contains a similar provision in para. 7 of Art. 285. Here also the dispatch of the notice is decisive. The buyer may rely on the communication only, if, within three months after the first notification of the defect, he sends a reminder that notice was given or gives fresh notice.

The buyer who fails to give notice does not lose all of his rights in any event. There is an exception which we shall point out when discussing Art. 44.

Article 40

There is another exception in Art. 40 which reads:

> The seller is not entitled to rely on the provisions of Art. 38 and 39 if the lack of conformity relates to facts of which he knew or could not have been

unaware and which he did not disclose
to the buyer.

In other words, the buyer retains his rights even
if he did not examine the goods and did not give
notice. It follows that under the Convention the
seller is obliged to disclose any defects of the
goods to the buyer. And, if the seller could not
have been unaware of the defects, he cannot use
the excuse that he did not know of the defects.
Thus he is also obliged to examine his goods
himself, to make sure that his goods conform with
the contract.

An interesting example of what is expected of
the seller is found in para. 1 of Art. 26 GCD:

> Before the goods are shipped, the seller
> shall be obliged to submit at his own ex-
> pense the quality of the goods to verifica-
> tion (test, analysis, inspection, etc.,
> depending on the type of the goods) in ac-
> cordance with the conditions agreed upon
> with the buyer; in case agreed upon con-
> ditions are lacking, then in accordance with
> the usual verification conditions existing
> in the seller's country with respect to the
> given goods.

And the GCD go on to provide rules for mass-
produced industrial and agricultural goods, consumer goods and food products, where only samples
are taken at random, machinery and equipment and
finally for large complete sets of equipment.

So far we have spoken only about quality. But
the same applies to quantity as well. Here I
refer back to Art. 35 where, as we have seen,
lack of conformity relates to quantity as well,
whereas many national laws treat short or partial
delivery as delay with different legal consequences.

If the seller ships 80 bicycles instead of

100, there are two possibilities. Either he will
enter the correct figure of the actual shipment
into the documents accompanying the goods or he
will write the figure stipulated by the contract.
If the way bill shows 80, it is clear that he is
aware of the lack of conformity with the contract, and therefore, no notice is necessary on
the part of the buyer. If the way bill shows 100,
he thinks he has shipped the whole lot, and thus
notice should be given.

Here one could point out that the seller would
have seen the difference if he had counted the
bicycles before shipment. But maybe he did count
them, and there were 100. And 20 disappeared
during carriage. The buyer does not yet know what
happened; he does not know why only part of the
goods arrived, and thus he cannot know whether
the seller could not have been unaware of the
non-conformity. Therefore, notice is necessary in
order for the buyer to retain his rights.

Art. 40 does not speak of the **time** of the
seller's knowledge, as for example in para. 3 of
Art. 35 where the knowledge of the buyer is
required at the time of the conclusion of the
contract. (The time of the conclusion of the
contract is also decisive under Art. 42 para. 1
and para. 2.)

In Art. 40 it could certainly not be the same
time. The goods may be all right at the time of
the conclusion of the contract but have deteriorated later on. In such a case the seller may not
ship them. It seems that the knowledge or better
the absence of knowledge of any defects in the
goods is required when the seller performs the
contract, that is, when he ships the goods.

In cases of differences in quantity, he may
become aware of the non-conformity even after
shipment by information which he receives from

the carrier. This should suffice for Art. 40 to apply. The seller may not rely on the absence of notice from the buyer if he, even after delivery, knew of the fact of his short delivery.

Article 41

As already mentioned earlier, non-conformity of the goods in regard to their being free from third party rights is dealt with separately in the Convention. Whereas the Hague Convention contained only one article dealing with this question, the Sales Convention has two separate articles, Art. 41 concerning third party rights in relation to title, and Art. 42 concerning third party rights in relation to intellectual property.

Art. 41 reads:

> The seller must deliver goods which are free from any right or claim of a third party, unless the buyer agreed to take the goods subject to that right or claim. However, if such right or claim is based on industrial property or other intellectual property, the seller's obligation is governed by Article 42.

The Convention regulates only the relations between the seller and the buyer, not those between the buyer and the third person. Whether it is possible or not to acquire title as a bona fide purchaser is outside the scope of the Convention (cf. Art. 4).

As far as the decisive time is concerned, the goods must be free from third party rights or claims at the time of delivery and not at the time of the conclusion of the contract for rea-

sons which we have already discussed in regard to
quality.

Rights and claims under Art. 41 may be rights
of title, for instance, the not uncommon reservation of title. A third party who has sold goods
to the seller under the condition that the title
to the goods shall pass only on full payment of
price and who has not been fully paid, may demand
the return of the goods under some legal systems,
(e.g., Art. 233 GIW).

Another right of title might be a pledge. Some
legal systems permit not only possessory but also
non-possessory pledges so that the seller could
deliver goods to the buyer which are pledged to a
third person.

The rights or claims of a third party mentioned in Art. 41 could extend to obligatory
claims if under certain agreements, like rent or
lease, a third party may claim possession of the
goods.

Whether the claim of the third party is justified or not and how the third party may pursue
his rights is likewise outside the scope of the
Convention. The right or claim of the third party, however, must be able to affect the buyer.

The buyer, of course, can agree to take the
goods subject to third party rights or claims as
he can agree to take goods with other defects.
This agreement need not be given expressly by the
buyer. It could also be construed if the buyer
definitely knows (and not only should know) of
the rights or claims of the third party and
nevertheless takes the goods without any reservation.

The buyer will usually agree to take goods
which are subject to third party rights if he
expects the right of the third party to soon
disappear.

The Convention speaks not only of **rights** of third parties, as is usual in many legal systems, but also includes **claims** of third parties and does not distinguish whether such claims are justified or not. The reason is that unjustified claims may also hinder the buyer in the use of the goods or at least may cause expenses, for instance, to defend a case in court even if the third party claimant has no chance of winning.

I already mentioned the decisive time for the existence of third party rights or claims, namely the time of the delivery of the goods. This time is very important especially in connection with unjustified claims. The seller must know of the claim. His obligation consists in refusing and contesting the claim and if necessary in defending a case. If, at a later time, a third party unjustly claims anything from the buyer, the seller cannot be held responsible.

Article 42

I already mentioned that ULIS did not have a separate article on intellectual property rights. Opinion is divided whether Art. 52 of ULIS included such rights or not. Honnold[13], relying on Tunc[14], does not think so, whereas, according to Dölle[15], ULIS extended to intellectual property rights as well.

Be it as it may, the reason why UNCITRAL decided to draft a separate article was to restrict the liability of the seller[16] in accordance with the principle of territoriality which governs most of intellectual property rights. In the light of this principle, the restriction of the liability of the seller is justified. The restriction relates to time and place as well as to knowledge of the seller and of the buyer and to special demands of the buyer.

Art. 42 speaks of industrial property or other intellectual property. The notion intellecutal property includes industrial property and is used more and more to denote patents, trade marks, models, denomination of origin, copy rights and others.

Art. 42 reads:

> (1) The seller must deliver goods which are free from any right or claim of a third party based on industrial pro- perty or other intellectual property of which at the time of the conclusion of the contract the seller knew or could not have been unaware,...

As in Art. 41, it is not only rights but also claims and, as we have assumed, also false or invalid, unjustified claims. In contrast, it is not the time of delivery of the goods which counts, but the right or claim must have already existed at the time of the **conclusion** of the contract; otherwise, the seller could not have known it.

The time of the conclusion of the contract has been chosen because, between that time and the date of delivery, third parties could acquire rights that the seller could not have foreseen or prevented and which he could not have taken into consideration. This risk falls on the buyer.

The seller could not have been unaware of the third party's right if he had been careful in examining the existing patent situation. It would be impossible, however, to conduct patent re- searches on a world-wide scale.

Art. 42, therefore, continues:

> ... provided that the right or claim is based on industrial property or other intellectual property:

(a) under the law of the State where
     the goods will be resold or other-
     wise used, if it was contemplated
     by the parties at the time of the
     conclusion of the contract that the
     goods would be resold or otherwise
     used in that State; or
(b) in any other case, under the law of
     the State where the buyer has his
     place of business.

The seller's responsibility to deliver goods
which are free from third party rights or claims
based on industrial property or other intellectual property rights always applies only to one
country, either the country of the buyer or, if
the goods would be resold or used in another
country, to that country.

The parties must not necessarily have **agreed**
on this third country, but it must have been
contemplated by them, that is, they must have
taken this possibility into account, and not only
the buyer but also the seller.

In any case, their contemplation must have
been directed toward a **specific** country; theore-
tically, of course, the goods could be resold to
any country, unless there is a clause in the
contract which does not permit re-export.

As with the buyer's knowledge of quality defects, the buyer's knowledge of third party
rights also frees the seller from his liability.
Para. 2 of Art. 42 provides:

(2) The obligation of the seller under
     the preceding paragraph does not extend
     to cases where:
(a) at the time of the conclusion of
     the contract the buyer knew or
     could not have been unaware of the
     right or claim;...

In contrast to rights of title (Art. 41) where
the buyer must **agree** to take goods subject to
third party rights, here under Art. 42 in respect
to intellectual property rights, it is sufficient
that the buyer **knew** of the third party right or
even that he should have known. Another difference is the time. The buyer must agree to rights
of title at the time of delivery, but he must
have known of intellectual property rights at the
time of the conclusion of the contract.

When could the buyer not have been unaware? Is
he obliged to conduct research regarding the
patent situation in his country or the country of
destination? I don't think so. There are, however, contracts, where the parties agree that the
buyer has to examine the patent situation in his
or another agreed country and, accordingly, notify the seller about any existing industrial
property rights. Such an agreement is based on
the fact that in some countries it might not be
easy for foreigners to find out whether third
party rights exist within a reasonable time and
at reasonable expense. On the other hand, there
are countries which do not have a patent system
at all and which do not participate in corresponding international agreements. If goods are
delivered to those countries, there is no danger
of third party rights for either the buyer or the
seller.

A last restriction of the liability of the
seller in Art. 42 concerns instructions given by
the buyer. The obligation of the seller does not
extend to cases where

> (b) the right or claim results from the
>   seller's compliance with technical
>   drawings, designs, formulae or
>   other such specifications furnished
>   by the buyer.

Here, the buyer's knowledge of third party rights is not required; he may be absolutely ignorant in this regard. If he gives specific instructions to the seller, he has to bear the consequences. On the other hand, if the seller knows of third party rights, under general rules of good faith, he should call the buyer's attention to them. If then the buyer nevertheless insists on his order, the seller will not be liable to the buyer. Whether the seller is liable to the third party is a different matter which cannot be discussed here.

Article 43

As with non-conformity of the goods in regard to quality and quantity (Art. 39), the buyer is also obliged to notify the seller in regard to third party rights. Art. 43 provides:

(1) The buyer loses the right to rely on the provisions of Art. 41 or Art. 42 if he does not give notice to the seller specifying the nature of the right or claim of the third party within a reasonable time after he has become aware or ought to have become aware of the right or claim.

If the buyer does not notify the seller, he loses his rights under the Convention

(i)   to claim damages (Art. 45),

(ii)   to demand goods not affected by third party rights (Art. 46),

(iii) to fix an additional period of time for performance by the seller (Art. 47),

(iv)   to declare the contract avoided (Art. 49).

Thus far this does not differ from Art. 39.

However, whereas Art. 39 specifies a maximum
period of two years for giving notice, here there
is no such limit. National laws usually contain
time-limits for all kinds of notices whether they
concern quality, quantity or third party rights.

The Convention does not require immediate
notice. The buyer, as provided under Art. 39, has
to give notice within a reasonable time. A reasonable time may include a certain period for
contemplation by the buyer, for inquiry into the
legal situation by consulting his lawyer. The
buyer should not delay the notice beyond a time
that could no longer be regarded as reasonable.
The buyer must not wait. The reasonable time
already commences when the buyer **ought** to have
become aware of the third party right or claim.
The buyer may not carelessly neglect rights or
claims of third parties of which he receives
knowledge.

The buyer not only has to give notice, he also
has to specify the nature of the right or claim,
the steps that the third party has undertaken or
intends to undertake. The notification of the
buyer will enable the seller to take immediate
measures defending his (and the buyer's) rights
against the third party. If the buyer fails to
give notice in time, this may also have consequences as far as his ability to claim damages is
concerned. According to Art. 77, a party who
relies on a breach of contract must take measures
to mitigate the loss.

Para. 2 of Art. 43 provides an exception to
the notice requirement:

> (2) The seller is not entitled to rely
> on the provisions of the preceding
> paragraph if he knew of the right or
> claim of the third party and the nature
> of it.

Here we find a parallel to Art. 40 with some
differences. Here definite knowledge of third
party rights is required on the part of the
seller, whereas, in regard to non-conformity of
the goods, it was sufficient that the seller
could not have been unaware. In the case of non-
conformity, there is the additional requirement
that the seller did not disclose the non-conformity to the buyer.

The meaning of "and the nature of it" at the
end of Art. 43 is not quite clear. Is the nature
of the right of the third party a separate item
which the seller has to know? And may he rely on
the buyer's failure to give notice if he knew of
the right of the third party but not of its
nature? I don't think so. If the seller is already aware of the right or claim of the third
party, no notice is required on the part of the
buyer.

Article 44

The last article in Section II of Chapter II
of Part III is one which cannot be found in any
national law. I have already mentioned in connection with Art. 39 that failure to give notice
does not deprive the buyer of his rights in all
cases.

Art. 44 reads:

Notwithstanding the provisions of paragraph (1) of Article 39 and paragraph
(1) of Article 43, the buyer may reduce
the price in accordance with Article 50
or claim damages, except for loss of
profit, if he has a reasonable excuse
for his failure to give the required
notice.

Since this provision refers to para. 1 of Art.

39 and not to para. 2, it does not affect the
maximum period of two years for giving notice.
If there was no notice at all within two years,
the buyer loses all of his rights. Art. 44,
therefore, concerns the reasonable time requirement. During the discussion of Art. 39 at the
diplomatic conference, it was stressed that it
would not always be possible to give notice within a reasonable time after discovery of the non-
conformity of the goods. Examples of reasonable
excuses were not given. At least one could think
of impediments like <u>force</u> <u>majeur</u> which could have
prevented the buyer from giving notice. Honnold[17]
mentions a buyer who noticed a defect in the
goods but considered it to be unimportant and
only later discovered the significance of the
defect. According to Honnold,

> 'Excuse' may also apply when the buyer
> notifies the seller that the goods are
> non-conforming but fails to 'specify
> the nature' of the lack of conformity,
> as required by Article 39(1), because
> of the difficulty of making such a
> specification.

On this last point I disagree with Honnold. I
don't believe that the buyer would lose his
rights under para. 1 of Art. 39 so quickly.

Even if there is an excuse, the fact that the
buyer failed to give notice in time does not
remain without consequences; he loses some of his
rights. He may no longer require delivery of
substitute goods or require the seller to remedy
the lack of conformity by repair. He may not
declare the contract avoided and he may not claim
loss of profit.

Article 45

We turn now to the last section of Chapter II; this is Section III: Remedies for breach of contract by the seller. Under the Convention the notion "breach of contract" covers **all** failures of a party to perform **any** of his obligations. There is no distinction between main obligations and auxiliary obligations. And it does not matter whether the obligation had its origin in the contract, in a usage or in the Convention itself. Under certain conditions a breach of contract is considered to be fundamental.

Art. 25 provides:

> A breach of contract committed by one of the parties is fundamental if it results in such detriment to the other party as substantially to deprive him of what he is entitled to expect under the contract, unless the party in breach did not foresee and a reasonable person of the same kind in the same circumstances would not have foreseen such a result.

The consequences of fundamental breaches are more severe than those of ordinary breaches. Some remedies are available only for fundamental breaches.

A survey of all available remedies is given in Art. 45:

> (1) If the seller fails to perform any of his obligations under the contract or this Convention, the buyer may:
>
> (a)   exercise the rights provided in articles 46 to 52;
>
> (b)   claim damages as provided in articles 74 to 77.

Whereas the specific rights and their neces-

sary preconditions are dealt with in Articles 46
to 52, Art. 45 is the general basis for claiming
damages. Articles 74 to 77 deal only with the
definition and the calculation of damages, their
limitation and mitigation.

Comparing Section III of the Convention with
the GCD, we see that the most important differences between the two documents are contained in
this section. The GCD do not have a provision
similar to para. 1 litera (b) of Art. 45. Instead, the GCD provide different remedies for
different breaches of contract and penalties
(liquidated damages) for the main categories of
non-fulfilment of a contract. These penalties
provide maximum compensation; the parties are
precluded to claim damages in excess of the stipulated penalties.

The remedies of Section III of Chapter II are
parallel to those of Section III of Chapter III.
In addition to the remedies contained in these
two Chapters of Section III, there are more remedies available in Articles 71 to 73 in regard
to anticipatory breach and instalment contracts.

Under certain conditions the seller may be
exempted from certain consequences of a failure
to perform his obligations. If the conditions
described in Art. 79 are present, he does not
have to pay damages. And there are no remedies
for the buyer at all, if the seller's failure to
perform was caused by the buyer's act or omission
(Art. 80).

It should be mentioned here that not only the
obligations of the seller but also the remedies
of the buyer may be changed by the parties in
their contract.

The buyer may claim damages even if the seller
is not at fault for failing to perform his
obligations. And furthermore,

(2) The buyer is not deprived of any
right he may have to claim damages by
exercising his right to other remedies.

Therefore, the right to claim damages exists
either as an exclusive right or as a supplementary right besides the right to require performance, to reduce the price or to avoid the contract.

(3) No period of grace may be granted
to the seller by a court or arbitral
tribunal when the buyer resorts to a
remedy for breach of contract.

This provision demonstrates that the buyer's
remedies for breach of contract by the seller
should be taken exclusively from the Convention
and not from any national law. In case of a
breach of contract, the rights of the buyer arise
immediately at the time of the breach (or in case
of an anticipatory breach even before) and no
court or arbitraton may defer them.

Article 46

(1) The buyer may require performance
by the seller of his obligations unless
the buyer has resorted to a remedy
which is inconsistent with this requirement.

Thus, the buyer may not require performance if
he has chosen to reduce the price or avoid the
contract. The buyer may require performance by
the seller in regard to any obligation of the
latter, under the condition, of course, he did
not ignore the period for giving notice as required under Articles 39 and 43.

Whether the required performance will be able
to be enforced is a different matter. Art. 28 of
the Convention provides that...

a court is not bound to enter a judgement for specific performance unless
the court would do so under its own law
in respect of similar contracts of sale
not governed by this Convention.

The right to require performance includes the
delivery of the goods, or of any missing part
thereof, the handing over of documents, the curing of defects or the performance of all other
acts necessary to fulfil the contract as originally agreed.

(2) If the goods do not conform with
the contract, the buyer may require
delivery of substitute goods only if
the lack of conformity constitutes a
fundamental breach of contract and a
request for substitute goods is made
either in conjunction with notice given
under Art. 39 or within a reasonable
time thereafter.

This provision concerns goods which "do not conform with the contract"; in Art. 35 we have seen
what this means. I would not hesitate, however,
to also include goods which are not free from
rights of third parties. The delivery of substitute goods is, of course, significant above all
in regard to defective goods. But depending on
the circumstances and the kind of third party
right, it is conceivable that goods affected by
such a right could be replaced by substitute
goods not affected by rights of third parties.
The buyer may require delivery of substitute
goods only in case of a fundamental breach of
contract, and, furthermore, only if he is able to
make restitution of the goods in essentially the
condition in which he received them. This re-

quirement, as well as exceptions thereto, is
provided in Art. 82.

It is doubtful whether the requirement of a
fundamental breach is justified. The choice between delivery of substitute goods and repair of
the defective goods depends much more on the kind
of goods, the nature of the defect, and the
possibilities of the seller.

Thus under Art. 281 of the GIW, if the buyer
demands the elimination of the defect, the **seller**
is bound to chose between repair or replacement
of the defective goods. Similar rules are contained in Art. 75 GCD. Paras. 2 and 3 state:

> In presenting a claim for quality, the
> buyer shall have the right to demand
> either remedy of the discovered defects
> or reduction in the price of the goods.
> If the buyer demands remedy of defects,
> the seller shall remedy the defect
> without delay at his own expense or
> replace the defective goods.

Criteria for determining what constitutes a
fundamental breach in regard to the quality of
the goods are not found in the Convention. One
aspect would be the ability of the seller to remedy the defect within a reasonable period.

> (3) If the goods do not conform with
> the contract, the buyer may require the
> seller to remedy the lack of conformity
> by repair, unless this is unreasonable
> having regard to all the circumstances.
> A request for repair must be made
> either in conjunction with notice given
> under Art. 39 or within a reasonable
> time thereafter.

The right of the buyer to demand repair is not
to be found in all national laws. Therefore,
there was a certain amount of opposition against

the inclusion of such a provision. On the other
hand, this is the most common remedy in international trade as far as technical goods are concerned.

Whether the repair is unreasonable may depend
on technical difficulties or the amount of expense required. Repair could even be impossible
due to technical reasons.

As was already mentioned, I would not hesitate
to include the remedying of third party rights.
The seller could free the goods from third party
rights, for instance, by taking a licence or
buying a patent.

Article 47

(1) The buyer may fix an additional
period of time of reasonable length for
performance by the seller of his obligations.

(2) Unless the buyer has received notice from the seller that he will not
perform within the period so fixed, the
buyer may not, during that period,
resort to any remedy for breach of
contract. However, the buyer is not
deprived thereby of any right he may
have to claim damages for delay in
performance.

The buyer may fix an additional period of time
for performance by the seller; however, he is not
obliged to do so. Fixing an additional period of
time is not a prerequisite for avoiding the contract, if there is already a fundamental breach.
After expiration of the additional period, the
buyer is still entitled to require performance by
the seller.

By fixing an additional period of time, the

buyer demonstrates his interest in the performance. Even if there is a fundamental breach, avoiding the contract is not always the best solution for the buyer. The additional period has to be specified -- it does not suffice to ask for prompt delivery -- and has to be made known to the seller.

Article 48

(1) Subject to article 49, the seller may, even after the date for delivery, remedy at his own expense any failure to perform his obligations, if he can do so without unreasonable delay and without causing the buyer unreasonable inconvenience or uncertainty of reimbursement by the seller of expenses advanced by the buyer. However, the buyer retains any right to claim damages as provided for in this Convention.

The right of the seller to remedy any failure to perform his obligations relates to all his obligations. Thus, he may deliver missing goods, repair goods, deliver substitute goods, or spare parts.

The right of the buyer, however, to avoid the contract according to Art. 49 has priority. Therefore, the seller has no right to remedy his failure to perform if the buyer avoids the contract. On the other hand, the seller may remedy his failure to perform as long as the buyer did not declare the contract avoided.

(2) If the seller requests the buyer to make known whether he will accept performance and the buyer does not comply

> with the request within a reasonable
> time, the seller may perform within the
> time indicated in his request. The
> buyer may not, during that period of
> time, resort to any remedy which is
> inconsistent with performance by the
> seller.

If the buyer has the right to declare the contract avoided and has not done so, the seller is
in a state of uncertainty. He may end this uncertainty by requesting the buyer to make known
whether he will accept performance.

If the buyer demanded substitute goods according to Art. 46 para. 2, the seller may not remedy
the non-conformity by repairing the goods.

> (3) A notice by the seller that he will
> perform within a specified period of
> time is assumed to include a request,
> under the preceding paragraph, that the
> buyer make known his decision.
> (4) A request or notice by the seller
> under paragraph (2) or (3) of this
> article is not effective unless re-
> ceived by the buyer.

Here, we find a deviation from the general rule
in Art. 27 where it suffices to dispatch the
notice. In this specific case, the notice must
have been received by the buyer. "Received" could
perhaps be defined in the same manner as
"reached" under Art. 24.

Article 49

> (1) The buyer may declare the contract
> avoided:
> (a) if the failure by the seller to perform
>   any of his obligations under the con-

tract or this Convention amounts to a
fundamental breach of contract; or

(b)   in case of non-delivery, if the seller
       does not deliver the goods within the
       additional period of time fixed by the
       buyer in accordance with paragraph (1)
       of article 47 or declares that he will
       not deliver within the period so fixed.

There is no automatic avoidance. The buyer,
even in a case of fundamental breach, may have an
interest in keeping his right to demand performance. But he may also avoid the contract and
does so by a mere declaration. No other steps are
necessary and no activity of a court is required.

Avoidance may comprise national concepts of
rescission as well as termination. In case of a
contract for delivery of goods by instalments, it
can be avoided in respect of deliveries already
made or of future deliveries (Art. 73 para. 3).
The effects of the avoidance are governed by
Articles 81 to 84. Both parties are released from
their main obligations under the contract.

The buyer may declare the contract avoided
only under certain conditions: the possbility to
return the received goods in their original condition (Art. 82 para. 1), or in case of non-
conformity or of third party rights, the giving
of notice as required under Articles 39 and 43.
If the buyer did not reply to a request of the
seller under Art. 48, he may also not avoid the
contract during the period of time specified by
the seller.

(2) However, in cases where the seller
has delivered the goods, the buyer
loses the right to declare the contract
avoided unless he does so:

(a) in respect of late delivery, within
    a reasonable time after he has

become aware that delivery has been
made;

(b) in respect of any breach other than
late delivery, within a reasonable
time:

   (i)   after he knew or ought to
have known of the breach;

   (ii) after the expiration of any
additional period of time
fixed by the buyer in accordance with paragraph (1) of
article 47, or after the
seller has declared that he
will not perform his obligations within such an additional period; or

   (iii) after the expiration of any
additional period of time
indicated by the seller in
accordance with paragraph (2)
of article 48, or after the
buyer has declared that he
will not accept performance.

As long as the buyer does not declare the
contract avoided, he has to reckon with performance by the seller. In general, there is no
period of time within which the buyer must declare the contract avoided. However, under certain conditions, when the seller has delivered
the goods, the buyer loses the right to declare
the contract avoided if he does not do so within
a reasonable time.

Article 50

If the goods do not conform with the
contract and whether or not the price
has already been paid, the buyer may

reduce the price in the same proportion
as the value that the goods actually
delivered had at the time of the delivery bears to the value that conforming
goods would have had at that time.
However, if the seller remedies any
failure to perform his obligations in
accordance with article 37 or article
48 or if the buyer refuses to accept
performance by the seller in accordance
with those articles, the buyer may not
reduce the price.

The reduction of the price is a right of the
buyer which he may exercise by unilateral declaration. The price may not be reduced if the seller
remedies any failure in accordance with Art. 37
or Art. 48 or if the buyer refused to let the
seller remedy the non-conformity.

The decisive time for the calculation of the
price difference between proper goods and non-
conforming ones is not, as in some national legal
systems, the time of the conclusion of the contract but the time of the delivery of the goods.
The Convention does not stipulate at which place
or market the prices have to be compared; however, in view of the close relationship between
date and place of delivery, this place should be
decisive. It is not excluded, however, that buyers may consider the place of destination.

Article 51

This provision, which does not need any comment, reads as follows:
(1) If the seller delivers only a part
of the goods or if only a part of the
goods delivered is in conformity with
the contract, articles 46 to 50 apply

in respect of the part which is missing
or which does not conform.
(2) The buyer may declare the contract
avoided in its entirety only if the
failure to make delivery completely or
in conformity with the contract amounts
to a fundamental breach of the contract.

Article 52

(1) If the seller delivers the goods
before the date fixed, the buyer may
take delivery or refuse to take delivery.

It is up to the discretion of the buyer whether he accepts early delivery or not. If he refuses to take delivery, he, in any event, has to
take steps to preserve the goods (Art. 86). If
the buyer takes early delivery, as a rule he
likewise has to fulfil his own obligations earlier, that is, examine the goods, give notice of
non-conformities, pay the price.

Similar provisions are contained in Art. 12
para. 1 and Art. 51 GCD or in Art. 44 para. 2
GIW.

As far as the obligation of the buyer to
examine the goods under Art. 38 is concerned, in
case of early delivery it has to be taken into
account that the buyer might not yet be ready and
that due to this circumstance the period "as
short as is practicable" might be somewhat longer.

By taking early delivery, the buyer may incur
additional expenses or even losses. These may be
claimed by the buyer only if he makes such an
indication at the time of taking delivery. Otherwise, early delivery and its acceptance will be

considered as a change of contract and in this case no damages may be claimed.

(2) If the seller delivers a quantity of goods greater than that provided for in the contract, the buyer may take delivery or refuse to take delivery of the excess quantity. If the buyer takes delivery of all or part of the excess quantity, he must pay for it at the contract rate.

In this case as well, the buyer has to preserve the goods if he refuses to take delivery.

NOTES

1. United Nations Conference on Contracts for the International Sale of Goods, Vienna, 10 March to 11 April 1980, Official Records (New York 1981) p. 179 et seq.

2. The elaboration of the Convention by UNCITRAL and its working group has been reported and analysed in great detail in the German Democratic Republic. See F. Enderlein, "Vorbereitung einer Konvention über den internationalen Warenkauf" 31 AWID (1975) 5. Beilage Recht im Aussenhandel; F. Enderlein and J. Völter, "Ergebnisse der Arbeit der UNCITRAL für ein einheitliches Recht über den internationalen Warenkauf" 51 AWID (1977) 31. Beilage Recht im Aussenhandel; F. Enderlein, "Zur Ausarbeitung einer Konvention über den Abschluss internationaler Kaufverträge durch die UNCITRAL" 52 AWID (1977) 32. Beilage Recht im Aussenhandel; F. Enderlein and H. Wagner, "Die XI. Tagung der UNCITRAL" 40 AWID (1978) 38. Beilage Recht im Aussenhandel.

3. J. Honnold, Uniform Law for International

Sales under the 1980 United Nations Convention (Deventer 1982).

4. Allgemeine Bedingungen für die Warenlieferung zwischen den Organisationen der Mitgliedsländer des RGW (ALB/RGW 1968/1975 i.d.F. 1979) Bekanntmachung vom 12.10.1979, GBl. II 6/1979 p. 81 et seq.

5. See report of the second session of UNCITRAL Yearbook vol. I: 1968-1970 (New York 1971) p. 98.

6. For the GCD see also Manfred Kemper, Heinz Strohbach, Hellmut Wagner, Die Allgemeinen Lieferbedingungen des RGW 1968 in der Spruchpraxis sozialistischer Aussenhandelsschiedsgerichte -- Kommentar (Berlin 1975).

7. See G. Willma, "Zu einigen Problemen der Anwendung der ALB RGW-Finnland" 44 AWID (1981), 55. Beilage Recht im Aussenhandel p. 8.

8. See Fritz Enderlein, Dietrich Maskow, Monika Stargardt, Konvention der Vereinten Nationen über die Verträge für den internationalen Warenkauf, Konvention über die Verjährung beim internationalen Warenkauf, Protokoll zu ändern der Konvention über die Verjährung beim internationalen Warenkauf -- Kommentar (Berlin 1985).

9. See F. Enderlein, "La réglementation de la vente internationale de marchandises dans le droit de la R.D.A. (Une comparison avec le projet d'une convention sur la vente internationale de marchandises)" 2 D.P.C.I. (avril 1977), tome 3, pp. 123-138.

10. See Dietrich Maskow, Hellmut Wagner, Kommentar zum Gesetz über internationale Wirtschaftsverträge -- GIW -- vom 5. Februar 1976, 2nd ed. (Berlin 1983). This Code is published in English in the series Commercial, Business and Trade Laws, "German Democratic Republic" (Dobbs Ferry, New York 1984).

11. A German translation of this Code was pub-

lished in 1974 by the Czechoslovakian Chamber of Commerce in Prague.

12. See the commentary to the 1980 edition of the INCOTERMS by Frédéric Eisemann and Werner Melis (Vienna 1982).

13. J. Honnold, <u>supra</u> n. 3, at p. 290.

14. André Tunc, <u>Commentary of the Hague Conventions of 1st July 1964 on the International Sale of Goods and on the Formation of Contracts of Sale</u>, published by the Ministerie van Justitie (The Hague).

15. Dölle and Neumayer, <u>Einheitskaufrecht</u> (München 1976). Art. 52 EKG marginal No. 6 refers to Art. 333 of the Czechoslovakian Code which was drafted according to Art. 52 of ULIS.

16. Rolf Herber, <u>Wiener UNCITRAL-Übereinkommen über internationale Warenkaufverträge vom 11. April 1980)</u> (Köln 1983) p. 26.

17. J. Honnold, <u>supra</u> n. 3, at p. 284.

CHAPTER SIX

OBLIGATIONS OF THE BUYER UNDER THE UN CONVENTION ON CONTRACTS FOR THE INTERNATIONAL SALE OF GOODS

LEIF SEVÓN
Ministry of Justice, Helsinki

1. General remarks

1.1.   A first glance at the UN Convention on
Contracts for the International Sale of Goods
supports the view that the obligations of the
buyer and the remedies for breach of those obligations are fairly simple issues in international
sales of goods. Of the 101 Articles of the Convention only 13 appear under the heading "Obligations of the Buyer." These provisions form part
of Part III of the Convention dealing with the
rights and duties of the seller and the buyer
under a contract of sale.

As in many other cases, the first glance
is misleading. Problems relating to payment in
international sales are both frequent and severe.
This does not necessarily mean that these problems are complex from a legislative point of
view. With a few exceptions, they are dealt with
in the contract. Compared to the great variety of
obligations of the seller and the different kinds
of breach of contract by the seller, the obligations of the buyer are relatively simple. For

that reason less text is needed to describe the
obligations of the buyer.

In addition, many provisions of the Convention other than those found in Articles 53-65
affect, directly or indirectly, the obligations
of the buyer and the remedies for breach of
contract by the buyer. In Part I of the Convention (Articles 1-13) dealing with the sphere of
application and general provisions, the non-
mandatory character of the Convention is stated
(Article 6). In this part of the Convention there
is also a provision on usages (Article 9) and on
the choice of the relevant place of business in
cases where a party has several places of business (Article 10). These provisions are relevant
for the understanding of Articles 53-65. In Part
II of the Convention (Articles 14-24), which
concerns the formation of contracts for the international sale of goods, one may find a definition of "offer" (Article 14) describing when a
proposal for concluding a contract is sufficiently definite. This provision is relevant when
interpreting Article 55. In Part III of the Convention dealing with the Sale of Goods (Articles
25-88), the general provisions (Articles 25-29)
and the provisions common to the obligations of
the seller and the buyer (Articles 71-88) are
directly applicable to the obligations of the
buyer.

This proves that the provisions on the
obligations of the buyer in Articles 53-65 cannot
be studied isolated from the rest of the Convention. They can be properly understood only as
part of a whole set of provisions dealing with
the cooperation or lack of cooperation between
the seller and the buyer.

1.2. In order to understand the provisions on the obligations of the buyer, it is also useful to recall some of the features of the elaboration of the Convention. The starting point was the 1964 Hague Conventions relating to a uniform law on the international sale of goods (ULIS) and to a uniform law on the formation of contracts for the international sale of goods. These Conventions did not seem to meet with international approval. After the United Nations Commission on International Trade Law (UNCITRAL) was established, the Commission set up a Working Group to consider the comments and suggestions by States on the Hague Conventions in order to "ascertain which modifications of the existing texts might render them capable of wider acceptance by countries of different legal, social and economic systems, or whether it [would] be necessary to elaborate a new text for the same purpose..."[1]

The UNCITRAL Working Group started its analysis of ULIS from the beginning of the Convention and soon reached the provisions on the seller's obligations. Many of the solutions on structure as well as on drafting were discussed thoroughly in that context. Later, the same solutions were adopted in relation to the obligations of the buyer and the remedies for breach of contract by the buyer. It was suggested that the same reasoning on which the Working Group had based its decisions in relation to the obligations of the seller also apply to those of the buyer, i.e., that a unified structure avoids gaps, cross references and inconsistencies, that it makes it possible to place all provisions on what the buyer shall do together and that repetitive and overlapping provisions can be avoided.[2]

It was also deemed useful to cast the provisions on the obligations of the buyer in the

same form as those dealing with the obligations
of the seller. The parallelism between the two
sets of provisions has been referred to on several occasions during the preparation of the
draft.[3]

The similar drafting of provisions dealing
with different realities may cause reactions
similar to those of Pawlov's dogs: Reference to a
period of time of reasonable length (Articles 47
and 63) or to an impediment beyond a party's
control (Article 79) may be a signal calling for
identical reactions by the judge or arbitrators,
or by the parties, irrespective of whether the
problems arise in the context of late performance
of the seller or of the buyer. The consolidated
system of remedies for breach of contract may
hide the fact that the situations differ and that
one should not treat a delay on the part of the
buyer on similar grounds as in cases where the
seller has delivered goods which do not conform
with the contract. However, this risk can be
overcome by educating readers of the Convention
and is mitigated by the fact that it is easier to
see the differences when one is confronted with a
specific problem.

1.3. In Article 53, which describes the obligations of the buyer, reference is made to two
sets of obligations. First, the buyer must pay
the price. This may be described as his main
obligation. Secondly, the buyer must take delivery of the goods. The Convention contains provisions describing the contents of these two obligations of the buyer in case the parties have not
defined them in their contract. In addition, the
Convention envisages that the buyer may have
other obligations. As far as these are concerned,
no attempt is made to specify or describe them in

the Convention, which only contains provisions on remedies for breach of such obligations.

In this paper, the different obligations of the buyer and the remedies for breach of these obligations will be discussed separately. The discussion will mainly be limited to the buyer's obligation to pay the price.

2. Payment of the price

2.1. The problems arising in relation to the price are at least those of "what?", "where?" and "when?".

Normally the parties agree on the price as well as on the time and place for payment. It follows from the non-mandatory character of the Convention that the parties may derogate from the Convention on these points. On the other hand, the Convention does not deal with the validity, in other respects, of the agreed provisions on the price under national law. They may be in conflict, e.g., with rules on the regulation of prices or on foreign exchange. Nor does the Convention provide an answer to the question what effect such rules of law would have if invoked in a court outside the country where the provisions have been enacted. The fact that one of the parties has concluded a contract containing provisions on the price which are in conflict, e.g., with that party's national law on foreign exchange does not necessarily preclude a court in another country from deciding in accordance with the provisions of the contract.

2.2. Calculation of the price. The Convention contains two provisions on the calculation of the price when this issue has not been settled in the contract.

2.2.1. Net weight. Under Article 56, if the price is fixed according to the weight of the goods, in case of doubt it is to be determined by the net weight. This is only a rule for interpretation of an unclear contract. Another result may follow from the contract itself or from practices established between the parties or from usage.

The provision in Article 56 does not purport to answer the question of whether the buyer is entitled to keep the packaging. This would normally seem to be the case. A different result may follow from the contract, usage or practices established between the parties.

2.2.2. Open price. Article 55 deals with the question of how the price is to be calculated if the contract has been validly concluded but does not expressly or implicitly fix or make provision for determining the price.

This provision was a problem throughout the preparation of the Convention. Attention was already drawn to it in the replies and comments by governments to UNCITRAL on the Hague Conventions of 1964.[4] Differences of opinion persisted until the issue was settled in Committee I of the Vienna Conference.[5]

The difficulties were due to the fact that under the law of some states, a contract of sale must necessarily set forth the price or provide a mechanism for determining the price. This seems to be the case under Austrian, Belgian, Dutch, French and Soviet Law. For these countries and others having a similar rule, the Convention represents a philosophy different than that on which their national law is based.

Article 55 must be read together with Article 14. Under Article 14 a proposal for con-

cluding a contract constitutes an offer only if
it is sufficiently definite. This is the case if
the proposal indicates the goods and expressly or
implicitly fixes or makes provision for determining the quantity and the price. The question then
arises whether there is a conflict between Articles 14 and 55 or whether the latter provision
lacks meaning.

This question is interesting from a theoretical point of view. It might, however, also be
interesting to ascertain its practical importance. The situation envisaged in Article 55 is
unlikely to arise in large contracts. It is unlikely that the parties would not fix the price
of the goods or a method for determining the
price when concluding a contract in writing. Such
a situation would thus hardly arise in regard to
a State which has made a declaration under Article 96: A written contract not containing any
such provision on the price would certainly be a
rare bird.

It is sufficient under Article 14 that the
proposal implicitly fixes or makes provision for
determining the price. The relation between the
two Articles would not seem to pose any problems
when the parties have agreed, explicitly or implicitly, that the price may be fixed by a third
party. Whether it would also be sufficient to
provide that the buyer shall pay the price generally charged for such goods at the time of delivery, seems to be uncertain, at least in some
legal systems. Recent French case law seems to
indicate that a reference to the price usually
charged for similar goods at the same place might
not be sufficient even if explicitly made.[7]

On the other hand, in cases where a practice has been established between the parties as
to the price, the parties would, under Article 9,

be bound by this practice. In these cases there
would be little doubt that the parties have implicitly referred to a price to be determined
according to previous practice.

The main reason for opposition to the proposals requiring that the contract must set forth
the price or a method for determining the price
was that this requirement might lead to strange
results in situations where a buyer has an urgent
need for goods, e.g., spare parts for a machine,
and orders them by phone, no reference being made
by either party to the price. A rule under which
no contract is considered to have been validly
concluded unless it provides at least for a method of determining the price, would then cover not
only a situation where the buyer immediately
after ordering the goods informs the seller that
he actually does not need them, but also situations where the seller ships the goods and the
buyer takes delivery of and uses the goods. The
result would not seem to be totally unacceptable
in the first case. On the other hand, one may
consider the possibility that the seller has
started production and incurred costs in an effort to assist the buyer. The result would seem
quite unacceptable in cases where the goods have
been used up by the buyer, who then informs the
seller that no contract was ever concluded and
that he therefore need not pay for the goods.

It seems unlikely that any legal system
would leave the matter there. One would probably
find a way out by resorting to other construc-
tions to reach an acceptable result. One could
imagine a great variety of methods. The judge
might probably find -- to the surprise of the
parties -- that they had indeed agreed implicitly
on a price. One could also apply different doc-
trines on unjust enrichment or other similar

methods in order to oblige the buyer to compensate the seller for the value of the goods. These
solutions bring the problem outside the scope of
the Convention and thus outside the scope of
unification.

When dealing with buyers from countries
requiring the price to be settled in or determinable from the contract, sellers ought to be careful not to start production of the goods or
dispatch them until agreement on the price has
been reached. If it is possible for the seller to
determine the price at that stage, not knowing
what the actual cost of production and shipment
will be, it might be possible for him to invoice
the buyer and, if the invoice is not protested,
maintain that the buyer must have accepted the
price indicated therein.

On the other hand, a rule requiring that
the price be determined in or determinable from
the contract might be inconvenient to buyers as
well. A buyer who has ordered goods without settling the price may find that no goods are delivered and that he has no remedies for such a
delay as no contract of sale has been concluded.

2.2.3. Other issues. The Convention does not
contain detailed provisions on what is considered
to be included in the price and what costs the
seller may charge separately. Some conclusions
can, however, be drawn from different provisions.

Under Article 35 (2)(d) the goods do not
conform with the contract unless they are contained or packaged in the manner usual for such
goods. It follows from this provision that packaging is part of the seller's obligation and that
the cost for packaging must be calculated in
setting the price. Again, an agreement, usage, or

practice established between the parties may lead
to a different result.

One may also assume that the costs for
transportation and other measures to bring the
goods to the place of delivery must be taken into
account when calculating the price and may not be
charged separately.

2.3. Place of payment. Under Article 57, if the
buyer is not bound to pay the price at any other
particular place, he must pay it to the seller at
the seller's place of business. If payment is to
be made against the handing over of the goods or
of document, the buyer must pay the price at the
place where the handing over takes place.

2.3.1 Effects of the rule on place of payment.
Under Article 57, the buyer has to bear the costs
and risk for the transfer of an amount corresponding to the price to the seller's place of
business at the time of conclusion of the contract. If the seller has more than one place of
business, the relevant place of business is the
one which has the closest relationship with the
contract and its performance, not only in regard
to payment of the price. The uncertainty inherent
in this provision is unlikely to cause problems
in practice as the place of payment is often
stated in the contract. In addition, payment is
usually made only after the seller has received
an invoice. The invoice may indicate which place
of business the seller considers to be relevant,
and such a statement may be interpreted as acceptance of payment being made at that place. On the
other hand, the buyer is not bound by such an
indication. It may well be that the seller, for
his own convenience, wishes payment to be made at
a particular place. The buyer may, in spite of

such a reference, pay the price at the seller's place of business which has the closest relationship with the contract.

A reference to a bank account in an invoice may normally also be interpreted as the buyer's declaration of acceptance to make payment at the bank instead of at the seller's place of business. In regard to this point it may readily be assumed that practices have been established between the parties.

Read together with Article 58, Article 57 states that if there is a delay in the transfer of the amount, e.g., due to lack of the authorization of transfer by the appropriate authorities or to a mistake by the buyer's bank, thus having the effect that the amount is not available at the place of payment in time, there is a breach of contract on the part of the buyer. As was noted above, the provision also has a bearing on the distribution of costs between the parties.

Under Article 57(2) the seller must bear any increase in expenses incidental to payment which is caused by a change in his place of business subsequent to the conclusion of the contract. The provision only deals with the distribution of costs. The fact that there is a change in the seller's relevant place of business does not seem to alter the buyer's obligation to pay the price at the right moment at the new place of business. If this is the case, the question arises, but remains unanswered in the Convention, whether a delay in payment caused by late information by the seller of the new place of payment is to be considered a breach of contract by the buyer and whether that would also be the case if the buyer can offer payment at the original place of business in time. It would seem

that the answer may be negative in both cases in
view of the provision in Article 79(1).

Article 57(1)(b) deals with the place of
payment when payment is to be made against the
handing over of the goods or of documents. If the
contract provides that payment is to be made
against a bill of lading or on CAD or COD terms,
the provision settles the problem of errors or
delay in transmission of the payment. If the
documents are to be presented at the seller's
place of business, there is a delay in payment if
payment is not made when the documents are presented in accordance with the contract. If there
is a delay in the transmission of the amount
which the buyer has paid upon presentation of the
documents at his place of business, this is no
longer any concern of the buyer.

The provision on place of payment seems to
have caused problems in some jurisdictions because under national law a party may be entitled
to bring suit at the place where payment is to be
made.[8] However, this result does not follow from
the Convention. During the Vienna Conference an
attempt was made to clarify that the Convention
did not settle the question of jurisdiction and
that it was thought inappropriate to solve this
problem in the Convention. If the result is
deemed inappropriate, it can be altered by amend-
ing national law.

2.4.   Time for payment. Article 58 deals with
the time for payment. The basic rule is that the
goods should be exchanged for payment of the
price. The seller is not obliged to extend credit
to the buyer and the buyer is not required to pay
until he receives the goods or documents controlling their disposition.

2.4.1. Documents controlling disposition. The expression "documents controlling their disposition" clearly covers the situation where the goods are to be delivered only against surrender of the documents. This would be the case with a bill of lading where, at least under the applicable legal rules, the carrier may only deliver the goods to the person presenting the bill of lading.[9] However, this does not correspond to current reality. Since the goods often arrive at the port of destination prior to arrival of the bill of lading, they are often handed over to the consignee although he cannot present the bill of lading.

The expression would also seem to cover a warehouse receipt entitling the holder to claim the goods.

It is uncertain whether the expression covers international way bills issued under the CMR and CIM Conventions governing carriage by road and rail respectively. Under these documents the carrier is required to deliver the goods to the consignee named in the document. The sender may appoint another consignee, but he may do so only if he can produce the relevant copy of the way bill. Having acquired the way bill, the consignee/buyer is thus protected against dispositions by the seller/sender.[10] It is to this extent that the holder of the way bill controls the disposition of the goods, which would seem sufficient for the purposes of Article 58(1).

Article 58(2) deals with the situation where the contract involves the carriage of goods. This expression covers cases where the seller is required or authorized to ship the goods. The contract does not involve carriage if the buyer takes delivery at the seller's place of business or if the buyer makes arrangements for the goods to be shipped.[11]

Where the contract involves carriage, the seller may dispatch the goods on terms according to which the goods or documents controlling their disposition will not be handed over to the buyer except against payment of the price. The impact of the provision with reference to the time of payment seems to be that the seller may not, unless agreed upon in the contract, require payment before dispatching the goods. On the other hand, the provision states that an arrangement whereby the seller dispatches the goods but does so on terms enabling him to retain control over them until payment is made, does not amount to a breach of contract.

2.4.2. Exchange of goods for price.   Under Article 58(1) and (2) the seller may retain control over the goods until payment is made. Article 58(3) states that the buyer is not bound to pay the price until he has had an opportunity to examine the goods, unless the procedures for delivery or payment agreed upon are inconsistent with his having such an opportunity.

The reason for the exception at the end of the provision is that buyers sometimes put pressure on the seller by refraining from taking delivery of the goods on the alleged ground of non-conformity. When the goods have arrived at the port of destination, the seller has incurred costs of transportation. Normally the goods cannot be sold to another buyer at the port of destination at a price corresponding to the contract price. If that would be possible, the buyer would be likely to take delivery of the goods. The seller may protect himself against such claims for reduction of the price by having a provision included in the contract specifying a procedure for delivery according to which the buyer may not inspect the goods until payment has been made.

If the provision is included for this reason, there would seem to be no ground for objecting to a demand by the buyer to inspect the goods before they are dispatched even if the procedures for delivery or payment would be inconsistent with an inspection at the place of destination.

An agreement according to which payment is to be made against transport documents while the goods are in transit would normally be inconsistent with an opportunity to inspect the goods at the place of destination before payment is made. It is doubtful whether the buyer has the right to inspect the goods at the place of destination if payment is to be made against documents after arrival of the goods.[12] At least under Scandinavian law, payment against transport documents would probably be considered a procedure inconsistent with such a right of inspection. If the buyer has not used the possibility to inspect the goods before they are dispatched, as envisaged above, he would not be in the position to defer payment until he has had an opportunity to inspect them.

This means that the buyer runs the risk of having to pay although the seller has delivered goods which do not conform to the contract. This risk is to some extent, but not completely, diminished by the rules in transport law on the duty of the carrier to insert a reservation in the transport document if the goods do not conform to the description in the document. In addition, the buyer may improve his position by re-

quiring a certificate of quality in order to
quarantee that he receives what he pays for.

2.4.3. Payment without request.   Article 59
states that the buyer must pay the price on the
date fixed by or determinable from the contract
or the Convention without the need for any request or compliance with any formality on the
part of the seller. This provision makes it clear
that payment is not subject to any formal demand
by the seller in order to become due. Such rules
exist at least in some European legal systems.[13]
The provision is not designed to deal with the
question whether the buyer is required to pay
before he has received an invoice. In cases where
the buyer does not know the price until he receives an invoice, he cannot pay the price earlier. In other cases usage may call for an invoice in order to trigger the buyer's obligation
to pay the price.

2.5. Extension of the obligation to pay the price

2.5.1. Price generally charged.   The Convention
answers few questions relating to the amount that
the buyer is obligated to pay. In Article 55
dealing with a situation in which the contract
does not expressly or implicitly fix the price,
it is stated that in such cases the buyer shall
pay the price generally charged at the time of
conclusion of the contract for such goods sold
under comparable circumstances in the trade concerned. The provision does not refer to the
prices charged by the seller. It was felt important to eliminate the possibility of the seller
charging excessive prices.[14] The rule adopted
achieves this result. It has the flexibility
needed in cases where the quality of the seller's

goods is higher than that of other sellers in that it refers to the price generally charged for "such goods." However, the provision does not lead to an appropriate result in cases where the prices charged by the seller are lower than those generally charged. In order to deal with such cases, one would have to construct an implicit reference to the price charged by the seller.

2.5.2. Other issues. The Convention does not deal with questions such as the currency in which payment shall be made. National law would thus apply on this point. At the Vienna Conference a proposal was made to provide for situations where payment in the currency stipulated by the contract is not possible. According to the proposed rule, the seller would be entitled to require equivalent payment in the currency of the buyer's place of business. However, it was thought that these problems were much too complex to be dealt with in this way. The proposal was therefore rejected.[15]

Nor does the Convention deal with the question of whether the seller is obliged to accept partial payment. A proposal making it clear that this is not the case was rejected on the grounds that this problem was not practical.[16]

Traditionally, the buyer's obligation to pay the price consisted of handing over the seller an amount of money corresponding to the price. Today, this is an unusual method of payment. More often the buyer arranges for the seller to receive payment in the form of a claim against the bank to which the buyer transfers the amount or where he has an account, or which otherwise has agreed to pay the seller an amount corresponding to the price. The Convention does not deal with the manner in which payment is to be made. Whether the buyer may pay the amount to the seller's bank or has to transfer the amount to the seller's place of business is left to national law. The issue may arise in cases where there is a banking strike at the seller's place of business.

The Convention extends the obligation to pay the price beyond the traditional handing over of money. According to Article 54, the buyer's obligation to pay the price includes taking such steps and complying with such formalities as may be required under the contract or any laws and regulations to enable payment to be made.

As pointed out above, this provision indicates that the buyer must bear the costs for measures necessary to enable him to pay the price. In addition, the provision enables the seller to resort to remedies for breach of obligation to pay the price if such steps are not taken or formalities complied with in time.

If the contract provides that the buyer shall arrange for the issuance of a letter of credit or a guarantee for payment by a certain date, the seller may resort not only to measures available to him in case of an anticipatory breach by the buyer but also to remedies for breach of contract by the buyer, if the letter of credit or guarantee has not been issued by that date.

Application for a license to transfer money abroad is, no doubt, a formality that may be required under the relevant national law. Nevertheless, the fact that such an application has not been filed by the date normally necessary in order to obtain such a license in time can hardly be treated as more than an anticipatory breach of contract. There is always the possibil-

ity that the authorities may surprise everyone by
a speedy handling of the application so that
payment may be made in time.

**2.6.   Remedies for breach of obligation to pay
the price.**   The remedies for breach of contract
by the buyer are described in Articles 61-65. The
provision on avoidance in Article 64 is supplemented by Article 72 on avoidance prior to date
for performance and by Articles 81-84 on effects
of avoidance. In addition, under Article 71 the
seller may suspend his performance in certain
cases. The provisions on preservation of the
goods are also important in an evaluation of the
system of remedies.

Some of the remedies described in Articles
61-65 are available to the seller irrespective of
the kind of breach by the buyer. Other remedies
are available only for breach of a certain obligation. This Section of the Convention actually
contains three sets of remedies consolidated into
a single text.

The Convention does not describe in detail
the relation between the different remedies a-
vailable to the seller. The relation is not as
complex as in cases of breach of contract by the
seller.

In some cases the seller may choose between requiring performance by the buyer or declaring the contract avoided, e.g., if the breach
by the buyer is fundamental. If it is uncertain
whether this is the case, the seller may fix an
additional period of time for performance by the
buyer and declare the contract avoided if performance is not rendered within that period. In
certain cases this choice is open to the seller
only for a limited time. In still other cases the
seller may not declare the contract avoided but

has to adhere to a requirement for performance. This remedy is not available to him if he has resorted to a remedy which is inconsistent with a requirement for performance. Once the seller has declared the contract avoided, he cannot change his mind and require performance.

Irrespective of whether the seller declares the contract avoided or requires performance, he may claim damages. This is explicitly stated in Article 61(2).

In case of breach of the obligation to pay the price, the seller may require performance by the buyer, avoid the contract, and claim damages.

2.6.1. Claim for the price. If payment is not made in time, the seller may require the buyer to pay the price. Such a requirement may be presented irrespective of an extension of the delay. Even if the delay amounts to a fundamental breach of contract, the seller may choose to require payment. He may do so even if he has the right to sell the goods under the provisions on preservation of the goods in Article 88. If he chooses to sell the goods or is under an obligation to do so, thereafter he may claim the balance between the price and the proceeds from the sale.

If the seller has fixed an additional period of time for payment, during this period he may not, under Article 63(2), resort to any remedy for breach of contract. It may be asked whether he still may require the price to be paid during this period. It seems that fixing an additional period of time for payment of the price is one way of requiring payment. It is difficult to see any reason why such a requirement may not be repeated during the fixed period.

Under Article 54 the buyer's obligation to

pay the price includes taking such steps and complying with such formalities as may be required under the contract or any laws and regulations. The right to require the buyer to pay the price thus includes the right to require him to take such steps as, e.g., arranging for a letter of credit to be issued or applying for a license to transmit exchange abroad.

Under Article 79(1) a party is not liable for failure to perform any of his obligations if he proves that the failure was due to an impediment beyond his control. According to Article 79(5), nothing in that Article prevents either party from exercising any right other than to claim damages. It would seem that the seller is entitled to require payment even if the buyer is exempted from damages. The implications of this are not all that clear. Presenting such a requirement may affect the seller's right to interest on the price if under national law such a demand is necessary. Since interest, according to the Convention, does not fall under the heading of damages, the provision in Article 79(5) would also apply to interest.

The main problem that may arise in regard to the right to require payment follows from the relation between Articles 62 and 28 on specific performance. This issue seems to be important in trading with the United States. The question of whether an action for the price is to be regarded as an action for specific performance in all cases has been discussed at length, and there seems to be little to be added by someone not familiar with the Uniform Commercial Code.[17] Since a court might, pursuant to the Uniform Commercial Code, award the price in cases where the buyer has accepted the goods or the goods were lost or damaged within a commercially rea-

sonable time after the risk of loss passed to the
buyer, the problem would presumably not arise in
those cases. In other situations it seems uncertain how the question would be solved under the
UCC. In case it is feared that the seller would
not be entitled to recover the price if the goods
are still in his possession, he would be well
advised to resell the goods and claim the balance
from the buyer.

2.6.2. Avoidance. Under Article 64(1) the seller
may declare the contract avoided if the failure
to pay the price amounts to a fundamental breach
of contract or if the buyer does not pay the
price within the additional period of time fixed
by the seller. If the buyer declares that he will
not pay the price during the additional period,
the seller may, however, declare the contract
avoided even before the additional period of time
lapses.

The provision on avoidance after lapse of
the additional period of time is supplemented by
Article 63. From that provision it may be concluded that the seller can avoid the uncertainty
arising from the concept of a fundamental breach
by fixing an additional period for payment. In
order to serve that purpose the length of the
period must be defined. It is not sufficient that
the seller expresses his wish to receive payment
as soon as possible without delay or uses other
similar terms. Instead he would have to specify
either the date on which he may resort to declaring the contract avoided in case payment has not
been made or specify the number of days after
which he will do so. Secondly, the seller must
make it clear that he is fixing the period for
the purpose of being able to declare the contract
avoided. This requirement would not be met if he

indicates that it would be nice to receive payment by a certain date.

The additional period must be of reasonable length. In cases of payment it may be preferable to measure this period in days, and a fairly
limited number of days at that, or in the case of
goods, the price of which is subject to rapid
changes, even in hours. This would certainly be
the case if the buyer has already received the
goods in his possession. But a similar rule might
apply in other cases too, as it may be deemed
unnecessary to consider the possibility that the
buyer has not arranged for the financing of the
transaction at this stage when payment should
actually have already been made.

The provision on the additional period is
based on the assumption that payment has already
been delayed when the period is fixed. Nothing
would seem to prohibit an arrangement according
to which the contract states that the seller is
entitled to declare the contract avoided if payment is not effected within a fixed period.

In case of the buyer's delay to take steps
to enable payment to be made, the Convention
clearly accepts the possibility of the seller
acknowledging that he shall declare the contract
avoided if the steps in question have not been
taken within a fixed period. On the other hand,
it would not seem possible for the seller to
require that contractual measures other than
those already delayed be speeded up in relation
to what the contract requires. If the buyer has
not taken steps in order to arrange for a letter
of credit to be issued, the seller may fix an
additional period for that arrangement, but not
for receiving the money unless there is an anticipatory breach on the part of the buyer in
that respect.

During the period thus fixed the seller may not resort to any remedy for breach of contract. This provision clearly covers a situation where the seller declares the contract avoided for the same reason which made him fix the period. Fixing a period means that the seller accepts not to declare the contract avoided on that ground during the period. However, during that period some other ground for avoidance may arise. A situation could be imagined where the buyer, during the additional period, refuses to take delivery of the goods and this refusal amounts to a fundamental breach of contract. It would not seem necessary to read the Convention in such a way that the contract could not be avoided because of a fundamental breach in taking delivery only because the seller has fixed an additional period for payment of the price.

Article 63(2) of the Convention deals with a situation where the seller may declare the contract avoided although he has fixed an additional period of time. If the buyer declares that he will not pay within that period, or if the seller otherwise receives notice from the buyer that he will not do so, the seller may resort to other remedies. This provision seems to entitle the seller to declare the contract avoided immediately even if the delay has not amounted to a fundamental breach of contract. Under this provision avoidance is possible upon such a declaration by the buyer.

If the delay in effecting payment amounts to a fundamental breach of contract, the seller may delcare the contract avoided without having to fix an additional period of time. The seller runs the risk that his estimation of what constitutes a fundamental breach will not be shared by others. However, he would be wise to act on the

assumption that there not be too much tolerance
with respect to delay in payment.

Under the Convention the contract may be
declared avoided for delay in payment irrespective of whether or not the buyer has already
taken delivery of the goods. This rule, which
runs contrary to at least both the existing and
proposed Scandinavian law[18] and to German and
Anglo-American law[19], may cause concern to other
creditors of the buyer who may see assets vanish
on which they have based their decision to grant
credits to the buyer. This may, in particular, be
the case as the Convention does not require the
seller to declare the contract avoided within any
specific period of time. He may obviously resort
to this remedy as long as payment is not made.
Under Article 64(2)(a) the seller cannot declare
the contract avoided owing to late payment after
having become aware that payment has been made.

Under Article 64(1) the seller may declare
the contract avoided if the buyer's failure to
perform amounts to a fundamental breach of contract or if the buyer does not pay the price
within the additional period fixed by the seller.
It follows from Article 72 that the seller may
declare the contract avoided at an earlier stage
if it is clear that the buyer will commit a
fundamental breach of contract. If the buyer
cancels his order for the goods, the seller may
assume that the buyer has also declared that he
does not intend to pay the price and may thus
declare the contract avoided. If, under Article
71, the seller has been entitled to suspend performance of the contract and the buyer's conditions deteriorate further, the seller may also be
entitled to declare the contract avoided. When
the seller cannot base his actions on a declaration of the buyer, he always runs the risk that

his estimation of the situation is not shared by others. It may be held that he himself has failed to perform his obligations and that the buyer is entitled to declare the contract avoided. In any case, the seller would be well advised to inform the buyer of his intention to declare the contract avoided before doing so.

Article 72 gives the seller the right to declare the contract avoided because of an anticipatory breach by the buyer. It does not obligate him to take such a step. The provision serves the purpose of protecting the aggrieved party. As the seller may even resort to a requirement for performance after the buyer's breach has amounted to a fundamental breach, it can hardly be assumed that the buyer could, at this stage, require the seller to take steps to mitigate his damage. In this context attention may be drawn to a provision in the proposed Nordic Sale of Goods Acts. Under Sec.58(2), if the buyer cancels an order for goods to be manufactured on his account, the seller is obliged to suspend manufacture, provided that this would not cause him substantial inconvenience or that he would not run the risk of the buyer refusing to compensate him for the loss incurred as a result of the cancellation.

In view of the description of the obligation to pay the price in Article 54, it may be assumed that anticipatory breach of the obligation to pay the price will be of limited use.

2.6.3. Damages. It follows from Article 61(1)(b) that the seller is entitled to damages if the buyer fails to perform any of his obligations. Article 78 seems to indicate that the seller is entitled to damages to the extent his losses are not covered by interest.

If, in cases where the buyer does not pay
the price, the seller declares the contract a-
voided and resells the goods within a reasonable
time after avoidance, Article 75 provides that
the seller may recover the difference between the
contract price and the price in the substitute
transaction. If, as usually seems to be the case,
the price in the substitute transaction is lower
than the contract price, the difference is recoverable under the heading of damages. Alternatively, the seller may choose not to reveal the
price of the substitute transaction but to claim
damages under Article 76 for the difference between the contract price and the current price of
such goods.

The costs for preservation of the goods in
cases where the buyer does not pay the price and
the seller, for that reason, does not hand over
the goods to the buyer, do not fall under the
heading of damages but are recoverable under
Articles 85 and 88(3). The seller is entitled to
recover these costs, to the extent they are reasonable, from the proceeds of the sale, obviously
irrespective of the reason for the buyer's failure to perform his obligations. If no such obligation exists, e.g., because the goods do not
conform with the contract, these costs are, of
course, not recoverable.

If the price in the substitute transaction
is higher than the contract price, the seller may
withhold from the proceeds an amount corresponding to the cost for preservation.

2.6.4. Interest. If the buyer fails to pay the
price, under Article 78 the seller is entitled to
interest on the sum in arrears. The Convention
establishes only the right to interest but deals
neither with the rate of interest nor with the

time for which interest may be calculated. Thus
these matters must be decided according to the
law applicable to the contract.

3.   Taking delivery

3.1.   Obligation to take delivery. The Convention does not deal at any great length with the
buyer's obligation to take delivery of the goods,
which is defined in Article 60. According to this
provision, the obligation to take delivery consists of doing all the acts which could reasonably be expected of the buyer in order to enable
the seller to make delivery and, on his part, in
taking over the goods.

The extent of the obligation to take delivery is not defined in great detail. It clearly
covers obligations relating to the transmission
of the goods from the seller to the buyer. It is
less clear whether this obligation also covers
the duty to provide information relevant to the
production of the goods. This issue, which is
partially covered by Article 65, is relevant with
respect to the remedies available to the seller
in cases of breach of obligation. It may be
assumed that the obligation to enable the seller
to make delivery covers these situations too.[20]

As can be seen from the situation just
discussed, the extent of the obligation to do all
the acts which could reasonably be expected of
the buyer in order to enable the seller to make
delivery, depends heavily on the contract. If the
buyer is obliged to provide information during
the production or to participate otherwise in it,
e.g., by delivering components for the ultimate
product, Article 60(a) might be applicable and
the remedies for failure to take delivery would
thus apply. This would, however, be modified to

the extent another result would follow from Article 65.

Where the contract of sale involves carriage of the goods and the buyer participates in the arrangements for the carriage, the extent of the buyer's obligation depends on the type of arrangements. The obligation covers the duty to enter into a contract of carriage. It might also cover obligations relating to the loading of the goods and their storage during carriage or at the destination.

The duty to take over the goods relates to the physical possession of them. Since references in the Convention to the buyer also cover persons acting on his behalf, it would seem that the obligation referred to in Article 60(b) also covers cases where the carrier refuses to accept the goods for carriage, e.g., because of their dangerous nature, if the buyer should have informed the carrier of the nature of the goods in advance. This obligation also covers the late arrival of a carrier engaged by the buyer at the place where the buyer is to take over the goods. Lastly, it covers the obligation of the buyer himself to take over the goods after carriage arranged by the seller as well as in cases where the contract calls for the seller to make delivery of the goods by placing them at the buyer's disposal at the seller's place of business or at another particular place.

Under Article 86(2), if goods dispatched to the buyer have been placed at his disposal at their destination and the buyer exercises the right to reject them, in certain situations he must take possession of the goods on behalf of the seller. Here one does not speak of taking delivery and it is doubtful whether the remedies for failure to take delivery apply in a case such as failure to take possession.

3.2.   Remedies for failure to take delivery.   If the buyer fails to take delivery of the goods, the seller may require him to do so, declare the contract avoided and claim damages.

3.2.1. Requirement to take delivery.   The seller may require the buyer to take delivery of the goods as long as he has not resorted to a remedy which is inconsistent with this requirement. Again, what is covered by the reference to an inconsistent remedy, is avoidance. The ground for declaring the contract avoided is irrelevant: It is the remedy, not the reason for resorting to it, that is inconsistent with a requirement for taking delivery.

   If the buyer has neither paid the price nor taken delivery, the remedy may be used together with, or separately from, a requirement for payment. Situations can be envisaged where the seller is more anxious to receive payment than to force the buyer to take delivery of the goods. He may therefore present these requirements simultaneously or separately.

   In cases where the buyer has paid the price but fails to take delivery, the seller may require him to take delivery.

   The use of the remedy is limited by Article 28 on specific performance. When dealing with buyers from countries where the legal system limits the resort to specific performance, a seller should have a closer look into that system in order to find a suitable remedy before requiring the buyer to take delivery of the goods.

3.2.2. Avoidance. The provisions on avoidance of the contract upon the buyer's failure to take delivery of the goods start at the same point as those in respect of failure to pay the price. This does not necessarily mean that the remedy of avoidance operates in the same manner in these two situations.

First, let us assume that the buyer has neither paid the price nor taken delivery of the goods. In cases where the seller has granted the buyer a credit, failure to take delivery may serve as an indication of an anticipatory breach of the obligation to pay the price. It might possibly cause the seller to suspend his performance in accordance with Article 71(1)(b). On the other hand, avoidance due to the failure to take delivery also serves as an independant remedy. The seller should, however, be careful in resorting to avoidance in these cases. The situations where the mere failure to take delivery would amount to a fundamental breach are presumably few.

Secondly, one may consider the case where the buyer has paid the price but fails to take delivery of the goods. Again, it is hard to envisage a great number of cases where the remedy of avoidance for failure to take delivery would be available. As in the previous case, situations can be imagined where the seller necessarily needs to dispose of the goods.

If the buyer has paid the price but not yet taken delivery of the goods, according to article 64(2)(a) the seller must exercise his right to declare the contract avoided before he has become aware that the buyer has taken delivery.

In both cases it might be wiser to resort to the provisions on preservation of the goods.

These provisions may be sufficient in dealing
with the problems that the seller may have. This
is the case if the seller is still in possession
of the goods or otherwise able to control the
disposition of them, e.g., by means of a transport document or a warehouse receipt in his possession.

Instead of awaiting the time at which the
breach in taking delivery amounts to a fundamental breach of contract, the seller may fix an
additional period of time for taking delivery. It
would seem that this period cannot normally be as
short as that which might be envisaged in the
case of late payment. During this period the
seller may not resort to any remedy for breach of
contract. As was mentioned above, this provision
would probably not prohibit the seller from requiring the buyer to take delivery, but it would
prohibit him from avoiding the contract for the
reason that the buyer has not taken delivery. On
the other hand, if the seller has fixed a period
for taking delivery, this would probably not
restrain his right to declare the contract a-
voided because of a delay in payment occurring
during the given period.

If the buyer does not take delivery of the
goods within the fixed period, the seller may
avoid the contract. This right of avoidance is
subject to the provision in Article 64(2)(b). If
the buyer has paid the price, the seller must
exercise his right of avoidance within a reasonable time after the expiration of the fixed period
or after the buyer has declared that he will not
take delivery of the goods. This provision, which
is designed to prevent speculation on the part of
the seller, leads to the result that if the
contract is not avoided within that time, it
cannot be avoided at all. Still, the seller may

sell the goods under the provisions on preservation of the goods. In that case, he is entitled to compensation for the cost of preservation. In addition, he is presumably also entitled to claim the balance between the contract price and the proceeds from the substitute transaction. This seems to be the case even if Article 75 only deals with situations where the contract has been avoided. Otherwise, the provision would lead to the result that the seller would have to preserve the goods until their value is entirely consumed by the costs of preservation.

3.2.3. Damages. The seller is also entitled to compensation for loss caused by the buyer's failure to take delivery of the goods. The amount of compensation is to be calculated on the basis of Article 74. Under that Article damages consist of a sum equal to the loss, including loss of profit suffered by the seller as a result of the breach. If the seller has resold the goods, the proceeds from the resale are to be taken into account in calculating the difference between the contract price and the price in the substitute transaction. On the other hand, the seller would seem to be entitled to compensation for loss of profit even if he resells the goods. The resale would indicate that the seller has lost a market and thus suffered loss of profit in one sale. However, one could also envisage cases where he would not be entitled to compensation for loss of profit.

4.   Other obligations of the buyer

The buyer may also have other obligations under the contract; however, no effort has been made to describe them in the Convention. On occasion the question may obviously arise whether such obligations are part of the obligation to take delivery, as described in Article 60, or whether they are to be separated from that obligation.

Although the Convention does not deal with the obligations themselves, it provides for remedies for failure to perform them. The seller may require performance of these obligations; he may fix an additional period of time for their performance; and he may declare the contract avoided in case the failure to perform them amounts to a fundamental breach of contract. However, even if the seller has fixed an additional period of time, the conclusion of that period of time does not entitle the seller to declare the contract avoided. The requirement of a fundamental breach prevails in these cases too. The right to declare the contract avoided is limited by the fact that this right must be exercised within a reasonable time after the seller knew or ought to have known of the breach. In addition, the seller may claim damages for the loss caused by the failure to perform the obligation.

NOTES

1. Report of the United Nations Commission on International Trade Law on the work of its second session (1969), at para. 38, <u>UNCITRAL</u> <u>I</u> <u>Yearbook</u>, p. 99.
2. Report of the Secretary General: Issues presented by chapters IV to VI of the Uniform Law on the International Sale of Goods, at para. 22-35, <u>UNCITRAL</u> <u>V</u> <u>Yearbook</u>, pp. 83-85, and Progress report of the Working Group on the International Sale of Goods on the work of its fifth session,

at para. 37-41, <u>UNCITRAL</u> <u>V</u> <u>Yearbook</u>, p. 33.

3. See, e.g., Progress report, <u>supra</u> n. 2, para. 42, and criticism at para. 56, and note by the Secretary General: Analysis of comments and proposals by Governments relating to Articles 56 to 70 of the Uniform Law on the International Sale of Goods, at para. 28, <u>UNICITRAL</u> <u>IV</u> <u>Yearbook</u>, p. 34.

4. Analysis of replies and comments by Governments on the Hague Conventions of 1964: Report of the Secretary General, at para. 125-126, <u>UNICITRAL</u> <u>I</u> <u>Yearbook</u>, pp. 173-174, where two Governments criticized the corresponding provision of the Hague Convention on the ground that the law should not permit the conclusion of a contract without a price or at least a clear indication as to the means for determining the price.

5. <u>United</u> <u>Nations</u> <u>Conference</u> <u>on</u> <u>Contracts</u> <u>for</u> <u>the</u> <u>International</u> <u>Sale</u> <u>of</u> <u>Goods.</u> <u>Official</u> <u>Records</u>, pp. 363-364. The Article was adopted in the plenary after a vote, <u>Official</u> <u>Records</u>, p. 211.

6. Denis Tallon, "The Buyer's Obligations under the Convention on Contracts for the International Sale of Goods," in N.M. Galston and H. Smit, eds., <u>International</u> <u>Sales:</u> <u>The</u> <u>United</u> <u>Nations</u> <u>Convention</u> <u>on</u> <u>Contracts</u> <u>for</u> <u>the</u> <u>International</u> <u>Sale</u> <u>of</u> <u>Goods</u> (New York 1984), pp. 7-11.

7. Ibid.

8. Ulrich Huber, "Der UNCITRAL-Entwurf eines Uebereinkommens über internationale Warenkaufverträge," 43 <u>RabelsZ</u> (1979) pp. 512-513; J. Honnold, <u>Uniform</u> <u>Law</u> <u>for</u> <u>International</u> <u>Sales</u> <u>under</u> <u>the</u> <u>1980</u> <u>United</u> <u>Nations</u> <u>Convention</u> (Boston 1982), p. 343.

9. Report of the Secretary General, <u>supra</u> n.2, at para. 14.

10. Selvig, <u>Fra</u> <u>kjøpsrettens</u> <u>og</u> <u>transportrettens</u>

grenseland [The Functions of Transport Documents in Sales] (Oslo 1975), p. 55.

11. Commentary of the Draft Convention on Contracts for the International Sale of Goods, prepared by the Secretariat, Official Records, p.64.

12. Ibid., p. 47 at para. 8.

13. J. Honnold, supra n. 8, at p. 350; D. Tallon, supra n. 6, at pp. 7-14 - 7-16.

14. Report of the first committee, Official Records pp. 120-121, and Summary Records, Official Records, pp. 363-367.

15. Report of the first committee, Official Records, p. 120, and Summary Records, Official Records, pp. 362-363.

16. Official Records, p. 370.

17. Allan Farnsworth, "Damages and Specific Relief," 27 Am.J.Comp.L. (1979) pp. 249-250; J. Honnold, supra n. 8, at pp. 355-359; Jan Hellner, "The UN Convention on International Sales of Goods," in Ius Inter Nationes, Festschrift für Stefan Riesenfeld, Berkeley-Kölner Rechtsstudien (1983), at pp. 87-88; Jacob S. Ziegel, "The Remedial Provisions in the Vienna Sales Convention: Some Common Law Perspectives," in N.M. Galston and H. Smit, supra n. 6, at pp. 9-30 - 9-32.

18. Scandinavian Sale of Goods Acts Sec.28(2). It is proposed that this rule be retained in the new Acts, Nordiska Köplagar. Förslag av den nordiska arbetsgruppen för köp. NU 1984:5, Sec.60(3). [Nordic Sale of Goods Acts. Proposal by the Nordic Working Group for Legislation on Sale of Goods].

19. J. Hellner, supra n. 15, at pp. 94-95; J.S. Ziegler, supra n. 15, at p. 9-32.

20. U. Huber, supra n. 8, at p. 515.

CHAPTER SEVEN

PROVISIONS COMMON TO THE OBLIGATIONS OF THE SELLER AND THE BUYER

JELENA VILUS
Professor of Law, Novi Sad/Belgrade

Introductory remarks

The provisions common to the obligations of the seller and of the buyer are found in Articles 71 - 88 of the Vienna Convention, which means that 17 articles are devoted to these obligations. This number shows that it was considered to be in the interest of the parties to regulate their common obligations rather thoroughly.

In connection with these obligations the following questions will be analyzed:
- Anticipatory breach and installment contracts,
- Damages,
- Interest,
- Exemptions,
- Effects of avoidance of contract, and
- Preservation of the goods.

Before analyzing the above questions, we should point out that these obligations cannot be completely understood without taking into account certain standard notions of the Convention such as:

- Fundamental breach of contract (Art. 25);
- Reasonability in regard to persons (Art. 25),
  time (Articles 73, 75, 79), notice (Articles
  72, 88), circumstances (Art. 86);
- Specific performance (Art. 29); and
- Duty to cooperate (Art. 77).

Many of these standard notions are more familiar to the lawyer of the common law system than
to the civil law lawyer; nevertheless, they are
basically the same and fairly well known to businessmen in the international sale of goods.

I.   ANTICIPATORY BREACH AND INSTALLMENT CONTRACTS

In regard to anticipatory breach of contract,
the basic question is whether the party that
doubts the performance of the other party has the
right to suspend or avoid the contract prior to
the date for performance. In other words, if the
situation and the circumstances change during the
performance of the contract and one of the parties is of the opinion that the other will not be
able to fulfill his obligations, the question
arises whether this party should wait until the
other party becomes insolvent, for instance, or
whether in such a case he himself should decide
to suspend performance of his obligations and
demand additional guarantees. On the other hand,
what would happen if his evaluation of the other
party's ability to perform is groundless and the
other party subsequently suffers financial loss
as a result of the anticipatory breach? These
dilemmas will have to be solved by arbitrators or
judges deciding disputes involving international
contracts of sale and were the same problems
which were discussed at the Vienna Conference
during preparation and adoption of the relevant
provisions.

It should be mentioned that there is a similar institution in the domestic law of civil law countries known as <u>non</u> <u>adimplety</u> <u>contractus</u> (precontractual non-performance).

1. Suspension of performance

As provided by Art. 71, one of the contracting parties may suspend his obligations if, after the conclusion of the contract, it becomes evident that the other party will "not perform a substantial part of his obligations." However, it is not sufficient that this is foreseeable on the basis of a subjective evaluation of one of the parties and may also be the ground for an abuse. Instead, the Vienna Convention insists on two additional conditions: a serious deficiency in his ability to perform or in his creditworthiness; or his conduct in preparing to perform or in performing the contract.

Here it is perhaps of interest to mention that the Uniform Law on the International Sale of Goods (ULIS) refers in Art. 73 to a difficult "economic situation of the other party," which was considered too narrow as a condition for suspension of performance. Of course, it could be questioned whether the ULIS provision was, in fact, broader than that of the Vienna Convention.

It should be emphasized that it indeed may prove difficult to determine what is to be regarded as "a serious deficiency" in performance ability and what kind of conduct "in preparing or in the performing the contract" will be sufficient as a ground for the other party to suspend his obligations.[1] In order to protect the other party, the text emphasizes that suspension of obligations is possible only if there are adequate grounds to conclude that the other party

will not perform a substantial part of his obligation. It should be pointed out that if anticipatory breach is performed without a good reason,
then that party will be in breach of contract.

Needless to say, in many cases application of
the provisions of this article may prove to be
difficult and may even lead to abuse since the
provisions give rather broad power. A decision to
suspend performance may entirely depend on one
party's subjective evaluation of the other's
ability to perform.

However, risks of this kind cannot be fully
avoided in international trade. Nonetheless, it
is not surprising that many delegates at the
Vienna Conference were in favor of deleting this
article.

a) Preventing the handing over of the goods to the buyer

In case the seller has already dispatched the
goods before the grounds for suspension become
evident, he, nevertheless, "may prevent the handing over of the goods to the buyer even though
the buyer holds a document which entitles him to
obtain them," for instance, a Bill of Lading.

The most common situation referred to in Art.
71 is the case when the goods are in transit. In
such circumstances there is a common law institution called **stoppage in transitu**[2] which the seller can use when the buyer has delivered the
documents to a third person. This is clear from
the formulation of Art. 71 which emphasizes that
"the present paragraph relates only to the rights
in the goods as between the buyer and the seller." The view is held that in such cases the
seller cannot claim the goods from a third party

on the basis of the Convention, but he might do so under the applicable national law.[3]

b) Sending notice

The party who suspends his performance under Art. 71 is obliged to **send notice immediately** "to the other party and must continue with performance if the other party provides adequate assurance of his performance." This rule applies irrespective whether the suspension occurs before or after the goods have been dispatched. It has been noted that this provision is under the influence of bank guarantees -- a practice that was not used as widely before the Vienna Convention and therefore was not provided for in the Hague Uniform Law. The question, however, remains open as to whether or not a bank guarantee for reimbursement of payments under the contract will be considered an "adequate assurance."

Suspension of the performance of the first party may last: a) until the other party performs his part of the obligations; b) until the first party gets "adequate assurance;" c) until the other party announces that he intends to avoid the contract; or d) until the expiration of the limitation period.

In case the party suspending performance suffers losses as a result of his not having received adequate assurance, he has the right to claim compensation regardless whether or not the contract is avoided.

2. Anticipatory breach involving fundamental breach of contract

Art. 72 of the Vienna Convention provides for

special rules in cases where there is a fundamental breach of contract.

Although Art. 72 is a logical continuation of the preceding article, its consequences are quite different. Whereas under Art. 71 the contract continues to exist while only its performance has been suspended, the provisions of Art. 72 permit avoidance of the contract "if prior to the date for performance it is clear that one of the parties will commit a fundamental breach of contract." It should, however, be pointed out that suspension of the contract under Art. 71 may lead to avoidance of the contract as well.

The party intending to declare the contract avoided must be absolutely sure that there is indeed a fundamental breach of contract.

Since this provision is also found in ULIS[4], it is relevant to cite A. Tunc who holds that such a provision is fully justified since it would not be

> right that one party remains bound by
> the contract when the other has, for
> instance, deliberately declared that he
> will not carry out one of his fundamen-
> tal obligations or when he conducts
> himself in such a way that it is clear
> that he will commit a fundamental
> breach of contract.[5]

There are, however, other views according to which such a right may be dangerous since, even if there is a breach, this does not necessarily mean that the contract will not be fulfilled. It is not always easy to provide clear proof of a fundamental breach of contract except in exceptional cases, for instance, bankruptcy of the debtor. In other words, there is the possibility that abuse may arise, especially in cases where the creditor has the opportunity to conclude a

contract with other partners under better conditions.[6]

Similar fears were expressed at the Vienna
Conference by many delegates of developing countries who insisted especially on the condition
that the party intending to declare the contract
avoided must inform the other party of his intention so as "to permit him to provide adequate
assurance of his performance." The industrially
developed countries were against this, pointing
out that two things had been mixed up, i.e.,
suspension of performance and the right to avoid
the contract.

In order to satisfy both demands, a compromise
was reached. Accordingly, para. 2 of Art. 72
provides that "if time allows" (compromise to the
developed countries), "the party intending to
declare the contract avoided must give reasonable
notice to the other party in order to permit him
to provide adequate assurance of his performance"
(compromise to the developing countries).[7] An
exception to this rule is provided for in para. 3
of Art. 72 in cases where it is absolutely clear
or obvious that the other party "will not perform
his obligations."

3. Installment contracts

Art. 73 represents, in principle, application
of the rule of Art. 72 in the special case of
installment contracts. The basic problem concerns
whether installment contracts should be considered as one contract, i.e., in their totality,
whereby a difficulty of performance in regard to
one installemnt would affect the contract as a
whole, thus avoiding the whole contract, or
whether they should be regarded as a series of
separate contracts. Since abuses are possible in

cases involving installment contracts, the rights and duties of the parties should be analyzed very carefully.

II. DAMAGES

In connection with damages, the Vienna Convention first specifies the damages for breach of contract (Art. 74), then deals with the questions of purchase or resale of goods when the contract is avoided (Articles 75 and 76), and finally reminds the party who relies on a breach of contract to "take such measures as are reasonable in the circumstances to mitigate the loss" and states the consequence for parties failing to do so (Art. 77).

1. Calculation of damages -- influence of common law notions

The rule of Art. 74 provides that
damages for breach of contract by one party consist of a sum equal to the loss, including loss of profit, suffered by the other party as a consequence of the breach.
However, the same article contains the exception to this rule, according to which
such damages may not exceed the loss which the party in breach forsaw or ought to have forseen at the time of the conclusion of the contract, in the light of the facts and matters of which he then knew or ought to have known, as a possible consequence of the breach of contract.
This notion of calculating damages has been taken from the common law system; the same idea

was also incorporated into the Hague Uniform Law
(Art. 82). In the common law system the sum of
the damages is not limited in cases involving
tort liability. However, in the field of contract
liability the basic question concerns how remote
the loss is from the cause of the damage. This is
the so-called remoteness of damages which is
based on the well-known British case of **Hadley v.
Baxendale** (1854). It, in fact, means that the
party liable for loss will be liable only for the
loss which he "forsaw or ought to have forseen"
at the time of the conclusion of the contract. In
his commentary of ULIS, Tunc points out that such
a concept is found in many legal systems. Furthermore, he states:

> If one of the parties considers, at the
> time of the negotiations preliminary to
> the contract, that breach on the part
> of the other party would cause him
> exceptionally heavy loss, he may always
> make this known to the other party.[8]

Calculating damages in the way provided by
Art. 74 may be regarded as just. Namely, limiting
the damages to the foreseeable loss purports,
inter alia, to protect the debtor from unjusti-
fiable claims on the part of the creditor. The
purpose of this article is to place the party
suffering the loss in the same economic position
he would have been in had the contract been
performed. The special rules concerning loss of
profit were necessary because in certain legal
systems loss (perte) does not include loss of
profit (gain manqué).

It may be observed that the criterion according to which it is judged whether or not the
party is liable is both subjective ("forsaw") and
objective ("ought to have forseen").

In spite of the fact that the Vienna Conven-

tion has introduced a fairly good rule on the
calculation of damages, this is nevertheless a
delicate question. In view of the fact that the
relevant circumstances vary from case to case,
arbitrators and judges will have problems determining an amount of damages that is just in certain cases.

2. Damages involving avoidance of contract

The rule adopted in most legal systems, and
the Vienna Convention as well, is that, in addition to avoidance, the party aggrieved by the
breach may always claim damages to compensate for
the loss caused by avoidance.

Art. 75 of the Vienna Convention reads as
follows:

> If the contract is avoided and if, in a
> reasonable manner and within a resona-
> ble time after avoidance, the buyer has
> bought goods in replacement or the
> seller has resold the goods, the party
> claiming damages may recover the dif-
> ference between the contract price and
> the price in the substitute transaction
> as well as any further damages recover-
> able under article 74.

According to Tunc, this rule "could not be
otherwise."[9] The condition provided for in Art.
75 is that the replacement purchase or the resale
must be made "in a reasonable manner and within a
reasonable time" after avoidance. Here the term
"reasonable manner" is to be interpreted as the
duty of the buyer to buy the goods at the lowest
possible price and of the seller to sell them at
the highest possible price. The "reasonable time"
starts to run at the time when the aggrieved
party avoided the contract.

The relevant provisions of Art. 76 should be taken into account when calculating differences in price[10], and the relevant provisions of Art. 74 when calculating additional compensation[11].

There are occasions when the buyer or seller does not make a replacement purchase or resale, respectively, but instead, due to a breach of contract, prefers to avoid the contract. In such cases the question arises as to how compensation should be calculated. This situation is known in all legal systems; in the civil law countries the so-called **abstract damages** are calculated, as opposed to **concrete damages** which occur when a purchase in replacement or resale took place and are thus easier to calculate.

If there was no purchase in replacement or resale under Art. 75, Art. 76 provides that the party claiming damages may...

> recover the difference between the price fixed by the contract and the current price at the time of avoidance as well as any further damages recoverable under article 74.

In the same article "current price" is defined as...

> the price prevailing at the place where delivery of the goods should have been made or, if there is no current price at that place, the price at such other place as serves as a reasonable substitute, making the allowance for differences in the cost of transporting the goods.

There are several points which should be mentioned in connection with Art. 76. First, the time of **avoidance of contract** may in practice be difficult to ascertain and could therefore lead to abuse. For instance, the party who plans to

avoid the contract may speculate by waiting to
avoid the contract at a time which, fiancially
speaking, is more favorable for him.

In order to keep possible abuses to a minimum,
Art. 76 provides that in cases where the party
claiming damages has avoided the contract "after
taking the goods," the "current price of such
taking over shall be applied instead of the current price at the time of avoidance."

In regard to the place where the current price
is to be determined, Art. 76 refers to: a) "the
place where delivery of the goods should have
been made," or alternatively b) "if there is no
current price at that place," then "such other
place as serves as a reasonable substitute." It
should also be mentioned that Art. 76 reminds the
contracting parties that "the allowance for differences in the cost of transporting the goods"
should be added.

3.   Duty to cooperate in case of breach

Art. 77 of the Vienna Convention contains the
rule according to which

> a party who relies on a breach of con-
> tract must take such measures as are
> reasonable in the circumstances to
> mitigate the loss, including the loss
> of profit, resulting from the breach.

According to Tunc, this rule, which is the same
as that in Art. 88 of ULIS, is found in numerous
codes of European countries and is often pro-
pounded by the courts of common law countries.
Thus Tunc concludes, "Its reasonableness is evident."[13] Furthermore, the same article provides
that if the party who is obliged to take the
necessary measures to mitigate the loss fails to
do so, then "the party in breach may claim a

reduction in damages in the amount by which the
loss should have been mitigated." It is obvious
that this is a very serious obligation on the
part of the "creditor," the party who relies on
breach, i.e., the innocent party, since the sanction consists of a "reduction of damages."

Indeed, the creditor should attempt to undertake everything possible in order to diminish the
loss or at least to prevent its increase, and
thus this rule may be regarded as just and fair.

III. INTEREST

The provisions on interest were the subject of
great controversy and differences of opinion both
in ULIS and at the Vienna Convention. On the one
hand, there were those who wanted to delete these
provisions altogether, whereas, on the other
hand, others favored detailed provisions regulating the legal consequences in cases where the
buyer fails to fulfill his major obligation,
i.e., to pay the price.

Art. 78 reads as follows:

If a party fails to pay the price or
any other sum that is in arrears, the
other party is entitled to interest on
it without prejudice to any claim for
damages recoverable under article 74.

This article differs to a great extent from
the provision in ULIS on interest.[14]

At the Vienna Conference the developing countries were very concerned about the article governing calculation of the interest rate. An increase of the interest rate by 1 %, as was suggested by some countries, was considered by the
developing countries to be extremely high, although it was suggested, for instance, by the
International Chamber of Commerce, that the in-

terest rate should be increased by 2 %. Furthermore, it was proposed that the interest rate
should be similar or identical to the prevailing
rate at the main financial center of the debtor
or the capital of the debtor's country. However,
it was argued that in certain countries the main
financial center and the capital are not the same
place, for instance, in the USA, in Switzerland
and other countries. Moreover, the Muslim countries argued that provisions on interest would be
contrary to Islamic law which forbids arrangements on interest. Consequently, it was difficult
to agree on a solution that would satisfy the
majority.

While the provisions of Art. 78 do not mean
much to many, on the other hand, others consider
them to be useful since they enable the creditor
to claim not only interest but also compensation
under Art. 74, which is not possible in some
countries.

The question of interest is important in view
of Art. 84(1) which provides that "if the seller
is bound to return the price, he must also pay
the interest on it from the date on which the
price was paid." This is the universally accepted
practice, in the Muslim countries as well, and
therefore it is indeed difficult to understand
why the efforts to regulate this question met
with such opposition.

IV. EXEMPTIONS

The question of exemptions which is regulated
by Art. 79 of the Vienna Convention is extremely
important -- both from a practical and a theoretical point of view. In certain cases one of the
parties may be confronted by such a change in
circumstances that he is either unable to con-

tinue his obligations or, if he does, they will
become an extremely heavy burden to him. All
countries have special rules governing such situations, and therefore it was only natural to
incorporate provisions on exemption into the
Vienna Convention, as was also the case in ULIS.
However, in this field, as in many others, the
notions of common law and civil law differ. As a
result, the international drafters wanted to
create a new concept by amalgamating different
ideas, which, of course, has its positive and
negative aspects.

According to the provisions of Art. 79 of the
Convention, a party is released from liability[15]
when his failure to perform is due to an impediment beyond his control if: a) he could not
reasonably be expected to have taken the impediment into account; b) the impediment could not
have been avoided; and c) the party was not able
to overcome it.

1. General rule on exemptions

It should be pointed out that at the very
outset many problems arose in connection with the
drafting of the rule on exemptions. Whereas ULIS
(Art. 74) refers to **circumstances**, the Vienna
Convention speaks of an **impediment**. Tunc maintains that the sole purpose of such provisions is
to "provide an answer to the question whether
[the] party" that has failed to perform his obligation "should or should not be liable for
damages."[16]

During the debate it was pointed out in the
working group at the annual sessions of the Commission and at the Vienna Conference that the
main problem arose from the fact that the article
attempts to combine the concepts of vis major

(force majeure, act of God) and frustration (imprévision).

Both ULIS and the Vienna Convention took "the middle road" by connecting the subjective and objective circumstances, which did, and probably will lead to controversy and differences of opinion. Many thought that this combination was very unfortunate since it causes confusion by trying to combine different things. Vis major should exempt the party from paying damages, whereas frustration releases him entirely from his obligations.

It was probably due to these different viewpoints that the drafting group and the Vienna Conference adopted the provision contained in para. 5 of Art. 79 according to which

> nothing in this article prevents either
> party from exercising any right other
> than to claim damages under this Con-
> vention.

2. Other grounds for exemptions

Situations in which the party's failure to perform any of his obligations is due to the failure by a third person whom he had engaged to perform the whole or part of the contract are governed by Art. 79 of the Vienna Convention. In such cases the party may be exempted from liability under the conditions set forth in para. 2 of Art. 79.

3. Temporary impediment

According to para. 3 of Art. 79, the exemption has effect only "for the period during which the impediment exists." Therefore, the exemption from liability ceases to exist either on the date for

performance or the date on which the impediment
was removed.

In case the impediment amounts to a fundamental breach of contract, the innocent party has
the right to avoid the contract.

4. Duty to send notice

The party exempted from liabiity to pay damages under Art. 79 "must give notice to the other
party of the impediemnt and its effect on his
ability to perform." The risk is borne by the
sender in case the "notice is not received by the
other party within a reasonable time after the
party who fails to perform knew or ought to have
known of the impediment."[17] This party will be
liable for damages resulting "from such non-
receipt."

5. Self-made failure

The provision of Art. 80 of the Vienna Convention reads as follows:

> A party may not rely on a failure of
> the other party to perform, to the
> extent that such failure was caused by
> the first party's act or omission.

It was suggested that this provision should be
included with those dealing with good faith, in
which case its sphere of application would have
been broader. Nevertheless, the view prevailed
that it is more closely related to exemptions and
duty to cooperate in cases of impediments.

V. EFFECTS OF AVOIDANCE

The Vienna Convention contains four articles
on the effects of avoidance. The general rule is

found in Art. 81, while Articles 82, 83, and 84 specify the concrete duties of the seller and buyer in cases of avoidance of contract.

1. General rule

According to Art. 81, "avoidance of the contract releases both parties from their obligations under it, subject to any damages which may be due." This means that "the seller need not deliver the goods and the buyer need not take delivery and pay for them."[18] The main consequence is that both parties are free in the sense that they are released from the duties and obligations assumed under the contract, except the obligation to pay damages.

In some legal systems avoidance of the contract eliminates all rights and obligations under the contract. In view of this, Art. 81 expressly states:

> Avoidance does not affect any provision
> of the contract for the settlement of
> disputes or any other provisions of the
> contract governing the rights and obli-
> gations of the parties consequent upon
> the avoidance of the contract.

The purpose of these provisions is to prevent complete termination of the contract, including those provisions dealing, e.g., with penalty clauses (liquidated damages), applicable law, arbitration and similar provisions, all of which will help the party relying on the avoidance take recourse to remedies provided by the Convention and the applicable law. On the other hand, the Vienna Convention does not say that these provisions are valid[19]; it merely provides the rule according to which avoidance of the contract "does not effect such provisions."

It should be pointed out that there is no similar provision in ULIS.[20] This was considered "unfortunate" since in the absence of such a provision, it might appear that a choice of law clause, a choice of forum clause, an arbitration clause or a liquidated damages clause would be ineffective once the contract is avoided.[21]

If one of the parties has performed the contract, entirely or in part, this party "may claim restitution from the other party of whatever the first party has supplied or paid under the contract." In some cases restitution will not be possible, for instance, restitution of the received goods. This, however, could not occur with respect to the seller's duty to refund the received price. In such exceptional cases the provisions of Art. 82 of the Convention shall apply.

2. Special rules on effects of avoidance

Para. 1 of Art. 82 provides that the buyer loses his right to declare the contract avoided if he is unable to return the goods in substantially the same condition in which he received them. This rule simply recognizes the effect of natural causes on the condition of the delivered goods. On the other hand, the goods to be returned do not have to be the same goods that were received; rather they must be "substantially in the condition in which" the goods were received.[22]

The rule in para. 1 of Art. 82 shall not apply in the following cases: a) if the impossibility of the buyer to return the goods "substantially in the condition in which he received them... is not due to his act or omission"; b) if the goods have perished or deteriorated, in whole or in part, "as a result of the examination provided

for in article 38"; and c) if the goods, or part
of them, have been sold in the normal course of
business or have been consumed, or transformed by
the buyer in the course of normal use "before he
discovered or ought to have discovered the lack
of conformity."

The Commentary prepared by UNCITRAL points out
that the right of either party to require restitution may be thwarted by other rules which fall
outside the scope of the international sale of
goods. In this context it is stressed:

> If either party is in bankruptcy or
> other insolvency procedures, it is
> possible that the claim of restitution
> will not be recognized as creating a
> right in the property or as giving a
> priority in the distribution of the
> assets. Exchange control laws or other
> restrictions on the transfer of goods
> or funds may prevent the transfer of
> goods or money to the demanding party
> in a foreign country.[23]

According to the Commentary, these and other
similar legal rules may reduce the value of the
claim of restitution, but they do not affect the
validity of the rights between the parties.

If the buyer loses his right to avoid the
contract or to request replacement of the goods,
he nevertheless, "retains all other remedies
under the contract and this Convention." As provided by Art. 83 of the Convention, this means
that the buyer has retained the right to damages
(Art. 45), to repair of the goods (Art. 46), or
to reduction of price (Art. 50).

A rule that is known in many legal systems and
has also been accepted by the Vienna Convention
obliges the party who must return the goods or
refund the price to also account for any benefit

which he has received by virtue of having had possession of the money or the goods. Under Art. 84, if the seller is obliged to refund the price, "he must also pay interest on it from the date on which the price was paid."[24] This obligation is rather "simple" and almost automatic, regardless of the fact that the Vienna Convention, as was pointed out earlier, does not provide for a rule to determine the amount of interest.

On the other hand, when the buyer benefited from the goods, he is obliged by para. 2 of Art. 84 to "account to the seller for all benefits which he has derived from the goods or part of them." This obligation on the part of the buyer would apply in the following cases: a) if he must make restitution of the goods or part of them, and b) if it is impossible for him to make restitution of all or part of the goods or to make restitution of all or part of the goods substantially in the condition in which he received them, "but he has nevertheless declared the contract avoided or required the seller to deliver substitute goods."

VI. PRESERVATION OF THE GOODS

Preservation of the goods is regulated in Articles 85 - 88 of Section VI which contains rules guaranteeing the rights of the buyer. Irrespective of which party bears the risk for loss or damage, the basic rule obliges the person who has possession or control of the goods to "take such steps as are reasonable in the circumstances to preserve them." Accordingly, Art. 85 of the Convention obliges the seller to take such steps "as are reasonable in the circumstances" to preserve the goods. In such a case, the risk will normally have passed to the buyer; thus, the

significance of this rule is that it releases the
buyer from liability for loss resulting from the
seller's failure to preserve the goods.[25] The
seller, however, is entitled "to retain [the
goods] until he has been reimbursed his reasonable expenses by the buyer."

In connection with the provisions of Art. 85
it should be pointed out that **reasonable** circumstances and **reasonable** expenses are common law
notions which provide standards according to
which a judge or arbitrator can evaluate the
necessary steps and expenses.

Art. 86 deals with the problem of preserving
the goods in the opposite case, i.e., when the
goods have beeen received by the buyer and he
intends to reject them. In such a case he has the
same obligations as the seller under Art. 85.

If the goods have been dispatched to the buyer
but the buyer, intending to reject them, has not
taken possession of them, para. 2 of Art. 86 provides:

> ...he must take possession of them on
> behalf of the seller provided that this
> may be done without payment of the
> price and without unreasonable incon-
> venience or unreasonable expense.

Here, as in the preceeding article, we have the
common law notions of "inconvience" and expenses
which are considered to be "unreasonable." Since
this rule is taken from ULIS, we refer to Tunc
who points out that in the given circumstances it
must be assumed that the buyer will "ordinarily
be better placed than the seller to take care" of
the goods.[26] The buyer is released from this
obligation "if the seller or a person authorized
to take charge of the goods on his behalf is
present at the destination."

The rule of Art. 87 of the Convention, which

can be found in many national laws and in ULIS
(Art. 93) as well, reads as follows:

> A party who is bound to take steps to
> preserve the goods may deposit them in
> a warehouse of a third person at the
> expense of the other party provided
> that the expense incurred is not unrea-
> sonable.

If the goods are subject to rapid deterioration or the party who is bound to preserve them
in accordance with Art. 85 or 86 would incur
unreasonable expense in doing so, this party is
entitled to sell them. The same rule applies "if
there has been an unreasonable delay by the other
party in taking possession of the goods or in
taking them back or in paying the price or cost
of preservation." In all of these circumstances
"a reasonable notice" of the intention to sell
must be given to the other party. After selling
the goods, the party exercising this right under
the Convention may retain out of the proceeds of
sale "an amount equal to the reasonable expenses
of preserving the goods and of selling them." In
this case he is bound to account to the other
party for the balance. In connection with para. 3
of Art. 88, it is pointed out in the Commentary
that if the party selling the goods has other
claims arising out of the contract or its breach,
under the applicable national law he may have the
right to defer the transmission of the balance
until the settlement of those claims.[27]

NOTES

1. In the <u>Commentary</u> <u>to</u> <u>the</u> <u>Draft</u> <u>Convention</u>
prepared by UNCITRAL, it is mentioned that this

may be the case when the buyer fell behind in his payments to the seller in respect of other contracts. (A)CONF.97(5), p. 159.

2. According to the American Uniform Commercial Code (Art. 2-705), "the seller may stop delivery of goods in the possession of a carrier or other bailee when he discovers the buyer to be insolvent..."

3. T.C. Hartley, The Uniform Law on the International Sale of Goods... and the Draft Convention on Contracts for the International Sale of Goods prepared by UNCITRAL, vol.II (London 1979) p. 7/3.

4. Only para. 1 of Art. 72 of the Vienna Convention has been taken from ULIS (Art. 76), which provides:

> Where prior to the date fixed for performance of the contract it is clear that one of the parties will commit a fundamental breach of contract, the other party shall have the right to declare the contract avoided.

5. A. Tunc, Commentary of the Hague Convention (The Hague 1966) p. 88.

6. Ph. Kahn, Etude comparée des Conventions de la Haye et Projet de Convention preparé par CNUDCI (Bruxelles 1979) p. 69.

7. The notion "reasonable notice" is not clear and may be interpreted in various ways. In the French version of the same article we find the term dans les conditions raisonable, which sounds better although similar doubts may arise as well.

8. A. Tunc, supra n. 5, at p. 92.

9. Ibid. p. 94.

10. At the Vienna Conference it was disputed whether the "contract price" and the "price fixed by the contract" are the same. Many were of the opinion that the contract price is provided ob-

jectively and precisely by the contract, which is not necessarily the case with the price fixed by the contract.

11. The additional expenses may include, e.g., the cost for transportation or for delay in delivery of the goods bought in replacement by the buyer.

12. It should be pointed out that Art. 76 speaks of the **price fixed** by the contract, whereas Art. 75 refers to the **contract price.**

13. A. Tunc, supra, n. 5, at p. 96.

14. Art. 83 of ULIS reads as follows:
> Where the breach of contract consists of delay in the payment of the price, the seller shall in any event be entitled to interest on such sum as is in arrear at a rate equal to the official discount rate in the country where he has his place of business or, if he has no place of business, his habitual residence, plus 1%.

15. B. Nicholas, "Force Majeure and Frustration," Am.J.Comp.L. (1979) p. 232. The author explains that the English term "exemption" could be explained by force majeure, cause étrangère, "impossibility, "frustration," Wegfall der Geschäftsgrundlage.

16. The main problem was whether to provide a detailed rule, in which case the text might be difficult to understand, or to have a short rule, in which case there would be room for application of the national law, which, however, was also not regarded as a satisfactory solution.

17. This rule is the exception to the rule found in Art. 27 of the Convention.

18. Commentary, supra n. 1, p. 175.

19. In Art. 4 the Convention expressly provides that it does not deal with "the validity of the contract or of any of its provisions or of any usage."

20. The only effect of the avoidance according to para. 1 of Art. 78 of ULIS amounts to release of both parties "from their obligations thereunder, subject to any damages which may be due."

21. In some legal systems, after avoidance of the contract all these clauses terminate with the rest of the contract. Therefore, the provision in the Vienna Convention provides a mechanism to avoid such results.

22. In the French text of the Convention the term <u>sensiblement</u> <u>identique</u> (almost identical) is used as the equivalent of "substantially." Although there is no definitiin of the term "substantially," it is held that it should be interpreted as a condition which the seller is not supposed to refuse to take.

23. <u>Commentary</u>, <u>supra</u> n. 1, at pp. 176-177.

24. Art. 78 provides:

If the party fails to pay the price or any other sum that is in arrears, the other party is entitled to interest on it, without prejudice to any claim for damages recoverable under article 74.

25. T.C. Hartley, <u>supra</u> n. 3, at p. 7/21.

26. A. Tunc, <u>Commentary</u>, <u>supra</u> n. 5, at p. 98.

27. <u>Commentary</u>, <u>supra</u> n. 1, at p. 197.

CHAPTER EIGHT

PASSING OF RISK
IN INTERNATIONAL SALES OF GOODS

BERND von HOFFMANN
Professor of Law, Trier

The passing of risk is one of the classic topics of sales law. It is also one of the main preoccupations of the parties in international sales transactions. The practical needs of international transactions differ widely from the established concepts of national sales law. The UN Sales Convention made a fresh start on the passing of risk problem with an original approach differing remarkably from conventional wisdom, yet trying to be close to practical needs.

The aim of this paper is to explain the new system and its policies against the background of comparative national law, international trade usages, and the instruments of international transport. It does not attempt to give an exhaustive account of all the problems connected with the passing of risk. In particular, it leaves aside the effect of the seller's breach of contract on passing of risk, a problem which is alluded to in Art. 70 of the UN Sales Convention and can only be dealt with properly in the context of remedies of the buyer.[1]

I.   GENERAL PART

1.   The Issue

The typical aim of a sale of goods transaction
is that goods in the hands of a seller pass into
the hands of the buyer who is then entitled to
use the goods and dispose of them according to
his wishes. The shorthand expression of this
ability of the buyer is that he is called the
owner of the goods. In some cases this
transaction is very straightforward: B enters
the shop of A, asks for a bottle of wine, pays
the purchase price in cash and takes the bottle
with him. In this example, the conclusion of the
contract and its completion (delivery of the good
and payment of the purchase price) are done simultaneously. Very often a sales transaction is
more complex and involves an element of **time**
between the conclusion of the contract and its
completion. Again a simple example: B telephones
wine seller A and orders 12 bottles of red wine
Chateau Lafite 1978. They agree that B will go to
A's shop the next day to pick up the 12 bottles.
In this example, there is a time element between
the conclusion of the contract and delivery of
the goods. Let us now assume that during the
night between the conclusion of the contract and
the intended delivery of the goods thieves break
into the seller's shop and take all his bottles
of Chateau Lafite including the 12 bottles which
have already been boxed for the purpose of
transport to the buyer; or a fire breaks out in
the shop damaging the bottles. Let us further
assume that the seller took all reasonable
precautions to prevent theft or fire.
In this situation two legal problems arise.
First, the buyer wants to know whether the seller

is still bound by his obligation to deliver 12
bottles of wine and, in particular, whether the
buyer is entitled to claim damages aiming at the
recovery of his positive interest (Erfüllungs-
interesse). The answer of the Convention is that
in case of supervening impossibility of delivery,
the seller is discharged of his obligation (Art.
97(1)). This means that the risk of performance
is borne by the buyer. This question, however, is
outside the scope of this paper.

The second question, which is precisely the
scope of this paper, concerns the following: Is
the buyer obliged to pay the purchase price even
if he did not receive the goods for which he
undertook to pay the price?

It is a common denominator of all legal systems that from a certain point in the development
of a sales transaction the buyer remains bound to
pay the purchase price even though he did not
receive the goods for which he contracted. This
is the problem of passing of risk from the seller
to the buyer.[2] It is dealt with in Articles 67-70
of the UN Sales Convention. Art. 66 recognizes
the principle of passing of risk by providing
that "loss of or damage to the goods after the
risk has passed to the buyer does not discharge
him from his obligation to pay the price..." The
problem now is to identify the point in the
development of the sales transaction at which
risk of payment passes from the seller to the
buyer.

2. Comparative Law[3]

Comparative law teaches that there are three
main points to which passing of risk in sales
transactions may be linked:
a) The conclusion of the contract,

b) The transfer of ownership from the seller to
   the buyer,
c) The transfer of physical possession from the
   seller to the buyer.

a)   Conclusion of the Contract

This principle can be traced to Roman law. The
Institutes of Justinian expressly state that the
risk passes to the buyer at the conclusion of the
contract even if the buyer is not yet in possession of the goods.[4]

The shorthand formula is _Periculum_ _est_ _empto-_
ris. This rule has been adopted, e.g., in Europe
by Art. 1496 of the Dutch B.W., Art. 1452 of the
Spanish C.c. and Art. 185 of the Swiss O.R. In
Switzerland, however, the rule has been critized
by legal writers and has been restrictively construed by the Federal Court.[5]

b)   Transfer of Ownership

This principle finds support in the legal
proverb _res_ _perit_ _domino_. This rule, which also
appears to be of Roman origin, was developed by
the proponents of natural law (Grotius, Pufen-
dorf) during the 17th Century.[6] It has been a-
dopted by the French Code civil (Art. 1624/1138
(2) and Art. 1465 of the Italian Codice civile.
It is also part of the English Sale of Goods Acts
of 1893 and 1979.[7] It has to be noted, however,
that under these legal systems the transfer of
ownership, to which the passing of risk is
linked, is already effected at the time of the
conclusion of the contract. Therefore, as a matter of practice, the rule _periculum_ _est_ _emptoris_
is also retained under the principle of linking
risk of loss to the transfer of ownership.[8]

c)   Transfer of Physical Possession

§ 446 of the German Civil Code links passing of risk to the transfer of possession to the buyer. It has been followed by Art. 522 of the Greek Civil Code. The same principle can be found in the Swedish Act of 1905 relating to the purchase and exchange of goods (Art. 17); also the US Uniform Commercial Code (sec. 2-509 (3)) establishes the general rule that the "risk of loss passes to the buyer on his receipt of the goods," thereby deviating from common law tradition.

d)   Comparative Evaluation[8a]

An analytical evaluation of the best starting point for the passing of risk has to take into consideration different arguments. There are several reasons to link risk allocation to the transfer of physical possession of the goods. First, as long as the seller is in physical possession of the goods, it is only he who can take measures for the prevention of risks of loss and damage. If goods are damaged or lost while in the possession of the seller, there is a strong presumption of his negligence. Therefore, the buyer who is requested by the seller to pay the purchase price for goods that are in possession of the seller will inevitably respond that the loss is due to the negligence of the seller. Thus a rule that links risk of loss to possession minimizes litigation on negligence. Secondly, the goods are covered by the risk insurance (e.g., fire insurance) of the seller as long as they are on his premises. It would be impractical to request the buyer to insure goods that are still in the care of the seller. Finally, it is easier for

the seller to press a claim against the insurance
company.

There is an argument which has been put forward in favour of linking the passing of risk to
the conclusion of the contract. It has been said
that an early passing of risk is an invitation to
the buyer to take possession of the goods as
early as possible. The transfer of risk, it has
been said, is the price for the laziness of the
buyer in collecting the goods.[9] This argument,
however, presupposes that the seller is always in
the position to deliver physical possession to
the buyer at the time of the conclusion of the
contract. This, however, is in conflict with
practice: At the conclusion of the contract the
seller is often not yet the owner of the goods
sold to the buyer. Even if he is the owner, he
may have stored the goods outside his premises
and be unable to deliver them immediately. Therefore, one can only blame the buyer for not taking
immediate possession of the purchased goods provided the seller has ownership and physical possession of the goods at the date of the contract.
Making these elements conditions of a transfer of
risk to the buyer would also enhance litigation
between seller and buyer in case of loss.

3. Particularities of International Sales

a) Contracts involving Carriage

This presentation of the problem of passing of
risk started with a simplified model case: A
cash sales transaction in which the buyer takes
the goods from the shop of the seller. The typical international sales transaction is characterized by greater complexity. The buyer living in a
foreign country normally is not prepared to phys-

ically take the goods from the seller's premises; also the seller is not equipped to bring the goods to the premises of the buyer situated in a foreign country. Normally they agree that the seller will make the necessary arrangements for the transport of the goods to the buyer. This typical transaction should be illustrated by an example: A manufacturer of agricultural machines has his place of business in Belgrade. He sells 20 machines to an import company located in Alexandria, Egypt. The seller undertakes to provide for transport to Alexandria. The practical means of transport in this particular situation is the following: The machines are transported by railway from Belgrade to Rijeka, then shipped from Rijeka to Alexandria.

b) Transport Documents, Bill of Lading

For reasons of simplicity, let us now concentrate on sea transport. Normally, the seller concludes a maritime contract of affreightment with the carrier. In this contract the seller is called the "shipper." The carrier issues the shipper a document, the bill of lading which contains two elements:
1. An acknowledgment of the carrier that he has received the goods,
2. A promise to hand over the goods to the person holding the bill of lading[10].

The buyer can collect the goods from the carrier at the port of destination only when he has the bill of lading in his hand. The bill of lading, therefore, is an essential document that enables the buyer to collect the goods. In a certain sense, the bill of lading represents the goods that are transported.

The bill of lading often has a very important

ancillary function connected with payment of the price. Since the bill of lading represents the transported goods, handing it over to the buyer against payment of the purchase price gives a security for payment of the purchase price equivalent to the retention of the goods until payment in cash sales. The seller often does not want to trust the willingness and ability of the buyer to pay after he has received the goods. Therefore, he may request a letter of credit from a bank in the buyer's country by which the bank undertakes to make payment on receipt of the transport documents. Such a letter of credit is usually confirmed by a correspondent bank of the buyer's bank in the seller's country. In such so-called irrevocable letters of credit, the seller gets the purchase price from a bank in his own country upon receipt of the bill of lading. The bank in the seller's country sends the bill of lading to the bank in the buyer's country that has issued the letter of credit which, in turn, hands it over to the buyer. As letters go faster than freight, the buyer has the bill of lading in his hands before the ship has arrived in his country.

c) Passing of Risk

The central topic concerning passing of risk in international sales of goods is the sales contract involving carriage. The general policy on risk allocation that was developed above is that risk should be linked to physical possession. This policy, however, is not very helpful in contracts involving carriage. During the time of carriage neither the seller nor the buyer is in physical possession of the goods. Therefore, the general criterion of risk allocation has to

be adapted to the transport situation. There is
some support to link the passge of risk to one of
the following criteria:

(1)   Transport cost,

(2)   "Delivery,"

(3)   Transfer of documents.

(1) Transport Cost

It has been suggested that the risk be allo-
cated to the party contractually bound to pay the
cost of transportation. This had been the rule of
the US Uniform Sales Act section 19, subsection
5. There is also some support for such a rule in
older British authorities.[11] The reason for this
rule is obvious: A seller who pays the carrier
and the insurance company thereby impliedly acknowledges that it is his duty to bring the goods
to the buyer. Any accident during transport is
therefore assumed to be at that party's risk;
insurance cover paid by the seller again implies
that he assumes to suffer the risk of loss.

This argument disregards contractual practice.
Let us assume that in case the seller is entitled
to repayment of his expenses for carriage and
insurance, the buyer has to take the risk of loss
during the transport process. It should be clear
that such an obligation to repay these costs is
very onerous for the buyer. He cannot calculate
the costs in advance and it is very difficult for
him to prove that the seller charged him an
unreasonably high transport cost. Moreover, the
seller frequently has made general arrangements
with carriers and insurance companies for discount rates which will make the overall transaction not only more predictable, but also cheaper.
And, indeed, international commercial practice
reflects these considerations: In most cases the

seller assumes the mentioned obligations. Shift-
ing the burden of payment of transport and insurance costs to the seller is to the advantage of
the buyer. It then seems unsatisfactory to automatically link to this another advantage: to
shift the burden of risk of loss from the buyer
to the seller. Such an automatic link between
risk of loss and payment of transportation cost
could have the effect that sellers would be less
inclined to accept the obligation to pay the
transportation cost and insurance.

There is another argument in favour of this
link between the obligation to provide for transport and risk: If, on the one hand, the seller
has to pay for the transport and the buyer, on
the other hand, has to bear the risk of loss
during transport, the danger exists that the
seller will look for the cheapest carrier and
insurer. This keeps his expenses low, but en-
hances the risk of loss of the buyer. If the
seller who chooses the carrier also has to bear
the risk of loss, he will look carefully for a
reliable carrier even if that implies higher
cost.[12]

This argument certainly has some appeal in
those cases in which the seller gets the purchase
price by means of a letter of credit immediately
after he has presented the shipping documents.
Nevertheless, the argument does not hold ground
for other export transactions. In many transactions, payment of the purchase price is not due
on shipment of the goods but only on presentation
of the bill of lading by the seller's representative to the buyer at the port of destination. In
such cases the seller runs the risk that the
buyer does not pay upon presentation of the bill
of lading. Therefore, his interest in safe carriage of the goods remains: If the buyer does not

pay, the seller can sell the goods again or
retain the insurance premium for goods lost or
damaged. He is therefore interested in safe carriage and correct insurance even if the risk of
loss is assumed by the buyer.

It has been the historical achievement of the
CIF clause to clearly dissociate risk of loss
from the obligation to pay transport cost and
insurance.[13]

In the movement for international unification
of sales law, the idea of linking risk of loss to
payment of transport cost (in cases of loss) has
not been accepted. Whereas the Hague Sales Law
only expressed a rule against a necessary link of
transport cost and risk of loss[14], the UN Sales
Convention does not mention such a link at all.

(2) Delivery

During the preparation of the Hague Sales Law,
there was widespread agreement on the principle
that risk of loss should pass from the seller to
the buyer at the moment when he has done all the
steps required by the contract. Art. 97(1) of the
1964 Uniform Law in the International Sale of
Goods states:

> The risk shall pass to the buyer when
> delivery of the goods is effected in
> accordance with the provisions of the
> contract and the present law.

This formula of linking the passage of risk to
"delivery" has been praised by several authors,
but it has also been critized for theoretical and
practical reasons.

The main **theoretical** argument against such a
link is the following: The concept of delivery
has been used in the Hague Sales Law for the
solution of different legal issues: It defines

the performance of the seller's obligations (Art. 30); it also marks the passing of risk from the seller to the buyer (Art. 97(1)), the date of payment of the purchase price (Art. 71) and the moment of identification of unascertained goods to the contract.[15]

This solution of different legal issues by one and the same concept necessarily makes the concept abstract and impractical. This conceptual approach, moreover, disregards that different policies may rule different issues. Take the example already quoted supra: B orders by telephone 12 bottles of Chateau Lafite 1978 from A to be taken from A's shop the next day. A collects 12 bottles from the cellars and boxes them. The following night the box is stolen. It is true that in this situation the seller has complied with his contractual obligations and therefore is not liable for damages for breach of contract. This does not necessarily imply that risk of loss passes to the buyer with the effect that the buyer is liable to pay the purchase price.[16] Practical considerations may advise postponement of risk of loss to the date the goods are actually handed over to the buyer.

There are two other practical objections against the use of delivery as the critical point for passing of risk. First: In the Hague Sales Law delivery means fulfillment of all contractual requirements by the seller. A seller who hands over defective goods to the buyer has not met his contractual obligations; he has not delivered. It follows that the risk remains with the seller even when the buyer has the goods in his hands.[17] Second: The possible connection of risk of loss with the handover of transport documents remains unresolved (infra 3).

(3) Handover of Documents

The second argument against linking the passing of risk to delivery may be illustrated by our above-mentioned case: Agricultural machines have been sold by a Belgrade seller to a buyer in Alexandria. Let us assume that the goods were damaged as a result of a ship collision in the Adriatic Sea before the seller sent the bill of lading to the buyer. There is considerable argument as to whether or not the seller has already fulfilled his contractual duty of delivery by handing over the goods to the carrier or whether handing in the transport documents is also part of the delivery. There is widespread agreement in several legal systems (France, England, CSSR)[18] to combine the handover of transport documents with the passing of risk. The legal rules of other systems, such as the US Uniform Commercial Code[19], and of several INCOTERMS clauses[20] are in opposition to such a link. The problem was discussed at length during the preparation of the Hague Uniform Law but it has not been expressly solved in that Convention.[21]

In favour of linking risk of loss to handing in the transport documents is the argument that the seller who keeps the transport documents in his hands reserves control over the goods. The buyer only gets control of the goods when he receives the transport documents. On the other hand, the reservation of a security interest in the goods (like reservation of title by the seller) generally is not regarded as a sufficient ground to reverse the general rules on risk allocation. Moreover, linking passing of risk to the surrender of documents can lead to practical difficulties. One example: Goods are shipped from Rijeka on March 1 and arrive at Alexandria on

April 1. The shipping documents are handed over
to the buyer on March 15. By then it may be clear
that the goods were damaged during shipment, but
it is not clear on which particular date the
damage occurred. Last but not least, damage is
usually discovered only after arrival. Therefore
the buyer is closer to the assessment of damage
than the seller.

(4) Typological Approach

It was the policy of the UN Sales Convention
not to use the ambiguous word "delivery" as the
critical point for the transfer of risk in all
international sales. The Convention replaced that
conceptual approach with a typological one.[22]
It distinguishes between different transport
situations and gives a clear cut answer in which
event risk passes to the buyer for each of them.
In the previous example (3), Art. 67 clarifies
that risk passes to the buyer "when the goods are
handed over to the first carrier for transmission
to the buyer in accordance with the contract of
sale..." The fact that the seller is authorized
to retain documents controlling the disposition
of the goods according to an express provision of
the Convention does not affect the passing of
risk (Art. 68).

4.   Incoterms. General Conditions of Sales (CMEA, ECE)

Export and import traders have long been aware
of the problems inherent in the carriage of goods
sold to different countries. They have developed
several types of clauses describing in a short-
hand form the respective obligations and risks of
seller and buyer concerning the international

carriage of goods. Particular consideration is
given in these clauses to the passing of risk
from the seller to the buyer. Such clauses were
originally forumulated for the international
carriage of goods by **sea**. Later they were developed for international carriage by **rail** and by
airplane. It seems, however, that for international carriage by **road** no such clauses have yet
been introduced.

a) Incoterms[23]

After the First World War the understanding of
these basic commercial terms in different countries was the object of inquiry in business circles. This showed that despite international
agreement on the respective duties of seller and
buyer in the international business community,
national differences of understanding persisted
as to several obligations. The International
Chamber of Commerce invited business circles of
its member countries to develop a common understanding of those terms which seemed to be internationally acceptable. This unification attempt
was the "International Rules for the Interpretation of Trade Terms" (INCOTERMS) which were first
published in 1936. They were later followed by
Incoterms 1953 and in 1980 the International
Chamber of Commerce recommended that an explicit
reference to INCOTERMS be added when using these
trade terms in order to make it clear that they
are to be interpreted in accordance with INCO-
TERMS. In many export contracts specific reference has been made to INCOTERMS.
The question remains, however, whether or not
the rules of interpretation as set out in INCO-
TERMS are relevant in those instances in which
no express reference to INCOTERMS has been made

by the parties. The alternate solutions are that
in these instances the national trade terms either of the forum, of the place of formation or
performance of the contract, or of the country of
the party whose obligations are involved shall
apply.[24] Article 9(2) of the UN Convention makes
reference to the usage which in international
trade is widely known to be observed by parties
to contracts of the type involved in the particular trade concerned. In regard to the parallel
provision in the Hague Sales Convention, there
was some dispute among legal writers as to whether or not INCOTERMS constitute a usage that is
binding for the interpretation of their terms.[25]
The materials of the UN Convention constantly
refer to INCOTERMS.[26] Therefore, it seems that in
the interpretation of those standard terms INCO-
TERMS should prevail not only over the UN Convention but also over national trade terms.

An important reservation has to be made in
regard to the actual world-wide use of INCOTERMS.
In the United States, the American Foreign Trade
Definitions of 1941 are still in current use;
also, many countries in the Far East which have
the US as their most important trading partner
adopt the American definitions.[27]

The different clauses in INCOTERMS provide for
a wide variety of points at which the risk passes
from the seller to the buyer in contracts involving carriage.

Under the term "free on rail" (FOR) risk
passes to the buyer when the seller has delivered
the goods into the custody of the railway authority at the agreed place. In the same way, under
the clause "freight or carriage paid to (named
point of destination)" the seller bears all risk
for the goods until they have been delivered into
the custody of the first carrier.

The **port of shipment** is the point for passing
of risk in the clauses "free alongside ship"
(FAS), "free on board" (FOB), "cost and freight"
(C+F) as well as "cost, insurance, freight"
(CIF). The purpose of these clauses is that the
specific risk of shipment is at the buyer, whereas the seller is regarded as being closer to the
risk of land transport before shipment.

The alternative connection point for carriage
by sea contracts is the **port of destination.** This
port may be located in the country of the buyer
or (as in Switzerland, Austria and Hungary) in
the port of the country next to the buyer. The
port of destination is the point for passing of
risk according to the clauses "ex ship" and "ex
quay." According to the latter clause, it is the
seller who has to pay customs duties.

It should be noted that INCOTERMS also provide
for clauses "ex works" and "delivered" (to a
named place of destination in the country of
importation). Under the first clause the risk
already passes at the seller's place of business.
Under the second clause it does not pass until
the goods arrive at the buyer's place of business.

INCOTERMS only describe the usual meaning of
the standard clauses concerning carriage in international business without indicating preference for any of the clauses. This has to be seen
against the background that the ICC did not want
to show any preference for one of these clauses
and that the different arrangements are the re-
flection of different market conditions that may
change very quickly.[28] It is obvious that in a
seller's market the clause "ex warehouse" is used
more frequently than in a buyer's market which
will show preference for the clause "delivered."
In sea transport the market situation will proba-

bly be reflected in those clauses which opt for
the port of shipping or those opting for the port
of destination.

2) CMEA GENERAL CONDITIONS OF DELIVERY[29]

The general conditions of delivery of goods
between organizations of the member states of the
Council for Mutual Economic Assistance (CMEA) of
1968 undertake to give an order of preference to
different clauses according to the type of transportation involved. As to **carriage by rail**, the
usual clause "FOR" is modified in comparison with
INCOTERMS in so far as the seller bears the risk
not only until the goods are put under the custody of the railway of the seller's country but
also until they are transferred from the railway
of the seller's country to the next railway receiving the goods (§ 5(b)). The same policy is
true for carriage by road. In this eventuality
the risk passes to the buyer at the moment when
the goods are examined by border customs of the
country next to the seller's country, even if the
goods are delivered by the seller's means of
transport to the buyer (§ 5(b)). As to **transport
by sea**, preference is given to the moment when
the goods pass the ship's rail at the port of
shipment (§ 7(b)). As to **carriage by air**, risk
passes with the surrender to the air carrier in
the seller's country.

The common denominator behind those rules is
that the seller takes transit risk for damage
occurring within his own country. The buyer takes
all other transit risks, even when transport is
effected by the seller's own staff. This policy
reflects the responsibility of state-trading
organizations for acts within the territory of
that state and cannot be exported to trade with

countries belonging to different economic systems.

c) ECE General Conditions of Sale[30]

Another source reflecting international trade
usages are the general conditions of sale promul-
gated under the auspices of the Economic Commission for Europe of the United Nations (ECE). The
General Conditions for the Supply of Plant and
Machinery for Export No. 188, 1953[31] show a preference for a sale "ex works." This implies that
risk passes from the seller to the buyer already
while the goods are on the premises of the seller. The same is true for the ECE General Conditions of Sale for the Import and Export of Dura-
ble Consumer Goods and of Other Engineering Stock
Articles, No. 730, 1961 (Clause 5).[32] The more
recent General Conditions of Sale for Fresh Food
and Vegetables including Citrus Fruit of 1979[33]
(clause 31) do not give preference to any of
these clauses but -- like INCOTERMS -- leave it
entirely to the parties to determine the applicable clause.

II. THE CONVENTION

1. Contract Involving Carriage (Art. 67)

The first rule concerning passing of risk is
established in Art. 67. The basic policy is expressed in Art. 67(1)(first sentence):
>   If the contract of sale involves
>   carriage of goods... the risk passes to
>   the buyer when the goods are handed
>   over to the first carrier...
This sentence already raises two questions:

a) When does a contract of sale involve carriage of goods?
b) Who is the first carrier?
Art. 67(1)(second sentence) gives an exception to the basic rule (infra c): Art. 67(2) deals with a prerequisite of passing of risk: the identification of goods to the contract (infra b).

a) Contract Involving Carriage of Goods

The term "contract of sale involving carriage of goods" is already mentioned in the chapter concerning obligations of the seller (Art. 31(a)). In regard to the obligations of the seller concerning the delivery of goods, the said article makes the following distinctions:
- The seller is bound to deliver the goods at a particular place (Bringschuld)[34],
- The contract involves carriage of goods (Versendungskauf),
- The seller only has to place the goods at the buyer's disposal at the seller's place of business (Holschuld).

From the context it becomes clear that the obligation to deliver the goods at a particular place is the exception which has to be specifically agreed upon by the parties. In the case of silence of the contract, the question arises whether or not the seller has to hand the goods over to the first carrier or whether he only is obliged to place the goods at the buyer's disposal at his own place of business.

The Convention does not give a specific rule of interpretation for this event. Therefore, the silence of the parties concerning whether or not the contract involves carriage has to be construed in each particular case. One has to take into account the understanding of a reasonable

person, all facts relevant to the case, the usages of the parties and international trade usages (Art. 8(3)); Art. 9(2)). Accordingly, it
seems that there are very few cases in which an
international sale is concluded with the seller
not being involved in carriage. It has been
pointed out that this provision could apply when
the seller and buyer are relatively near each
other and the buyer has access to trucks that can
conveniently go to the seller's place of business.[35]

Let us come back to the case in which a buyer
from Egypt orders several agricultural machines
from a seller in Belgrade. The seller accepts the
order and there is no agreement on delivery of
the goods to a specific place nor do the circumstances of the case suggest that the buyer wants
to go to Belgrade in order to take delivery of
the machines there. Therefore, the normal consequence is that the seller has to send the goods
to the buyer. It may be interesting to ask who
has to arrange for the carriage of goods in a
situation where there has not been a specific
contractual agreement concerning the carriage.
Art. 32(2) of the Convention says:

> If the seller is bound to arrange for
> carriage of goods, he must make such
> contracts as are necessary for carriage
> to the place fixed by means of
> transport appropriate in the circum-
> stances and according to the usual
> terms for such transportation.

This clause does not specify under which circumstances the seller is bound to arrange for carriage of the goods. The commentators seem to be
silent on this point. It seems to me, however,
that in case the contract involves the seller in
the carriage of goods and the contract does not

provide for specific ways of sending the goods,
it is up to the seller to arrange for carriage of
the goods according to the terms provided for in
Art. 32(2). Such an obligation, however, does not
bind the seller to arrange for insurance (Art.
32(3)). Therefore, it remains up to the buyer to
effect insurance; the seller, however, is obliged
to provide the information necessary for conclusion of the insurance contract.

b)   The First Carrier

Let us stick to our introductory case. The
Belgrade seller has accepted the buyer's order
for several machines. The contract directs no
specific means of transport. In accordance with
usage, the seller decides to take the machines by
railway from the railway station in Belgrade to
Rijeka Port railway terminal and then ship them
via Athens to Alexandria. He requests a local
truck carrier to bring the machines from his
factory to the railway station. During the transport from the factory to the railway station
there is a car accident in which the machines are
heavily damaged. Is the seller entitled to request payment from the Egyptian buyer? The question is whether or not the local truck company
which had to transport the goods from the factory
to the railway station was the first carrier.
This problem seems to have been discussed at
length during the preparation of the Hague Sales
Convention.[36]
It seems that the uniform view has been that
local transportation cannot have the effect of a
passing of risk to the buyer. This is also valid
for the UN Convention.
The next question is whether or not transport
by the staff of the seller can be regarded as

transport by the first carrier. Take our initial
example. The Belgrade seller has his own trucks
and chooses to transport the machines to Rijeka
with his own trucks and not by railway. Midway
between Belgrade and Rijeka the goods are damaged
in an accident. Under the Hague Sales Law[37] and
also the UN Convention, the prevailing opinion is
that transportation by the staff of the seller is
not equivalent to transportation by an independent carrier. Above all, there is a practical
argument in favour of leaving the risk with a
seller who undertakes transportation: The goods
remain physically in his hands. He is closer and
can thus take preventive measures easier than the
buyer.

I do not believe that it is a good policy to
leave the risk with the seller. It penalizes a
seller who provides transportation services that
are quicker or cheaper than those of established
transport organizations. Only in these eventuali-
ties (economy, rapidity) is he entitled to replace his own service by existing carriers. It is
certainly true that the burden of proving that
the loss or damage was not due to an act of the
seller (or of his staff) is upon the seller. When
the seller has presented such evidence, there is
no reason why he should not be discharged from
the risk of loss during transport effected by his
own staff. In the end, this policy I suggest
operates in favour of the buyer: He is the person
who profits from specific measures of the seller
to compete in transport with other established
institutions.

c) Handover at Particular Places

The traditional trade terms "FAS," "CIF,"
"FOB" reflect the idea that when carriage in-

volves land transport as well as sea transport,
the risk passes to the buyer only at the port of
shipment and not already when the goods are
handed over to the first land carrier. During the
discussions of the Hague Sales Law it had been
suggested that a special rule be made for sea
transport.[38] This suggestion was rejected as a
general rule, and the UN Sales Convention also
does not provide for such a general rule. Nevertheless, Art. 67(1)(second sentence) can be explained by that policy: If the seller is bound to
hand the goods over to a carrier at a particular
place, the risk does not pass to the buyer until
the goods are handed over to the carrier at that
place. Let us give an example: The buyer in
Alexandria orders several agricultural machines
from the seller in Belgrade with the provision to
ship the machines from Rijeka to Alexandria. In
this situation the seller is bound to hand the
goods over to the sea carrier at Rijeka. The
result is that the seller bears the risk of loss
during the land transport from Belgrade to Rijeka
even though this transport has been effected by
the railway as the first carrier. The splitting
of transit risk between the seller and the buyer
presents practical problems in determining the
place where the damage occurred. Therefore, this
exception should be construed narrowly.[39]

The first example for narrow construction is
where the port of shipment has not been provided
for at the conclusion of the contract but by a
later instruction of the buyer to the seller.
Such subsequent choice should not affect the
passing of risk.[40]

Also in cases where the parties have agreed on
alternative ports, e.g., UK-port, Amsterdam/
Antwerp, Hamburg/Le Havre, Deutsche Nordseehäfen,
the aim of such a clause is to enable shipment at

the port from which the next vessel is departing
to the destination of the goods. In this situation the identification of the "particular place"
where the goods are to be handed over to the
carrier depends on an act of the **carrier** after
the conclusion of the contract. Such alternative
determination of a particular place, whereby the
place is specified only after the conclusion of
the contract, should have no effect on the passing of risk.[41]

Provided a particular place has been agreed
upon between seller and buyer, the risk passes
when the "goods are handed over to the carrier at
that place." Traditional trade terms are more
specific on the transfer of risk between seller
and buyer in contracts involving sea transport.
They alternatively provide that risk passes when
the goods are delivered by the seller **free alongside ship** or when they have effectively **passed
the ship's rail.** The first clause puts the risk
of loading on the buyer; the latter on the seller. Art. 67(1)(second sentence) is not so sophisticated: It lets risk pass when the goods
enter into the physical possession of the carrier. In regard to the Hague Sales Convention, it
was suggested that in contracts involving sea
transport risk regularly pass to the buyer only
when the goods have effectively passed the ship's
rail, even if they have previously been put in
the physical possession of the carrier.[42]

In view of the different trade usages concerning passing of risk in sea transport (alongside
ship or passing the ship's rail), it seems that a
uniform international trade usage cannot be determined that has prevalence over the provision
of the Convention. Therefore, the physical handover to the sea carrier is decisive.

d) Identification of Goods to the Contract (Art. 67(2))

This is a very obscure provision that has limited practical interest and normally is neglected by commentators of the Convention. Nevertheless, it is worthwhile to go into it as it shows some interesting pecularities of the transfer of risk problem unknown to national laws.

The starting point is very simple. B telephones A and orders 12 bottles of wine Chateau Lafite 1978. Risk then passes -- according to conventional wisdom -- to B only when A takes the bottles out of his wine cellar, boxes them, and writes the buyer's name on the box. If the seller has done all these steps before the goods are destroyed, then risk has passed to the buyer. The procedure carried out by the seller was to "appropriate" goods which hitherto have been unascertained. The UN Convention now uses the term "identification" instead of "appropriation" which is a term of English law. Identification means that it becomes obvious that goods of the seller have become connected with a particular contract.

In contracts involving carriage, identification of goods may give rise to particular problems. Normally, the name of the buyer is marked on the goods, or the person entitled to claim delivery from the carrier may be inferred from the shipping documents, in particular the bill of lading. Therefore, in this case the bill of lading entitles the buyer to receive goods that are clearly identified to the contract by the shipping documents.

Nevertheless, in many cases the buyer is not named as consignee in the bill of lading.[43] The seller often prefers to send the goods to himself as the consignee at the port of arrival. This is

particularly true in situations in which payment
has not been received by way of letter of credit.
Then the seller wants to maintain the possibility
of disposing of the goods in case the buyer does
not procure payment on the presentation of the
bill of lading. Therefore, the bill of lading is
not an appropriate means of identifying the goods
to the contract. In this situation a **notice of
dispatch** of the goods to the carrier is regarded
as sufficient for the identification of the goods
to the contract.

Such a notice of dispatch provides identification of goods to the contract after the risk has
passed from the seller to the buyer: handing the
goods over to the first carrier or to the sea
carrier. The question arises whether or not such
identification has retroactive effect. Many laws
support the viewpoint that an identification of
goods to the contract that took place after the
goods have been lost does not have retroactive
effect. The opposite view, however, has also been
defended. Art. 100 of the Hague Sales Convention
excluded the passing of risk from the seller to
the buyer only in those situations in which the
buyer knew or should have known at the time of
sending of the document that the goods handed
over to the carrier have been lost or damaged.
This implies that according to the Hague Convention identification of goods to the contract
generally had retroactive effect. Art. 67(2) of
the UN Convention uses clear language; in our
example risk only passes when the seller gives
notice to the buyer. It is true that such a rule
produces the probability of dispute whether or
not the damage occurred before sending notice. On
the other hand, it avoids dispute on the question
whether or not the seller was <u>bona</u> <u>fide</u> in sending the notice. It also encourages the seller to

send the notice to the buyer without delay. And
normally it should be possible for the seller to
send the notice of dispatch immediately after he
has handed over the goods to the carrier.

2. Sale of Goods during Transit (Art. 68)

In a particular type of international sales
transaction, the goods are already in transport
at the time of the conclusion of the contract
between the seller and buyer. Let me give an
example: An American corn exporter ships corn
from New York to Rotterdam. He has a contract
with a European buyer CIF Rotterdam. The contractual time of delivery in the contract gives
the seller a certain time period within which he
can choose whether to use the quantity of corn
afloat to meet his existing contractual delivery
obligations towards his buyer or to look for
another buyer with whom he may agree on a more
favourable price than in his previous contract.
He can then fulfill his original contractual
obligation by sending another shipment of corn.
It should be noted that the prices of commodities
vary considerably with time, and therefore a sale
of goods afloat enables the seller to speculate.[44] Let us assume that the cargo of corn has
been shipped by the seller on April 15 and sold
to a European importer on April 20. The seller
hands over the bill of lading to the buyer on the
date of the sale. Upon arrival the corn is found
to have been damaged by sea-water.

The question now arises whether the seller or
the buyer has to bear the risk of loss. The
general rule -- as we have seen -- is that the
buyer bears the risk of loss from the time of the
handover to the first carrier. In this particular
case, the handover to the first carrier has been

effected before the contract between the seller and the buyer was concluded. Therefore, the question is whether or not the buyer has to bear the transit risk even for the time before conclusion of the contract. The alternative would be to make the risk pass only from the time of conclusion of the sales contract. The practical inconvenience of this latter solution is that it is very difficult to determine when damage occurred to the goods in transit. Therefore, such a rule leads to disputes. Moreover, the general argument that the buyer who inspects the goods is closer in order to press a claim against the carrier or the insurance company is also valid for risks that occurred before the conclusion of the contract. It seems that there has been an international trade usage, at least in Europe, which makes risk pass retroactively to the buyer for the whole sea transport.[45] This rule has been recognized in the Hague Sales Law (Art. 99).

The UNCITRAL Draft of the Sales Law contained a similar provision (Art. 80), which, however, gave rise to strong protests on the part of the delegates of a number of developing countries who pointed out that such a commercial usage contradicted the interests of buyers in developing countries.[46]

The most impressive argument against the retroactive passing of risk was that it is unacceptable for the buyer to assume the risk for the time before conclusion of the contract if the goods had not been **insured** prior to that date.[47]

The following compromise has finally been agreed upon: Normally, the risk in respect of goods sold in transit passes to the buyer only at the conclusion of the sales contract (Art. 68 (first sentence). There is, however, an important exception. The risk passes to the buyer

retroactively from the time of the handover to
the carrier "if the circumstances so indicate."
The question remains open as to which circumstances indicate such a retroactive passing of
risk. It is clear from the wording of that exception that the parties need not agree **expressly** on
retroactivity but that such an agreement can be
implied from the circumstances of the sales
transaction. It has been reasonably argued that
under the typical circumstances indicating retroactive passing of risk, the seller, in execution
of the sales contract, hands over the buyer an
insurance policy payable "to the order of the as-
sured" endorsed by the seller to the buyer.[48]

3.   General Residual Rule (Art. 69)

It has been stated that the characteristic
feature of international sales transactions is
that they involve carriage obligations of the
seller. Only in exceptional cases is the whole
transport obligation assumed by the buyer (as in
"ex works" contracts). Therefore -- in contrast
to purely international sales transactions -- the
rule on passing of risk in sales not involving
carriage by the seller has only a subsidiary
function. Art. 69(1) covers those situations. The
principle is that risk passes from the seller to
the buyer at the time the buyer takes over the
goods at the seller's place of business. Therefore, the risk remains with the seller during the
time period the buyer is permitted but not contractually bound to take over the goods. If the
buyer is to take over the goods by the end of
May and the goods are stolen on May 28, the risk
of loss is still at the seller. The reason behind
this rule is that the seller who has the goods in
his hands is closer to their custody than the

buyer. The rule is preferable to INCOTERMS "ex works" which makes risk pass to the buyer as soon as the goods are placed at his disposal.

The question remains whether or not a breach of contract by the buyer can effect a transfer of risk to him. Art. 69(1) makes risk pass to the buyer if he does not take over the goods in due time. From that time on he commits a breach of contract by failing to take delivery when the goods are placed at his disposal. The latter means that goods have been identified to the contract by the seller (cf. Art. 67(2)). Art. 69(1) does not expressly cover the situation in which a breach of contract by the buyer does not consist of a refusal to take delivery but of a refusal to do other acts that according to the contract have to be done by the buyer prior to delivery. A typical case of such a breach of contract may occur when the buyer is bound to make payment on delivery but refuses to do so. In this situation, the buyer does not fail to take delivery, but it is the unpaid seller who refuses to deliver to the buyer.

It is true that an amendment proposed by the German delegation with the aim of effecting the passing of risk to the buyer in all cases in which he prevents delivery by a breach of contract was not adopted.[49] However, I believe that systematic coherence demands that delivery prevented by a breach of contract on the part of the buyer lets the risk of loss pass to the buyer. This argument is supported by the policy consideration that passing of risk is one of the elements which may encourage the buyer to meet his contractual obligations.

III.   CONCLUSION

The legal effect of the rules concerning the passing of risk is that, as all provisions of the UN Sales Convention, they are non-mandatory. Therefore, the specific provisions on passing of risk that have been agreed upon by the parties as well as established by international trade usages prevail over the rules of the Convention. We have seen that, in export trade, standard trade terms such as ex works, CIF and FOB give very precise definitions of the passing of risk, especially when they are interpreted in the light of INCO-TERMS.

The Convention itself did not attempt to present rules for the interpretation of these trade terms. Such an effort might have had the positive effect of promoting an even greater international uniformity of interpretation of these terms than that guaranteed by INCOTERMS.[50] The important drawback of such an effort, however, would be that it would lead to a "petrification" which is in contradiction to the notion of commercial usage. Commercial usage is in a permanent state of development and takes continual notice of new technical and documental developments. It is not difficult to anticipate that the further development of container transport[51] and of "multi-modal" transport documents[52] will influence future trade practices concerning the passing of risk. Therefore, the reluctance of this Convention in formulating trade terms wisely recognizes the respective roles of international trade usage and the Convention in the development of international trade: Priority is given to trade usage, enabling dynamic development and adaptation, whereas the Convention -- replacing national statutes -- provides a subsidiary framework.[53]

In its choice of a model for the rules on the
passing of risk, the Convention did not rely on
precedence in national legislations or on traditional legal concepts. It refuses to link passing
of risk to the conclusion of the contract, to the
transfer of property, to the execution of the
seller's contractual obligation (delivery) or to
payment of the transport cost. The main reason
for the lack of such a general rule for the
passing of risk seems to be that it would be
unable to cope with the practical needs of different types of international contracts involving
carriage. Trade terms, as reflected by INCOTERMS,
show that none of the classical systems of linking passing of risk to a certain event has been
accepted by the commercial world. Therefore, this
Convention does not offer one general criterion
for the transfer of risk but rather a typology
covering different situations:
- Contract involving carriage,
- Contract involving carriage to a particular
  place,
- Sale of goods in transit,
and then gives a general residual rule.

On the whole, the underlying policy for risk
allocation in contracts involving carriage is the
following: In export sales, goods are normally
insured against transportation risks. Therefore,
the main question concerning risk allocation is
whether it is easier for the seller or the buyer
to claim compensation for loss and damage from
the insurance company. The practical consideration after goods have been sent to the buyer is
that only the buyer can discover transit damage.
The consequence is to let the buyer suffer the
loss, thus keeping the seller out of the dealings
with the insurance company. The other way around,
letting the seller suffer the loss would make the

transaction with the insurance company more difficult: First the seller has to be informed of
the damage by the buyer and then recover the
damage from the insurance company. The risk of
loss allocation has therefore become a question
of balancing the respective inconveniences of
buyer and seller. Such a model of risk allocation
is unfamiliar to national systems;[54] I am confi-
dent, however, that it will be accepted by the
international commercial community for which this
Convention has been designed.

NOTES

1. On this topic cf. J. Honnold, Uniform Law for
International Sales (Deventer 1982) pp. 385-390.
2. According to P.M. Roth, "risk is an elusive
concept." This statement, however, is only true
when the different legal issues raised by one
factual event are not distinguished from each
other. "The Passing of Risk" 27 Am.J.Comp.L.
(1979) p. 291 et seq.
3. For a recent comparative study cf. G. Hager,
Die Gefahrtragung beim Kauf (Frankfurt/M. 1982).
4. I. 3, 23, 3; D. 18, 6, 8 pr. quote classical
authors for support of the opinion; it is, however, a matter of dispute whether or not this
principle had already been part of the classical
law. Cf. P. Jörs/W. Kunkel/L. Wenger, Römisches
Recht 3rd ed. (Berlin 1949) p. 228.
5. B.G. 18.4.1958, B.G.E. 84 II 158.
6. Cf. G. Hager, supra n. 3, at p. 39.
7. SGA 1893 (s. 20 (1), s. 18 rule 1); SGA 1979
(sec. 20, sec. 18 rule 1).
8. Remarkable agreement between French and English law is noted by G. Hager, supra n. 3, at p.
57.

8a. Those policies have been stressed mainly by P.M. Roth, <u>supra</u> n. 2, at p. 296, and J. Honnold, "Uniform Law and Uniform Trade Terms," in N.Horn and C.M. Schmitthoff (eds.) <u>The Transnational Law of International Commercial Transactions, Studies in Transnational Economic Law</u>, vol. 2 (Deventer 1982) pp. 161-162. They are apparently influenced by the "Economic Analysis of Law" Movement. Cf. <u>infra</u> n. 54.

9. H. Giger, <u>Berner Kommentar zum Schweizerischen Privatrecht</u> VI, 2/1 (Bern 1973) Art. 185 Rz. 24. Contra: B. von Hoffmann, <u>Das Recht des Grundstückskaufs. Eine rechtsvergleichende Untersuchung</u> (Tübingen 1982) p. 197.

10. For a short introduction to the nature of bills of lading see C.M. Schmitthoff, <u>The Export Trade</u> 7th ed. (London 1980) p. 345.

11. J.Ph. Benjamin, <u>A Treatise on the Law of Sale of Personal Property</u> 8th ed. (London 1950) p. 337.

12. On this argument, cf. H. Grossmann and D. Doerth, <u>Das Recht des Überseekaufs</u> vol. 1 (Mannheim/Berlin/Leipzig 1930) p. 143 f.

13. Ibid. cf. p. 144 f.

14. Art. 101 only says: "The passing of risk shall not necessarily be determined by the provisions of the contract concerning expenses." This does not exclude, however, presumptions in favour of such link.

15. P. Schlechtriem, "The Seller's Obligations Under the United Nations Convention on Contracts for the International Sale of Goods," in <u>International Sales ...</u>, (ed.) Parker School of Foreign and Comparative Law (New York 1984) pp. 6-7.

16. Ibid, at pp. 6-10.

17. For criticism cf. K. Neumayer, "Zur Revision des Haager Einheitlichen Kaufrechts..." in <u>Festschrift E. von Caemmerer</u> (Tübingen 1978) pp. 955-

986 (985); P.M. Roth, supra n. 2, at p. 295; C. Angelici, "La disciplina del passaggio dei rischi," in La vendita internazionale (Milano 1981) p. 226.

18. For references see H. Dölle and K. Neumayer, Kommentar zum Einheitlichen Kaufrecht (München 1976), Art. 97 Rz 55.

19. S. 2-509 (1 a).

20. Cif; C & F.

21. Cf. H. Dölle and K. Neumayer, supra n. 18, at Art. 97 Rz 55.

22. C. Angelici, supra n. 17, at p. 228.

23. F. Eisemann and J. Ramberg, Die Incoterms heute und morgen (Wien 1980); J. Ramberg, "Incoterms 1980," in Horn and Schmitthoff (eds.), supra n. 8a, at pp. 137-151.

24. For a discussion of this problem see B.von Hoffmann, "Zur Auslegung von Formularbedingungen des internationalen Handelsverkehrs," AWD (1970) pp. 247-253.

25. Pro: Y. Loussouarn and J.-D.Bredin, Droit du Commerce international (Paris 1969) p. 676. Also the German Federal Court construed the FOB clause in conformity with INCOTERMS even when the contract did not contain an express reference to those rules (BGH, 18.6.1975. RIW/AWD (1975) p. 578); B. von Hoffmann, supra n. 24, at p. 252; F. Eisemann and J. Ramberg, supra n. 23, at p. 34 et seq.; contra: H.-J.Mertens and E. Rehbinder, Internationales Kaufrecht (Frankfurt/M. 1975), Art. 9 Rz 42; H. Dölle and W. Junge, supra n. 18, at Art. 9 Rz 18 expressly reserve the future development of INCOTERMS towards an international trade usage.

26. In particular the Secretariat of UNCITRAL makes specific reference to INCOTERMS for the interpretation of trade terms used in contracts, in its commentary to the UNCITRAL Draft of March

14, 1979 (A/Conf. 97-5) pp. 82, 198.

27. J. Ramberg, supra n. 23, at p. 151.

28. F. Eisemann and J. Ramberg, supra n. 23, at p. 25 et seq.

29. Cf. Szasz, A Uniform Law on International Sales of Goods -- The CMEA General Conditions (Budapest 1976); J. Jakubowski, CMEA General Conditions of Contract," in Horn and Schmitthoff, supra n. 23, at pp. 153-157.

30. Cf. H. Cornil, "The ECE General Conditions of Sale," 3 JWTL (1969) pp. 390-412.

31. Reprinted in K. Zweigert and J. Kropholler, Sources of International Uniform Law I (Leiden 1971) p. 90; cf. L. Goffin, "Les conditions générales de vente à l'exportation de biens déquipement" 1 D.P.C.I. (1975) pp. 215-224.

32. Reprinted in K. Zweigert and J. Kropholler, supra n. 31, at pp. 149-153.

33. UN/ECE General Conditions of Sale. For Fresh Fruit and Vegetables Including Citrus Fruit (1979) ECE/AGRi/40.

34. Remarkably enough, the Convention does not specifically mention the obligation to deliver goods at the buyer's place. Such contracts are not infrequent in Continental Europe. Cf. P. Schlechtriem, supra n. 15, at pp. 6-10.

35. H. Dölle and K. Neumayer, supra n. 18, at Art. 97 Rz 15.

36. Ibid. Art. 97 Rz 15 reproduces the discussions in detail.

37. Ibid., at Art. 97 Rz 15 (para. 2); P. Schlechtriem, Einheitliches UN-Kaufrecht (Tübingen 1981) p. 82.

38. J. Honnold, supra n. 1, at p. 368.

39. Cf. L. de Vries, "The Passing of Risk in International Sales under the Vienna Sales Convention as compared with Traditional Trade Terms," 17 European Transport Law (1982) p.504:

"for it is ancient usage, indeed, that a particular and (more or less) strict rule as regards
passing of risk as implied in each trade term
cannot -- once agreed upon -- be made invalid...
made by changing subsequently the modalities of
taking over..."

40. Ibid., p. 503.

41. Ibid., p. 504.

42. H. Grossmann and D. Doerth, supra n. 12, at
p. 257 s.

43. H. Dölle and K. Neumayer, supra n. 18, at
Art. 96 Rz 16.

44. E. Rabel, Das Recht des Warenkaufs, vol. 2
(Berlin/Tübingen 1958) p. 335.

45. Cf. the references in Dölle and Neumayer,
supra n. 18, at Art. 99 Rz 7.

46. Report of the United Nations Commission on
International Trade Law on the Works of its 10th
Session (Vienna, 23 May - 17 June 1977) (A/32/17)
UNCITRAL Yearbook VIII (Vienna 1977) p. 63: "the
representative of the Philippines expressed a
reservation... in that the provisions of that
paragraph were not consistent with logic. It was
stated that it was inconceivable that the buyer
should bear the risk of loss or damage to the
goods prior to the time that the contract was
concluded. Also the view had been expressed in
the committee that if the paragraph accorded with
international commercial practice, that practice
was one of the developed world. UNCITRAL should
take into account that the Resolutions of the
General Assembly which laid down the framework of
a new international economic order. If UNCITRAL
wished to carry out its mandate to make ULIS more
acceptable to countries of widely different economic and social backgrounds it should not ignore
these General Assembly Resolutions." Cf. the
position of the representative of Finland, ibid.,

stressing the arguments in favour of the retroactive passing of risk.

47. P. Schlechtriem, <u>supra</u> n. 37, at p. 82, N. 366.

48. J. Honnold, <u>supra</u> n. 1, at p. 372; P. Schlechtriem, <u>supra</u> n. 37, at p. 82; the same position already had been advocated by Neumayer concerning Art. 99 of the Hague Sales Law. Cf. H. Dölle and K. Neumayer, <u>supra</u> n. 18, at Art. 99, 11, 13.

49. Cf. P. Schlechtriem, <u>supra</u> n. 37, at p. 83.

50. Cf. <u>supra</u> n. 27 where some reservations on the actual worldwide use of INCOTERMS are noted.

51. Cf. J. Basedow, "Die Incoterms and der Container oder wie man kodifizierte Usances reformiert," 43 <u>RabelsZ</u> (1978) pp. 116-146 (144-144).

52. K. Grönfors, "Container Bills of Lading -- A New Trend in Documentation," in <u>Festschrift Schmitthoff</u> (Frankfurt/M. 1974) pp. 187-205. N.R. McGilchrist, "In Perspective -- ICC rules for a Combined Transport Document," 1 <u>Lloyds Mar. Comm.L.Q.</u> (1974) pp. 25-28; W.D. Mapp, "Documentary Problems of Intermodal Transport," 12 <u>JWTL</u> (1978) pp. 514-547). Incoterms 1980 did not yet take into account these new practices, cf. J. Ramberg, <u>supra</u> n. 23, at p. 147.

53. J. Honnold, <u>supra</u> n. 8a, at p. 171.

54. It should be noted that the theoretical analysis of that model can draw benefit from R.A. Posner, <u>Economic Analysis of Law</u> 2nd ed. (Boston/ Toronto 1977) pp. 74-79.

CHAPTER NINE

GENERAL PRINCIPLES
OF EUROPEAN CONTRACT LAW

ULRICH DROBNIG
Professor of Law, Hamburg

This contribution does not directly deal with the international sale of goods, the central theme of this book. Specifically, it does not deal with those "general principles on which it [the Vienna Sales Convention] is based"; these general principles of the Convention are to serve as a yardstick for solving those matters which, though governed by the Convention, are not expressly settled in it.[1]

What, then, **is** the relevance of general principles of contract law, generally speaking and for the international sale of goods in particular?

I. THE SIGNIFICANCE OF GENERAL PRINCIPLES OF CONTRACT LAW

1. General principles of law in general

The distinction between specific legal provisions and general principles of law is probably as old as legislation. It is bound up with such basic divisions as the Roman distinction between leges and jus, or the general distinction between law and justice. The Vienna Sales Convention, Art. 7(2), also uses this division. This is not the place to go into the historical or theoretical details of this general distinction.[2]

Nor shall we deal here with the status and significance of general principles of law in individual legal systems, such as "socialist legality" in the Socialist countries of Eastern Europe[3], the "principles of Islamic law" in certain Islamic countries[4], or "good faith and fair dealing" in Western legal systems[5].

It is worth noting that "general principles of law" are particularly relevant for supranational and international legal systems. The most prominent example is furnished by public international law; one of its sources are the "general principles of law recognized by civilized nations";[6] in the absence of express provisions in treaties this source is of major practical significance. Important illustrations on the supranational level are to be found in the law of the European Communities. The Treaty instituting the European Economic Community provides in Art. 215(2) that the tort liability of the Community must be determined by the "general principles of law of the member states"; the European Court of Justice has had frequent occasion to develop general principles in this area of law. Without any statutory basis at all, this Court has also attempted to introduce a system of basic rights for the citizens of the Community. Here again, the court has strived to develop general rules based upon the systems of fundamental rights of citizens recognized in the member states of the Community.[7]

Our concerns here will be more specific: What is the relevance of general principles of contract law, first, for the unification of law, and second, for the application of law?

2. General principles of contract law and the unification of aspects of contract law

The unification of law proceeds spontaneously, without any overall planning, by very different sponsors and at various political levels. Efforts have concentrated so far on certain types of contracts, especially in the field of transportation: The contract for international carriage by rail has been unified for Western Europe, on the one hand, and for Eastern Europe, on the other hand.[8] The contract for the international carriage of goods by road is regulated in another instrument, which has been elaborated by another sponsor.[9] The Warsaw Convention of 1929 with subsequent amendments governs international air transportation and is "administered" by the International Civil Aviation Organization.[10] Various aspects of contracts for international maritime transport are regulated by a number of instruments, most of which have been elaborated by the International Maritime Committee, some recent ones by the Inter-Governmental Maritime (Consultative) Organization (IMCO, now IMO), a body attached to the United Nations.[11]

In the field of sales, we have the truly universal effort of the Convention for the International Sale of Goods of 1980 (CISG), the potentially universal Uniform Law of Sales of 1964 (ULIS) and, at the regional level, the "General Conditions for Deliveries of Goods" of the member countries of the Council for Mutual Economic Aid (CMEA or Comecon) of 1958, with subsequent revisions.[12]

The record of individual sponsors is not better. The Council for Mutual Economic Aid, where one may expect the highest degree of planning, has regulated four types of contracts: for deliv-

ery of goods, i.e., sales; for installation of
plant and machinery; for repair of machinery,
tools and equipment; and for cooperation and
specialisation of production.[13] On the other
hand, the European Communities are in the course
of elaborating harmonised rules on insurance
contracts, on door-to-door contracts and on certain credit transactions of consumers,[14] inter
alia.

What we see at the universal level and at the
regional level is rather unsatisfactory: It is a
conglomerate of uniform instruments governing a
few individual types of contracts; and this conglomerate is more often than not quite inco-
herent. Occasionally it consists only of fragments, sometimes regulating no more than individual contract clauses, such as penalty clauses[15],
or a specific form of conclusion of a contract,
such as door-to-door contracts.

None of these unified rules on certain types
of contracts or aspects of contracting can and
does offer exhaustive rules on contracts. They
usually do not cover the problems of substantive
validity, of contracting through agents, of as-
signment, of special aspects of performance, etc.
All uniform rules are fragments, some more and
most less complete; but nowhere is there a complete code of contracts.

It is a function of general principles of
contract law to fill the gaps existing within the
various individual pieces of unified contract
law. This function is particularly important for
the larger authorities drafting uniform legislation, such as regional organisations. They also
require a guideline for coordinating future
drafting efforts.

3. General principles of contract law as <u>lex contractus</u>

General principles of contract law may also serve directly as a source of law. This occurs when the parties agree upon them as governing their contract[16].

It is true, such choice-of-law clauses are not very frequent; especially, they hardly ever occur between private parties. By contrast, such clauses sometimes do occur in major agreements between a state (or a state enterprise) and a foreign enterprise, often a multinational company. Thus, a number of concession agreements for the exploration and exploitation of oil resources in Arab-speaking countries contain a choice-of-law clause stipulating that the agreement be subject to, and governed by, the "general principles of law" or "the principles of law normally recognised by civilised nations in general".[17]

It must be noted, however, that the validity of a choice-of-law clause referring to "general principles of law" is not entirely beyond doubt. There are writers who would regard such clauses as invalid because their contents are too vague[18]. On the other hand, several arbitrators[19] and writers[20] have confirmed the validity of such clauses, at least for agreements between a state and a foreign enterprise.

I should mention one further function of general principles of contract law, a pedagogical one: General principles, by virtue of their being abstracted from details, may be of considerable assistance for the student. They help to give a bird's-eye view of a complex area of law; and contract law, in many respects, is quite complex since it is designed to cope with a vast number of extremely different transactions.

II. THE SOURCE OF GENERAL PRINCIPLES OF EUROPEAN CONTRACT LAW

It is almost of the essence of "general principles of law" that they are not laid down by any legislative action (supra I 1). They are nowhere readily formulated -- rather they have to be elaborated.

The process of elaborating general principles of contract law is the same as that employed to elaborate any other general principles of law: It is by a comparison of national systems of contract law.[21]

The general principles of contract law which I shall discuss here are qualified as being "European". This requires some explanation. I shall base my discussion primarily on some of the major West and Central European systems of contract law, especially English, French and German. I am less familiar with the East European legal systems; they will, therefore, be dealt with only marginally. Moreover, for the sake of comparison, my attention will focus on the foreign trade contracts of the Socialist countries; both the economic function and the legal regulations of this particular type of contract appear to be closest to the general West European type of commercial contract.

We shall shortly explain the underlying economic reason (infra III). The other two types, i.e., civil law contracts with citizens and between citizens and especially plan contracts are more peculiar to the special conditions of the East European countries. They are therefore less suited to serve as bases for the elaboration of general principles of European contract law.

III. FREEDOM OF CONTRACT

The first and supreme principle of European contract law is the freedom of the parties to contract. The freedom of contract has three distinct aspects: Each party is free to decide whether it wishes to contract at all; with whom it wishes to contract; and on which terms it is willing to contract.

Freedom of contract in its three aspects is the basic principle of European contract law because it expresses on the legal level the basic economic system, namely that of the market economy. The economic system of the market economy rests on the assumption that every citizen is best qualified to determine for himself whether he needs supplies or wishes to sell, who will best serve his needs and on what conditions. If all these three decisions are to be made by every individual for himself, he must be granted freedom of contract as to whether at all, with whom and on what terms he wishes to contract.

The economic rules of the market economy govern the foreign trade even of the Socialist countries; this is why it is justified to include the regime for foreign trade contracts of the Socialist countries among the bases of comparison from which general principles of European contract law can be drawn (supra II).

The context between freedom of contract and a system of market economy is best proved by contrasting these twin principles with the opposing two principles, a planned economy with planned contracts. In the so-called economic contracts of the Socialist countries the supreme principle is the plan. The dominating role of the plan, though, is mitigated in current practice by systems of moderate planning which leave considera-

ble autonomy to the state enterprises and therefore also some degree of freedom of contract.

Although a basic principle, freedom of contract as such is rarely spelt out in legislation.
On the level of uniform law, freedom of contract
is usually expressed only in provisions allowing
the parties to exclude the uniform law or to
derogate from any of its provisions.[22]

IV. CONCLUSION OF CONTRACT

Few general principles are more firmly established than the basic rules on the formation of a
contract. The well-known mechanism of offer and
acceptance is recognised everywhere in Europe: A
contract is concluded if one party's offer is
accepted by the other party.

A very detailed, broad and careful comparative
study has been devoted to this subject; it has
elaborated 26 general rules on individual aspects
of the formation of contracts.[23]

The existing uniform rules on international
sales of goods contain, or are supplemented by,
uniform rules on the formation of such sales
contracts. All of these uniform rules are also
based upon the idea of offer and acceptance.[24]

There is thus an exceptionally broad area of
agreement as to the principles governing the
formation of a contract. For present purposes,
this conclusion must suffice. It may merely be
noted in passing that the general principles on
the formation of a contract by offer and acceptance are not free from doubt in certain marginal
situations, for instance, if one party contracts
under standard conditions.

V. VALIDITY OF CONTRACT

In the related field of validity of contracts, the situation is quite different. The difficulties in this area are due in part to the legal complexities and to divergent social policies, in part also to conceptual complications. Let me try to clarify at least the basic issues although, in many respects, agreement on the solutions is not yet in sight.

The problems of validity of contract may be subdivided into three separate issues: first, the binding effect of contractual promises; second, defects of consent; and third, illegality and immorality. I shall briefly comment on each of these three issues.

1. The binding effect of contractual promises[25]

In the legal systems of the world one may find two approaches with respect to the binding effect of contractual promises: Some countries use internal criteria in order to determine the binding nature of contractual promises, whereas other countries take into account external factors.

The first group comprises the German-speaking, the Scandinavian and probably also the East European countries. Here a contractual promise is binding on the promisor, provided only it is intended by him to be legally binding. Whether the latter intention is present, is to be ascertained by interpretation of the promise. Unilateral legal acts, such as an offer to conclude a contract, are therefore, as a rule, binding upon the author. Sometimes, however, the law interferes by imposing certain conditions, especially a form requirement, e.g., for the promise to make a gift.

By contrast, in many other countries the binding nature of a contractual promise depends upon
the presence of an external factor called **cause**
in the Romanic world and "consideration" in the
Anglo-American orbit. Although the details vary
considerably, in the present context[26] the contents and the functions of **cause** and "consideration" can be reduced to the following rule: A
contractual promise is binding if there is a
counterperformance by the other party or the
promise of such a counterperformance.

Consequently, it is certain that at least a
bilateral contract imposing obligations on each
party, such as a sales contract, is valid.

On the other hand, unilateral promises, such
as an offer or a modification of a sales contract
affecting the obligations of only one of the
parties are, as a rule, not binding. Consequently, provisions like Art. 16(2) and Art. 29(1)
CISG which recognise the irrevocability of an
offer in certain circumstances and the power of
the parties to modify a contract by "the mere
agreement of the parties" are deviations from the
common law of the anglophone and the francophone
countries.

The general principle which can be formulated
as to the binding character of a contractual
promise is narrow in theory although broad as to
its practical implications. It reads: Contractual
promises in a contract providing for mutual obligations of both parties are binding.

2. Defects of consent[27]

The validity of contracts may also become
doubtful by the presence of defects of consent,
such as mistake, fraud or duress.

In the recent past, UNIDROIT in Rome, one of
the major agencies for the academic preparation
of a broad unification of private law, has
launched some efforts of comparative analysis in
this field. These comparative efforts first resulted in a draft on uniform rules relating to
the substantive validity of international sales
contracts.[28] After UNCITRAL decided not to include these rules in its proposals for a new
uniform sales law, UNIDROIT reconsidered and has
generalised these rules so as to make them applicable to international contracts of any type.[29]

The general principles elaborated in this
field deal with the grounds, the procedure and
the effects of avoidance. Suffice it to say here
that the principles strive to restrict the
grounds for avoidance by admitting avoidance only
if the other contracting party knew or ought to
have known of the defect, or if it has caused the
defect of consent.

It should be mentioned that the term "avoidance" in this context has a meaning which differs
from the meaning in which CISG uses the same term
in various provisions.[30] In the context of defects of consent, "avoidance" means according to
all European legal systems that a contract becomes void ex tunc. In the context of the uniform
sales laws "avoidance", by contrast, means that a
contract is terminated ex nunc. This confusion of
terms is quite unfortunate; it is due to the fact
that different sponsors have elaborated the various texts; and it illustrates at the same time
the need of general principles as an instrument
for discovering inconsistencies between various
international instruments.

3. Illegality and immorality

Before dealing with the substance, a systematic observation is in order. Most legal systems deal with illegal and immoral contracts <u>tel</u> <u>quel</u>, i.e., under the heads of illegality and immorality.

Not so the Romanic countries. There, the peculiar institution of **cause** fulfills also the function of invalidating illegal and immoral contracts.

The method by which this is achieved is well demonstrated by French law. Code civil Art. 1108 mentions four requirements for a valid contract, the fourth being "Une cause licite dans l'obligation". And Art. 1133 then provides that

> La cause est illicite, quand elle est
> prohibée par la loi, quand elle est
> contraire aux bonnes moeurs ou à l'or-
> dre public.

Thus, a contract with an illegal or immoral **cause** is treated, in effect, in the same way as an illegal or immoral contract.

As to substance, two issues arise: First, **when** is a contract illegal or immoral? And second, what is the **effect** of an illegal or immoral contract? It will be obvious that in this area generalisations are impossible. Prohibitions express moral convictions or social policies. It will be very difficult to find a common denominator for these basic values. This is true even within a regional association like the European Community -- except the provisions enacted by this Community itself which are binding upon all the member states.

VI. BREACH OF CONTRACT IN GENERAL

After having dealt with three positive aspects of contracting, namely freedom, conclusion and validity of contract, I shall now devote several sections to breach of contract; first to the concept of breach of contract and then to its consequences.

1. The Concept

Is breach of contract a unitary institution or is it merely a name which comprises several, but distinct cases of violating a contractual obligation?

A brief survey reveals that breach of contract as a unitary institution of contract law is not familiar to all legal systems. The concept as such is derived from Anglo-American law. But a unitary approach is also adopted in the Romanic legal systems; there it is called non-performance.

By contrast, German law and some legal systems inspired by it (such as Austrian and Swiss law) do not use a unitary approach. Instead they distinguish between the various causes of breach, especially between impossibility of performance, delay, and all other instances of breach; in addition, following Roman traditions, defects of individual goods are dealt with on a special basis. This sytem of splitting up breach of contract into several more or less separate institutions has proved to be quite inadequate in many respects because it gives rise to difficult problems of delimitation.

Under the impact of comparative law and the unification of sales law there is now a strong tendency in German academic writings to adopt the

unitary approach. Indeed, both the Uniform Sales
Law and the Vienna Convention use the basic and
unitary concept of "breach of contract".[31] The
unity of the concept of breach of contract may
therefore now be regarded as widely, although not
yet generally accepted.

2. Responsibility for Breach

In theory, two radically different systems
confront each other: The Anglo-American principle
of strict liability for any breach of contract,
on the one hand, and the Continental principle
that breach of contract presupposes responsibility of the non-performing party, on the other
hand.

In practice, however, the opposition between
these two basic approaches is considerably mitigated by concessions of both sides: Anglo-
American law recognises certain instances where
the non-performing party, although he is strictly
liable on princple, is nevertheless absolved from
liability for a breach of contract. This is primarily achieved by implying in the contract
limits of the non-performing party's contractual
guarantee.

Nor do the Continental legal systems pursue
their basic idea of requiring the non-performing
party's fault in all cases. Important exceptions
are the non-performing party's strict liability
if he owes a generic performance (rather than a
species) and the strict guarantee for defects of
goods sold. Another important mitigation of the
basic principle are (rebuttable) presumptions of
responsibility for breach of contract.

Also the East European Socialist countries
follow in essence the Continental approach. Penalty clauses which are obligatory for many in-

stances of breach of contract oblige the non-
performing party to pay by virtue of such non-
performance alone.[32]

On the other hand, damages only fall due if
the non-performing party is responsible for the
non-performance; but this responsibility is presumed.[33]

The uniform laws for sales essentially follow
the Anglo-American theory of strict liability for
breach of contract. The seller or the buyer is
liable for breach of contract if he has not
performed any of his contractual obligations,
unless he proves that there was a ground for
exemption from liability. A non-performing party
is exempted from liability if the failure to
perform was due to an impediment beyond his control that he could not be expected to have taken
into account at the time of contracting or to
have avoided or to have overcome its consequences.[34] The limit of contractual liability
thus coincides with _force_ _majeure_.[35]

Although there is a high degree of convergence
in the direction pointed to by the uniform rules
on sales, the existing divergencies between the
different basic approaches are still considerable. It is not yet possible to formulate a general principle as to the non-performing party's
liability for a breach of contract.

VII. ENFORCED PERFORMANCE

1.   Performance _in_ _natura_

If a party does not perform a contract although performance is possible, the question
arises whether the other party may claim performance.

Here again the world is divided between Anglo-

American law, on the one hand, and the Continental legal systems, on the other hand.

Under Anglo-American common law, there is no
claim for specific performance. However, equity
has intervened and grants specific performance if
the normal sanction of damages would be inadequate. This is so, e.g., if the goods sold are
unique. The economic background of these rules is
that the aggrieved party can ordinarily be expected to go into the market, acquire a substitute performance and liquidate the damages which
he has sustained.

On the Continent, the sanctity of contract is
regarded as implying the opposite principle,
namely the claim for performance. Also the East
European Socialist countries embrace the principle of "real performance". However, the economic
reasons for this identity of principles differ;
consequently, also the application in practice of
the principle is quite divergent.

In the market-economy countries, an aggrieved
party, especially in commercial relations, usually will not bother with bringing a claim for
performance, waiting to obtain judgment and then
attempting to levy execution. This would be much
too expensive in terms of time, effort and money.
Rather, the aggrieved party will procure a substitute performance and then claim damages. In
practice he thus will act like his brother in
England or the United States. By contrast, the
socialist principle of "real performance" is
taken seriously in the Eastern European countries
with strictly planned economies. For this, there
are both political and economic reasons: Since in
a planned economy contracts serve to implement
plans, both the aggrieved party and the non-
performing party would deviate from their planned
tasks if the one does not perform and the other

does not insist on performance. Moreover, there
is usually no functioning market at which the
aggrieved party can procure a substitute performance.

In view of these economic factors and the
practice which has developed as a result of them,
a true dichotomy exists between market-economy
countries, on the one hand, and planned-economy
countries, on the other hand.

And yet, even the market-economy countries are
still heavily influenced by the impact of their
diverging basic approaches. This impact is so
strong that the two uniform sales laws were unable to achieve harmony on this point. While both
laws grant claims for enforced performance,[36]
they reserve each Contracting State the power to
refuse to enforce such a claim where enforced
performance would be contrary to the lex fori.[37]

This reservation in favour of the lex fori
must be regretted. An intensified comparative
effort shows that it is well possible to work out
a rule which covers all cases in which Anglo-
American law refuses specific performance and
where in the Continental market-economy countries
the aggrieved party is not used to insist on
performance in natura. This general principle
provides:

1. Payment of **money** can always be demanded;
2. Any **other performance** may also be demanded,
   except where
   a) there is factual or legal impossibility;
   b) performance would involve the non-perform-
      ing party in unreasonable effort or ex-
      pense;
   c) the performance consists of services or
      work of a personal character;
   d) the aggrieved party may reasonably obtain
      performance elsewhere; or

e) the aggrieved party does not require performance within a reasonable time after he
knows or ought to know about the non-performance.

This general principle as to enforced performance covers, however, only market-economy countries; it is not relevant for Socialist countries
with a strict planning regime. However, arbitration practice of the CMEA countries shows that at
least in foreign trade the principle of real
performance plays a minor role.[38]

2. Judicial penalties

Judicial penalties, like contractual penalty
clauses, serve to reinforce a judicial order for
performance. The penalty is to induce performance.

However, the European countries are divided as
to the admissibility of a judicial penalty. In
England, compliance with a decree of specific
performance, as of any other decree in equity,
can be sanctioned by a penalty for contempt of
court. French courts have developed the as-
treinte, which was sanctioned by the legislator
in 1972. The Benelux-countries have concluded a
convention providing for the judicial penalty.[39]
In England, the penalty is paid to the state
treasury, whereas in the other countries it goes
to the aggrieved party. In any case, it is not a
kind of liquidated damages but is awarded in
addition to the damages.

Germany and other West European countries do
not accept a judicial penalty or only in very
narrow limits. This aversion is based upon its
penal character or, on payment to the aggrieved
party, because the latter is then unduly en-
riched.

In view of this controversial situation there is obviously no general principle with respect to judicial penalties as a means of securing performance of a contract.

VIII. DAMAGES

1. General function

The place and function of damages for breach of contract is complementary to the place and function of a claim for enforcing performance. Where the latter claim is the primary remedy, as in the Continental market-economy countries (see _supra_ VII 1), a claim for damages can only be of secondary importance. Where, on the other hand, a claim for specific performance is, in principle, excluded -- as in the Anglo-American orbit -- damages are the primary remedy.

Treitel has well illustrated the difference between the two approaches: Under English common law an employee who is wrongfully dismissed by his employer cannot sue for the agreed remuneration but only for damages. These consist of the agreed remuneration. Continental laws, by contrast, would award the same sum, but as the agreed remuneration.[40] While the practical result will often be the same, the underlying theories are quite different.

In view of the general principle as to enforced performance at which we have arrived for the market-economy countries (_supra_ VII 1), we can also answer the question as to the place and function of damages for breach of contract. Since an aggrieved party can primarily claim performance _in_ _natura_, damages are a secondary remedy. However, practically speaking, in view of the long catalogue of exceptions to the principle of

enforced performance, an aggrieved party will
more often take recourse to damages than to specific performance. Thus, although a secondary
remedy, damages will in effect be of great practical importance.

2. Damages as compensation for loss

In most legal systems it will be regarded as a
truism to say that damages should compensate the
loss of the aggrieved party -- neither more nor
less. However, neither of these two apparently
obvious rules is accepted everywhere.

a) Damages exceeding the loss

The rule that damages should not exceed the
loss, while accepted by most legal systems is not
followed by all. Anglo-American law sometimes
awards damages beyond the aggrieved party's loss,
especially nominal damages -- a symbolic compensation even if the aggrieved party has not suffered any loss; and sometimes multiple damages --
in order to coerce the non-performing party to
perform.[41]
However, it would seem that these peculiarities of Anglo-American law are on the retreat. In
particular, nominal damages were popular as a
substitute for a declaratory action which formerly had not been, but now is being admitted.

b) Limits of recovery derived from the conditions of the non-performing party

While damages, generally speaking, may not
surpass the aggrieved party's loss, more often
they do not even reach it. Here, as elsewhere in
most legal systems, the non-performing party

often is given special consideration. The limits
of recovery are in part derived from the conditions of the non-performing party and in part
from circumstances of the aggrieved party.

Most legal systems limit damages out of consideration for the non-performing party, and they
do so by a great variety of techniques: By requiring that the non-performing party was at
fault; or that he foresaw or could have foreseen
the loss; or that he "adequately" caused the
loss. In this context it is impossible to explain
and compare all of these various approaches towards the limiting of damages; this has been done
elsewhere.[42]

As is well known, the uniform sales laws have
adopted the Anglo-American foreseeability test.[43]

By contrast, the CMEA General Conditions for
Deliveries combine the requirements of a causal
connection and of fault on the part of the non-
performing party.[44]

In view of the great diversity of approaches
it is not yet possible to formulate a general
principle as to the limits of recovery of damages
derived from the conditions of the non-performing
party.

c) Limits of recovery derived from the conditions of the aggrieved party

We shall now turn to those limitations of
recovery which are derived from the conditions of
the aggrieved party.

In this respect, two types of loss clearly
stand out: The first is loss suffered by the
aggrieved party which results from his own unreasonable behaviour or his failure to take reasonable steps to mitigate his loss. The second ground
for limiting recovery is the presence of savings

or gains which result from the breach of contract.

These two heads of limiting the aggrieved
party's loss and therefore of his compensation
seem to be very widely recognised. The aggrieved
party's burden of mitigating the loss is also
expressly spelt out in the uniform sales laws.[45]

3. Interest

For the very frequent case of delay in payment
of money, most legal systems have fixed as damages a lump sum called statutory interest. England is a lonely exception; but this has been
criticised and the English Law Commission has
proposed to introduce a statutory interest on
contractual obligations to pay money. The duty to
pay interest may therefore be regarded as a general principle.

Details, however, differ, especially the computation of the rate of interest. Also the question whether the creditor may claim additional
damage is answered differently, probably because
of the different rates of interest.

IX. TERMINATION OF THE CONTRACT

The third major remedy of the aggrieved party
-- apart from enforced performance and damages --
is termination of the contract. For the reason
mentioned earlier I avoid using the term "avoidance" here, thus deviating from the terminology
of the uniform sales laws (supra V 2). In some
situations termination will be the only effective
remedy, e.g., when the non-performing party is
insolvent and can neither perform his obligations
nor pay damages.

1. Prerequisite

Today most legal systems agree in effect on the most important condition for allowing the aggrieved party to terminate the contract: The non-performance complained of must be of a serious nature. This criterion is expressed quite differently: English law requires breach of a condition and not of a mere warranty; in France where the contract, unless otherwise provided by the parties, can only be dissolved by judicial decision, the judge will not pronounce the dissolution unless there is a "grave reason"; in Germany, a main obligation of the contract, and not merely an incidental one, must be violated. The uniform sales laws express the same idea by distinguishing "fundamental" and other breaches of contract; only the former empower the aggrieved party to terminate the sales contract.[46]

CISG Art. 25 defines a fundamental breach of contract as follows:

> ...it results in such detriment to the other party as substantially to deprive him of what he is entitled to expect under the contract, unless the party in breach did not foresee and a reasonable person of the same kind in the same circumstances would not have foreseen such a result.

The difficulties of applying such a definition can fortunately be remedied to some degree by the German _Nachfrist_ procedure: The aggrieved party may fix an additional period of time of reasonable length for performance; upon its expiry the aggrieved party may terminate.[47]

The expiry of the additional period of time fixed by the aggrieved party thus converts any breach into a fundamental breach.

2. Consequences

Termination puts an end to the contract. The parties have to return what they had already received.

One consequence of termination deserves to be mentioned expressly: In most countries, despite his termination of the contract, the aggrieved party is entitled to ask for any damages which may be due. This rule has also been adopted in the uniform sales laws.[48]

However, German law regards the effect of termination as being so absolute as to withdraw the basis for claiming damages for breach of contract, namely the contract. Obviously, this dogmatic solution is not satisfactory in practice.

Here again, as in so many other instances, comparison with the laws and experiences of other countries helps one to obtain a critical view of his own law and suggestions for its improvement.

NOTES

1. Art. 7(2) CISG. See P. Volken, infra chapter two, p. 42.

2. For a recent historical and comparative survey cf. R. David, "Sources of law," International Encyclopedia of Comparative Law (I.E.C.L) vol.II ch. 3 (1984) s. 19-38.

3. Cf. I. Szabo, "The Socialist Conception of Law," I.E.C.L. vol. II ch. 1 (1975) s. 98-105.

4. Cf. Art. 1(2) Civil Code of Libya.

5. Cf., e.g., the overwhelming role of Treu und Glauben in German law.

6. Cf. Art. 38(1)(c) of the statute of the International Court of Justice.

7. D. Feger, Die Grundrechte im Recht der Europäischen Gemeinschaften (1984); M. Dauses, "La protection des droits fondamentaux dans l'ordre juridique communautaire," 20 Rev. trim. dr. eur. (1984) pp. 401-424; P. Pescatore, "The context and significance of fundamental rights in the law of the European Communities," 2 Human Rights L.J. (1981) pp. 295-308.

8. Convention relative aux transports internationaux ferroviaires (COTIF) de 1980, Zeitschrift für den internationalen Eisenbahnverkehr (1984) p. 33.
CMEA: Accord concernant le transport international des marchandises par chemin de fer (SMGS) de 1966, in K. Zweigert and J. Kropholler, eds., Sources of International Uniform Law/Sources du Droit uniforme international/Quellen des internationalen Einheitsrechts vol. II (1972) F 291; Agreement concerning International Passenger Traffic (SMPS) of 1966, in K. Zweigert and J. Kropholler, E 293.

9. Convention on the Contract for the International Carriage of Goods by Road (CMR) of 1956, in K. Zweigert and J. Kropholler II, supra n. 8 at E 280.

10. Convention for the Unification of Certain Rules Relating to International Carriage by Air of 1929, in K. Zweigert and J. Kropholler II, supra n. 8 at E 248.

11. F. Berlingieri, "Il comité maritime international, le sue origine, la sua storia ed il suo futuro," 81 Dir. mar. (1979) p. 148 et seq.; A. Xerri, "The Contribution of the Comité Maritime International to the Movement for the Unification of Maritime Law," Rev.dr.unif. (1977) II 87; S. Mankabady, ed., The International Maritime Organization (1984).

12. For CISG see, e.g., J. Honnold, Uniform Law

for International Sales under the 1980 United
Nations Convention (Boston 1982).
For ULIS cf. K. Zweigert and J. Kropholler I,
supra n. 8, at E 137.
For the CMEA General Conditions for Deliveries of
Goods of 1968, cf. ibid. at E 155.
13. For delivery of goods, cf. supra n. 12; for
the General Conditions of Installation... related
to the Mutual Delivery of Machinery and Plant of
1962, cf. K. Zweigert and J. Kropholler I, supra
n. 8, at E 153; for the General Conditions of
Service for Machinery, Plant and Other Products
of 1962, cf. ibid. at E 154; for the General
Conditions on Specialisation and Cooperation in
Production of 1979, cf. Gesetzblatt der Deutschen
Demokratischen Republik 1979 II 50.
14. For the (amended) proposal of a Directive on
door-to-door contracts of 1978, see O.J.E.C.
(1978) no. C 127 at p. 6.
For the (amended) proposal of a Directive on
Consumer Credit of 1984, see O.J.E.C. (1984) no.
C 183 at p. 4.
15. Convention Benelux relative à la clause
pénale (1973).
16. For details and references see, e.g., R.
Schlesinger and H.-G. Gündisch, "Allgemeine
Rechtsgrundsätze als Sachnormen im Schiedsge-
richtsverfahren," RabelsZ (1964) p. 5 with ample
reference.
17. E.g., Art. XXIII (K) of the Petroleum Concession Agreement between the Arab Republic of Egypt
and several oil companies of 1975, in P. Fischer,
A Collection of International Concessions and Related Instruments vol. I (1981) pp. 191, 294;
Art. 7 (I) of the Supplemental Agreement Between
the Government of Kuwait and BP (Kuwait) Ltd. ...
of 1966: ibid. II (1982) pp. 192, 199. For a
recent instructive survey of contractual clauses

see P. Weil, "Principles généraux du droit et contrats d'Etat," <u>Le</u> <u>droit</u> <u>des</u> <u>relations</u> <u>écono-</u> <u>miques</u> <u>internationales.</u> Etudes <u>Goldman</u> (Paris 1983) pp. 389-392.

18. F.A. Mann, "The Proper Law of Contracts Concluded by International Persons," 35 <u>Brit.Yb.</u> <u>Int.L.</u> (1959) pp. 44,45; J. Verhoeven, "Droit international des contrats et droit des gens," 14 <u>Revue</u> <u>belge</u> <u>dr.int.</u> (1978/1979) p. 218; P. Weil, <u>supra</u> n. 17, at pp. 404-405, 410; W. Wengler, "Les principes généraux du droit en tant que loi du contrat," 71 <u>Rev.crit.dr.i.p.</u> (1982) pp. 484-490.

19. B.P. v. Libya (1973), 53 <u>I.L.R.</u> (1979) pp. 328-329 per Lagergren; Texaco v. Libya (1977), 53 <u>I.L.R.</u> pp. 452-454 per Dupuy; LIAMCO v. Libya (1977), 62 <u>I.L.R.</u> pp. 175-176 per Mahmassani. See also the instructive survey by P. Weil, <u>supra</u> n. 17, at pp. 392-397.

20. Art. 2 of the Resolution of the Institut de Droit international of 1979, cf. 58 II <u>Annuaire</u> (1980) p. 192; K.-H. Böckstiegel, <u>Der</u> <u>Staat</u> <u>als</u> <u>Vertragspartner</u> <u>ausländischer</u> <u>Privatunternehmen</u> (1971) pp. 110-119, 374; J.-F. Lalive, "Contrats entre états ou entreprises étatiques et personnes privées," 181 <u>Rec.</u> <u>des</u> <u>Cours</u> (1983 III) pp. 47-48, 103-104; Lord McNair, Q.C., "The General Principles of Law Recognized by Civilized Nations," 33 <u>Brit.Yb.</u> <u>Int.L.</u> (1957) pp. 7-10; H. Kipp, "Verträge zwischen staatlichen und nicht-staatlichen Partnern," 5 <u>Berichte</u> <u>der</u> <u>Deutschen</u> <u>Gesellschaft</u> <u>für</u> <u>Völkerrecht</u> (1964) pp. 182-188; K. Zweigert, "Verträge zwischen staatlichen und nichtstaatlichen Partnern" ibid. pp. 204-214; R. Schlesinger and H.-G. Gündisch, <u>supra</u> n. 16, at pp. 14, 29, 30-31, 38-44; M. Virally, "Un tiers droit? Réflexions théoriques," <u>Le</u> <u>droit</u> <u>des</u> <u>rela-</u> <u>tions</u> <u>économiques</u> <u>internationales.</u> Etudes <u>Goldman</u>

(Paris 1983) pp. 382-385.
21. W. Lorenz, "Rechtsvergleichung als Methode zur Konkretisierung der allgemeinen Grundsätze des Rechts," Juristen-Zeitung (1962) p. 269.
22. CISG Art. 6; cf. ULIS Art. 3. Cf. CMEA General Conditions for Deliveries, preamble para. 2 which permits contractual modifications under certain broad conditions.
23. R. Schlesinger, Formation of Contracts 2 vols. (1968).
24. CISG Articles 14-24; GMEA General Conditions for Deliveries § 1-4; ULFIS.
25. An excellent comparative discussion in K.Zweigert and H. Kötz, 2 An Introduction to Comparative Law (1977) p. 77 et seq.
26. We are not dealing here with the function of cause as a necessary element of a transfer of assets.
27. Cf. K. Zweigert and H. Kötz, supra n. 25, at p. 81 et seq.
28. I Rev.dr.unif. (1973) p. 60 et seq.
29. UNIDROIT Study L-Doc. 20 (1982).
30. CISG Articles 26, 49, 64, 81-84.
31. ULIS Articles 10, 26(1), 27(1), 28, 30(1), 32(1), 32(3) etc.; CISG Art. 25, title of sections III in chapters II and III, Articles 49(1)(a), 51(2) etc.
32. CMEA General Conditions for Deliveries § 67 B(2).
33. CMEA General Conditions for Deliveries § 67 D(1)(d), (3).
34. See especially CISG Art. 79(1); similarly ULIS Art. 74(1).
35. Cf. D. Tallon, "Réflexions comparatives," Les effets du contrat dans les pays du Marché Commun (1985) pp. 297 et seq., 302.

36. ULIS: Articles 24(1)(a), 26(1), 30(1), 41(1)(a), 42(1) etc. CISG: Articles 46, 51(1), 62.

37. ULIS: Art. 16 and Art. VII of the ULIS Convention; CISG: Art. 28.

38. See report on a conference of the presidents of the arbitration tribunals at the chambers of commerce of the member countries of the CMEA held in 1983, in 72 AW Recht im Aussenhandel (1984) pp. VII-VIII.

39. See supra n. 15.

40. G. Treitel, "Remedies for Breach of Contract," I.E.C.L. vol. VII ch. 16 (1976) s. 40.

41. Cf. Treitel, ibid. at s. 46-47.

42. Cf. the thorough analysis by Treitel, ibid. at s. 40-118.

43. ULIS Articles 82, 86; CISG Art. 74.

44. § 67 D (1)(c) and (d), (2) and (3).

45. ULIS Art. 88; CISG Art. 77. Cf. also CMEA General Conditions for Deliveries § 67 D(4).

46. CISG: Articles 49, 51(2), 64, 72, 73; ULIS: Articles 24(1)(b), 26(1), 30(1), 43, 45(2), 52(3), 55(1)(a), 62(1), 66(1), 70(1)(a).

47. § 326 BGB. Uniform sales laws: CISG Articles 47, 49(1)(b), 63, 64(1)(b); ULIS Art. 27(2), 31(2), 44(2), 62(2), 66(2).

48. CISG Art. 81(1)(first sentence); ULIS Art. 78(1).

CHAPTER TEN

THE VIENNA CONVENTION AND STANDARD FORM CONTRACTS

JAN HELLNER
Professor of Law, Stockholm

1. Everyone is aware of the current importance of standard form contracts for international sales. Yet there is no explicit reference to such contracts in the United Nations Convention on Contracts for the International Sale of Goods (hereinafter referred to as the Vienna Convention). Article 6 of the Convention simply states that the parties may derogate from or vary the effect of any of the provisions of the Convention. After seeing this provision, one might believe that the relationship between the Convention and standard form contracts is simple. However, there are a number of complications, and I shall deal with some of them.

There are three principal issues which are often intertwined:

(1) How do the rules of the Convention interact with the standard form contracts now in use?

(2) To what extent do the rules of the Convention correspond with the law embodied in modern standard form contracts?

(3) How will national rules on the control of standard form contracts function with regard

to contracts of sale subject to the Vienna Convention?

In discussing various questions involving these issues, I shall be chiefly concerned with three sets of standard terms: "The Incoterms," revised by the International Chamber of Commerce (ICC) in 1980; "The General Conditions for the Supply of Plant and Machinery for Export, prepared under the auspices of the United Nations Economic Commission for Europe" (known and hereinafter cited as the "ECE 188 contract"); and "The Uniform Customs and Practices for Documentary Credits (1983 revision)," issued by the ICC.

2. Already at an early stage of the preparation of what has now become the Vienna Convention, there was a discussion on the relation between the proposed text of the new law and standard form contracts. It was said that the text did not pay sufficient attention to what was called "the living law" (le droit vif) found in standard forms. This criticism was chiefly voiced by the French Professor Edouard Lambert. Ernst Rabel, spiritus rector of the project for unifying the law of international sales, replied to this criticism in an article dedicated to his critic.[1] He admitted the importance of standard form contracts but gave a number of reasons why a uniform law would be useful even when such contracts were employed. The law would fill in the gaps left by the standard form contracts; it would unify the mandatory law which could not be touched by the standard form contracts; it would suppress differences in the interpretation of standard form contracts due to different mentalities of various national legislators; it would be useful as a basis for the law of standard form contracts; it would influence arbitration; and it would be useful as a general law, as opposed to the diversities of national legislation. An expression that Rabel used is that the law should provide an "infrastructure" for standard form contracts.

We may note that Rabel speaks of the unification of mandatory rules as an advantage, in spite of the fact that neither the draft nor later versions, including the final Convention, contain any such rules. He was thinking primarily of rules regarding invalidity of contracts because of fraud etc., and rules concerning passing of property, bankruptcy and similar matters. He also admitted that achieving unity in this field was particularly difficult. The problems of introducing control of standard terms had not yet attracted attention. I shall return to this matter at the end of this essay (<u>infra</u> 11).

Much later, in 1961, another Frenchman, Dr. Philippe Kahn, raised the criticism that the Uniform Law -- or rather the 1956 draft, the text that had been available to him -- was based to an unsatisfactory extent on earlier legislation and case law rather than on the requirements of modern trade, as manifested in standard form contracts.[3] He pointed out that contracts of sale differ greatly, depending chiefly on the kinds of goods that are concerned. His criticism will be summarised briefly here since it serves as a background for my later discussion.

According to Kahn, at the one extreme we find sales of commodities such as grain, silk, coffee, oil, sugar etc., which are bought and sold in great quantities in international markets. For the sale of commodities, strict rules on the duties of seller and buyer and on the remedies for breach of contract are required. Such con-

tracts generally contain an element of speculation, and gains and losses reflect fluctuations
in price. Accordingly, damages depend on developments related to price, and if there is a breach
of contract by the seller, the damages will be
the same whoever the buyer is. If the goods are
non-conforming and the buyer declares the contract avoided, the seller can generally sell them
elsewhere without great difficulty, even if at a
lower price because of the defect.

At the other extreme, for sales of complex machinery, above all machinery specially manufactured for the buyer, more lenient rules are suitable. The avoidance of such a contract will hurt
the seller badly and often will not be very
advantageous to the buyer either, who may then
have to wait a long time for the delivery of
another machine. For this reason, avoidance of
the contract is not a suitable remedy except in
extreme cases. The buyer's loss and the corresponding damages will depend less on fluctuations in price than on the individual situation
of the buyer, in particular on the effect of a
breach of contract on his production. Often the
seller cannot foresee these consequences for the
buyer, and, therefore, cannot predict the amount
of damages covering the whole loss of the buyer.
When there is a defect in a machine, the most
important remedy is the duty of the seller to
remedy the defect.

The gist of Kahn's criticism is that the differences between various kinds of goods were not
reflected in the 1956 draft. The situation has
not changed much since Kahn wrote his book. However, there are some changes in the rules that
bear on the peculiarities of various goods. In
the Vienna Convention we find a rule concerning
remedies for breach of contract -- inserted at a

fairly late stage -- according to which a buyer
is permitted to require the seller to remedy non-
conformity by repair (Art. 46(3)). Another change
is that the rules in the 1964 Uniform Law on the
International Sale of Goods (see Art. 28) that
introduce special remedies for breach of contract
in a sale of goods for which a price "is quoted
on a market where the buyer can obtain them" have
been omitted from the Vienna Convention. These
changes can be regarded as a sign that the Convention is less concerned with commodities and
more concerned with machinery and similar goods.
But this does not change the fact that the Convention is intended to apply equally to all kinds
of goods, regardless of differences between them.

3. As is now apparent, we must assume that the
Convention will be supplemented by standard form
contracts in a number of cases. The first question will therefore be how the mechanism for the
introduction of such forms operates during the
formation of a contract. If both parties agree
that a certain standard form is to apply -- as is
fortunately by far the most common case -- there
is no difficulty. If they do not agree, problems
arise.

The relevant provision, Art. 19 para. (1), refers to "a reply to an offer which purports to be
an acceptance but contains additions, limitations
or other modifications." It is generally assumed
that this provision applies not only to individual terms but also to terms contained in standard
form contracts.[4] The article primarily concerns
cases in which, before performance of the contract has begun, one party maintains that he has
not entered into a contract, whereas the other
claims that he has.[5] We can imagine that buyer B

offers to buy goods from seller S, who replies affirmatively but refers to or sends over a standard form contract. B, who does not like the standard form contract, or who has changed his mind, prefers not to enter into the contract.

The first possibility is that the reference to the standard form contract does not involve any modification at all. This case is not as improbable as might first appear. It is thus possible that a reference to the "Incoterms" in a contract between two continental European parties would be regarded merely as a confirmation of what would apply even without such a reference. There will then be no opportunity for B to withdraw from the contract by invoking the reference to the Incoterms. On the other hand, if the seller is a Swede and the buyer an American, it is more likely that the reference to the Incoterms would be regarded as a modification. The second possibility is that the reference to the standard form contract is regarded as a modification but not a "material" one. B must then give notice of his objection "without undue delay" (para. (2)). If he does not, the terms of the contract are those of the offer with the modifications contained in the acceptance. If he does object, the primary result is that there is no contract, but presumably in many cases the negotiations will continue.[6] The third possibility is that the alteration is material, and then B is not bound to the contract, even if a long time passes without his having objected. There is a description in para. (3) of what constitutes materiality. This description is such as to make most standard form contracts modify the terms materially. Para. (3) mentions, for instance, "settlement of disputes," which means that an arbitration clause in a standard form contract

will be considered to alter the terms materially.[7] ECE 188 may be mentioned as an example of a
standard form contract which contains an arbitration clause.

In my opinion, these rules are not well suited
to standard form contracts, of which there are
many different kinds. The distinctions between
additions which do not modify the contract, those
that modify the contract but not materially, and
those that modify the contract materially, cause
difficulties which may be hard for the parties to
observe and can scarcely be justified. As for the
third group, which is probably the most common,
it seems curious that the party receiving a reply
which purports to be an acceptance but which
contains a reference to a standard form contract,
has no duty to react, apparently not even if he
notices the difference and its importance. If he
does not react, no contract exists (because it
lapses if the counteroffer is not accepted).

As mentioned earlier, Art. 19 is primarily
concerned with cases in which the disagreement
between the parties becomes apparent before performance has begun. There is another situation to
which Art. 19 may also possibly apply. This is
the famous "battle of forms." When a contract has
been performed, and thus there is no practical
possibility to maintain that no contract exists,
it is discovered that each party has sent his
standard form contract to the other and that
there are differences between them. The question
will be whose contract is to prevail.

If the differences are so slight that they
will not be considered as "material" modifications, it might be possible to apply Art. 19
para.(2), mentioned earlier, according to which
the terms of the contract are those of the offer
with the modifications contained in the accep-

tance. But if a number of communications have
passed between the parties, it may be uncertain
which one is to be considered the acceptance. It
might further be argued that if part of Art. 19
is applicable, the whole of it should be.[8] However, since the differences will be material in
most instances and the rule in Art. 19 is, in
this case, that there is no contract, little
guidance can be found.

The preferable view seems to be that "the battle of forms" should not be judged at all by the
rules on offers and counter-offers.[9] This view
is reinforced by the fact that at the Vienna Conference in 1980, the Belgian delegation proposed
that the Convention should include a rule on "the
battle of forms." This proposal was rejected.[10]
If we assume that Art. 19 should not be applied
at all to the "battle of forms," the question
arises as to which rules should apply. To this
question I have no answer; there are a number of
different solutions.[11]

4. Let us now direct our attention to the rules
on **delivery** in the Vienna Convention and compare
them with the corresponding provisions in the
Incoterms. Delivery is dealt with in Articles 31
and 32 of the Convention. Art. 31 contains the
main provisions, whereas Art. 32 has some supplementary rules of minor interest in this connection. Accordingly, we should direct our attention
to Art. 31.

Art. 31 covers three cases, numbered (a) to
(c), or rather four cases, if we include the introduction to the article. The first case is that
the seller is bound to deliver the goods at a
particular place (the introduction). The three
other cases (a, b and c) presuppose that he is

not so bound. If the contract of sale involves carriage of the goods, delivery consists in handing the goods over to the first carrier for transmission to the buyer (a). The other two cases need not concern us much; they refer to two different situations in which the contract does not involve carriage of goods. The gist of the rules (b) and (c) is that the goods are delivered at the seller's place of business.

In the Incoterms we find rules for the interpretation of a great number of so-called "trade terms," the best-known of which are "f.o.b." and "c.i.f." Together, the Incoterms provide a very comprehensive set of possibilities for regulating delivery, passing of risk, distribution of costs, etc. I do not intend to examine these various clauses; my intention is rather to look at Art. 31 of the Convention from the point of view offered by the Incoterms.

If a contract contains an explicit reference to the Incoterms, no problem arises. The Incoterms are so complete that there is no need to supplement them with the rules of the Convention. They have been "derogated" by the contract.

If a trade term is used but there is no explicit reference to the Incoterms, and if it is not indicated by any other fact (such as the "previous course of dealing" of the parties) that the Incoterms or some other set of provisions are to apply, it is more uncertain whether Art. 31 of the Convention has any significance. Some relevant possibilities may be mentioned.

The trade term "c.i.f." does not mention the place of delivery, since it states the place of destination, in spite of the fact that it denotes a shipment contract in the sense that delivery is effected when the goods are shipped. Is such a contract one in which "the seller is not bound to

deliver the goods at any particular place" and to
which, accordingly, Art. 31 rule (a) should apply? The consequences would be that when there
is first a land transportation by an independent
carrier and then a carriage by sea, the goods are
delivered when they are handed over to the land
carrier. However, in international usage -- which
is amply confirmed by the Incoterms -- goods sold
c.i.f. are not delivered until they have been
loaded in the ship.[12] It seems clear to me that
in this case the common interpretation must prevail over the words of the Convention. A similar
question might be asked concerning a sale which
does not involve carriage of the goods. But in
this case the question has less importance,
since, according to both the Convention and the
interpretation of the clause "ex works" in the
Incoterms, delivery consists of "placing the
goods at the buyer's disposal" at the seller's
place of business (Art. 31(b)(c) of the Convention).[13]

It is a more difficult matter to decide what
is meant by the expression "the contract of sale
involves the carriage of the goods." Is it sufficient that, according to the contract, it appears that the goods must be transported, or
should it be required that the seller has contracted to transport the goods? Expressed in
trade term language, are goods sold "free carrier" or "ex works" when the contract contains no
direct indication? In my opinion, the latter view
must be correct. If the seller has not undertaken
to perform any part of the transportation, his
duties should not depend on where it is possible
to find an independent carrier.[14] The Incoterms
will not help us in this case, since they are
concerned with the interpretation of various
clauses. The ECE 188 contract, for example,

states explicitly that when there is no indication in the contract of the form of sale, the
goods are to be considered to be sold "ex works."

The principal function of Art. 31(b) is to
provide a rule for the cases in which it is clear
that the seller has a duty of transportation but
no further indication of the extent of his duties
can be found. The rule that handing over the
goods to the first carrier, rather than shipping
the goods in a ship, constitutes delivery makes
the Convention rule coincide with the trade terms
"Free carrier... (named point)," "Freight or carriage paid to," "Freight or carriage and insurance paid to" which were introduced by the 1980
revision of the Incoterms. The Convention rule
thus differs from the old and well-known terms
"f.o.b.," "c & f" and "c.i.f.," each of which
provides that if sea transportation is included,
the goods are not delivered until they have been
loaded in the ship. This is a policy decision by
the Convention which is noteworthy.[15]

5. As for the rules on <u>passing of risk</u>, there are
two principal types of legal technique. One is to
link the passing of risk to delivery and provide
that risk passes on delivery (with certain exceptions). The other is to provide separate rules on
delivery and on passing of risk. Both the Convention and the Incoterms employ the latter technique. The rules of the Convention on passing of
risk (Articles 66-70) do not contain any reference to delivery. The Incoterms contain separate provisions, in the form that they state from
which moment the buyer must bear all risks.

However, even with the latter technique, there
is a clear correspondence between delivery and
passing of risk, as can be found in particular by

comparing Articles 31 and 67 of the Convention. Therefore, the same characteristic features and problems that were mentioned previously can be found in the rules on passing of risk.

We may note that a rule regarding passing of risk which has no counterpart in the Incoterms is found in Art. 68 of the Convention. It applies to goods sold in transit. The explanation is that since the Incoterms are mainly concerned with the relation between the first seller and the first buyer, it does not contain any clause which deals with the situation when the first buyer sells them while they are in transit.

In addition, the Convention contains various rules which constitute exceptions to the general principles for the passing of risk, referring chiefly to the conduct of the buyer. Most of these exceptions are not dealt with by the Incoterms. In the absence of such provisions in the Incoterms, guidance must be sought in the Convention's rules. These seem therefore to have greater importance for the passing of risk than for delivery.

6. With regard to the **"handing over of documents"** the Convention contains only one, very short rule (Art. 34). However, when payment is to be effected by a documentary credit, we must observe that the Uniform Customs and Practices for Documentary Credits contain a number of detailed rules regarding the documents that are accepted by banks for such credits. Although the Uniform Customs refer primarily to the relations between the buyer and the bank that the buyer instructs to open such a credit, the seller who has contracted for a documentary credit must be assumed to have agreed to comply with the rules found in the Uniform Customs. Thus, the Uniform Customs may supplement the Convention's rule. The risk of a conflict between the two sets of rules is not very great, especially since the Convention pre-scribes in Art. 34 that the documents must be handed over "at the time and place and in the form required by the contract."

7. The provisions of the Convention on **remedies for breach of contract by the seller** (Articles 45-52) are rather complicated and cannot be de-scribed in detail here. Only some significant details will be pointed out. On the whole, the rules are common to all breaches of contract, although certain rules apply only to late deliv-ery and non-delivery, whereas others refer only to non-conformity.

In case of **late delivery and non-delivery** the buyer may, according to the Convention, usually require performance (Art. 46). He can avoid the contract if either the breach is fundamental (Art. 49(1)(a)) or he has set a <u>Nachfrist</u> and the goods have not been delivered within it (Art. 49(1)(b)). He may claim damages in all cases of delay (Art. 45(2), 47(2)) unless the seller is exempted under Art. 79. The rules, especially the one concerning damages, must be considered to be strict regarding the seller.

The Incoterms do not contain any provisions on breach of contract. The ECE 188 contract, on the other hand, contains ample provisions on reme-dies. These will therefore be considered in what follows. In contrast to the case with the Conven-tion, there is no uniformity in the remedies for late delivery and non-delivery, on the one hand, and for non-conformity (defects), on the other hand.

The provisions regarding the consequences of
late delivery (or non-delivery) in the ECE 188
contract differ entirely from those of the Convention. The primary remedy is a reduction of the
price by a percentage which is to be fixed in the
contract and which is computed on each complete
week of delay. There is a maximum reduction,
which is also to be fixed by the contract. For
the period when the reduction operates, the contract cannot be declared avoided and no damages
can be awarded. Only if delivery has not been
effected at the expiration of the maximum period
for reduction of the price can the buyer declare
the contract avoided and claim damages. Damages
cover only the loss suffered by the buyer after
the period of reduction has expired. Even for
such damages there is, in general, a fixed limit
stated in the contract.

Our first conclusion must be that this system
is entirely different from that of the Convention. Its system of avoidance and damages has
been replaced by a system of reduction of price,
the remedy of avoidance with a right to damages
being available only in extreme cases.

The second conclusion is that, like other
standard form contracts used in the sale of machinery, the ECE 188 contract reflects the features of sales of machinery which were pointed
out by Dr. Kahn (supra 2). This theme need not be
developed further here. But it is pertinent to
ask whether the Convention should not have taken
more account of contract practices relating to
sales of machinery. My answer is no. Since the
percentage of reduction of the price will be a
matter of negotiations between the parties, and
the height of the percentage plays a dominant
role in deciding the character of the remedy, it
would almost be impossible to insert suitable

rules into a convention. On the other hand, we must acknowledge that in the case of sales of machinery, the situation might be very awkward for the seller, if the Convention is not replaced by a standard form contract.

8. As for **non-conformity**, the Convention gives the buyer a number of remedies. He may require substitute goods provided that the breach is fundamental (Art. 46(2)), he may require the seller to remedy the lack of conformity unless this is unreasonable (Art. 46(3)), he may claim a reduction of the price (Art. 50), he may declare the contract avoided if the non-conformity amounts to a fundamental breach of contract (Art. 49(1)(a)), and finally, he is always entitled to damages, unless the seller is exempted under Art. 79.

If we look at the ECE 188 contract, we find the corresponding provisions under the heading "guarantee." In the first place, a guarantee period must be fixed. If a defect appears during this period, the seller's duty is to remedy the defect. We may ask what happens if he does not succeed in remedying the defect within a reasonable time. The answer is found in para. 9.13:

> If the Vendor refuses to fulfil his obligation under the Clause or fails to proceed with due diligence after being required to do so, the Purchaser may proceed to do the necessary work at the Vendor's risk and expense, provided that he does so in a reasonable manner.

No other remedy for non-conformity is mentioned. Clearly, in this respect as well, there is a considerable difference between the ECE 188 contract and the Convention.

Although the text of the ECE 188 contract does not contain any reference to the possibility of the buyer declaring the contract avoided, in the commentary by the experts on the ECE 188 contract, we find the following statement (Sec. 21):

> The Turkish and Yugoslav experts asked what would happen in the case of an irremediable defect, i.e. if the Purchaser were unable to carry out the necessary repair when the Vendor failed to do so. In their opinion, the General Conditions should have contained a provision on this subject giving the Purchaser the right to recover damages and to automatic termination of the contract. The Working Party thought it unnecessary to consider this extremely remote eventuality in which, moreover, the results described by the Turkish and Yugoslav experts could be obtained simply by applying the general principles of law; for in all European countries the total failure of the Vendor to fulfil his obligations would give the Purchaser the right to recover damages. Moreover, non-fulfilment of his obligations by the Vendor would be considered as a ground for termination under the law of most countries, except that of the Netherlands, where it would be necessary to apply to the courts for that purpose.

As for damages because of non-conformity, the provisions of the ECE 188 contract are somewhat vague since the only clear provision states:

> It is expressly agreed that the Purchaser shall have no claim in respect of personal injury or of damage to

property not the subject matter of the
Contract or of loss of profit unless it
is shown from the circumstances of the
case that the Vendor has been guilty of
gross misconduct.[16]

However, this provision in the text of the contract should be compared with the statement in
the commentary of the experts quoted above.

It seems clear that we are facing a new aspect
of the interaction between a standard form contract and the Convention. Even the semi-official
commentary to the ECE 188 contract admits that it
must be filled out with "general principles of
law" found in "European countries." If the Convention is applicable to a contract of sale, the
Convention rather than some national legal system
must provide the "general principles" that are
assumed to exist. On the other hand, the Convention's rules are obviously much stricter regarding the seller than the "general principles"
mentioned in the commentary. It is clear that the
group of experts who framed the ECE 188 contract
did not expect avoidance and damages to enter
into play except in extraordinary circumstances.
The explicit exclusion of compensation for "loss
of profit" in the ECE 188 contract differs entirely from the general principle of computing
damages in Art. 74 of the Convention.[17]

The difficulty lies deeper than in reconciling
the two texts and deeper than in explaining the
contents of the ECE 188 contract by reference to
the kind of goods to which it refers, even if
this is part of the explanation. The essential
difficulty lies in the fact that whereas the
Convention aims at justice between the parties,
the ECE 188 contract protects the interests of
the seller better than those of the buyer. Whereas the contract is explicit in limiting the obli-

gations of the seller in a number of respects, it maintains silence on his duties when a defect cannot be remedied. This silence puts the buyer at a disadvantage. The criticism raised by the Turkish and Yugoslav experts, together with the awkward answer given by the rest of the Working Party, brings this feature out.

Here it is impossible to discuss what a court or arbitrators should do when confronted by such a situation. However, we shall touch upon this matter in another context shortly when dealing with the control of standard form contracts which are governed primarily by the Convention (see infra 11).

9. Let us now turn briefly to the **buyer's breach of contract** and look at the rules in the light offered by the Uniform Customs and Practices. As has been mentioned before (supra 6), these rules must, when the contract between seller and buyer states that the latter is to open a documentary credit, be taken to also include the provisions of the Uniform Customs.

The failure to open such a credit may be held to constitute a breach against the obligation of payment, which includes taking "such steps... as may be required under the contract..." (Art. 54). Accordingly, this failure is not only an anticipatory breach but a breach in itself. Since, according to the contract, the credit generally shall be opened at some time before the seller is to deliver the goods, the buyer has an obligation that is to be performed before the seller's performance.

If the buyer fails to perform one of his obligations, the seller, according to the Convention (Art. 61), has a number of remedies open to

him. What we should look at here is the remedy of
declaring the contract avoided. He may do so
immediately if the breach is fundamental (Art.
64(1)(a)) and after the expiration of a _Nachfrist_
if it is not fundamental (Art. 64(1)(b)).

In my opinion, these rules are not satisfactory when the buyer has the obligation to open a
documentary credit. The seller should always be
allowed to declare the contract avoided if the
buyer does not open the credit within the fixed
time. The seller may depend on the exact fulfil-
ment of such an obligation, and he should not be
required to prove that the breach is fundamental.
This is especially the case when the credit is
transferable and the seller may need to transfer
the credit immediately to the party from whom he
has himself bought the goods that he is to deliver to his buyer.[18] The seller should not have
to offer proof that such is the case or that in
some other way the breach is to be considered
fundamental.

10. One of the most discussed provisions of the
Convention is Art. 79 which deals with **exemptions.** At the same time, it can be expected to be
the most seldom applied provision since practically all standard form contracts of a general
character, and many of those which are rudimen-
tary in most respects, contain _force majeure_
clauses. Most of these clauses differ from Art.
79, _inter alia_, by describing in detail what
kinds of events constitute _force majeure_, although it is customary to supplement the enumera-
tion of various events with a general provision
exempting a party from other circumstances beyond
its control. Here we shall deal only with one

special feature of Art. 79, i.e. the consequences
of a seller being exempted.

According to the express provisions of Art.
79(5), nothing in the article prevents either
party from exercising any right other than to
claim damages under the Convention. This means
that even if the seller is exempted, the buyer
retains his right to declare the contract avoided
if the breach is fundamental or if there is no
delivery within the Nachfrist. The buyer may even
claim performance of the contract.[19] For the sale
of commodities, which can easily be sold and
bought in world markets, such rules may be suitable. For the seller of machinery, the fact that
the buyer can declare the contract avoided as
soon as the breach becomes fundamental (or even
earlier by using the device of the Nachfrist) may
prove serious.

We find that the ECE 188 contract contains
provisions on the effects of force majeure which
differ entirely from the Convention. The main
effect is that the period within which delivery
is to be effected is extended "as far as is
reasonable having regard to all the circumstances
of the case" (Sec. 7.2). This means that no
remedies at all are available while force majeure
operates. Since the period of delivery is extended, there is no breach of contract. However,
the extension cannot continue for an indefinite
period. Under Sec. 10.3 of the ECE 188 contract,
both parties can terminate the contract if "the
performance of the Contract within a reasonable
time becomes impossible." We may note that both
parties, both the one whose performance is delayed and the other party, are entitled to declare the contract avoided. It cannot be excluded
that a party whose performance is delayed because
of force majeure will in this way be allowed to

escape from an unfavourable contract. If the
contract is terminated in this way, special provisions apply to the division of expenses incurred in respect of the contract (Art. 10.4-6).

This is another example of a standard form
contract containing provisions of a type which
differ greatly from the system of the Convention.
We admit that it would have been an almost
impossible task to frame rules that would be
suitable for both sales of commodities and sales
of complex machinery. But once more we must
realize the importance of permitting the
Convention to be replaced by standard form
contracts suited to special kinds of goods.

11. Finally, we shall turn to the <u>control</u> <u>of</u>
<u>standard</u> <u>terms</u>, an important matter in modern
contract law. The attitude of the Vienna Convention is simple: Art. 4(a) states that the Convention is not concerned with the validity of the
contract "or of any of its provisions." This
means two things: there are no rules in the
Convention itself that will interfere with the
provisions of a contract to which it is applicable, and the fact that a contract is subject to
the Convention will not prevent courts or arbitrators from enforcing national rules on invali-
dation of contract terms.

As we are now dealing with national law, it is
necessary to restrict the discussion. For various
reasons, I shall limit myself to three systems,
the English, the West German and the Swedish. Of
these, I can claim familiarity only with the
Swedish system, which will be apparent in what
follows.

Before dealing with special questions, we
might ask whether there are sufficient practical

reasons for exercising control over international contracts. It might be argued that control should be limited to national contracts, especially contracts with consumers, and that courts and arbitrators should not interfere with international contracts. In my opinion, this is too simple a view. Among the standard examples of contracts that favour one party unduly are those of automobile manufacturers with their sub-contractors, and these are often international contracts. A Volvo car, for instance, contains numerous and important parts that have been manufactured outside Sweden. We cannot start by assuming that all contracts between manufacturers and sub-contractors should be automatically exempted from the control exercised over national contracts.

Even the ECE 188 contract, which has been prepared by an international organization, contains clauses that must be considered unsatisfactory. It states inter alia that the buyer shall have no claim in respect of personal injury (see supra 8). This provision is directly contrary to principles that are universally accepted at present, not to mention the Council of Europe Convention and the draft of the ECE directive on products liability. As we have seen, according to the commentary, the contract's provisions on remedies for a defect are supposed to be supplemented by general principles of law (supra 8). If there were no commentary, or if it is considered not to have persuasive force, a court might find that the only way of allowing termination and damages for a serious irremediable defect is to exercise a right of control of the contract provisions.

12. Control of standard form contracts may assume various forms. One is **preventive control**, by which certain clauses in standard form contracts are prohibited for the future by courts or by administrative authorities. Under the German AGB-Gesetz (Gesetz zur Regelung des Rechts der Allgemeinen Geschäftsbedingungen) 1976, a chamber of commerce or an organization for the purpose of protecting business interests may start proceedings for the prohibition of specified clauses (Art. 13(2) Rules 2 and 3). This procedure might be applied to international contracts as well. Sweden has a new statute that entered into force on July 1, 1984, under which certain organizations can bring suit against enterprises for an order of prohibition of specific clauses.[20] Suppose that a suit based on this rule would be successfully brought against a manufacturer of automobiles. In this case the manufacturer would undoubtedly be enjoined from using these clauses in contracts with foreign parties as well. It is too early to make predictions about the possible influence of the new statute on international contracts.

13. It is more interesting to look at the **control of contracts that have been concluded,** as this enters more directly into the sphere of application of the Vienna Convention.

The **United Kingdom**'s Unfair Contract Terms Act of 1977 deals to a considerable extent with "standard terms of business" (see particularly Sec. 3). The Act limits the validity of exemptions for breach of contract (Sec. 3(2)(a)). However, it contains an express exception for international contracts (Sec. 26). Although the

wording of this rule is complicated and somewhat
obscure, it seems to exclude most, if not all,
contracts to which the Convention can apply.[21]

On the other hand, the English doctrine of
"fundamental breach," as far as it survives recent precedents, makes no exception for international contracts. The **Suisse Atlantique** case
provides an example.[22] The consequences this
doctrine will have for contracts subject to the
Convention cannot even be surmised by a foreign
observer.

The **German AGB-Gesetz** contains no exemption
for international contracts. It even contains an
express rule making it applicable to some contracts to which German law does not apply in
other respects (Sec. 12). On the other hand, the
detailed provisions of Secs. 10 and 11, which
make certain types of clauses void either condi-
tionally or unconditionally, do not apply to
contracts in which the party dealing with a party
who employs a standard form contract is also a
merchant (Sec. 24). But the "general clause"
(Sec. 9), which declares all standard terms invalid that contrary to good faith and honour
disfavour the other party unduly, can be applied
to contracts between merchants as well. It is
difficult to judge the implications of these
provisions for international contracts.

As for the general clause found in the German
Civil Code Sec. 242, which appeals in a very
general way to the notion of good faith and
honour in the application of a contract, I can
only make a guess. Nevertheless, it seems proba-
ble that a German court would consider the implications of Sec. 242 regarding Geschäftsgrundlage to be irrelevant for contracts subject
to the Convention, since the Convention contains
its own rules on exemptions (Art. 79). On the

other hand, in so far as Sec. 242 invalidates unduly oppressive contracts (<u>Knebelungsverträge</u>), my guess would be that a German court would not hesitate to extend such application to international contracts as well. But these are, of course, only the surmises of a foreign observer.

In **Swedish** law the relevant provision is the new "general clause" that was inserted into the Contracts Act (Sec. 36) some years ago.[23] There is a fair amount of case law on its application, but most of it deals with consumer contracts and all of it with national contracts. The provision itself makes no exception for international contracts. There is an important decision dealing with a commercial contract between two Swedish enterprises, in which the Supreme Court of Sweden accepted the validity of a clause exempting a seller from liability for consequential loss[24], although it was pleaded that the clause was invalid according to Sec. 36. In this case the Court referred, <u>inter alia</u>, to the ECE 188 contract and cited its provisions as a ground for accepting the exemption as valid. Even if it is clear from this case that the Swedish Supreme Court is prepared to accept such deviations from statutory sales law as are consistent with modern business practice, it does not follow that the court will not interfere with clauses in international contracts that it considers unjust and unreasonable.

In view of what has been stated above about the law of the three countries, it appears that there is no certainty as to the control that national courts will apply to international contracts. Above all, there is no unity.

14. As a conclusion to the preceding brief survey, a few remarks can be made. The Vienna Convention, like national systems of sales law, cannot alone satisfy the need for diversity and variation in sales relations. As before, we shall have to rely on standard forms to achieve this diversity. This observation does not imply any criticism of the Convention. It is necessary to have rules which can act as an "infrastructure" -- to borrow Ernst Rabel's expression -- for standard form contracts. The question is whether the Convention fulfils this function.

On the whole, the diversity is not greater than appears necessary, although we could wish for greater clarity on a number of points. However, in some cases, the need for interaction with standard form contracts does not seem to have been observed sufficiently. This is particularly true for the part that deals with formation of contracts. The Convention lacks rules for the introduction of standard terms into contracts, and it does not solve the problem of the "battle of forms." If, as the result of this omission, the Convention will be applied instead of standard form contracts that are better suited to special goods, or special methods of transportation, or special methods of payment, the result might be unfortunate.

It is perhaps also to be regretted that the Convention does not deal with the problem of control of standard terms in contracts. The main reason for this is simple. At the time when work on the Convention began, the discussion on such control for contracts of sale had hardly started. But during the long period of preparation, this discussion has become vivid, and a number of countries have introduced such control, both by legislation and by various devices which permit

the courts to exercise considerable discretion.
Unification of such control seems as desirable as
any other part of the unification of sales law.
However, it must be admitted that attaining
agreement on such a subject would probably have
been even more difficult than reaching the unity
that has now been achieved.

NOTES

1. E. Rabel, "L'Unification du droit de la vente
internationale, ses rapports avec les formulaires
ou contratstypes des divers commerces," Recueil
d'études en l'honneur d'Edouard Lambert Paris
1938), reprinted in E. Rabel, Gesammelte Auf-
sätze, vol. 3 (Tübingen 1967) p. 837.
2. Ibid. p. 654.
3. Ph. Kahn, La Vente commerciale internationale
(Paris 1961) p. 20 et seq.
4. See e.g. J. Honnold, Uniform Law for International Sales under the 1980 Convention (Boston
1982) p. 190 et seq. The corresponding rule in
the Uniform Commercial Code (§ 2-207) fulfils a
similar function. For a general discussion see
Ontario Law Reform Commission, Report on Sale of
Goods (Toronto 1979, Ministry of the Attorney
General), vol. 1, p.81 et seq.
5. Ibid. pp. 190, 192.
6. Ibid. cf. p. 193.
7. Cf. P. Schlechtriem, Einheitliches UN-Kaufrecht (Tübingen 1981) p. 42 et seq.
8. Ibid. at p. 44.
9. Cf. Lord Denning's judgment in Butler Machine
Tool Co. Ltd. v. Ex-Cell-O Corporation (England)
Ltd. [1979] 1 All E.R. 965.
10. See United Nations Conference on Contracts
for the International Sale of Goods, Official

Records (New York 1981) p. 96.

11. See e.g. P. Schlechtriem, "Kollidierende Standardbedingungen und Eigentumsvorbehalt," Zum Deutschen und Internationalen Schuldrecht, P. Schlechtriem and H.G. Leser, eds. (Tübingen 1983) p. 1. It can be noted that Art. 33 para. 3 of the International Commercial Contracts Act of the German Democratic Republic contains an express provision on the "battle of forms." This provision codifies the "last shot" principle.

12. I.C.C. rule A 4 on the c.i.f. term Cf. D.M. Sassoon, C.I.F. and F.O.B. Contracts (2 ed. 1975) p. 35. As for American law see Uniform Commercial Code § 2-320 (2)(a). But cf. J. Honnold, supra n. 4, who seems to confuse the traditional c.i.f. clause with the new "Freight or Carriage and Insurance Paid to..." clause, which differs from the c.i.f. clause precisely by making handing over to the first carrier constitute delivery, even if he is a land carrier.

13. I.C.C. rule A 2 on the "ex works" clause.

14. See, however, J. Honnold, supra n. 4, p. 237 et seq. Honnold states that the provision on sales not involving carriage is most likely to apply when the seller and buyer are relatively near each other and the buyer operates trucks that can conveniently come to the seller's place of business. But he seems to overlook that the "ex works" solution can be and is in fact often used on other occasions as well. The buyer can, for example, employ a forwarding agent to take care of the transportation when goods are sold ex works. Honnold mentions UCC § 2-509 (1), which refers to cases where "the contract requires or authorizes the seller to ship the goods by a carrier," but he does not mention that UCC § 2-308 -- which is the provision that corresponds to Art. 31 of the Convention -- states that unless

otherwise agreed, the place for delivery of the goods is the seller's place of business.

15. Cf. J. Honnold, supra n. 4.

16. See para. 9.16 of the contract.

17. Cf. J. Hellner, "Consequential Loss and Exemption Clauses," 1 Oxford Journal of Legal Studies (1981) p. 13.

18. It has been suggested that the seller is permitted to avoid the contract immediately if payment is a "fixed obligation"; see U. Huber, "Der UNCITRAL-Entwurf eines Übereinkommens über internationale Warenkaufverträge," (1979) Rabels Z p. 413 (516); cf. J. Hellner, "The UN Convention on International Sales of Goods -- an Outsider's View," Ius inter Nationes, Festschrift für Stefan Riesenfeld (Heidelberg 1983) p.71 (92). This view opens an easy way of overcoming the restrictions apparent in the Convention's system of remedies.

19. The obligation to perform even when performance is impossible is a curious feature. Cf. P. Schlechtriem, supra n. 7, p. 97.

20. Lag (1984:292) om avtalsvillkor mellan näringsidkare.

21. Cf. Bejamin's Sale of Goods, 2nd ed. (London 1981) p. 822.

22. Suisse Atlantique Société d'Armement Maritime S.A. v. N.V. Rotterdamsche Kolen Centrale [1967] 1 A.C.361. Cf. Benjamin on Sales, supra n. 21, p. 472 et seq.

23. See J. Hellner, "Contracts and Sales," An Introduction to Swedish Law, ed. S. Strömholm (Stockholm 1981) p. 207 et seq.

24. Nytt Juridiskt Arkiv 1979 p. 483. Cf. Hellner, supra n. 17, p. 34 et seq.

CHAPTER ELEVEN

THE INTERNATIONAL SALES PRICE AS BASIS FOR CUSTOMS VALUATION

HANS van HOUTTE
Professor of Law, Louvain

Most customs duties are levied on the basis of the value of the imported goods (ad valorem). In the major trading countries the general criterion for customs valuation, i.e., the administrative appraisal of goods for the imposition of this ad valorem duty, is the "transaction value" (Part I). The transaction value refers to the sales price (part II). Although the sales price and the transaction value are not the only criteria (part III), they are very important for customs assessment. Thus drafters of international sales contracts have to be aware of the customs implications of the sales price. Adequately drafted price provisions might indeed result in lower customs duties and permit advantageous customs planning.

I. Transaction Value in Customs Valuation

Until 1980 the seller and buyer did not have much leeway to influence the customs valuation of imported goods. Article VII of the General Agree-

ment on Tariffs and Trade (GATT), applicable
among most trading nations, excluded valuation on
an arbitrary or fictitious basis. It left customs
authorities the choice of basing their valuation
either on the actual value of the imported merchandise or on the basis of the value of similar
merchandise of foreign origin[1]. However, the
actual value of the goods was seldom retained.
Instead, import duties were usually levied on the
basis of the price at which similar foreign merchandise was sold or offered for sale[2]. Although
GATT had forbidden assessment on the basis of
"the value of merchandise of national origin,"
the United States even valued certain products at
the level of the domestically-produced articles
with which the goods competed[3].

Since 1980 the major trading nations have
adopted new and uniform valuation criteria. Ad-
herring to the Customs Valuation Code (CVC) elaborated under the auspices of GATT, they have
incorporated its detailed set of valuation criteria into their domestic law.[4] At present, the
CVC is reflected, for instance, in section 402 of
the amended Tariff Act (1930) of the United
States[5] and in many EEC regulations applied by
the ten Member States of the European Communities[6]. Most socialist states, however, have not
adopted the CVC as they are reluctant to adhere
to GATT rules such as the CVC. Moreover, developing countries hesitate to adopt the CVC because
customs duties, which are more easily admini-
strated than income taxes, are a main source of
their government revenue. Hence, they generally
uplift duty values. Furthermore, their valuations
are frequently approximate and adaptable entry by
entry. Many developing countries apparently prefer these patterns to the more disciplined and
uniform system of the CVC which reduces the po-

tential for artificially inflated customs appraisals. In order to attract signatories, the drafters of the CVC were willing to grant developing countries five years in which to implement the Code. Although this concession has succeeded in attracting but few developing countries until now[7], it may be expected that more developing countries will adhere to the CVC in the near future[8]. At present, already more than 70 % of international trade is imported under the CVC, thus making it a major instrument of international trade.

The CVC has made the "transaction value" the principal basis for valuation. Determined by the actual sales price of the imported merchandise, the transaction value is thus an individualized criterion for each importation. It is unaffected by the prevailing market price or the price at which competitors sell the product. About 90 - 95 % of all imports under the CVC are assessed on the basis of the transaction value. Only when one of the very few grounds for exclusion of this standard is present should other valuation criteria be used. Its general application has undoubtedly reduced the disparity in customs treatment that previously existed among nations and deflected international trade from its normal course. Consequently, the uniform criterion of the transaction value has been a major step towards equal treatment in customs valuation.

However, CVC terms such as "transaction value" run the risk of being interpreted and applied differently by customs administrations within one country. Some parties, for instance, the EEC and the USA, have reduced this risk by issuing administrative rulings and centralizing the judicial review of customs decisions. Within the EEC, any domestic court which has to review

administrative customs decisions may ask the
European Court of Justice in Luxembourg for a
prejudiciary ruling on the correct interpretation
of the CVC as incorporated in the EEC-customs
regulations; domestic courts of last resort are
even obliged to do so. The decisions of the Court
of Justice become part of EEC law and bind customs officials and courts of the Member States.
These decisions thus promote uniform interpretation of the customs law throughout the EEC. In
the USA judicial review is even more centralized,
the Court of International Trade having exclusive
jurisdiction over customs matters. Review of its
decisions may only be exercised by the Court of
Appeals for the Federal Circuit.

Moreover, at the international level, i.e.,
among different states, uniform interpretation is
encouraged by two institutions: the GATT Committee on Customs Valuation and the Technical Committee on Customs Valuation[9]. The GATT Committee
decides on trade policy matters and occasionally
on matters of principle not directly covered by
the CVC. Thus, it has already decided on the
valuation treatment of interest and of software
carriers. However, the main attempt at achieving
uniform interpretation may be attributed to the
Technical Committee on Customs Valuation, a body
which operates within the GATT framework but
under the auspices of the Customs Cooperation
Council (CCC). This Committee has already issued
and published[10] some forty interpretative guidelines called "advisory opinions," "commentaries,"
explanatory notes," "case studies" or "studies"[11]. In addition, the CCC centralizes information on the application of the CVC by different
countries [12]. The decisions of the GATT Committee
and the Technical Committee are not legally binding under international law. However, GATT com-

mittee decisions are formally adopted by the
parties and often incorporated into domestic
law[13]. The Technical Committee rulings are carried out by the parties which, moreover, have to
report to the Committee on their implementation.
Thus, the transaction value that is generally
used as the basis of customs valuation has to be
interpreted in the light of the authoritative
guidelines of the GATT Committee and the Technical Committee.

II. Sales Price as Basis for the Transaction Value

The transaction value revolves on the sales
price of the imported goods, i.e., "the price
actually paid or payable for the goods when sold
for export to the country of importation" (CVC
art. 1). The term "sale," however, is not precisely defined. It should be taken in its broadest sense, but exclude in any event hire, leasing
or loan which do not imply transfer of property[14]. Moreover, it is not clear what "sold for
export" implies. When the goods are sold from the
country of exportation directly to the country of
importation, they are undoubtedly "sold for export." However, are they also "sold for export"
when the country of importation is not known at
the moment the merchandise leaves the country of
exportation, e.g., when the goods are sold "en
route"? Countries have held different views on
this matter. The United States, for instance, has
maintained that the buyer has to be known when
the goods are exported; the EEC has taken a more
lenient view. Recently the Technical Committee
has stated that "sold for export" does not require a sale in a specific country of exportation, but only a sale with the view to export[15].

Customs officers may not reject the sales price on the sole ground that it is too low or lower than the prices of other transactions. It is even irrelevant whether this price yields some profit to the seller or buyer. Low prices may entail anti-dumping measures, but are unobjectionable from a customs point of view[16]. High prices are not an impediment either. Customs officers may levy duties on inflated sales prices regardless of lower market prices. French customs thus levied high duties on goods which were overpriced in order to expatriate money out of France in spite of exchange controls[17].

Contracts usually express the price in an amount of money; this contract price will generally be used as the basis for customs valuation. The contract price is usually taken over in the invoice. In fact, customs officers rely primarily on the invoice rather than on the contract. When no appropriate invoice price is available, the sales price has to be determined on the basis of the contract provision. Moreover, prices may be invoiced in a currency other than that of the country of importation. Customs officers then have to compute the sales price in local currency at the prevailing exchange rate at the time of importation. When the contract contains a fixed exchange rate, custom officers generally have to rely on this contractual rate for their valuation[18]. Contracts may also contain formulas for determining the final sales price on the basis of costs of labor, prices of raw materials, overhead expenses, currency fluctuations and quality. When the final sales price has not been determined by an invoice on the basis of the review provision at the time of importation, the sales price payable at the time of importation should be computed on the basis of the price review clause. Such a clause does not even preclude valuation when some of its variables do not come into play until after importation; the final customs valuation may then be delayed until computation of the price is possible[19]. In brief, contract drafters should be aware that price review clauses might complicate customs valuation.

Since sales prices are composed of different elements, they can only be an objective basis for customs valuation when reduced to a common denominator. The CVC specifies how sales prices have to be adjusted for valuation purposes. Only adjustments provided for in the CVC may be carried out; others are impossible. Adjustments are facilitated or even become superfluous when the invoice contains adequate price specifications or when separate invoices are drafted for different elements of the transaction. Therefore, the sales contract -- especially its price provisions -- should contain the necessary elements and directives for customs-minded invoicing. There are at least three reasons for this: 1) the contract may help to confirm the invoice price if challenged; 2) valuation becomes more predictable if based on the agreed invoice price without the need of further adjustments, thus eliminating an important source of surprises leading to time-consuming quarrels with the customs administration; 3) well-structured price provisions in contracts may result in the most beneficial customs regime within the legal limits of the CVC.

The CVC only concerns imported goods, i.e., tangible property. Under the CVC, incorporal property as such is not valued for custom purposes and may consequently be imported free of duty. As a result, the contract and the invoice should separate the price for duty-free imported services, know how, and processes from that of

the tangible goods subject to valuation. Drafters
might even make separate contracts for both types
of transactions.

Royalties or license fees for patents, trade-
marks and copyrights raise delicate questions.
These tangibles are, in principle, not subject to
customs valuation. However, royalties may be a
condition of the sale of goods, for instance,
when the buyer had to accept to pay not only the
stated sales price but also some royalties for
the goods. These royalties are then in fact part
of the global sales price and have to be added to
the stated sales price for valuation purposes if
not already included therein. Contract drafters
should phrase dutiable royalties in terms of a
fixed amount per unit rather than as a percentage
of the proceeds in order to simplify their valuation. Most royalties, however, need not be included in the sales price as they are unrelated
to the import transaction and only concern repro-
duction or distribution of the goods after importation. Their payment might be a term of the sale
but not a condition thereof. In contracts and
invoices these royalties should in any event be
stated separately from the royalties to be included in the sales price for valuation purposes
and even better, to prevent any risk of confusion, they should be the subject of a separate
contract and invoice[20].

Software, another intangible, merits special
mentioning. Software that is necessary for the
operation of imported computer hardware is part
of the transaction value of the computer hardware
and should be included in its sales price for
valuation purposes. However, some software, e.g.,
application programs, can be imported independently from hardware. In the past, some states
have refrained from levying customs duty on such

software; others have levied duties on the disks or other carriers in which the software was incorporated. The GATT Committee has considered these two possibilities and decided that the parties may opt to levy duties either on the total value of the software and carrier or on the software carrier only[21].

Commissions are another example of intangibles which have to be added to the sales price under the CVC if not yet included. Thus commissions for a selling agent have to be added to the price of agency importations to named customers[22]. Only "buying commissions," i.e., "fees paid by an importer to his agent for the service of representing him abroad in the purchase of the goods being valued," remain duty free[23]. The contract, hence, should specify whenever payments concern duty-free "buying commissions" and state that these commissions have to be listed separately in invoices. Moreover, the contract should make clear that the agent to whom commissions have to be paid acts on behalf of the buyer and not the seller.

Whenever the production of the imported goods required engineering, development, design, tools, plans or sketches carried out elsewhere than in the country of importation, the costs of these "assists" have to be included in the transaction value and thus might as well be included in the contract or invoice price. Most often these assists were not made exclusively for the imported goods but for the production of other items as well. According to the CVC, in this case only a portion of these costs should be taken into account, "apportioned as appropriate." In order to facilitate customs adjustment, contract drafters could indicate this proportion in the contract and the buyer should only be billed for this portion[24]. Moreover, as the list of "dutiable assists" is exclusive and appears not to contain research costs, the latter should be priced separately in the contract and on the invoice[25].

In addition, contract drafters should make specific provisions as to the costs of other sales-related performances and require separate billing. Storage costs subsequent to the purchase are not part of the transaction value and thus should not be included in the global sales price billed.[26] If the buyer agrees to pay these costs, he should stipulate in the contract that these costs have to be billed separately.

Drafters should also make special provisions as to the transportation costs. The CVC preferred not to impose uniformity as to the extent to which transportation expenses have to be included in the transaction value. For instance, the United States still values imported merchandise on a FOB (franco on board) basis, i.e., transportation costs excluded -- while the EEC assesses on CIF (cost, insurance, freight) basis. As a matter of fact, the EEC only includes transportation from the exporter's country to the place of introduction into the EEC. For goods carried by road or inland waterway, this will generally be the port of unloading or the place where the first customs office is located; for goods carried by air or rail, it is the place where the frontier of the EEC is first crossed[27]. Contract drafters should take into account the extent to which transportation costs form part of the transaction value in the country of importation. For merchandise imported into a country assessing on FOB prices, the contract should state the sales price ex works and provide for a separately invoiced transportation price. When, on the contrary, merchandise is imported into a country including transportation to its border in the assessable sales price, the contract should include these costs in the sales price and provide that the duty-free transportation costs within the importer's country be billed separately[28].

Construction, erection, maintenance or technical assistance for industrial equipment occurs after importation. These and other costs for works undertaken after importation are not dutiable, provided that they are distinguished from the price actually paid or payable for the imported goods[29]. Consequently, the contract and the invoice should identify these costs separately from the proper sales price. Similarly, duties and taxes imposed after importation do not form part of the transaction value on the date of importation[30]. They should be invoiced separately whenever the seller has to recover them from the buyer.

The sales price "actually paid or payable" constitutes the basis for the transaction value. Interest on credit granted by the seller according to the terms of payment are not considered to be part of the price actually payable for the imported goods[31]. The seller sometimes grants a discount on the contract price for prompt or advance payment of the imported merchandise (e.g., a 5 % discount on payment within 30 days). Such a discount reduces the price actually payable by a percentage which may be considered as credit costs for delayed payments. When the goods were paid with reduction of the discount before valuation, the discount may, of course, be deducted from the original sales price. When, on the contrary, no payment has been made at the time of valuation, reference to the discount in the contract and invoice might justify deduction of the discount from the actual contract price

for valuation purposes[32]. Quantity discounts,
i.e., reductions after the buyer has purchased a
specified number of items, may be deducted from
the originally agreed sales price from the moment
the agreed quantity has been exceeded. In that
event the invoices consequently should deduct the
quantity discounts from the original prices. The
contract should contain specifications to that
effect.

The contract sales price remains relevant when
different shipments for reason of size or geo-
graphical distribution imply separate invoicing.
The invoiced prices of each delivery should then
reflect the apportioned value of the global contract sales price[33].

III. Limitations to the Sales Price as Basis for Customs Valuation

The invoiced sales price, even adjusted as
described above, is not the only basis for customs valuation. This sales price may need additional corrections or may even not be usable at
all.

Additional corrections to the invoiced sales
price are necessary when the sale concerns goods
classified under different customs headings and
subject to different rates. In that event the
sales price as invoiced has to be split up and
apportionated among the different goods[34]. The
invoiced sales price does not suffice either when
the buyer has directly or indirectly supplied
goods or services at reduced costs or free of
charge to the seller for the production of the
merchandise. The profit of materials, components
or tools consumed in the production thus delivered (which is not reflected in the invoice)
has to be added to the invoice price [35]. Similar-

ly, the costs of dutiable assists or royalties
(see supra) paid to third parties and not reflected in the seller's invoice have to be added
to the invoiced price[36].

The sales price may not be used at all for
customs valuation in a few exceptional cases. The
seller can impose restrictions (other than geo-
graphical) on the use or disposition of goods
that substantially affect the value of the goods.
For instance, he may impose lawful price maintenance or other resale restrictions. Sales
prices then do not reflect the customs value of
the goods and cannot be used. Moreover, in barter
transactions the price is not expressed in money
but in merchandise. In this case, customs authorities cannot rely on the money value of the sales
price, but have to assess the market value of the
barter transaction[37]. Furthermore, the sales
price may also -- but exceptionally -- be set
aside when the sale occurs between related companies. Transactions between related companies
are of great importance in international trade
because many manufacturers operate their foreign
distribution. Customs officials fear that they
might charge too low a price in order to reduce
duties. Formerly, transfer prices between related
companies were generally suspected to be distorted and were very often uplifted. However,
inter-company pricing does not need to be artificial. Indeed, personnel advancement on the
basis of profitability and company accounting
often prevent distorted transfer pricing in inter-company sales. Possible advantages of lower
customs duties are generally set off largely by
higher income taxes in the country of importation. Consequently, the CVC has taken a more
lenient view on inter-company pricing. The sales
price between related companies is maintained

when the importer can prove it has not been influenced by the relationship, i.e., that the value of the imported merchandise "closely approximates" the customs value of goods of a similar nature[38]. Finally, sales prices may be set aside when the customs can prove them to be artificial. Customs authorities may, therefore, always examine the accuracy of the price specifications in the contract and invoice. If they can prove artificially specified prices to evade customs duties, the specified price is set aside[39].

If valuation cannot be based on the contract price, it has to be based on the transaction value of identical or similar goods. If these criteria do not succeed, the value may be deducted from the resale price or computed on the costs of production[40]. If a buyer would prefer these criteria to valuation based on the sales price, he could even prevent the applicability of the latter, for instance, by accepting restrictions on the use of the goods in the sales agreement.

Conclusion

Sales prices almost always constitute the basis for customs valuation under the CVC. Invoices should specify the elements of the price and separate the value of dutiable merchandise from the price of other items. Customs planning requires that sales contracts contain the necessary arrangements to that effect.

NOTES

The author wishes to thank Mr. C. Van Walleghem of the Customs Cooperation Council (Brussels) for the information he provided. The views expressed in this article, however, are those of the author.

1. General Agreement on Tariffs and Trade, art. VII, 2 (a), 55 U.N.T.S. 194. In 1984, 90 states were full-fledged members of GATT and 31 states de facto respected GATT. Thus, Gatt is followed by nearly all countries of the "Western" and the "third" world as well as Czechoslovakia, Hungary, Poland, Romania and Yugoslavia.
2. E.g., the "price on a sale in the open market," the criterion of the Brussels Valuation Convention (1950) (171 U.N.T.S. 305, see annex I, art. I (1)) -- became widely accepted during the 1950s and 1960s.
3. This "American Selling Price" had already been introduced in 1922. Since it antedated the GATT Agreement, its legality was alledgedly preserved under art. 1 (b) of the GATT Protocol of Provisional Application (the "grandfather clause") which exempted existing legislation from the application of art. VII of the GATT Agreement.
4. See the "Agreement on implementation of Article VII of the General Agreement on Tariffs" concluded on April 12, 1979 as one of the culminations of the Tokyo Round (1973-1979), T.I.A.S. 9619; Official Journal (hereafter: O.J.) 1980 L 71, applicable as of June 1984 in Australia, Austria, Belgium, Botswana, Canada, Czechoslovakia, Denmark, Finland, France, Federal Republic of Germany, Greece, Hungary, Ireland, Italy,

Japan, Luxembourg, Malawi, the Netherlands, New Zealand, Norway, Romania, South Africa, Sweden, Switzerland, the United States and also followed in the non-signatories Bulgaria, Lesotho and Swaziland.

See moreover the commentaries published in the earliest period of the CVC: H. Glashoff, "Der 'Verkauf von Waren' im neuen Zollwert-System," Recht der Internationalen Wirtschaft (1980), pp. 626-634; G. Koschel, Das neue Zollwertrecht, (Köln 1980); O. Schwarz, Zollwertrecht in der EWG. Auf den Grundlagen des GATT Customs Valuation Code (Köln 1981); S. Sherman, "Reflections on the new custom valuation code," 12 Law & Pol'y Int'l Bus. (1980) pp. 119-157; S. Sherman and H. Glashoff, A Businessman's Guide to the GATT Customs Valuation Code (Paris 1980); W. Snijder, "Customs Valuation in the European Economic Community," 11 GA. J.Int'l. & Comp. L. (1981) pp. 79-100; R. Van Raan, "The Valuation of Goods for Customs Purposes," Intertax (1981) pp. 126-133.

5. 19 U.S.C. 1401 a. Customs Service Decisions will be published in R. Sturm, Customs Law and Administration, 3rd ed. Binder 3, Oceana Publications.

6. See, e.g., Regulation 1224/80 O.J. 1980 L 134, as amended by Regulation 3193/80 (O.J. 1980 L 333) and by Regulation 320/85 (O.J. 1985 L 34); Regulation 1494/80 (O.J. 1980 L 154) for the interpretative notes; on the applicability to coal and steel products: O.J. 1980 C 130.

Moreover, European Communities, Customs Valuation (looseleaf) containing i.a. the EEC Conclusions, hereafter cited.

7. Only Argentina, Brazil, India, Spain and Yugoslavia have signed the Convention subject to reservation as to the effective date of implementation.

8. E.g., India, Portugal, Spain and Turkey.

9. CVC art. 18 and Annex II.

10. Customs Co-operation Council (ed.), Gatt Agreement and Texts of the Technical Committee on Customs Valuation (Brussels - looseleaf).

11. Advisory Opinions concern the application of the Code to particular sets of facts. **Commentaries** are comprehensive comments on the text of the Code. **Explanatory Notes** concern questions of a general nature arising directly from one or more provisions of the Code. **Studies** also concern general questions but only indirectly related to the interpretation of specific Code provisions or not intended for publication outside government circles. A **case study** analyzes a complex set of facts based on an actual commercial transaction.

12. The CCC will publish references to national rulings and decisions in the Gatt Agreement and Texts of the Technical Committee on Customs Valuation. (supra n. 10).

13. See infra notes 21 and 31. Moreover, e.g., Regulation 220/85 on interests (O.J. 1985 L 25).

14. Advisory Opinion 1.1.

15. Advisory Opinion -- Annex IV to Doc. 32.350.

16. Commentary 3.1.

17. See European Court of Justice, Procureur de la République v. R. Chatain (Sandoz), case no. 65/79, 1980, ECR 1345 and Procureur de la République v. S. Wilner, (Victory) case no. 54/80, 1980, ECR, 3673. However, the Court ruled that the fiscal and financial authorities were not bound by the overvaluation for purposes other than the application of the customs tariff. For levies on unusual elevated transportation costs (e.g., by air instead of by ship) European Court of Justice, C. Edding v. Hauptzollamt Hamburg, case no. 27/70, 1970 ECR 1035.

18. CCC - Custom Valuation (commentary on the

Brussels Nomenclature Convention), 4 B. VI and VII; EEC Conclusion no. 1.

19. Commentary 4.1. See also <u>Finland</u>, ruling TVR 61, TH 13/303/81 of 7 April 1981; <u>U.S.A.</u>, ruling no. 543094 of 30 March 1984.

20. CVC art. 8.1.c and Annex I, interpretative note to art. 8. See also advisory opinions nos. 4.1 - 4.6. Regulation 3158/83 on the incidence of royalties and license fees in customs value, 1983 <u>O.J.</u> L. 309. Sherman, <u>supra</u> n. 4, art. 147-148; Snijder, <u>supra</u> n. 4 at p. 91. <u>Finland</u>, ruling TVR 130, TH 44-45/303/81, KHO 4386/27/81 of 21 July 1981.

21. Decision of the Committee on Customs valuation, adopted during its 10th Meeting on 24 September 1984, GATT Doc. VAL/8/Add. 1.

22. E.g., <u>Finland</u>, ruling TVR 62, TH 9/303/81 of 7 April 1981.

23. CVC art. 8, 1 (a) (i) and Annex I, interpretative note to art. 8, para. 1; EEC conclusion no. 14. However, Snijder, <u>supra</u> n. 4 at p. 96.

24. CVC art. 8, 1 (c); case study; <u>U.S.A.</u>, ruling no. 542519 of 21 July 1981, TAA no. 35:

> The method of apportionment used will depend on the detail in the documentation provided by the importer. If the entire anticipated production using the assist is destined for exportation to the United States, the value might be apportioned over the first shipment if the importer wishes to pay duty on the entire value at one time... over the entire anticipated production.

EEC Conclusion no. 13.

25. Sherman, <u>supra</u> n. 4 at pp. 145-146.

26. Commentary 7.1. See, e.g., European Court of Justice, <u>Enka</u> <u>v.</u> <u>Dutch</u> <u>customs</u>, case no. 38/77, 1977 <u>E.C.R.</u> 2203.

27. Regulation 3177/80 on the place of introduction, O.J. 1980 L 335; Regulation 3178/80 on air transport costs to be included in the value for customs purposes, O.J. 1980 L 335; and amended: Regulation 321/85, O.J. 1985 L 34; Regulation 3179/80 on postal charges to be taken into consideration when determining the customs value of goods sent by post, O.J. 1980 L 335. See EEC Conclusion no. 6.

28. See, e.g., Court of Justice, Hauptzollamt Schweinfurt v. Mainfrucht, case no. 290/84, O.J. 1985 C 29.

29. CVC, Annex I, interpretative note to Article 1; EEC Conclusion no. 4.

30. Advisory Opinion 3.1; U.S.A. ruling no. 542451 of 4 June 1981, TAA no. 27.

31. Finland, ruling TVR 61, TH 13/303/81 of 7 April 1981; Sweden, ruling 196/81 of November 1981; U.S.A. ruling no. 542627 of 17 December 1981, TAA no. 43. Moreover, see Decision of the Committee on Customs Valuation of 26 April 1984, GATT Doc. VAL/6 and Regulation 320/85, O.J. 1985 L 34. However, U.S.A., ruling no. 542150 of 6 January 1981, TAA no. 14 and ruling 542275 of 11 June 1982, TAA no. 31.

32. Advisory Opinions 5.1 - 5.3; New Zealand, ruling 956/VAL/302 of 25 January 1984.

33. Commentary 6.1.

34. Commentary 8.1; EEC Conclusion no. 10.

35. CVC art. 8, 1 (b). See Finland, ruling TVR 93, TH 25/303/82 of 27 April 1982; U.S.A., ruling no. 542302 of 27 February 1981, TAA no. 18; ruling no. 542355 of 3 April 1981, TAA no. 21; Moreover ruling no. 542356 of 13 April 1981, TAA no. 24 (whether costs of acquisition or book value should be used); ruling no. 542948 of 29 November 1982, TAA no. 55 (component chips).

36. U.S.A., ruling no. 543070 of 28 July 1983.

37. Advisory opinion 6.1.

38. CVC art. 1 para. 1 (d) and para. 2, art. 15 para. 4. See also European Court of Justice, <u>Caterpillar</u> <u>Overseas</u> <u>v.</u> <u>Belgian</u> <u>State</u>, case no. 111/79, 1980, <u>E.C.R.</u> 773.

39. EEC Conclusion no. 9.

40. CVC art. 2-7.

CHAPTER TWELVE

UNIFORM SUBSTANTIVE AND CONFLICTS RULES ON THE INTERNATIONAL SALE OF GOODS AND THEIR INTERACTION

GIORGIO CONETTI
Professor of Law, Trieste

Practically speaking, a high degree of certainty regarding the applicable law in international trade transactions, especially in respect of international sales of goods, can be attained by uniform substantive law through the adoption of international conventions. Thus, a large number of States may agree to incorporate the uniform rules into their internal legal orders. This practice is deemed to offer a better solution than the alternative of the conventional unification of conflict-of-laws rules, as it seems capable of solving the problems arising from the conflicts of laws themselves.

This attitude is widely accepted notwithstanding the well-known fact that deriving an international uniform law from an international conventional source leads to serious problems regarding the determination of its scope in relation to the internal rules of general application as well as its classification and interpretation. The adoption of the two Hague 1964 Conventions (Convention relating to a Uniform Law on the Interna-

tional Sale of Goods and Convention relating to a
Uniform Law on the Formation of Contracts for the
International Sale of Goods), the 1974 UN Convention on Prescription in International Sales of
Goods, the 1980 UN (Viennna) Convention on Contracts for the International Sale of Goods, and
the 1983 UNIDROIT (Geneva) Convention of Agency
in the International Sale of Goods marks the
solidarity of the present preference which appears to be even too ample in attainments.

However, a quick glance at the uniform substantive provisions of these conventions suffices
to see that they cannot entirely avoid dealing
with private international law rules and problems
(e.g., see Art. 1(b) of the 1980 Vienna Convention or Art. IV of the 1964 Hague Conventions)
concerning the internal conflict-of-laws rules of
the Contracting States which, at times, have been
introduced as the result of international conventions on uniform choice-of-law rules. The relationship between the uniform substantive law of a
convention and the internal substantive and conflicts rules is one of ambivalence. Within the
internal legal order of a State it raises the
problem of interaction between the conventions'
rules on the sphere of application of the uniform
substantive law and the lex fori conflict-of-laws
rules; or within public international law it
leads to the problem of coordinating subsequent
uniform law conventions containing substantive or
conflict-of-laws rules. We shall see that the
latter problem is easier to solve than the former.

Sometimes the uniform substantive law itself
deals with the problem of its position within the
internal legal order as well as with the application of its rules with regard to other internal
legal orders. However, there is much uncertainty,

and the various texts contain a number of solutions, at times, several within one text itself.

Generally speaking, the problem can be presented by referring to the following models: a)
Uniform substantive law of conventional origin
could be considered as a system of mandatory
internal provisions whose sphere of application
is determined autonomously and which therefore
refrains from interfering with the lex fori conflict-of-laws rules, at least with those not
derived from another international convention;
in that case the question of interaction is
shifted to the level of the interrelated international agreements. b) Uniform substantive
law could be held to be a special internal law
since it prevails over the other general provisions of substantive law; however, just as this
substantive law, it is also subject to the lex
fori choice-of-law rules, both the general ones
and those incorporated into internal law in compliance with other international conventions. c)
Furthermore, one may regard the substantive law
introduced by a convention as special substantive
private international law that is separate from
the general substantive and conflicts laws of the
forum, and, in accordance with the given convention's scope, is to be applied to some well-
defined issues which link only the Contracting
States of the convention on a reciprocal basis,
as indicated by the convention's special rules on
its sphere of application. d) On the other hand,
the uniform substantive law could be applied only
when referred to by the autonomy of the parties
or when it functions as a connecting factor referring to the application of a legal order containing the uniform law; or e) when the contracting parties select the uniform provisions as
a special part of the internal law that can be

applied only when requested by the parties themselves as an expression of their contractual
autonomy within the limitations set by the internal public order of the law applicable to the
contract, as established in accordance with the
lex fori conflict-of-laws rules.

Odd as it may sound, this last approach to the
relationship of uniform substantive law of conventions and internal substantive and conflicts
rules is taken by some conventions on the international sale of goods. At present, it has also
turned out to be the favored approach of the
Italian courts in regard to the sphere of application of the 1956 Convention on the Contract
for International Transport of Goods by Road
(CMR).

At first glance, it seems obvious that the
first of the various solutions described above
seems preferable and most suitable for establishing uniform substantive law by means of international conventions, i.e., to have identical substantive legal provisions on the same matters and
with the same sphere of application adopted by
the largest possible number of internal legal
orders. This is the main solution offered by the
1964 Hague Conventions; however, at the same
time, they have accepted a system of reservations
which allows the Contracting States to follow
other models. According to Art. III, it is possible to limit the uniform law's sphere of application to contracts whose parties have their places
of business or their habitual residences only in
the territory of different Contracting States
(model c). Otherwise, Art. IV provides that a
State which has previously accepted a convention
on conflict of laws on the same subject as that
of the 1964 Hague Conventions (reference to the
1955 Convention on the Law Applicable to the

International Sale of Goods) can apply the uniform law only when the conflict-of-laws provisions of the latter convention require the application of a legal order containing the uniform
law (model b). There is a further reservation in
Art. V of the first 1964 Hague Convention providing that the uniform law of the Convention shall
apply to a sales contract only if the parties
thereto have selected it as the law governing the
contract (model d). Furthermore, Art. 3 of the
uniform law permits the contracting parties to
exclude the application of the uniform law either
entirely or partially (model e, as negated).

The solutions adopted by the 1980 Vienna Convention are not as elective. Although the Convention qualifies the international character of
the sale by requiring that the contracting parties have their seats or places of business in
different States, it does not autonomously define
its sphere of application, as the two Hague Conventions do. Its application depends on the international character of the cases so that the
Convention is only applied when the States concerned are Contracting States (model c), or when
the lex fori conflict-of-laws rules of a Contracting State lead to the application of the law
of another Contracting State containing the uniform law which, after all, could be the lex fori
itself (model b). However, Art. 95 provides that
the reservation is not limited to the latter
solution. Thus, the general substantive applicable law would apply instead of the uniform one,
if, according to the lex fori conflicts rules,
the contracting parties' seats of business are
not in two different Contracting States. Furthermore, according to Art. 6, the contracting parties may exclude the application of the Convention, or derogate from it, or vary the effect

of its provisions (model e).

It is commonly known that the main solution adopted by the 1964 Hague Conventions has, for the most part, not been followed and that most of the Contracting States, with the exception of Israel, have availed themselves of the optional solutions offered by the reservation clauses of the Conventions. In accordance with Art. IV, Italy has made a reservation, limiting application of the uniform substantive law to cases where it is applicable by virtue of the 1955 uniform connecting factors. This reservation applies only to the first of the two 1964 Conventions, as it has been deemed, a bit superficially, that the 1955 Convention should not overlap with the 1964 Convention on the formation of sales contracts.

The 1983 Geneva Convention on Agency in the International Sale of Goods follows a pattern similar to the model of the Vienna Convention. Declaring itself to be a complementary text of the latter, the Geneva Convention has aligned its sphere of application to that of the Vienna Convention. Hence, after having defined its application ratione materiae in Art. 1 and restricted its sphere of application in Art. 3, the Geneva Convention states the requirements for recognizing the international character of agency relationships which can be submitted to the uniform law (i.e., at last two of the three parties, the principal and the third party, must have their places of business in different States, thus corresponding to the application requirements of the Vienna Convention). Then, in accordance with the Vienna system, it provides that in order for the Convention to apply, the agent must have his place of business in a Contracting State (model c) or that the private international law of the

lex fori lead to the application of the law of a
Contracting State containing the uniform law
(model b). Moreover, under Art. 28, the Contracting States may declare that they will not be
bound by the second rule stated above, thus con-
firming that the nature of substantive private
international law of the residual model c applies
only to some of the relationships involving some
of the Contracting States. Art. 5 permits the
principal or the agent, acting in accordance with
the principal's instructions, to agree with the
third party that the application of the Convention be excluded or derogated from.

The lack of success of the attempt at autonomous delimitation of uniform substantive law is
reflected in the application rules adopted by
this last Convention. This is also the result of
widespread criticism of the main solution of the
1964 Convention which scholars have considered to
be an immoderate claim of competence on the part
of the lex fori.[1]

In this statement I detect some misunderstanding of the real issues at stake. One must distinguish between the sphere of application of the
uniform substantive law and the necessity of not
extending application of the substantive lex fori
provisions beyond some fair limits in cases with
which they are not meaningfully connected. Although the uniform substantive law is incorporated in the internal legal order, its origin and
scope are different. Being set forth in an international agreement, it has the special aim of
governing cases that can be subjected to a uniform law, which at the same time constitutes an
international obligation.

The essential quality of the uniform substantive law is its applicability to those cases
specified by the restrictions it sets on its own

sphere of application, thus fulfilling its in-
trinsic international task of providing certainty
in contractual relations. The fact that this task
could be carried out by incorporating the uniform
law into the internal legal order should not be
misleading as far as its real nature and special
aim are concerned.

The general lex fori conflicts rules which
define the fair limits within which the substantive lex fori provisions are to be applied cannot
be assimilated to the special rules by which an
international convention defines the sphere of
application of its uniform law. Since these special rules comply with the international interest
to provide uniform legislation in a given field,
they may be regarded, vis-à-vis the general lex
fori conflicts and substantive rules, as a way of
conferring the character of mandatory law upon
the uniform substantive law.[2] In this way they
are guaranteed to satisfy the interest vested in
the particular convention.

However, in view of the fact that there are a
number of legislative texts of conventional origin containing uniform substantive or conflicts
rules for the international sale of goods (we
must now add the 1980 Rome Convention on the Law
Applicable to Contractual Obligations which, at
present, is in the process of receiving its first
ratifications), we must point out the problems
which arise as a result of the interaction of
their respective rules relating to their own
sphere of application. This is very difficult
since, as we have seen, some conventions offer
different alternatives.

The conflicts problems arising as the result
of overlapping uniform law conventions could be
settled by recourse to different techniques depending on our point of departure. Regarding them

as sources of uniform law, i.e., of international conventions that have taken place, we can deal with them by the means provided for by international rules of law, notably Art. 30 of the Vienna Convention on the Law of Treaties. On the other hand, we can choose the point of view of the internal legal order where the uniform substantive as well as conflicts rules of different conventional origins have been applied and then follow its own techniques of interpretation (e.g., the principles of speciality or those in favor of a socially valued outcome). However, here again we are confronted with the alternatives described above regarding the reciprocity of general and special conflict-of-laws and substantive rules.[3]

Nevertheless, as far as the uniform law conventions on the international sale of goods are concerned, we are able to make use of the "compatibility clauses" which most of them contain in regard to their respective application. This includes Art. IV of the 1964 Conventions, Articles 9 and 99 of the 1980 Vienna Convention and Articles 21, 23, 24 and 25 of the Rome Convention. As for the first interaction, i.e., between the 1955 conflict-of-laws Convention and the two 1964 uniform substantive law Conventions, doubts have been raised as to the feasibility of the reservation provided for in Art. IV that every problem arising from the concurrence of the 1955 private international law rules be accounted for.[4] First of all, the concurrence between the sphere of application of the two systems still ought to be explained since the international sales of goods, as defined in Art. 1 of the 1955 Convention, could be interpreted as not entirely covering those sales qualified as international under the 1964 Conventions. As a result, the

reservation provided for in Art. IV of the 1964
Conventions could be inadequate to guarantee that
the uniform conflict-of-laws rule have priority.

By virtue of Art. 3 of the 1964 Conventions
and Art. 6 of the 1980 Vienna Convention, the
contracting parties have the freedom to entirely
or partially exclude application of the respective convention. This does not seem to contradict
the 1955 conflict-of-laws rules if it is regarded
as contractual autonomy within the applicable
law. However, some difficulties may arise if, on
the other hand, it is regarded as the freedom to
choose the connecting factor.

The 1973 Convention on Prescription (Art. 37)
and the 1980 Vienna Convention (Art. 90) contain
an identical compatibility clause that above all
may be taken into account when answering the
question whether they are to prevail over the
1955 private international law Convention. With
the same wording, the two U.N. Conventions acknowledge that they shall "not prevail over any
international agreement which has already been or
may be entered into, and which contains provisions concerning the matters" within their jurisdiction "provided that the parties have their
places of business in States parties to such
agreement." The 1983 Agency Convention contains a
similar provision in Art. 23 which, however,
refers only to other agreements containing provisions of substantive law. Accordingly, Art. 23
does not apply in respect of the 1955 Convention
but only in respect of conflict-of-laws rules of
the lex fori to which it refers in Art. 2(1)(b)
or from which it may derogate in accordance with
Art. 2(1)(a).

Therefore, when the sphere of application of
the two U.N. Conventions mentioned above overlaps
with that of another convention, as is the case

when the States where the contracting parties
have their places of business are Contracting
States of both the former and latter conventions,
the latter shall prevail. This clause may result
in the exclusion of the 1980 Vienna Convention
when a uniform conflict-of-laws rule of conventional origin, that is common to the two States
involved, refers to the law of a third State
where the Vienna Convention is not in force, but
where, for instance, the 1964 Conventions could
be in force.

Of course, this only occurs when a third State
is involved, as it is well known that Art. 99 of
the 1980 Convention does not allow a Contracting
State to be, at the same time, party to the 1964
Conventions. On the other hand, Art. 38 of the
1973 Prescription Convention permits a Contracting State which is party to an existing convention on the international sale of goods to declare that it shall apply the Prescription Convention "exclusively to contracts of international sale of goods as defined in such existing
convention." Thus, a State that has made use of
this last reservation as well as the reservations
provided by Art. IV of the 1964 Conventions con-
ceding priority to the 1955 Convention could
attain a very coherent regime which links the
three systems together. Obviously, it is not
possible to construct a unique system linking the
1955, 1964 and 1980 conventions, since a choice
must be made between the latter two, with the
consequences as described above.

In addition, some coordination is attained
when the application of the 1980 Convention depends on a conflict-of-laws rule of the _lex_ _fori_
as this could be the one introduced by the 1955
Convention.

The maximum of flexibility that can be granted

in such compatibility clauses is undoubtedly
contained in Art. 21 of the 1980 Rome Convention
on the Law Applicable to Contractual Obligations.
In regard to the relationship between this and
other conventions, it is stated that the Rome
Convention shall not affect the application of
any international convention to which a Contracting State is or becomes party. Such broad wording
seems to cover every type of international convention on uniform conflict-of-laws rules and
uniform substantive law having its own rules on
its sphere of application.

Articles 23 and 24 of the Rome Convention
permit the Contracting States, after the Convention has entered into force, to either adopt a
new choice-of-laws rule for any particular category of contract within the scope of the Convention, or to become party to a multilateral convention to lay down rules of private international law concerning one of the subjects governed by
the Rome Convention. This can only take place
after having carried out a consultation procedure
that may be requested by any other signatory
State.

From these clauses it can be deduced that,
even if interference with the Convention regime
is allowed by the adoption of new single conflict-of-laws rules for special matters or particular categories of contracts, there is no freedom left to the Contracting States to create or
enter into a new general system of conflict-of-
laws rules for contractual obligations that, on
the whole, would aim at replacing the Community
Convention.[5]

One question still remains open inspite of the
negative solution presented in the Convention's
Explanatory Report by Giuliano and Lagarde. That
is, does the consultation procedure provision

also apply to new conventions on uniform substantive law in the field of contractual obligations, where it is often possible to find some single accessory private international law rules? Furthermore, one must keep in mind that uniform substantive law conventions could, by virtue of their own rules, determine their sphere of application in a way that would interfere with the Rome Convention's system of conflicts rules.

Anyway, Art. 25 of the Rome Convention also permits the consultative procedure in the case of international agreements not covered by Art. 24 when a Contracting State maintains that the unification achieved by the Convention could be affected by their conclusion. Then, when the rules on the sphere of application in uniform substantive law conventions are intended, as special rules, to derogate from the <u>lex</u> <u>fori</u> choice-of-law rules, thus conferring the character of mandatory law upon their uniform law, coordination between the Rome Convention and the uniform substantive law convention could be achieved in accordance with the clauses on mandatory rules of the <u>forum</u> in Art. 7 of the Rome Convention as well as those of the law of the country with which the situation has a significant connection.

NOTES

1. See mainly L.I. de Winter, "La loi uniforme sur la vente internationale des objects mobiles corporels et le droit international privé," <u>NTIR</u> (1964), p. 271 et seq.; R.D. Kollewijn, "Les Conventions relatives à une loi uniforme sur la

vente internationale et le droit international
privé," NTIR (1965), p. 219 et seq.; A. von
Overbeck, "Le champ de l'application des règles
de conflit ou de droit matériel uniforme prévues
par les traités," Annuaire (1979), p. 97 et seq.;
S.M. Carbone, "L'ambito di applicazione e i cri-
teri interpretativi della Convenzione di Vienna
sulla vendita internazionale" (The sphere of
application and criteria for interpretation of
the Vienna Convention on International Sales),
Riv.dir.int.priv.proc. (1980), p. 513 et seq.

2. On this nature of the uniform law, see A.
Malintoppi, "Les rapports entre droit uniforme et
droit international privé," Recueil des Cours III
(1965) pp. 1-87.

3. On problems of interaction among uniform law
conventions, see F. Majoros, Les conventions
internationales en matière de droit privé, t. II,
Le droit des conflits des conventions (Paris
1980); P. Volken, Konventionskonflikte im IPR
(Zürich 1977); B. Dutoit and F. Majoros, "Le
lacis des conflits de conventions en droit privé
et leurs relations possibles," Rev.Crit. (1984)
pp. 565-596; with special reference to the coordination of the 1964 Conventions with the upcom-
ing UNCITRAL draft, see R. Monaco, "Relationship
between the two Conventions on sale adopted at
The Hague in 1964 and the future conventions
resulting from the work being done by UNCITRAL,"
Italian Yearbook of International Law (1977) pp.
50-60.

4. On the relations between the 1964 Conventions
with private international law, see K. Zweigert
and U. Drobnig, "Einheitliches Kaufgesetz und
internationales Privatrecht," RabelsZ (1965), p.
146 et seq.; K.H. Nadelmann, "The Uniform Law of
International Sales of Goods: a Conflict of Laws
Imbroglio," 74 Yale LJ (1964-65), p. 456 et seq.

5. For this interpretation, see I.F. Fletcher, Conflict of Laws and European Community Law (Amsterdam/New York/Oxford 1982) p. 153.

CHAPTER THIRTEEN

INTERNATIONAL SALES AND SECURITY INTERESTS WITH AN OUTLINE OF CONFLICTS LAWS

HANS HOYER
Professor of Law, Vienna

The Vienna Convention on the International Sale of Goods is said to be uncomplicated and easily understood and applied even by merchants who have to deal with it. This is undoubtedly an advantage of the Convention over the two Hague Conventions dealing with the same topic. The Vienna Convention does not use primarily legal or scientific terms (i.e., what is usually called "legal shorthand") which are loaded with preoccupations and prejudices in varied and manifold ways; on the contrary, the main detriment of the Hague Convention on the Formation of Sales Contracts is said to be its dogmatic and highly specialized technique, especially in view of its application by merchants of developing countries.

This applies primarily to those who are not familiar with the application of a judicial system derived from Roman law (civil law system). In world-wide trade a non-dogmatic instrument may therefore be advantageous. One has, however, to take into account that the choice of a non-dogmatic instrument can cause considerable prob-

lems when it is incorporated into national substantive law. Therefore, it is legitimate to
raise the question how gaps are to be filled[1]
which emerge within the scope of the Convention
itself, on the one hand, and from the confrontation of the Convention and national substantive
law, on the other hand. Outside the scope of the
Convention, the filling of gaps requires the
solution of choice-of-law problems in order to
determine the applicable law and last, but not
least, to apply it. The way of dealing with these
problems is the topic of this paper.

I. INTRODUCTION

It should first be explained why the relationship between the sales rules of the Convention and national rules on security interests is
apt to increase the awareness and understanding
of problems arising in the field of application
of the United Nations Convention for the International Sale of Goods. The topic at stake is not
within the scope of the Convention, but -- quite
the reverse -- lies outside, excluded by the
Convention, like all other matters dealing with
transfer or reservation of property, acquisition,
loss or expiration of security interests. Nevertheless, between the Convention and the problems
we intend to deal with, there are some clear
common grounds and, on the other hand, even elements of uncertainty. Most of the latter questions lie within an analytic framework and can be
said to be of primary importance. One of the
crucial points is to know the contractual prerequisites for a transfer or a reservation of title
which are required by the applicable national law
in order to comply, in a given case, with the
rules of the Convention. In fact, different ele-

ments, such as time limits, specific exclusion of
rights or "intended purposes," special forms of
contracts, declaratory acts leading to contracts,
the access to and the requirement of publicity of
registration have their impact on both the formation of a sales contract as well as on its substance and form. Whereas in the field of contracts some spirit of solidarity -- sometimes an
historically grown uniformity -- seems to be
present, the situation is quite different as to
questions relating to the transfer of title, the
reservation of property, or the transfer or reservation of a secured transaction.

First of all, the institution "contract" was
derived and has been clearly based on Roman law.
Therefore, generally speaking, concurring opinions of the courts relating to the prerequisites
and legal effects of voluntary actions, agreements etc. are almost a natural -- at least not a
surprising -- consequence. Within property law,
various domestic (i.e., national) laws tend to
form three main groups of transfer and acquisition of property or expiration of security in
rem.

Furthermore, one must take into account that
Art. 41 of the Convention obliges the seller to
warrant that the delivered goods are free from
any right or claim of a third party. However,
according to Art. 4(b), it is clear that "the
effect which the contract may have on the property in the goods sold" is not governed by the UN
Convention but is a question of domestic law. It
is part of the issue whether the obligation is
still due or not. Attention will be devoted to an
analysis of the following concepts:

Part A
- The three main systems of transfer and acqui-

sition of property or expiration of security in
rem (II);
- Protection of the contracting party as a <u>bona
fide</u> purchaser (III);
- Interdependence between the obligation and the
security (IV);
- Specific prerequisites for acquisition of
security (including reservation of proprietary
rights) (V);
- Expiration of security (VI).

This discussion, however, will not cover
guarantees or other security leading, e.g., to a
person's liability only.

Part B
- Conflict of laws (VII).

This final part deals with conflict-of-laws
problems relating to the questions of substantive
law enumerated <u>supra</u> (III - VI). We will present
a comparative survey of matters remaining outside
the scope of the Vienna Sales Convention as well
as some principles of comparative conflict of
laws.

P A R T   A

II. THREE MAIN SYSTEMS OF TRANSFER AND ACQUISI-
TION OF PROPERTY OR EXPIRATION OF SECURITY
IN REM

A. The following introductory remarks should be
made:

1. The distinction between the law of obligations and the law of property was developed by
legal writing (doctrine). Therefore, this classi-

fication is traditional in legal systems influenced by the Pandectist School, for example, the
German BGB, the Italian Codice civile [of 1942]
and the Swiss ZGB. Other legal systems tend, at
first glance, to neglect the differentiation
between _jura_ _in_ _rem_ and _jura_ _in_ _personam_, e.g.,
the Austrian General Civil Code of 1811 (ABGB).
The ABGB distinguishes between "real rights"[2] and
"personal rights"[3]. This distinction, however,
covers neither the classification of "real property" -- "personal property" on the one hand,
nor "mere claims" on the other, as made in the
common law. Nevertheless, in both cases interpretation and application of the law are influenced
by Pandectist tradition. An approach between
Pandectist and common law bodies of law can be
observed.

The third group lacks this scheme. The French
Code civil [4] does not provide for security in
rem, i.e., security rights, in the 2nd Book[5] but
rather in the last section of the 3rd Book on
special contracts. Hence, a special conveyance
contract is unknown since a contractual act operates as a conveyance of ownership. This legal
construction does not render public disclosure of
certain legal acts unnecessary. Quite to the
contrary, publicity will be required when "real
rights" in goods are transferred by a person who
does not own them or who cannot yet dispose of
the goods. The historical reasons for this development will be dealt with later.

2. It should also be stressed that we are only
dealing with part of a general issue, namely the
question of when and how the transfer of property
or power of disposal _erga_ _omnes_ is completed.
Other problems such as the passing of use and
benefits or the passing of risk are not dealt

with here. Nor will we devote attention to the question of when and how goods intended for transfer can be seized by creditors of the transferrer or of the transferee.

3. The three main systems mentioned above (<u>supra</u> II) do not suggest a final investigation of all possible ways of effecting conveyance. Therefore, we cannot speak of an exhaustive typology in the sense of a universal comparative law. The typology developed by the domestic laws of the Roman-Germanic legal family will be given preference. The virtue of this method lies in the object itself: Common and dissimilar features serve as a paradigm that can easily be understood in the light of their mutual historical background. Then, the European comparatist finds himself more familiar with legal systems belonging to the Roman-Germanic legal family, because African or East-Asian legal systems have quite a different historical and cultural background. Note, however, that we do not wish to belittle the latter.

Finally, since the sale of goods encompasses movables only, we will obviously not deal with immovables. Their consideration would extend rather than substantiate the issue.

B. The three systems have in common the fact that they are **embedded** in the **Justinian Code**[6] on the one hand, and were influenced by Germanic law, the **gewere** signifying the right to a <u>de facto</u> physical control, on the other hand. However, the conclusions differ widely. Two antipodal and one moderate position should be emphasized, the latter of which is not the result of a compromise since one of the former positions was developed at a much later stage.

1. The French Code civil represents the oldest view. Generally, the **principle of consent** (<u>Konsensprinzip</u>) suffices for the acquisition of ownership. Thus no special conveyance contract, i.e., a <u>traditio</u> according to Roman law is needed.[7] However, public disclosure[8] is more important when a right of pledge is to be established.[9] Most legal writers support the view that this special solution is based on the fact that a contract of pledge is not a consensual but rather a conveyance contract.[10] In French law, a clear distinction is not always made between "real rights" and "personal rights." Thus, miscellaneous forms[11] weaken the system, and as a result, the assertion that chattel mortgage is governed by the principle of causal tradition[12] (i.e., for the validity of which a legal title is required) does have substance.

The principle of consent underlies the British Sales of Goods Act (ss. 17, 18) as well as the US Uniform Sales Act (ss. 18, 19).

Legal systems based on this principle offer a clear-cut solution for the multiple sales problem: The first purchaser becomes the owner of the goods because any subsequent purchaser (of the same goods) would have bought them from a person who was no longer entitled to sell them.

The French Code civil, however, provides for a special rule. According to Art. 1141, a <u>bona fide de facto</u> possessor (having actual custody of the goods) will be considered the owner in a multiple sales case.[13] This leads to another question: Under which conditions can a <u>bona fide</u> purchaser acquire an incontestable legal position?

In summary, the genuine principle of consent enjoys unrestricted validity in cases involving succession of title, provided public disclosure is not required in order to ensure an _erga_ _omnes_ effect. Public disclosure is complied with by a _de_ _facto_ or fictitious (i.e., constructive) conveyance, by registration etc.

2. The second oldest theory is represented by the **principle of transfer.** As was mentioned above, this theory is regarded by some as a compromise, which is correct from a historical point of view.

The principle of transfer encompasses first of all the mutual agreement between the contracting parties (i.e., the contract as such) and, in addition, conveyance of the goods. The legal nature of conveyance has been disputed by legal writers, some of which have considered conveyance to be a kind of "_de_ _facto_ transfer"; others have argued that conveyance is a (partly independent) "legal act"; still another group has preferred to classify it as a "causal legal act," while a fourth group has insisted on the classification of an "abstract legal act," which enables an indisputable legal position to be acquired without taking into account the underlying valid and effective legal obligation (i.e., cause).

Some legal systems still adhere to the principle of conveyance (_traditio_);[14] others have returned to it after having favored the principle of consent awhile.[15] Obviously, unanimous agreement has been achieved on one point: Under certain conditions the _traditio_ is obsolete and can be replaced by other solutions. For example, when the contracting party is already in possession of the goods he intends to acquire, a mutual agreement will suffice. This mode of acquisition was known in Roman law as _traditio_ _brevi_ _manu_. Therefore, it is a mere technical question whether this _traditio_ is to be regarded as an anticipated conveyance,[16] as a special form of conveyance

standing for a surrogate[17] or a subsequent approval of a completed de facto transfer for a
special purpose, namely for inducing legal consequences to be effective at a later time.

The anticipated legal effect of an intended
conveyance by way of a declaration of the parties, such as the classical constitutum possessorium, leads to considerable problems. At the
time, however, only lack of public disclosure
seemed questionable, with doubts being expressed
primarily about the transfer of property as such.
In addition, a problem arose which is not to be
discussed here but nevertheless deserves to be
mentioned: the question whether and under which
conditions goods intended for transfer can be
seized by creditors of the transferrer or of the
transferee. It seems unlikely that third parties,
for example, are able to attribute the goods to
one or the other contracting party. Unencumbered
property was not so much the object of suspicion
as the right to be paid which could not be identified by third parties.[18] The right of pledge in
this context will be discussed later.

For policy reasons the doctrine has introduced further alternatives: a) the order to hold
in possession, and b) direct conveyance by the
first to the last contracting party of an entire
chain. The former (so-called Besitzanweisung)
requires the mutual consent of transferrer and of
transferee. This agreement is then communicated
to the third party who had been holding the goods
in possession for the transferrer, ordering him
to hold them from then on in possession for the
transferee. The second legal act mentioned a-
bove[19] corresponds to a series of interrelated
orders. Both of these acts deserve attention but
will not be dealt with here.

In the group of legal transactions we were

discussing earlier, the <u>traditio</u> is to be qualified as a "causal" conveyance. Accordingly, the
conveyance is legally related to the <u>causa</u>, i.e.,
the legal title establishing the contractual
agreement. This legal title is determined by its
objective nature. Therefore, ownership will only
be acquired if the contractual agreement is valid
and effective.[20] Recent discussions have suggested that the legal qualification of the <u>tradi-
tio</u> is still an open question.

This is even true in the Austrian legal system although the legislator clearly insists on a
legal title (<u>titulus</u>) **followed** by a means of
transfer, sc., conveyance (<u>modus</u>) as prerequisites for the acquisition of ownership.[21] Some
writers have expressed opposition to an independent agreement in rem connected to the contractual agreement by means of the legal title on the
ground that this would make the original distinction incomprehensible.[22] **Bydlinski** has cited
additional reasons why the agreement in rem cannot be an independent contract, emphasizing the
fact that the contracting parties give their
consent to conveyance by virtue of the contractual agreement.[23] However, doubts remain. First,
the text of the ABGB causes problems[24]; moreover,
the view sketched above would lead to the unbear-
able consequence that a transferrer would be able
to force upon the transferee an ownership that he
does not wish to acquire. Such a result cannot be
desirable.

3. The third point of view differs from the other
two in that it advocates the **doctrine of the
abstract real contract.** According to this doctrine, the validity of the contract of sale is
entirely independent of the validity of the real
contract (the actual performance of the former).

This "independence" involves abstraction as to both the content and form of the "real contract." By conveyance (real contract) the transferee will acquire property even though the contract of sale was initially void or subsequently has become so. However, the German conceptual division -- as we have just described it -- is not as clear-cut as it appears to be. A defect affecting the contract of sale will have its impact on the conveyance contract.[25] The same applies when under the terms, i.e., conditions of both contracts the parties agree that the validity of the "real contract" depends upon the validity of the "obligatory contract." It has also been argued that both contracts form a unitary transaction; thus the invalidity of the former would necessarily lead to voidance of the latter without any further considerations (condition, defect etc.) being needed. However, neither of these possibilities seems to be compatible with the doctrine of the abstract real contract in the strict sense of the term.

C. Once a right is acquired, especially a right in rem, problems arise in regard to the requirements for **continuous publicity** which must be satisfied in order to retain the right. A study of different legal systems has convinced us that mainly "limited real rights" such as the pledge are involved.

In some legal systems public disclosure is a prerequisite for the acquisition of limited real rights, which makes the problem seem less obvious. In this context it is worth mentioning security rights that are not transferred but rather registered, deposited in a court or public authority or merely labelled. Security rights requiring transfer and, in addition, some forms of registration do not fall under this category.

Most legal systems, however, require a contractual agreement and the transfer of security rights or some equivalent thereof for the establishment of "limited real rights." Under German law the validity of this legal transaction is not effected by lack of the possibility to recognize encumbrances.

French law, however, will only give _erga omnes_ effect to the transaction if the pledgee has exclusive possession -- whereas joint possession or restraint generally suffice -- and an official certificate referring to the transaction has been registered.[26] This certainty is an exception to the principle of consent. In regard to the rejection of _constitutum possessorium_ for lack of public disclosure, some authors refer to Art. 2076, others to Art. 2279 Code civil. The distinction seems to be of artificial importance. Therefore, it is not surprising that a _constitutum_ cannot establish a valid transfer of ownership by virtue of a security. Yet, not only general codes but also special laws repeal the strict principle of public disclosure, replacing it by judicial or official registration. The legislator thus neglects the fact that without the use of pledged property, the pledgor is undoubtedly put into a detrimental economic position.

Italian law[27] copes with the problem in a way similar to that of French law. Here, no official registration, but rather a dated certificate indicating the debt and the pledged item is required[28] if the debt exceeds a certain amount of money as the result of inflation. Exclusive possession by the pledgee or a third person (bailee) are still required.

Swiss, German and Austrian law insist upon "possession"[29] as a prerequisite for establishment and maintenance of the pledge. Only very specific movables, e.g., ships and some lifestock can be held in a so-called Fahrnisverschreibung, i.e., registered pledge, in Switzerland. Consequently, a pledge cannot be established by constitutum possessorium.

Spanish law provides for a possessory pawn[30] and a variety of chattel mortgages, e.g., mortgages on enterprises, industrial machinery and vehicles. It is interesting to note that a notarial contract of pledge and registration are required; in addition, an export ban is recorded on car licences in order to ensure realization of the pledge within the country.

III. PROTECTION OF THE CONTRACTING PARTY AS A BONA FIDE PURCHASER

Protection of the bona fide purchaser results in conflicting interests: The owner strives to protect his status against unjustified interference by third persons; on the other hand, the buyer is usually not able to recognize whether or not the holder of the goods owns them. This awkward situation is brought about by lack of sufficient publicity because the holder of the goods can be the owner and/or possessor. As long as the holder himself knows whether he can act as an owner, we do not forsee any problems.

Under Roman-Justinian law, derivative acquisition was governed by the principle nemo plus iuris transferre potest quam ipse habet. At the beginning, however, original acquisition of property was restricted to unattached property. The owner could file a rei vindicatio against anyone who did not acquire the goods from him. Disre-

garding the acquisition of a right through ad-
verse possession over a certain period of time,
we can clearly see that the Roman solution has
become quite inadequate in view of modern business transactions. For this very reason it is
absolutely necessary that a purchaser relying in
good faith on the "material circumstances,"[31]
i.e., that the seller is in possession of the
goods, be protected. Otherwise, he would be facing the risky probatio diabolica of ownership by
several previous owners. Mutatis mutandis, i.e.,
argumentum a maiori ad minus, the same is true
for the acquirer of a security in rem.

National legislators have solved the above-
mentioned conflicting interests in a remarkable
variety of ways. Some introduced a unitary regulation; others emphasized criteria such as exter-
ior circumstances, acquisition for or without
valuable consideration (payment), the type of
loss of possession, the licence to trade under
public law, or the de facto carrying out of the
trade or profession of the transferrer, the goods
etc.

1. The Roman law principle is advocated by **critical** scholars of the common law, stating that
every owner has the right to demand (judicially
by lodging an ownership complaint) his proprietary goods from any holder. Since strict application of this principle would lead to severe and
impractical consequences, moderating regulations
have been introduced[32] such as the protection of
bona fide acquisition "in market overt" and acquisition for valuable consideration "from a
mercantile agent." If the acquired goods have
been stolen from the owner, they will be returned
to him as soon as the thief is convicted for

theft. This rule does not apply to theft of money or negotiable instruments.

By application of the estoppel principle, a bona fide acquisition for valuable consideration will be valid if the bona fide acquirer was led to believe by virtue of the owner's conduct that the holder was entitled to dispose of the goods.

2. In **French law** Art. 2279(1) Code civil[33] attracts our attention. Under this rule, which concerns the possession of goods and is derived from the principle of consent, acquisition of property will be presumed if possession was acquired. Although we do not wish to go into the particulars of bona fide acquisition, the main prerequisites should nevertheless be mentioned.

Only corporal movables which are not the object of unalienable domaine public can be acquired bona fide. The acquirer must have the possession utile, including "custody" of the goods,[34] the intention to possess, the authenticity of possession as well as good faith at the moment of acquisition. If the actual entitled party has lost the goods out of his custody without consenting thereto,[35] the goods can be sought by the bona fide acquirer during a period of three years. If the bona fide purchaser has bought the goods at a market or trade fair, at a public auction or from a tradesman authorized to carry on such a trade,[36] the actual entitled party will be required to reimburse the purchase price. Special statutes introduce exceptions in the case of negotiable instruments. If possession is lost, a published "objection" will provide the lawful owner stronger protection.

Good faith of the pledgee is protected; however, he cannot redeem a pledge like the actual entitled party can reimburse the purchase price to a bona fide acquirer. Art. 2280(1) Code civil provides namely that the **purchase money** must be returned.

3. The **German legislator** provides for bona fide acquisition from a non-entitled party as well. According to §§ 932 et seq. BGB, the good faith of the buyer must pertain to the seller's right of property, whereas commercial law[38] simply demands reliance upon the power of diposal by the tradesman authorized to carry on such a trade. Some legal scholars allege that movable goods (which are restricted in German law to corporal property) acquired without valuable consideration, stolen goods and goods which have been lost cannot be acquired bona fide. This opinion is not entirely accurate. The bona fide party can acquire the property in goods without payment, but the previous owner can oblige the bona fide acquirer to return the goods by bringing an action on grounds of unjust enrichment.[39] Here, however, contrary to French law, the bona fide purchaser cannot claim reimbursement of the purchase price. Stolen goods and lost objects cannot be acquired bona fide. Yet, for the sake of smooth business § 935(2) of the German BGB provides for three exceptions to the general rule: money[40] and negotiable instruments and bona fide acquisition of stolen or lost objects. Bankers and money changers, however, cannot acquire transferable instruments in good faith if the loss of the securities had been announced during the current or previous year.[41]

4. According to **Swiss law**, the bona fide purchaser acquiring property or a pledge is protected in an absolute way, provided he, in reliance upon the seller's ownership, acquired it

from the person to whom the property was entrusted. If, however, the entitled person lost
the object without his consent, he can claim it
from the person who actually possesses it for a
period of five years. However, he is not entitled
to claim the money and negotiable instruments
from the bona fide purchaser. Goods bought by a
bona fide purchaser at a public auction, at a
market or from a tradesman authorized to carry on
such a trade must be restituted; however, only in
compensation for the purchase money.[42]

5. Italian law seems to have a straightforward
solution for the problem. An adequate legal title
(causa) and a completed conveyance are required
for a bona fide acquistion from a non-entitled
party.[43]. Transferable instruments can be acquired in good faith as well, if the acquisition
complies with the regulations on security trading.[44]

6. Austrian legal history is responsible for
particular rules on the bona fide acquisition of
property. The introduction of the German Commercial Code into Austrian law in 1939 implied, of
course, the introduction of the rules on bona
fide acquisition. In addition, the Austrian General Civil Code provides for the acquisition of
property in good faith as well. Hoping to bring
the two codes into conformity, the Austrian legislator added a fifth paragraph to § 366 HGB
(German Commercial Code), according to which the
rules that are more advantageous to the bona fide
purchaser are to be applied. Austrian civil law
provisions provide that property can be acquired
bona fide without payment by undistinguishably
merging money or transferable instruments (bearer
bonds) with the property of the acquirer[45] and by

transactions _inter_ _vivos_ by the sham heir.[46]
Property can be acquired in good faith for valuable consideration from a tradesman carrying on
any trade in accordance with §§ 366 et seq. HGB,
subject to the exceptions described earlier. In
addition, § 367 HGB restricts bona fide acquisi-
tions to the acquisition of property at a public
auction, from a tradesman authorized to carry on
such a trade, or by purchase from the person to
whom the owner himself had entrusted the property
for use, preservation, or any other purpose. Most
legal writers demand conveyance in order for the
acquisition to be valid. It should be noted,
however, that constitutum possessorium does not
suffice, neither does good faith restricted to
the power of dispostions for transactions not
underlying § 366 HBG.

IV. INTERDEPENDENCE BETWEEN THE OBLIGATION AND THE SECURITY

It is not surprising that a security (collat-
eral debt) depends on a principal debt. The debt-
or providing security will be interested in the
free disposition of his goods once the obligation
ceases upon payment of the debt. On the other
hand, a legitimate interest of the creditor in
the security can generally be denied if the secured debt was paid.

However, a thorough investigation of the ways
security can be provided reveals digressions from
the principle described above. This is due to the
structural differences between legal systems and
the system itself. We do not intend to go into
detail; yet, two main problems should be mentioned: Some security is merely extinguished upon
retransfer of the items serving as security back
to the party who had provided the security. This

will be the case when the items could not be
transferred with an implied (or constructive)
agreement of retransfer at the time of transfer.
On the other hand, some forms of public disclosure, especially those necessitating registration, require deletion of the security from the
register when it has ended or become obsolete.
These two alternatives lead to an additional
problem: The party to whom security has been
provided could misuse the public disclosure of
the items serving as security, thus enabling
third parties, in "reliance on the material circumstances," to acquire the security right and
the obligation as well (although the debt was
paid off). Moreover, the secured party, by the
prima facie significance of possession or custody
of the items, is able to provide ownership to
third parties.

A. So-called transfer of ownership by way of
security requires retransfer of ownership to the
party providing the security. We are usually
dealing with a mere contractual obligation of the
secured party to retransfer ownership. Therefore,
the party providing the security has just one
alternative to protect his interests: He will
insist upon simultaneous mutual performance,
i.e., payment of the debt due contingent upon
simultaneous retransfer of the items serving as
security.

Only those legal systems that acknowledge the
establishment of ownership by way of security
even without conveyance of the items serving as
security, i.e., the constitutum possessorium,
will permit an anticipated retransfer. This is,
as far as we know, the case only in Germany.

B. Publicity of security can be effected in two
ways: by the creditor having custody of the items
serving as security, or by registration. In the
former case, the parties can alter custody whenever they wish to do so; in the case of registration an entry can be deleted merely by produc-
ing the relevant documents and applying for deletion, unless, of course, the effects of registration cease upon lapse of time.

C. However, even without changing any means of
public disclosure, security rights may be extinguished if their legal validity, in accordance
with the principle of accessoriness, depends upon
the existence of the secured debt. This applies,
however, only where rights in rem and "elasticity" of ownership are main features of the relevant legal system. The theoretical construction
underlying this technique may be outlined as
follows: Limited real rights -- in fact only a
pledge will qualify in this context -- restrict
proprietary rights (ownership); however, with
their extinction the entire ownership is restored
to its original extent. After payment of the
secured debt, an action based on ownership (<u>rei
vindicatio</u>) provides sufficient protection to the
party furnishing security, as the party to whom
security has been provided cannot counteract by
insisting on an extinguished security right.

V. SPECIFIC PREREQUISITES FOR ACQUISITION OF SE-
CURITY (INCLUDING RESERVATION OF PROPRIETARY
RIGHTS)

The specific prerequisites for acquisition of
security should be explained in detail. In regard to the reservation of property and pledge,
all immovables recorded in a public register

should be mentioned first. Validity of security
requires, of course, compliance with all the
conditions of registration. Obviously, custody
must be established as well, if public disclosure
is desired. These conclusions, however, are not
at the heart of the problem.

The main question that arises in regard to
the registration of security rights for movables
concerns jurisdiction. The problem of jurisdiction does not arise when immovables are registered (whatever nature the registration system
may be) since jurisdiction in such cases is determined by the location of the immovables in
question. On the other hand, movables can be
taken from one place to another and thus entail a
wide variety of regulations.

As far as the registration of ships is concerned, jurisdiction is usually determined by the
ship's flag, subsidarily by the home port. Land-
locked states can register sea-going vessels as
well and provide for a fictious home port located
at a considerable altitude above sea level. Few
people are aware that Vienna's register of ships
comprises merchant vessels with a volume of
10,000 to 16,000 registered tons. The same is
true of the Swiss Navy, registered at Basle.

Acquisition of non-possessory pledge has been
subject to diverse regulations in **French law.** We
will not deal with the details of pledge secured
by enterprises in this context. Worth mentioning
are, however, pledges secured by motor vehicles
and investment goods. According to a law of 1934,
the seller of a motor vehicle can acquire a
pledge by registering at the licensing authority
(préfecture), provided he produces the written
contract of sale. This is a non-possessory pawn,
securing only a portion of the mercantile value
and limited in time.[47] The pledgee is hereby put

into the position of custodian. As to investment goods, certain goods (outillage et matériel d'équipement) are to be registered at a commercial court having jurisdiction for registration of the pledgee (nantissement).[48] For some goods security can be issued on the basis of a warehouse warrant that is an order paper. The warrant will be effective against third parties only if it was executed by the court. Under French law there are additional forms of pledges for other types of goods, each pledge differing slightly in the way it can be formally established and in its legal effect.[49]

In **Italian law**, machinery exceeding a certain value is secured by a hypothec in accordance with Art. 2762 codice civile. The security must be registered at the pretura, as must the reservation of proprietary rights on the machinery. The reservation of title is not[50] limited in time; however, the hypothec is restricted to three years. The pretura at the place where the machinery is located will have jurisdiction.

In **Swiss law**, Art. 1 of the Ordinance of the Federal Court (Bundesgericht) on the Registration of Reservation of Proprietary Rights provides that the Betreibungsamt (executing board) at the domicile of the acquirer will have jurisdiction. If the domicile is changed, the registration is effective for an additional three months.[51] This rule, which was also adopted by the Turkish Republic, leads to various practical problems concerning jurisdiction. These difficulties have not entirely been eliminated by a law on compulsory auction of immovable property procedure. Thus, it often occurs, for example, that the domicile of the user and the situs of the goods do not coincide, which can easily deceive third persons.

VI. EXPIRATION OF SECURITY

We could speak of an advantageous principle in this context if security were to expire at the moment it satisfied the aims set by the parties. For example, when the security is realized in favour of the secured claim and the claim is satisfied by other means, the principle of accessoriness mentioned in section IV above applies. Yet, the principle is subject to certain modifications depending on the specific forms of public disclosure for a particular security and the system of transfer -- still in force in some legal systems. Security in rem can extinguish as the result of certain events, e.g., destruction of the goods[52]; expiration of the time specified by statute for certain kinds of security; transfer of a security to a different place; absorption of the item serving as security (by merging it with other materials) or its consumption; the bona fide acquisition of unemcumbered goods by a third party etc.

In view of the great number of security rights and their possibility of expiration, it is impossible to include all or even most of the particulars. Therefore, we will present a brief survey to exemplify the problems at stake.

1. In legal systems where the **reservation of proprietary rights** does not require specific public disclosure, paying off the secured debt satisfies the prerequisite for the passing of property, and thus the security expires at that moment. Note that the secured debt must not necessarily be the purchase price obligation, especially if transfer of ownership by way of security demands no specific public disclosure.[53] The party who has received security but does not have

the item in his custody or possession, cannot
convey ownership to third parties. If registration is necessary in order for the reservation of
proprietary rights to be effective, as is the
case under Swiss law,[54] then deletion of the
entry will also be necessary. Otherwise, third
parties could acquire the property, not in reliance on the register but rather on the seller's
ownership that had not yet been extinguished.

In **French law** the reservation of proprietary
rights is also extinguished as the result of
bankruptcy of the purchaser. This rather surprising result of bankruptcy proceedings is based on
the fact that a rei vindicatio for movables in
the custody of the common debtor is barred to a
certain extent. This case law of the French
courts[55] was codified on July 13, 1967 in a
special statute redrafting bankruptcy law.

Thus, French law provides for expiration of
the reservation of proprietary rights as well as
of the seller's privilège[56] in case of bankruptcy
of the purchaser. The consequences are quite
clear: The security is invalidated in those cases
where such is useful and necessary.

2. With the exception of German law and in respect of trusts in the common law, public disclosure is required by nearly all legal systems
for the establishment and continuance of secured
rights, for ownership by way of security. The
policy argument that a creditor should be able to
realize security is obvious here. In this respect
Austrian law has rather rigorous rules, according
to which every (at least unconditional) retransfer of items serving as security extinguishes the
security.[57] The **Swiss** legislator is rather severe
as well; however, only in regard to temporary
suspension of the pledge.[58]

Neither in legal systems where no specific continuous public disclosure is required nor in others does the mere discharge of a secured debt result in automatic restoration of the property to the party who had provided security. Instead, a special retransfer is necessary. Of course, the parties, when concluding the security transaction, can stipulate retransfer of the items serving as security upon payment of the secured debt.

3. In regard to the **pledge,** two main groups can be distinguished. The first includes those legal systems which mention "real rights." Here, the problem of retransfer does not arise when a "limited real right" is redeemed. In this case the concept of "elasticity of property" has the effect that the limitation of a complete <u>jus</u> <u>in</u> <u>rem</u> simply expires. On the other hand, in the second group, retransfer of the items serving as security is required. Additional distinctions need to be made in cases where continuous public disclosure of the pledge is required or publicity is effected by registration. It may, for example, be necessary to discontinue public disclosure in order to extinguish all effects of the pawn which served as security. This may be the case where a third party can acquire a pledge <u>bona</u> <u>fide</u> from the pledgee even after the secured debt has been paid off. Moreover, expiration of a pledge may depend upon suspension of a subpledge, the existence of which prevents encumbrances from expiring.

4. Rights to retain property comprise the right of refusal to surrender. These rights are not "real rights" in the strict sense of the term. Since security is their very purpose, they usually expire together with the debt that is paid

off. No specific public disclosure is required,
and therefore, no special right must be retrans-
ferred. Hence, it can be said that they are
usually extinguished by voluntary waiver of custody.

P A R T   B

VII. CONFLICT OF LAWS

1. Scope of application of the Convention

The Vienna Convention on Contracts for the
International Sale of Goods represents a body of
uniform law containing no conflict-of-laws rules,
only substantive law. This qualification raises
the question whether the Convention applies automatically if all the prerequisites are fulfilled
(so-called _ipso iure_ application) or, alternatively, only if its application is orderd by
conflicts rules.[59] Still another problem is
whether the contracting parties can opt for the
application of the Convention or are entitled to
exclude it.[60] The Convention itself provides the
starting point for the solution of these problems.

The Convention is to be applied when its
autonomous prerequisites are established in principle.[61] Furthermore, the Convention provides for
so-called indirect application[62] when the conflicts rules of a Member or also Non-Member State
refer to the law of a Contracting State as the
applicable law,[63] provided that the parties have
their places of business in different states. If
a party has not been informed that the other
party's place of business is not in the state
where the contract was concluded, the Convention,
as specified in Art. 1(2), shall not apply. The

same idea can be found in Art. 10(a) in the words: "... having regard to the circumstances known to or contemplated by the parties at any time before or at the conclusion of the contract." Unanticipated application of the Convention should be avoided; therefore, it will not be applied if the foreign principal remained undisclosed to the other party.

According to the terms of the Convention, the parties can agree upon the application of the Convention as such, unless the conflicts rules lead to a different result. On the contrary, Art. 6 allows the parties to opt out the application of the Convention completely; they can even vary the effect of any provision.

The exceptions to the scope of application of the Convention provided for in Articles 2 and 3 are valid irrespective of the ground for invocation of the Convention.

2. Problems of connection outside the scope of the Convention

It seems inevitable to point out these problems since the choice of law of the parties is often likely to be linked to other elements. Obviously, the validity of a contract of sale -- not covered by the Convention -- is one example. Here the matter at stake does not involve questions of legal capacity, capacity to act or prohibitory exchange regulations, at least not subject to the parties' power of disposal. The scope of the law selected by the parties will certainly be significant as far as the conflicts rules, albeit few, are concerned in regard to permitting a choice of law in the field of property law. The same is true in systems where connecting factors point to the same applicable law for a debt to be secured and a security transaction (e.g., pawning etc.).

Thus, where it is determined -- either by a choice of law made by the parties or by statutory rules -- that the same _lex_ _causae_ is applicable both to the matters within the scope of the Convention and to peripheral matters as well, we are dealing with the uniform application of law, and the Convention becomes an integral part of the applicable substantive law. All the problems caused by the need of harmonization and the process of gap-filling are identical with those arising from the application of the uniform law of the Convention _vis-à-vis_ substantive law respectively.

The conflicts problems worth mentioning include the following: In Member States the question arises as to which law outside the scope of the Convention is applicable. On the other hand, in Non-Member States whose conflicts rules refer to the application of the Convention by reference to the law of a Member State, the question arises in regard to the scope of the Convention whether the reference to a foreign internal law remains a reference to the private international law rules outside the scope of the Convention. Similar questions arise if the parties agree that the Convention shall apply.

The genesis of the Convention clearly demonstrates that various conflict-of-laws problems had been expected. It is therefore not surprising that a reservation clause was introduced in Art. 95, according to which any State, at the time of ratification, may declare that it will not be bound to the indirect application specified in Art. 1(1)(b).

In this context, we may point out a transitional problem occurring prior to the coming into force of the Convention. According to the Convention, the parties can agree upon the application of the Convention as <u>lex</u> <u>contractus</u> despite the fact that, due to the lack of a sufficient number of ratifications, it has not yet come into force. Are we dealing here with the choice of private international law rules excluding the mandatory substantive law (that would otherwise be applicable) or is it merely the choice of a <u>lex</u> <u>contractus</u> within the framework of the mandatory substantive law? From the point of view of the law of a Non-Member State as the <u>lex</u> <u>fori</u>, the latter will be true. From that of a Member State, the former interpretation is unlikely, although it seems to comply with Art. 1(1)(b) of the Convention.[64] From the time of ratification until the coming into force of the Convention, Member States are to regard their own internal law and the applicable law as equivalent. Once the Convention is ratified, the Member States have no further influence on the day the Convention will take binding effect.

Another problem concerns the opting-out clause in Art. 6 of the Convention. It provides that the parties can exclude the application of the Convention or derogate from its provisions, both subject to the formal requirements stipulated by Articles 12 and 96. If the parties opt out the application of the Convention, the applicable law will be determined by the appropriate private international law rules. On the other hand, if merely some provisions are excluded or modified, the question arises as to which provisions will be applied and, in the case of modification, which character the modified provisions will assume.

This question can be answered straight away: Since the freedom of the parties to modify particular provisions is provided for by the Convention itself, any restrictions are delimited by the Convention, and not by the actual lex fori.

However, if the parties exclude some provisions, the answer is more complicated. We are not only faced with the exclusion of particular provisions as such, but also with the filling of corresponding gaps. Here, too, the Convention grants the parties the freedom to exclude some provisions. Therefore, the parties are authorized to fill the gaps caused by their contractual freedom as well, without any restrictions as to mandatory substantive law. If the parties fail to fill the gaps, the otherwise applicable law will be decisive. In this case there are two solutions available: The first provides recourse to the parties' choice of law in order to fill the gaps by application of its conflicts rules, while the second points to the Convention itself.

Art. 7 aims at a gradual process. In the interpretation of the Convention, emphasis is placed on its international character and the uniformity of its application as well as on the observance of good faith in international trade (para. 1).[65] In addition, the need to promote conformity is stressed: conformity with the general principles on which the Convention is based, and in the absence of such principles, conformity with the law applicable by virtue of the rules of private international law (para. 2). Thus, the Convention takes absolute priority, unless there are no general principles having legal authority; in the second instance, the law applicable by virtue of the private international law rules will be decisive.

In view of this basic principle, it is easy to justify that the law designated by private international law rules be applied to problems outside, yet still adjacent to the sphere of application of the Convention. In the latter case, a mere problem of "adaptation" of the Convention may arise. Adaptation within the scope of the Convention does not seem to be too difficult since the Convention, as was already mentioned, does not contain a systematic-dogmatic body of provisions. In fact, substantive law can therefore be determined without effort and consistently leads to the uniform law.

3. Hence, practically all the **private international law problems** to be dealt with lie outside the scope of the law of sales. Generally, it is the so-called "incidental question" (question préalable, Vorfrage) that we are concerned with. The Convention merely governs the formation of the contract ("formal approval") and the respective reciprocal rights and obligations of the parties. Consequently, private international law problems must be settled within the framework of the law of sales. According to Art. 4, the validity of the contract (legal capacity and the parties' capacity to contract, lack of consent as the result of duress, mistake, unsoundness of mind or otherwise, violation of boni mores and other grounds of nullity) and the effect of the contract on the property in the goods sold are issues excluded from the Convention and are thus to be governed by the applicable domestic law.

4. According to most domestic conflicts rules, the validity of a sales contract regarding the capacity of the parties is usually governed by a different substantive law than the one applicable to the question of lack of consent or the absence of a statute leading to voidness or relative nullity of the contract.

As a general rule, the capacity of a person
is governed either by the law of his nationality[66] or by the law of the person's domicile,
habitual residence or, at least, his simple residence in the country. The controversy on the law
of domicile and the law of nationality as the
personal law has been going on for many years and
is presumable well known. In common law systems
(the United Kingdom, the Common Wealth and the
United States) the personal law is the law of
domicile, whereas Continental Europe has changed
its policy on the matter. Until the first half of
the nineteenth century the law of domicile had
generally been advocated, save for some counter-
proposals in France. As a result of the ideas of
the French Revolution of 1784, nationalism became
popular. The principle of nationality, i.e., the
citizenship of a person determines the law applicable to his capacity, was introduced in the
French Code civil and adopted by other countries.
Countries with a considerable number of immi-
grants are interested in the amalgamation of such
groups and therefore claim that the principle of
domicile is more useful. Thus, some non-common
law countries e.g., Brazil, adhere to this principle.

Generally, lack of consent is governed by the
law of the contract itself. This is the concept
underlying Art. 4(a) of the Convention. It fails
to offer a solution for the problem that under
some laws: a) a contract afflicted with error is
void or voidable, or b) even unilateral amendments by one party are permitted. With regard to
lack of consent, the Convention falls short of
any specific rules. We thus have to inquire into
the spirit and purpose of the Convention in order
to fill the gap.

Under Art. 4 specific domestic rules relating

to the validity of the contract and introduced
for reasons of state interest, business and commerce, currency etc. are not to be interferred
with. Undoubtedly, protective measures taken by a
State must be governed by the law of this State
since these are sovereign acts. Whether foreign
courts are thus automatically obliged to respect
these measures, remains to be seen. Here, a dif-
ferentiated approach is recommended: If the contracting parties are linked by a convention,
e.g., a currency agreement, and are simultaneously confronted with matters of national concern,
the "interference statute" will apply. If this
prerequisite is not fulfilled, the courts are
under no obligation to apply such an agreement,
though nothing will prevent them from doing so in
the interest of the party involved.

The transfer and acquisition of property, the
acquisition and expiration of a security in rem
and the prerequisites for the protection of a
bona _fide_ purchaser give rise to considerable
problems.

Until the beginning of this century most
writers advocated the _lex_ _rei_ _sitae_ as the proper
law governing real rights including property,
pledge, mortgage etc. At the time, the _lex_ _situs_
coincided with the _lex_ _fori_. The latter was gradually introduced and became well established.
Increasing specialization has had, however, due
influence on the discussion of the proper law.
The _lex_ _rei_ _sitae_ still governs real rights relating to immovables, a point of view which has
been upheld until today, whereas the proper law
of matters dealing with real rights relating to
movables is subject to varied legislation. Some
recent codifications differentiate between "property" and "possession"; moreover, they have
introduced a special proper law for negotiable

instruments and created the category of intangible movables. In addition, distinctions are made between the means of transport (e.g., by ship, by airplane and helicopter, by hoovercraft [e.g., in India], by truck, railway, coaches and lorries), between so-called _res in transitu_ (whether the movables are import or export items), and even between contractual and statutory liens, pledges and the right to retain property. A thorough investigation of all recent statutes on conflict of laws reveals the mere conceptual character of an intended uniformity. In reality presuppositions and controversial conclusions still exist, while mutual agreement on the process of differentiation and even on classification has vanished. Nevertheless, some, although few, systematic or dogmatic concepts can be derived from the conflicts rules in recent statutes. Hence, we will attempt to trace the ideas underlying recent legislation on conflict of laws.

Basically, two maxims on the proper law governing real rights to movables have been advocated. The oldest view considers the personal status of the proprietor to be decisive. This principle, however, results in a vicious circle since the problem as to which of the two parties is entitled to enjoy proprietary rights is not solved. The rule _mobilia ossibus inhaerent_ (movables inherent in the bones), advocated by early writers, has been reactivated today and applied, e.g., to luggage and other movables carried by a traveler. For the purposes of conflict of laws, the old rule mentioned above applies to both regardless whether the personal law is a person's nationality or domicile (sc. residence).

The second maxim, the _lex situs_, avoids the vicious circle. However, notwithstanding the degree of certainty provided by the _lex rei si-_

tae, problems still arise as the result of a vicious transfer of the movables to another country (e.g., by the error of a third party or by the transfer of stolen goods).

Both concepts reflect a static background; however, they do not offer an explanation for the acquisition of real rights.

By contrast, the dynamic approach to the question "which law governs the creation of 'real rights'" seems to be more useful.[67] Here again we are faced with the three main systems of transfer and thus a differentiation is needed.

According to the doctrine of abstract real contract, the law of the country where the conveyance takes place will usually govern the transfer. With regard to the obligation (titulus), the doctrine of transfer leads to the same result. Here, however, the incidental question as to which national law governs the validity of the title complicates the application of this doctrine. Consequently, the proper law cannot be ascertained that easily. In this context we cannot deal with the various views that have been expressed on the subject of the incidental question. But we should devote attention to another problem.

Contrary to the former concept, the principle of consent to the transfer of property supports application of the law governing the obligatory contract (sc. executory agreement to transfer) in respect of the transfer as well. In this context there are two important exceptions to be pointed out.

First, the law of the place where a legal act takes place (lex loci actus) governs the bona fide purchase and its legal consequences (acquisition of property or of real rights). In order to ensure clear-cut solutions, formal require-

ments for acquisition, e.g., market overt, public
auction, tradesman authorized to carry on such a
trade etc. must be governed by the law of the
place where the goods were actually acquired.
Nevertheless, a _traditio_ _brevi_ _manu_ and a mandatory order to a third party as the custodian may
well be governed by the law of the place where
the goods are located.

Second, in some cases, continuous publicity
is required. The removal of goods from one place
to another will cause a change of the applicable
law governing the question of expiration of some
real rights due to the termination of continuous
publicity. On the other hand, acquisition of
these rights in the country from which the goods
were removed will be governed in accordance with
the law of this country.[68] The problem of the
change of jurisdiction caused by the removal of
movables from one place to another and the doctrine of vested rights (_droits_ _acquis_) seems to
remain unsolved. Public policy arguments might
lead to the exclusion of foreign law. The old
dictum _ubi_ _res_ _ibi_ _ius_ _est_ serves as the common
basis of these two exceptions.

The law governing the acquisition of property
and security applies to the expiration of security rights as well, even if there has been no
change of jurisdiction caused by transfer of the
goods from one place to another.[69] This result
can be achieved by broaching the incidental question again irrespective of the change of jurisdiction and the place of custody.

In one case, only the inner link between different substantive rules prevails: If a _bona_ _fide_
purchaser acquires proprietary rights in goods
free from any encumbrances, all security rights
previously acquired by another party will expire.

NOTES

1. The filling of gaps is a separate problem; P. Volken deals with it in this book at pp. 42-45.

2. Dingliche Sachenrechte are rights which a person enjoys in respect of a particular thing including the unrestricted right of disposal; they can be asserted against anybody (ius in rem).

3. Persönliche Sachenrechte give a person the right to bring a claim against another person (ius in persona, according to Pandectists ius ad rem).

4. Art. 2114 Code civil explicitly acknowledges the character in rem of the hypothecary law.

5. M. Ferid, Das französische Zivilrecht, vol. II (Frankfurt am Main/Berlin 1971) p. 877; see 3 A 1 where its content is correctly qualified as so-called "resting property law."

6. 1. 20 C de pactis 2,3: Traditionibus et usucapionibus dominia rerum, non nudis pactis transferentur.

7. See French Code civil, Articles 711, 1138, 1583.

8. See H. Mazeaud, Leçons de droit civil vol.III (Paris 1959) no. 66 et seq. Public disclosure has proved to be important for the registration of various pledges as well as chattel mortgages on water and aircraft. A pledge signifies the right to retain possession of another's property pending discharge of a debt.

9. French Code civil, Art. 2076.

10. Legal policy rather than doctrinal arguments on the topic can be found in H. Mazeaud, supra n. 8, vol. III, at no. 66.

11. M. Ferid, supra n. 5, vol. I, at p. 181, see 1 C 17.

12. H. Mazeaud, supra n. 8, vol. III, at no. 68;

in differentiating between a "contract of pledge" and a _traditio_, Mazeaud regards the latter as a legal act in the sense of a "real contract," i.e., specific performance of the contract.

13. This solution is derived from Art. 2279(1) of the French Code civil which reads: " en fait de meubles la possession vaut titre."

14. See Articles 609 and 1091 of the Spanish Codigo civil; Art. 3.9.2.1. of the Dutch Nieuw Burgerlijk Wetboek; §§ 425 et seq. of the Austrian ABGB; Articles 714 et seq. of the Swiss ZGB.

15. Articles 1447 et seq. of the Italian Codice civile (1865) were replaced by Articles 1476 et seq. and 1523 of the Italian Codice civile (1942).

16. However, if goods are transferred for the purpose of custody or loan etc., the transferrer, as a rule, does not intend to transfer ownership to the transferee.

17. E.g., cf. § 429 of the Austrian ABGB.

18. The _hypotheca_ _universalis_ _(generalis)_ of the revenue authority in Roman law still provides a leading negative example: These priority rights could not be identified by third parties and thus impaired business carried out in good faith.

19. So-called _Streckengeschäft_.

20. The Pandectist School adherred to the subjective _causa_ _traditionis_ characterized by excessive abstractness; consequently, a _causa_ merely presupposed by the parties, i.e., a constructive cause, proved to be sufficient. A direct parallel to the third and historically youngest view on the matter is mentioned _infra_.

21. See §§ 380 and 425 of the Austrian ABGB. According to § 381, a legal title is obligatory even for the acquisition of unattached property. This, however, is already reflected in the hered-

itary liberty to take possession of it.
22. G. Dulckeit, <u>Die Verdinglichung obligato-</u>
<u>rischer Rechte</u> (Tübingen 1951) p. 32; cf. K.
Larenz, <u>Lehrbuch des Schuldrechts</u>, 12th ed. vol.
II (München 1981) 11 ss.
23. F. Bydlinski, in H. Klang, <u>Kommentar zum ABGB</u>
2th ed. vol. IV/2 (Wien 1978) pp. 370-376.
24. § 425 ABGB advocates the doctrine of <u>titulus</u>
and <u>modus acquirendi</u> stating that: "The mere
title does not convey ownership. Ownership of
property, and all real rights in general, can be
acquired only through the legal formalities of
delivery and acceptance, except in cases determined otherwise by the law."
25. Quite a few problems remain unsolved: To what
extent does nullity of the contractual agreement
brought about by usury, for example, invalidate
the real contract?
26. French Code civil, see articles 2074 and
2076.
27. Italian Codice civile (1942), Art. 2786 ss.
28. "Scrittura con data certa," Italian Codice
civile, Art. 2787 al 2.
29. Not necessarily exclusive possession.
30. Introduced by the Law of December 16, 1954.
31. <u>Vertrauen auf den äusseren Tatbestand</u>. After
M. Wellspacher analyzed the problem in <u>Das Ver-</u>
<u>trauen auf äussere Tatbestände im bürgerlichen</u>
<u>Recht</u> (Wien 1906) the expression became <u>terminus</u>
<u>technicus</u>.
32. See especially the British Sale of Goods Act,
ss. 21-24.
33. The historical background of this rule is described by H. Kiefner, "Qui possidet dominus esse
praesumitur," 79 <u>Zeitschrift der Savigny-Stiftung</u>
<u>für Rechtsgeschichte</u>, (Romanistische Abteilung)
(Weimar 1962) p. 239 ss, p. 218 ss.
34. Either actual custody or custody of goods in

the care of a caretaker; constitutum possessorium
does not suffice; see H. Mazeaud, supra n. 8, no.
1622.
35. Although the wording of Art. 2279 (2) of the
French Code civil mentions only vol (theft) and
perte (loss), the doctrine and courts do not
consider the text as being exhaustive.
36. See Art. 2280(1) of the French Code civil.
37. "... le prix qu'il lui a coûte."
38. § 366 HGB (German Commercial Code).
39. See § 816(1) German BGB: "If a person without
title to an object makes a disposition of it
which is binding upon the person having title, he
is bound to hand over to the latter what he has
obtained by the disposition. If the disposition
is made gratuitously, the same obligation is
imposed upon the person who acquires a legal
advantage directly through the disposition."
40. Including foreign currencies.
41. § 367 German HGB.
42. See Articles 933-935 Swiss ZGB (Civil Code).
43. See Art. 1153 Italian Codice civile (1942).
44. See Art. 1994 Italian Codice civile (1942).
45. See § 371 ABGB.
46. See § 824 ABGB.
47. Depending on the type of motor vehicle and
the amount of credit, resp. 9 to 18 months.
48. For more details see E. Mezger, "Zur neuesten
Entwicklung des kaufmännischen Registerpfand-
rechts in Frankreich," 115 ZHR (1952) p. 150; see
also J. Féblot/E. Mezger, "Eigentumsvorbehalt und
Rücktrittsklausel bei Lieferungen nach Frankreich," 20 RabelsZ (1955) p. 662.
49. More details in M. Planiol/G. Ripert/J. Bou-
langer, Traité de Droit Civil d'après le Traité
de Planiol (Paris 1958) 1230 ss.
50. See Art. 1524 Italian Codice civile.
51. Art. 3 of the said Ordinance also states the

conditions under which registration must be carried out at the new domicile.

52. We will not deal with questions on compensation for damages, e.g., whether the owner of the goods and/or the party to whom security has been furnished can claim damages against the insurer or against the damaging party.

53. E.g., as in German law.

54. Cf. Articles 715 et seq. Swiss ZGB; the Turkish Republic adopted Swiss private law in the part mentioned as well.

55. Cass. Civ. 3.3.1935 D 1935. 1.313.

56. Art. 2102 no. 2 French Code civil.

57. The latest decision by the OGH (Austrian Supreme Court) dates from Dec. 14, 1983, published in various gazettes, at first in Juristische Blätter (1984) p. 550; however, inadequately analyzed by M. Schwimann.

58. See Art. 888 Swiss ZGB; and P. Tuor/B. Schnyder, Das schweizerische Zivilgesetzbuch (1965) p. 636: "... hebt zwar das Pfandrecht nicht auf, lähmt aber dessen Wirkungen solange, als sich die Sache beim Verpfänder befindet..." (the pledge is not extinguished, but its effects are suspended as long as the pledgor has the item).

59. See P. Volken, chapt. two supra, at pp. 25 et seq.

60. Ibid., at p. 35.

61. Art. 1(1)(a).

62. In German terminology Vorschaltlösung.

63. Art. 1(1)(b).

64. According to Art. 95, the parties can make a reservation clause with regard to this very rule. This problem obviously did not arise in the decisions on the Hague Conventions on Sales that have been published.

65. It is doubtful whether any international standards have been developed yet.

66. I.e., the so-called law of nationality (<u>lex</u>
<u>patriae</u>) as the personal law of the individual,
contrary to the domicile connecting factor.
67. The <u>bona</u> <u>fide</u> purchaser is considered <u>infra</u>.
68. Cf. H. Hoyer, "Sind Sicherungseigentum und
Pfandrecht gleich zu behandeln?" <u>Juristische</u>
<u>Blätter</u> (1984) p. 543.
69. Admittedly, some legal systems consider a removal unimportant if the goods were removed without permission of the entitled party who thus
lost custody of them.

CHAPTER FOURTEEN

THE GENEVA CONVENTION ON AGENCY IN THE INTERNATIONAL SALE OF GOODS

PETAR ŠARČEVIĆ
Professor of Law, Rijeka/Lausanne

I. INTRODUCTION

Conducting business in foreign countries through an agent is now a common practice. The institution of agency, which developed inter alia as a result of the division of labor, is known to all legal systems.[1] However, as Müller-Freienfels has emphasized,[2] for centuries the historical development of the law of agency has followed independent courses, e.g., in the common law and civil law systems. Not only do the legal situations involving agency differ in the two systems, but also the concepts, terminology, and the legal technique itself. In short, as Eörsi has said, both systems "have a structure of their own and the two structures mutually differ."[3]

Thus it is not surprising that the Rome Institute for Unification of Private Law (UNIDROIT) launched a research project on the unification of the law of agency as early as 1935. It wasn't, however, until nearly fifty years later that the UNIDROIT Draft Convention on Agency in the Inter-

national Sale of Goods (hereafter: Agency Convention or merely Convention) was adopted at Geneva
in 1983.

In order to gain a better understanding of
the efforts that have gone into the creation of
the Agency Convention, and, in particular, of the
solutions laid down in the Convention, it is
first necessary to make some introductory remarks
on the law of agency. This shall be done by
briefly pointing out some of the main differences
in the law of agency in the civil law and common
law systems.

1. In the common law, agency is defined as "the
relationship which exists between two persons,
one of whom expressly or impliedly consents that
the other should represent him or act on his
behalf [principal], and the other of whom similarly consents to represent the former or so to
act [agent]."[4] To greatly simplify the matter, it
can be said that the common law concept of agency
distinguishes between three different legal situations where: a) the agent names the principal
prior to the conclusion of the contract, b) the
agent acts as agent but does not name the principal, and c) the agent acts on behalf of an "undisclosed principal"[5] purporting to contract on
his behalf.

On the other hand, the civil law countries
make a distinction between direct and indirect
agency. Whereas the term **direct agency** refers to
legal situations where the agent acts not only on
behalf but also in the name of the principal, in
indirect agency the so-called commission agent
concludes contracts in his own name but for the
account of the principal. In the latter case, a
direct contractual relationship is established
between the agent and the third party as opposed

to direct agency where the contractors concluded
between the principal and the third party through
the agent.

2. These differences are also reflected in the
theoretical approaches to agency in the common
law and civil law systems. Today, the modern
theory of agency in the civil law is dominated by
the principle of separation which is based on the
abstract nature of authority. This principle
differentiates between the internal and external
aspects of agency by regarding the mandate, i.e.,
the contract which binds the principal and the
agent, as the internal aspect of the relationship, and the authority, i.e., the agent's power
to deal with the third party, as the external
aspect of agency.

The separation of agency into internal and
external aspects has also had its effect on civil
law legislation where there are two types of
rules on agency: the first of which governs, in
general, the external relations between the parties in regard to the authority, and the second
the internal relations of the parties in special
types of agency contracts. Schmitthoff was referring to the second type of rules when he once
stated that the theory of separation "has been
made workable by the necessary corollary of frag-
menting the agency concept into usually statu-
torily defined types of intermediaryship."[6]

The principle of separation is the underlying
concept of agency not only in Germany but in many
other civil law countries as well.[7] It should be
pointed out, however, that in civil law countries
where the Romanic influence was predominant -- in
France, Italy, and other countries which followed
the French Code civil -- the tendency was to
"regard the authority of the agent as a mere

aspect of the underlying contract,"[8] thereby
ignoring the distinction between the internal and
external aspects of agency.[9] Although this has
changed somewhat over the past few decades, the
French approach to agency is still evident in
some countries.[10]

In the common law the theoretical foundation
of agency is the doctrine of identity of the
principal and the agent; it has its expression,
e.g., in § 1 of the US Second Restatement Agency:

> Agency is the fiduciary relation which
> results from the manifestation of con-
> sent by one person to another that the
> other shall act on his behalf and sub-
> ject to his control, and consent by the
> other so to act.

By adopting the theory of identity, the common
law has developed a unitary concept of agency
which admits only few exceptions.[11]

3. Although both systems have developed their
own legal theories, the main problem remains the
same: How can it be justified that a contract
between the agent and the third party legally
binds the principal, while the agent "remains a
stranger to the rights and obligations" arising
from that contract.[12]

Thus it is not surprising that, in Schmitthoff's words, "in no branch of international law
is the cleavage between legal theory and commercial reality greater than in the law of agency."[13] Schmitthoff continues by pointing out that
the legal characteristic of various types of
intermediaryship, as elaborated by commercial
practice, are often at variance with the concept
of agency developed by legal theory.[14]

In view of the legal difficulties arising in
international trade as the result of the numerous

theoretical and legislative differences in the
field of agency law, the idea emerged that negotiations should be initiated with the aim of
unifying the law of agency in order to make it
"safer" for use in international trade.

II. EFFORTS TO UNIFY THE LAW OF AGENCY

1. The unification project initiated by UNIDROIT
in 1935 was interrupted during World War II, then
resumed in 1946. In 1961 two draft Uniform laws
were published, one on agency for private law
relations of an international character, the
other on contracts of commission in the international sale or purchase of goods.[15] The drafts,
however, were rejected by the common law countries on the ground that the solutions therein
conflicted with their theoretical and practical
approaches to agency.[16]

Thereafter, a Committee of Governmental Experts was convened by UNIDROIT to end the dead-
lock. Its decision to narrow the field in which
unification should be attempted resulted in the
draft text of a new Uniform law dealing with the
practical aspects of agency contracts of an international character for the sale and purchase
of goods.[17] In 1973 the draft text was sent to
the member countries of UNIDROIT for consideration. Six years later the Government of Romania
hosted a diplomatic conference with the purpose
of adopting the draft Convention on Agency.[18]
Although the Bucharest Conference did not achieve
its goal, it nevertheless made the drafters aware
that the Uniform law still dealt with too many
matters which were subject to sometimes very
different regulations under national laws.

At the request of the UNIDROIT Council in
1980, the preparatory work was continued by a

small group of well-known experts representing
the common law, the civil law and the Socialist
countries. Aware, on the one hand, of the need
for a uniform law on agency in the international
sale of goods, yet, on the other, of the great
number of "unbridgeable" legal differences, the
Group of Experts recommended that unification be
attempted only in respect of the external relations of agency, thus eliminating the internal
relations between the principal and the agent
from the scope of the Convention. Accordingly,
UNIDROIT proceeded by concentrating its efforts
on unifying the external aspects of agency "affecting the position of the third party to a
contract of international sale vis-à-vis both the
principal and the agent."[19]

Before turning our attention to the Agency
Convention, we should briefly mention two other
major efforts to unify the law of international
agency.

2. In 1976 the Commission of the European Communities proposed an EEC Council Directive to
coordinate the laws of the Member States in respect of self-employed commercial agents. In its
proposal the Commission explained that the various national regulations on agency created in-
equality and thus acted as a barrier to trade
transactions within the EEC. The legal basis,
provided by Council Directive 64/222 of 25 February 1964, proposed that intermediaries be guaranteed the freedom to establish and carry out the
business of commercial representation for the
commerce and industry of the EEC.[20] The fact,
however, that the Commmission based its proposal
on German law drew sharp criticism not only from
the English Law Commission but also from the
European Parliament. As a result, the EEC Commis-

sion submitted an amended draft of 29 January 1979. In view of the fact that the Directive attempts to cover a large group of specific types of agents, e.g., travel agents, literary and theatrical agents, advertising agents, stock-brockers etc., it is difficult to make accurate predictions as to its chance of success.

3. Another attempt to unify rules of agency law was undertaken in the field of private international law. In March of 1978, the Hague Convention on the Law Applicable to Agency was open for signature; however, at the end of 1984 the only signatory States were France and Portugal, and the only ratification that of Portugal of 4 March 1982. The main obstacle appears to be the scope of the Convention which is defined in very broad terms so as to apply "to any agency activity on behalf of another."[21]

III. THE 1983 GENEVA CONVENTION

Forty-nine countries participated at the Geneva Conference, held 13 January - 17 February 1983, while nine countries and various international organizations sent representatives with observer status. Although the adoption of the Agency Convention may be regarded as an achievement, it does not signify the end of the efforts to unify the substantive law of agency. First, as was mentioned above, only part of the subject matter of the institution of agency is governed by the Convention. Second, only six States signed the Convention when it was open for signature: Chile, France, Italy, Morocco, the Vatican, and Switzerland. Moreover, at present the Convention has not yet received a single ratification.

Past experience has shown that the entering into force of conventions is often a lengthy and tedious procedure in itself. Since the Agency Convention is closely linked to the 1980 UN Convention on Contracts for the International Sale of Goods (hereafter: Sales Convention), it is hoped that once the Sales Convention enters into force, this should speed up ratification of the Agency Convention. Nonetheless, one should not be overly optimistic when it comes to predicting how long it might take for the Convention to enter into force.

1. Structure of the Convention

The Agency Convention contains a total of 35 articles divided into the following five chapters: 1) sphere of application and general provisions (Articles 1 - 8), 2) establishment and scope of authority of the agent (Articles 9 - 11), 3) legal effect of the acts carried out by the agent (Articles 12 - 16), 4) termination of the authority of the agent (Articles 17 - 20), 5) final provisions (Articles 21 - 35).

Some of the provisions of the Convention, especially in chapters one and five, correspond to or have been taken over from the relevant provisions of the Sales Convention virtually unchanged. This, of course, was not coincidental. During the preparation of the Convention, one of the principal concerns of the drafting Committee was "to follow as closely as possible the structure of the first two chapters" of the Sales Convention and "to employ wherever possible and desirable the same language as that used in the relevant provisions of the Vienna Convention."[22]

2. Scope of application

2.1 Art. 1 provides that the Convention's provisions shall apply to those situations where the
agent has authority or purports to have authority
on behalf of the principal to conclude a contract
of sale of goods with the third person. Moreover,
the contract of sale must be international in
character. Under Art. 2(1) the international
element is determined by the places of business
of the principal and the third party, which, in
order to qualify as **international**, must be located in different States.

Since it is the principal and the third party, not the principal and the agent that must
have their places of business in different
States, it follows that the contract of sale must
be international in character, not the agency
contract. Accordingly, the place of business of
the agent is "totally irrelevant"[23] in determining the international character of the relationship. However, it is not irrelevant when it comes
to determining the applicability of the Convention.

It was once proposed that the Convention
should apply whenever one of the three parties
has its place of business in a Contracting State.
This proposal, however, was rejected on the
ground that in some cases only the agent, and
thus presumably his place of business, is known
to both the principal and the third party.[24] As a
result, the scope of application of the Convention is further restricted by the requirement
that the agent's place of business must be in a
Contracting State (Art. 2 (1)(a)). If this is not
the case, the alternative additional requirement
states that the rules of private international

law must lead to the application of the law of a
Contracting State (Art. 2 (1)(b)). It should be
noted that the second alternative may be subjected to the reservation provided under Art. 28
which allows a State to declare that it will not
be bound by Art. 2 (1)(b), i.e., that the choice-
of-law rules will not be applied. The effect of
such a declaration will be to broaden the applicability of the lex fori, thereby narrowing the
applicability of the Convention.

2.2 Although the place of business is of crucial
importance in determining the applicability of
the Convention, the Convention fails to define
the term. In connection with the Sales Convention, Schlechtriem has suggested that the place
of business can be presumed to have been established for some time and to have a certain amount
of authority.[25]

Since there are numerous situations where at
least one of the parties could have places of
business in more than one State, it is necessary
to determine which place of business is relevant.
In view of the fact that it is the contract of
sale that must be international in character,
Art. 8(a) specifies that the place of business
"which has the closest relationship to the contract of sale" is decisive for the purpose of
Art. 2.

If one of the parties does not have a place
of business, reference is to be made to his
habitual residence (Art.8(b)). However, this does
not mean that the place of habitual residence
will be decisive whenever a businessman concludes
a contract outside his place of business. It is
expected that this rule will be applied only
rarely in practice.

2.3 It was the intention of the drafters that the Agency Convention be applicable to the same cases falling under the Sales Convention. Thus, the Agency Convention applies to contracts not only for the sale of goods but also for the purchase of goods. This is not stated explicitly in Articles 1 and 2 of the Convention as it was considered sufficient to explain that the term **contract of sale of goods** is based on the language of the Sales Convention.[26]

The limitation of the scope of application of the Agency Convention to contracts of sale of goods has been criticized. As Stöcker has correctly pointed out, this will lead to problems of characterization. In certain cases, for example, it will be difficult to determine whether a contract is a sale of goods contract or perhaps an innominate contract containing elements of other contract types as well.[27]

2.4 On the other hand, the drafters were well aware that the Agency Convention will also apply to some cases not covered by the Sales Convention. For example, a contract concluded between an agent and a third party whose places of business are in the same country falls under the scope of the Agency Convention but outside that of the Sales Convention.

In addition to contracts, the Agency Convention also governs any act undertaken by the agent for the purpose of concluding a contract with the third party as well as the agent's acts related to the performance of that contract (cf. Art. 1(2)). Accordingly, in differentiating between the scopes of application of the two conventions, Bonell reminds us that the contract of sale proper will be governed by the Sales Convention, but "the effect of the acts carried out by the agent in connection with the conclusion of the sale contract" will fall under the scope of the Agency Convention.[28]

At this point it should be emphasized that the references to **performance of the contract** and **acts undertaken by the agent** in Art. 1(2) of the Agency Convention do not imply that the Convention governs questions such as the validity of the contract of sale. Only matters concerning the authority of the agent, e.g., whether the agent has the authority to conclude a contract or purports to have such authority, are governed by the Convention.[29]

2.5 During the drafting of the Convention it was suggested that the Convention's sphere of application should be broadened to include all transnational agency relationships relating to private law with few exceptions.[30] This, however, proved to be impossible, and thus Art. 3 further restricts the scope of the Convention by excluding specific agency relationships.

The agency of a dealer on a stock, commodity or other exchange is excluded from the scope of the Convention as this type of agency is usually governed by national rules which vary according to the nature of the particular market. Moreover, the agency of an auctioneer is excluded because of its special legal position between the buyer and seller. Following the precedence set by Art. 2 (c) and (d) of the Hague Convention on the Law Applicable to Agency,[31] the Convention excludes respectively agency by operation of law in family law, in the law of matrimonial property, or in the law of succession as well as agency by virtue of a decision of a judicial or quasi-judicial authority or subject to the direct control of such an authority. Finally, agency arising from

statutory or judicial authorization to act for a
person without capacity to act is excluded from
the Convention's sphere of application on the
ground that the Convention should not interfere
with national rules governing the authority to
act on behalf of persons without capacity in
cases where the power is not conferred by virtue
of a contract of agency.

The list of exclusions is enlarged by Art. 4
of the Convention which provides that the Convention shall not apply to representatives of a
company who act "by virtue of an authority conferred by law or by the constitutive documents of
that entity" (Art. 4(a)). Consequently, this
excludes the so-called procurist whose power is
based on statute.[32] Under Art. 4(b) trustees are
also excluded from the scope of application of
the Convention.

2.6 In view of what has been said above, the
Convention's sphere of application appears to be
very narrow. This impression, however, may prove
to be wrong in the light of Art. 30, which has no
equivalent in the Sales Convention:

1) A Contracting State may at any time
declare that it will apply the provisions of this Convention to specified
cases falling outside its sphere of
application.

2) Such declaration may, for example,
provide that the Convention shall apply
to:

a) contracts other than contracts of
sale of goods;

b) cases where the places of business mentioned in Article 2, paragraph 1, are not situated in Contracting States.

Art. 30 is unusual in respect of its form as well as substance. As far as its form is concerned, the provision may be regarded as a reservation; however, contrary to the substance of a reservation, it allows a Contracting State to extend the applicability of the Convention by making a declaration, the effect of which is to broaden the scope of the Convention to include other types of contracts and/or cases where the places of business of the principal and the third party are not in a Contracting State.[33]

It is surmised that the inclusion of Art. 30 might encourage more countries to ratify the Convention since its narrow scope of application, as specified in Articles 1 and 2, represents only a statutory minimum which can be extended by virtue of a declaration under Art. 30. Thus, this article enables a State to extend the application of the Convention so as to include cases which fall within the concept of agency in that country but are not covered by Art. 1 of the Convention.

3. Party autonomy

One of the basic rules in the law of international contracts is the rule of party autonomy: When concluding a contract, the contracting parties may select the law by which the contract is to be governed. Accordingly, the Convention provides for the so-called opting-out solution in Art. 5 which allows the parties to exclude or modify the rules of the Convention.[34] From Art. 5 it follows that in the event the parties select a national law to govern their contract, the applicability of the Convention is thereby excluded. If the parties agree that the Convention shall not apply but fail to select the applicable law,

the applicable law shall be determined in accord
ance with the rules of private international law.

On the other hand, the parties may agree to
exclude the application of or to modify the formulation of specific rules of the Convention.
Unless otherwise provided, all the provisions of
the Convention are subject to modification by
agreement of the parties. Individual provisions
may also be replaced by rules of standard forms
and general conditions, provided the latter satisfy the national prerequisites of validity.

4.   Interpretation and gap-filling

4.1 The wording of the rules in Art. 6 on the
interpretation of the Agency Convention is mod-
eled on Art. 7 of the Sales Convention. Therefore, we refer to Volken's analysis in chapter
two since his conclusions also hold true for the
interpretation and filling of gaps in respect of
the Agency Convention.

Nonetheless, it should be mentioned that the
observance of good faith in international trade
(Art. 6(1)) is one of the general principles of
the Convention which should be taken into account
whenever questions of interpretation or gap-
filling arise. It remains, however, to be seen
how this will be achieved in practice. A comparative analysis of several legal systems shows
that, in the absence of a common judicial body,
the same provision will undoubtedly be interpreted in different ways. Some legal systems, for
example, do not recognize court decisions as a
direct source of positive national law. Therefore, the courts of such countries cannot be
expected to extend any authority to judicial

decisions rendered by courts of other Member
States to the Convention. In view of this, it is
not surprising that a more unified international
approach to the process of interpreting international conventions is being sought.[35]

4.2 Since the Agency Convention does not provide
solutions for all situations which ought to be
governed by the Convention, the problem of gap-
filling cannot be avoided. As specified by Art.
6(2), gaps are to be filled in conformity with
the general principles on which the Convention is
based. Since the wording of this provision is
identical to Art. 7(2) of the Sales Convention,
the question has arisen as to whether this is an
indication that both conventions are based on the
same general principles, which, of course, is not
the case. In its Explanatory Report, the UNIDROIT
Secretariat has emphasized that the basic principles underlying the Agency Convention are laid
down in the following articles: Art. 1(1) and (4)
on the scope of the Convention, Art. 9(1) which
provides that the authorization of the agent by
the principal may be express or implied, Articles
13 - 19 etc.[36]

Furthermore, as specified by Art. 6(2), only
questions concerning matters governed by the
Convention should be settled in conformity with
the general principles on which it is based.
Accordingly, all matters excluded from the scope
of the Convention are beyond the reach of gap-
filling under Art. 6(2).

Gaps that cannot be filled in conformity with
the general principles laid down in the Convention are to be filled by the competent authority
deciding the case "in conformity with the law
applicable by virtue of the rules of private

international law" (Art. 6(2)). This is not a
conflict-of-laws clause but merely a reference to
the fact that the applicable national substantive
rules are to be determined by national choice-of-
law rules.

5. Usages and established trade practices

Art. 7(1) of the Convention provides that the
parties may agree to be bound by any usages as
well as practices established between themselves,
thus giving contractual effect to such usages and
practices.[37] It should be noted that trade usages
which are widely known to and regularly observed
by parties to the same type of agency relationship shall be considered impliedly made applicable by the parties unless otherwise agreed. This
means that in order to exclude a usage that is
widely known and regularly observed in that particular branch of trade, the parties to an agency
agreement falling under the Convention must explicitly agree that such usage shall not apply to
their agency relationship.

Referring to the contractual status of usages
as "an expression of the impossibility to provide
for everything in a contract," Goldštajn comments
on the hierarchy of the sources of the law for
international contracts, stating that usages have
priority over the provisions of the Convention as
well as those of the applicable national law.[38]

This is also true in the case of business
practices established between the principal or
the agent on one hand, and the third party on the
other. Since business practices as such are regarded as part of the contract, they are to be
applied prior to the Convention's rules and national substantive rules.[39]

6. Consumer protection as a general principle

As the result of significant changes over the past decade, today one is inclined to distinguish between so-called consumer transactions and other transactions, whereby special protection to consumers is provided for consumer transactions.[40] Under Art. 3(2) of the Agency Convention, the rules of the Convention cannot derogate from any national rule of law for the protection of consumers. Proposed by the Norwegian delegation, this provision aims to prevent potential conflicts between the Convention and national consumer protection laws.[41] During the drafting of the Convention, the question arose as to whether the rule should apply only to mandatory provisions of national law. Since consumer protection measures are sometimes embedded in non-mandatory enactments of national law as well, the word mandatory was finally deleted. As to the question whether reference should be made only to national rules of the applicable law, it was decided that both the words national and applicable should be deleted, the former on the ground that international rules such as the EEC special rules for the protection of consumers might also be applicable, and the latter because "the provision would obviously not contemplate an inapplicable rule of law."[42] As a result, Art. 3(2) reads as follows:

> Nothing in this Convention affects any rule of law for the protection of consumers.

7. Authority of the agent

The main problem in Chapter II arose in connection with the establishment of the agent's

authority. The question was how to confer authority upon the agent in a way that would guarantee
the agency relationship enough flexibiity so as
to promote international trade, yet on the other
hand be acceptable to countries with different
legal systems. As adopted, the basic rule of Art.
9 provides that "the authorization of the agent
by the principal may be express or implied." This
rule applies to all types of agency relationships
covered by the Convention irrespective of whether
the agent acts in his own name or in that of the
principal (cf. Art. 1(4)). In principle, there
are no requirements as to the form of the authorization (Art. 10).

Whereas the national legal systems of the
civil law and common law countries recognize both
express and implied authorization, this is not
the case in the Socialist countries where national legislation requires that the authorization be
express and, moreover, in written form. This made
it necessary to introduce Art. 11 which permits a
State to make a declaration under Art. 27 to the
effect that

> any provision of Article 10, Article 15
> or Chapter IV which allows an authori-
> zation, ratification or termination of
> authority to be other than in writing,
> does not apply where the principal or
> the agent has his place of business in
> that State.

In addition, it should be clarified that
although the basic rule in Art. 10 lays down no
requirements as to the form of the authorization,
this does not mean that the parties cannot stipulate formal requirements. Their right to do so is
guaranteed by the principle of party autonomy. In
cases where a particular form is required for the
contract to be concluded by the agent, it might

be well to ask whether this affects the form of
the authorization. The Convention provides no
answer to this question as no attempt was made to
bridge eventual differences or, as Badr puts it,
"to come up with a uniform rule on the form of
the authority in its relation to the form of the
agent's contract."[43]

7.1 The difference between implied and express
authorization is explained by Evans as follows:

> Implied authorization differs from ex-
> press authorization in the sense that
> agreement of the principal to the a-
> gent's acting on his behalf must be
> inferred from the conduct or from other
> circumstances, as for example by the
> principal's consenting to certain acts
> by the agent over a period of time
> which have not been expressly author-
> ized by him; the two notions share the
> common feature that the principal actu-
> ally intends the agent to act on his
> behalf.[44]

This conclusion might be correct; however,
the fact remains that at this point the Convention is dealing with a matter outside its scope,
i.e., the internal relations between the principal and the agent. Moreover, the mere reference
to "implied authorization" in the Convention
without a detailed explanation of the term invites municipal courts to provide their own interpretations, which obviously is not the way to
promote uniform interpretation.

7.2 One of the main practical problems arising in
the relationship between the principal and the
agent concerns whether an agent has the right to
perform a particular act which was not foreseen

at the time of authorization. Art. 9(2) of the
Convention provides that "the agent has authority
to perform all acts necessary in the circumstances to achieve the purposes for which the
authorization was given." In view of this broad
formulation and the fact that the Convention
presents no guidelines for determining which acts
are justifiable under Art. 9(2), it is left to
the courts to decide, in accordance with the
circumstances of the particular case, whether or
not the agent was acting within the scope of his
authority.

There are no restrictions as to the means of
proving that the principal conferred authorization upon the agent. Art. 10 explicitly states
that "it may be proved by any means, including
witnesses." This provision is important in that
it excludes any exceptions existing in national
procedural rules, including rules preventing
evidence by witnesses.

8. Legal effects of the agent's acts

Chapter III, the central part of the Convention, deals with the legal effects of the agent's
acts, thereby answering the question: Who is
bound by the acts of the agent?

8.1 In a typical case falling under Art. 12 of
the Convention, the agent acts within his authority and the third party knew or ought to have
known that the agent was acting on someone else's
behalf. It is irrelevant whether the agent acted
on behalf of a "named" principal[45] or a "disclosed" principal[46]. In both cases "the third
party knows that he is not contracting with the
agent personally, but with another person through

the agent."[47] It should be pointed out that the
decisive moment in regard to the third party's
knowledge or presumed knowledge that the agent
was acting as an agent is the time of the conclusion of the contract of sale.[48]

In such cases the legal effects of the a-
gent's acts are binding on the principal and the
third party, or as Art. 12 puts it: "...the acts
of the agent shall directly bind the principal
and the third party to each other." The general
exception, which covers situations where the
agent acts with the intention of establishing a
contractual link only between himself and the
third party, reads as follows: "unless it follows
from the circumstances of the case... that the
agent undertakes to bind himself only." This
would be the case, e.g., if the agent acts under
a contract of commission. Since this is the only
example cited by the Convention, it is left to
the courts to determine which other circumstances
may imply that the agent intended to bind himself
only.

8.2 Conversely Art. 13 governs situations where
the third party neither knew nor ought to have
known that the agent was acting as an agent at
the time of the conclusion of the contract. This
is actually a reference to the common law concept
of undisclosed principal.[49] At the same time,
however, it also governs the exceptional case
mentioned under Art. 12 above, i.e., where the
agent undertakes to bind himself only, for example, by acting as a commission agent. In both
types of cases the only existing contractual link
is that between the agent and the third party,
even though the agent was acting on behalf of a
principal.

According to Evans, Art. 13 "represents a
serious attempt to bridge the gap between the
Common law and the Civil law systems."[50]
Nevertheless, the compromise achieved in this
article is basically the civil law approach. As
Bonell points out, from the ivil law systems

> it adopts the general principle that
> the sales contract binds only the two
> parties who are directly involved, not
> only when the third party is unaware of
> the agency capacity of his co-contrac-
> tor, but also when his co-contractor is
> acting openly as a commission agent.[51]

Although the commission agent acts on behalf of
the principal, there are no legal links between
the principal and the third party. Accordingly,
the third party cannot claim any damages from the
principal, only from the commission agent. As a
result, the principal is actually the third person as long as the commission agent does not
relinquish his rights to the actual principal or
to the third party.

On the other hand, in the English doctrine of
undisclosed principal a person "who is not overt-
ly a party to a contract may acquire rights and
be subjected to liabilities."[52] Thus it follows
that an undisclosed principal can "sue and be
sued in his own name on any contract duly made on
his behalf, as long as the agent acted within the
scope of his authority in so contracting."[53]

In order to meet the exigencies of the common
law systems, the Convention provides as a correc-
tive measure "that the principal and the third
party may directly sue each other for the performance of the sales contract."[54] In this sense,
Art. 13(2)(a) and (b) specify that, if the agent
is not in a position to fulfill his obligations,
the principal may exercise against the third

party the rights acquired on the principal's behalf by the agent (a), and _vice_ _versa_ the third party may exercise against the principal the rights the third party has against the agent (b).

These rights can be exercised only after a notice of intention to exercise them has been given to the agent and the third party or principal. Upon receipt of such a notice of intention, the third party or the principal, as the case may be, may no longer free himself from his obligations by dealing with the agent (Art. 13(3)). Instead, the only rights to which the third party and the principal will have recourse are those in :he application of Art. 13(2).

It is of little or no importance whether the agent's failure or inability to fulfill his obligations is due to failure of performance on the part of the third party or because of other reasons.[55] Furthermore, the time fixed for the fulfillment of the obligations by the agent must not necessarily have lapsed; it suffices that the agent is not in a position to fulfill them.

8.3 In certain cases, as provided by Art. 13(6), the principal may not exercise against the third party the rights acquired on his behalf by the agent if it appears from the circumstances of the case that the third party, had he known the principal's identity, would not have entered into the contract.

The incorporation of the common law institution of undisclosed principal in Article 13 leads to problems that are characteristic of this type of agency relationship. Whether the third party would have refused to enter into a contract, had he known the principal's identity depends to a large extent on the type of business transaction

and other circumstances of the case. Whereas the
reasons for the third party's refusal may be
different in nature,[56] the decisive factor in
English practice is whether the identity of the
person with whom the third party is contracting
is material to the making of the contract. If so,
then "the failure to disclose the fact that the
agent is acting on behalf of a principal will
deprive the principal of the right to sue on the
contract."[57]

8.4 Sometimes only the agent knows the identity
of the other parties involved in the sales contract, as is the case, e.g., in undisclosed agency. At the request of the third party, the agent
may be obliged to disclose the name of the principal, provided he was not able to fulfill his
obligations to the third party due to the principal's failure of performance (Art. 13(4)). Conversely, if the third party fails to fulfill his
obligations under the contract to the agent, the
agent shall be obliged to communicate the name of
the third party to the principal (Art. 13(5)).

At this point, it is worth noting that the
Convention fails to provide sanctions for situations where the agent refuses to comply with
these provisions. This can be explained by the
fact that disclosing the names of the parties is
a matter concerning the internal relations between the principal and the agent which are not
governed by the Convention.

The inclusion of para. 7, which provides that
the agent may agree with the third party to
derogate from or vary the effect of Art. 13(2),
has been widely disputed. Although it refers to a
specific provision, the fact remains that Art.
13(7) repeats the general principle contained in
Art. 5 almost _verbatim_. Although different

sources have tried to justify the duplication,[58] we are still not convinced that it was necessary. Duplicating provisions will not facilitate the interpretation of the Convention; on the contrary, one may attempt to find some special meaning in the paragraph beyond the mere repetition of Art. 5.

9. Acts of the agent without authority

Whereas Articles 12-13 govern situations where the agent acts within the scope of his authority, in the situations governed by Articles 14-16 he acts outside the scope of his authority or without any authority at all. In regard to the legal effects of such acts, Art. 14(1) specifies that acts performed by an agent outside the scope of his authority or without authority do not bind the principal and the third party to each other.

9.1 In view of the fact that the basic rule of Art. 14(1) makes no reference to the relations between the agent and the third party, the question arises as to whether such acts produce contractual effects between them. Art. 14(1) is silent on this matter; however, Evans points out that,

> apart from the possible liability of the agent under Article 16, the circumstances of the case and in particular the intention of the parties as to whether the agent was binding himself will determine whether or not contractual relations have been established between him and the third party.[59]

9.2 The exception to the basic rule provides that the principal may not invoke the lack-of-authori-

ty objection against the third party, if his
conduct causes the third party reasonably and in
good faith to believe that the agent has authority to act on behalf of the principal and that the
agent is acting within the scope of his authority
(Art. 14(2)).

As in the English doctrine, the exception
does not refer to an attempt to establish implied
authority but rather **apparent authority**.[60] The
types of situations where apparent authority may
be invoked by the third party are limited under
the English doctrine. Cases in the English practice show, for example, that apparent authority
is invoked on the part of the third party because

> there is some representation either in
> the public documents of the company, or
> as a result of some conduct by the
> company, including, possibly the direc-
> tor himself with whom the outsider was
> dealing.[61]

On the other hand, the Convention fails to
restrict invocation of the lack-of-authority
objection to specific situations. As a result,
there are no set criteria to determine what specifically in the conduct of the principal can
lead the third party to believe that the agent
had apparent authority to act as he did. The
Explanatory Report is of no help in this matter.
Nonetheless, once the existence of apparent authority is established under Art. 14(2), the
consequence is clear: The principal may not invoke against the third party the lack of authority of the agent.

9.3 Art. 15 permits the principal to ratify an
act by an agent who acts without authority or
outside the scope of his authority. On ratification by the principal, the act shall produce the

same effects as if it had initially been carried out with authority. There are no requirements as to the form of the ratification, which accordingly may be express or merely inferred from the conduct of the principal (Art. 15(8)). This, however , is subject to the right of reservation under Art. 27. Accordingly, there are no formal requirements for ratification if neither the principal nor the agent has his place of business in a State that has made a declaration to the contrary under Art. 27.

9.4 The main issue at stake, however, concerns the third party: Is he obliged to accept such a ratification? Generally speaking, this will depend on whether the third party entered into the contract in good faith, i.e., believing that the agent was acting with authority or within the scope of his authority. Thus it follows that the third party may refuse to accept the ratification if he neither knew nor ought to have known of the lack of authority at the time of the agent's act. Furthermore, once he is aware of the agent's lack of authority, the third party must notify the principal of his refusal at any time prior to ratification. If the principal ratifies the acts of the agent but fails to do so **within a reasonable time**, the third party may refuse to be bound by such ratification, provided he gives prompt notice of his refusal (Art. 15(2)).

Conversely, if the third party knew or ought to have known of the lack of authority, in principle he may not refuse to become bound by a ratification, provided that the time agreed for ratification has not expired, or in the absence of such agreement, within **such reasonable time** as specified by the third party (Art. 15(3)). In interpretation of the term <u>reasonable time</u>, due

consideration is to be given to all relevant circumstances of the case.

9.5 The Convention also provides a solution for
cases where only partial ratification is given by
the principal. In such cases the refusal of the
third party is unconditional (cf. Art. 15(4)).

9.6 Turning to the opposite situation where there
is no refusal on the part of the third party, we
are confronted with another question: At which
moment does the ratification take effect? Whereas
the Draft Convention[62] specified that ratification was to take effect at the moment it came to
the attention of the third party, this solution
was modified in the final text. It was argued,
for example, that the solution did not cover
cases where the ratification reaches the office
of the third party but, for some reason, is not
brought to his attention until later. In view of
this possibility, the final text contains both an
objective and a subjective criterion:

> Ratification shall take effect when
> notice of it reaches the third party or
> the ratification otherwise comes to his
> attention (Art. 15(2)).

In this context it should be mentioned that the
word <u>reaches</u> is to be interpreted as the time "it
is delivered to his place of business or mailing
address."[63]

Once ratification has been given, it may not
be revoked (Art. 15(2)(2nd sentence). Moreover,
the ratification is effective irrespective of the
effectiveness of the agent's act, thus emphasizing that the acts are independent of each other
(Art. 15(6)).

9.7 Finally, the Convention indirectly governs situations where the act is performed on behalf of a legal entity that has not yet been created. This covers acts carried out by an agent on behalf of a corporation or other legal entity **before its creation**, which most likely means, in Bonell's words, "during the formation of a corporation or other business entity destined to acquire a legal personality." [64] In view of the fact that national solutions seem to be very divided as to whether ratification is possible after the creation of the personne morale, the Drafters compromised by adopting a choice-of-law rule rather than a substantive rule. Accordingly, "ratification is effective only if allowed by the law of the State governing its creation" (Art. 15(7)).

10. Relations between the agent and the third party

Up to this point our discussion has been concentrated primarily on the relations between the principal and the third party. In the event, however, that there is no ratification or ratification is refused, this brings the relations between the agent and the third party into play. This raises the question as to which rights the third party has against an agent who acts without authority or outside the scope of his authority.

There are various approaches to the question of the agent's liability in comparative law. In some legal systems the third party can choose between a claim for fulfillment of the obligations or payment of damages, e.g., in the German Federal Republic.[65] In other legal systems he may claim only those damages suffered by him "due to his reliance without fault on the validity of the contract."[66]

Although it may not be obvious at first glance, the Convention offers the first solution in Art. 16(1):

An agent who acts without authority or who acts outside the scope of his authority shall, failing ratification, be liable to pay the third party such compensation as will place the third party in the same position as he would have been in if the agent had acted with authority and within the scope of his authority.

The alternative, i.e., performance by the agent, is not explicitly stated in para. 1; however, it is understood that performance is the normal way for the agent to discharge his obligations if he himself is bound under the contract to the third party.

Again, the decisive factor is whether the third party knew or ought to have known that the agent was acting outside his scope of authority or without authority. If the third party had or ought to have had such knowledge, the agent shall not be liable for damages, and the third party's rights against him will be limited to those he has acquired under the contract of sale.[67]

11. Termination of the authority

It was already mentioned that the Convention's field of application is limited to the external relations of an agency contract between the principal or the agent on the one hand, and the third party on the other. Chapter IV on termination of the authority of the agent reminds us how difficult it can be to make clear-cut

distinctions between the external and internal
relations of an agency relationship.

After the decision to delete the internal
relations between the principal and the agent
from the scope of the Convention, it was uncertain until the very end of the Geneva Conference
whether the Convention would include a special
chapter devoted to termination of the agent's
authority. Those opposed to its inclusion argued
that the subject matter concerns primarily the
internal relations of an agency relationship.[68]
On the other hand, those in favor of its inclusion emphasized that it was in the interest of
all three parties that the Convention contain
rules not only on the establishment of the a-
gent's authority but also on the termination
thereof. Furthermore, they insisted that it is of
critical importance for the third party to be
aware of the facts leading to termination of the
agency relationship.[69].

As a result, the rules were finally incorporated into the Convention. However, at the time
of drafting it was emphasized that only such
grounds for termination should be included that
are already treated in a fairly uniform manner by
most national laws. Otherwise, as a supplementary
measure, the authority will also terminate when
the applicable law so provides (Art. 18).

11.1 According to Art. 17, the authority of the
agent is terminated: a) if there was an agreement
between the principal and the agent to this end,
b) if the transactions for which the authority
was created are completed, and c) if the authority was revoked by the principal or renounced by
the agent, irrespective of whether this is consistent with their agreement.

In regard to termination of the agent's authority by revocation or renunciation, the Explanatory Report points out that this ground
concerns only the external relations and is not
intended to affect the mutual rights and obligations between the principal and the agent themselves.[70]

11.2 The fact that the authority has terminated
shall affect the third party only if he knew or
ought to have known of the termination or the
facts which caused it (Art. 19). Since the Convention does not specify in which circumstances
the third party could have known or ought to have
known of the termination or the facts which
caused it, it is presumed that the principal
would have informed him as it is primarily the
principal's interests that are at stake.[71]

11.3 Objection was raised to the inclusion of the
final article of this chapter, which undoubtedly
concerns mainly the internal relations between
the principal and the agent. Art. 20 provides
that an agent whose authority is terminated shall
nevertheless remain authorized "to perform on
behalf of the principal or his successors the
acts which are necessary to prevent damage to
their interests" (Art. 20).
   The proposal to delete this provision was
finally defeated on the ground that it is also in
the interest of the **third** party to be aware of
the fact that the agent has remained authorized
to protect the principal from damage.[72]

12. Final provisions

Chapter V of the Convention contains 15 final
provisions, all of which except three (Articles

25, 29, and 30) have either the very same or
similar wording as provisions of the Sales Convention. Unifying the provisions of conventions
can be very useful, even if it be only the final
provisions. This eliminates _inter_ _alia_ problems
of application arising from conflicting or non-
uniform provisions and promotes above all the
international unification of legal rules.[73]

Whereas the attempt to unify the final provisions of the Agency Convention with those of
the Sales Convention is to be praised as a positive step towards achieving unification of legal
rules, there is another characteristic of the
Agency Convention which produces the very opposite effect. This is its rather wide range of
possibilities to exclude application of either
individual provisions of the Convention or the
Convention as a whole.[74] In addition to the
opting-out possibilities provided for in Articles
5 and 13(7) (_supra_ III. 3. and III. 8.4), several
other important reservations deserve to be mentioned.

In regard to the Federal State clause in Art.
24, it is well known that by virtue of a declaration, the Convention will not extend to all the
territorial units of that Contracting State.
Thus, if a party has his place of business in a
territorial unit to which the Convention does not
extend, it will not be considered to be within
the territory of a Contracting State (Art.
24(3)).

Furthermore, two or more Contracting States
having the same or closely related legal rules on
matters governed by the Convention may always
exclude the application of the Convention, provided that, in accordance with Art. 26(1), the
parties have their places of business in those
States. The same applies when a Contracting State

has the same or closely related legal rules as
one or more non-Contracting States (Art. 26(2)).
This means that, by making a declaration under
Art. 26, the Scandinavian States, for example, or
the member countries of the EEC or COMECON could
exclude application of the Convention in contractual relations among themselves.

At the request of the COMECON States still
another possibility to exclude the Convention was
introduced in Art. 29. Under this article, if all
or part of the foreign trade of a Contracting
State is carried on exclusively by specially
authorized organizations, the State may at any
time declare that, in cases where such organizations act as buyers or sellers, they shall not be
considered as agents in their relations with
other organizations having their place of business in the same State. Since foreign trade in
the COMECON States is carried out by special
export organizations, they expressed fears that
without such an escape clause their other organizations "might be considered to be principals for
the purpose of Art. 13(2)(b) and (4) and thus be
exposed to a direct action by the foreign third
party."[75]

Finally, the reservation possibilities under
Articles 27 and 28 should be briefly mentioned in
this context. Under Art. 27 a State whose legislation requires an authorization, ratification or
termination of authority in writing may exclude
any provision of Art. 10, Art. 15 of Chapter IV
which permits otherwise (supra III. 7.). A declaration under Art. 28 allows a State to exclude
application of the choice-of-law rules as specified by sub-paragraph b of Art. 2(1) (supra III.
2.1).

IV. CONCLUDING REMARKS

1. In view of the extreme differences existing among various national laws governing the institution of agency, the adoption of the Geneva Convention on Agency in the International Sale of Goods may indeed be regarded as an achievement.

When UNIDROIT initiated its unification project nearly five decades ago, it had visions of unifying all aspects of the law of agency. During the course of the negotiations, however, it became clear that UNIDROIT had launched a major undertaking with an admirable but overly ambitious goal. As a result, the scope of application of the proposed Draft Convention had to be narrowed.

Thus, with the adoption of the Agency Convention, UNIDROIT's original goal -- unification of the law of agency -- has been achieved only in part. Aware of this fact, the delegations to the Geneva Diplomatic Conference agreed in the Final Resolution of the Convention

> that the further development of international rules relating to the relations between principal and agent in agency in the international sale of goods would be an important contribution of international trade.

2. At the request of the Conference Delegations, the Governing Council of UNIDROIT has already instructed its Secretariat to prepare a report on the possibility and feasibility of establishing uniform rules to govern the relations between the principal and the agent, particularly in the field of the international sale of goods.[76]

If the decision of the Governing Council is to be taken as an indication of UNIDROIT's future

intentions, it appears that its unification efforts will continue to be restricted to agency
relationships in the international sale of goods.
In the light of Art. 30 óf the Agency Convention,
the question arises as to whether such a restriction is still possible. This, of course, presup-
pose˩ that, in the course of time, the Contracting States will make use of their right to broad-
en the scope of the Agency Convention by virtue
of a declaration under Art. 30.

3. Since the process of unification of law
does not end with the adoption of a convention,
one of the major problems yet to be solved concerns how to promote uniform interpretation of
the Convention's rules. In the absence of a common judiciary body, the interpretation of the
rather broad formulation used in some of the
provisions will be left to the national courts.
Since this may lead to differences in interpretation, it would therefore be desirable to establish a prompt and precise reporting system under
the auspices of UNIDROIT, the task of which would
be to gather and distribute information on national case law relevant to the Convention. However, this measure in itself will obviously not
be sufficient to guarantee uniform interpretation.

NOTES

1. W. Müller-Freienfels, "Law of Agency," 6 Am.
J.Comp.L. (1957) p. 165.
2. W. Müller-Freienfels, "The Law of Agency" in
Yiannopoulos (ed.) Civil Law in the Modern World
(1965) p. 77.
3. Gy. Eörsi, "Two problems of the unification
of the law of agency" in F. Fabricius (ed.), Law

and International Trade -- Recht und internationaler Handel, Festschrift für C.M. Schmitthoff
(Frankfurt 1973) p. 84.

4. See F.M.B. Reynolds and B.J. Davenport, Bow-
stead on Agency, 14th ed. (London 1976) p. 1.

5. An undisclosed principal is "one of whose
existence the third party is unaware, so that the
third party does not know that the person with
whom he is dealing is anybody's agent." G.M.L.
Fridman, The Law of Agency (London 1983) p. 221.

6. C.M. Schmitthoff, "Agency in international
trade" 129 Recueil des Cours (1971) p. 125.

7. E.g., Switzerland (OR, Articles 32 et seq.),
Czechoslovakia (International Trade Code, § 49 et
seq.).

8. M.J. Bonell, "The 1983 Geneva Convention on
Agency in the International sale of Goods," 32
Am.J.Comp.L. (1984) p. 719.

9. Ibid.

10. E.g., Austria and Spain. In Italy, the Italian Civil Code of 1942 adopted the theory of
separation.

11. C.M. Schmitthoff, supra n. 6, at p. 134.

12. See G.M. Badr, "Agency: Unification of material law and of conflict rules," 184 Recueil
des Cours (1985) p. 21.

13. C.M. Schmitthoff, supra n. 6, at p. 116.

14. Ibid.

15. "Explanatory Report" prepared by UNIDROIT
Secretariat, Diplomatic Convention for the Adoption of the UNIDROIT Draft Convention on Agency
in the International Sale of Goods, Acts and Proceedings of the Conference, I-II Rev.dr.unif.
(1983) p. 13.

16. Ibid.

17. Ibid.

18. The Conference was held in Bucharest from 28
May to 13 June 1979.

19. "Explanatory Report" supra n. 15, at p. 14.

20. On the EEC Council Directive, see O. Lando, "The EEC Draft Directive relating to self-employed commercial agents," 44 RabelsZ (1980) pp. 1-16; also J. Basedow, "Das Vertretungsrecht im Spiegel konkurrierender Harmonisierungsentwurfe," 45 RabelsZ (1981) pp. 196-217.

21. See the detailed analysis of the Convention by P. Hay and W. Müller-Freienfels, "Agency in the Conflict of Laws and The 1978 Hague Convention," 27 Am.J.Comp.L. (1979) pp. 1-49.

22. "Explanatory Report" supra n. 15, at p. 18.

23. M.J. Bonell, supra n. 8, at p. 727.

24. "Explanatory Report" supra n. 15, at p. 20.

25. P. Schlechtriem, Einheitliches UN-Kaufrecht (Tübingen 1981) p. 29.

26. See "Explanatory Report" supra n. 15, at p. 18. However, see also p. 63 ("Explanatory Notes" prepared by UNIDROIT Secretariat in Acts and Proceedings supra n. 15) for explanation why the word international was deleted in the final text.

27. H.A. Stöcker, "Das Genfer Übereinkommen über die Vertretung beim internationalen Warenkauf," 28 WM (1983) p. 780.

28. M.J. Bonell, supra n. 8, at p. 727.

29. "Explanatory Report" supra n. 15, at p. 19.

30. Preliminary Draft of 1955 (Art. 2), cited at Badr, supra n. 12, at p. 102.

31. Text published in 26 Am.J.Comp.L. (1978) p. 438.

32. E.g., see the German Commercial Code (HGB), §§ 48 et seq.

33. Cf. H.A. Stöcker, supra n. 27, at p. 784.

34. Cf. J. Honnold, Uniform Law for International Sales under the 1980 United Nations Convention (Deventer 1982) p. 106; also P. Schlechtriem, supra n. 25, at p. 21.

35. J. Honnold, supra n. 34, at p. 122.

36. "Explanatory Report" supra n. 15, at p. 17.

37. Cf. J. Honnold, supra n. 34, at p. 102.

38. A. Goldštajn, see p. 45 of this book.

39. Ibid, p. 46.

40. M.J. Bonell, supra n. 8, at p. 727.

41. Acts and Proceedings, supra n. 15, at p. 265.

42. Ibid., p. 399 (Farnsworth).

43. G.M. Badr, supra n. 12, at p. 113.

44. M. Evans, "Explanatory report on the Convention on Agency in the international sale of goods," I Rev.dr.unif. (1984) p. 113.

45. A "named" principal is "one whose name has been revealed to the third party." G.H.L. Fridman, supra n. 5, at p. 187.

46. A "disclosed" principal is "one whose existence has been revealed to the third party by the agent, but whose exact identity remains unknown." G.H.L. Fridman, supra n. 5, at p. 187.

47. Ibid.

48. M. Evans, supra n. 44, at p. 121.

49. see supra n. 5.

50. M. Evans, supra n. 44, at p. 119.

51. M.J. Bonell, supra n. 8, at p. 735.

52. G.H.L. Fridman, supra n. 5, at p. 221.

53. Article 13, paragraph 2(a) of the Convention.

54. Article 13, paragraph 2(b) of the Convention.

55. Cf. H.A. Stöcker, supra n. 27, at p. 782; also M. Evans, supra n. 44, at p. 123.

56. As Evans points out, the third party's refusal to enter into a contract with the principal may be due to competition, exclusive agreements, an international embargo, commercial policy. M. Evans, supra n. 44, at p. 129; in addition, even due to personal reasons.

57. G.H.L. Fridman, supra n. 5, at p. 227.

58. E.g., Bonell points out "that in practice it would be above all this provision that the agent or the third party, or both, would be interested

in excluding." M.J. Bonell, supra n. 8, at p. 737. He believes that such an exclusion would be used especially in general conditions and standard contracts. However, the summary records of the Plenary Meetings of the Geneva Conference fail to provide a convincing answer to justify the inclusion of the additional rule. ("Explanatory Report" supra n. 15, at pp. 342-345), as does Evans, supra n. 44, at p. 131.

59. M. Evans, supra n. 44, at p. 133.

60. On apparent authority see, e.g., G.H.L. Fridman, supra n. 5, at pp.319-322.

61. Ibid., p. 319.

As Diplock LJ defined it in Freeman & Lockyer v. Buckhurst Park Properties (Mangal) Ltd. [1964] 1 All ER 630 at 646, for apparent authority it must be shown in English case law:

> (a) that a representation that the agent had authority to enter on behalf of the company into a contract of the kind sought to be enforced was made to the contractor [ie the outsider contracting with the company]: (b) that such representation was made by a person or persons who had "actual" authority to manage the business of the company either generally or in respect of those matters to which the contract relates; (c) that he (the contractor) was induced by such representation to enter into the contract, ie that he in fact relied on it; and (d) that under its memorandum or articles of association the company was not deprived of the capacity either to enter into a contract of the kind sought to be enforced or to delegate authority to enter into a contract of that kind to

the agent. (cited at Fridman, <u>supra</u> n.
    5, at p. 321, note 14).
62. See Art. 16(4); see also the "Explanatory Report," <u>supra</u> n. 15, at pp. 40-41.
63. A similar solution can be found in Art. 24 of
the Sales Convention. Cf. J. Honnold, <u>supra</u> n.
34, at pp. 206-207.
64. M.J. Bonell, <u>supra</u> n. 8, at pp. 742-743.
65. § 179 BGB.
66. M.J. Bonell, <u>supra</u> n. 8, at pp. 743-744.
67. M. Evans, <u>supra</u> n. 44, at p. 141.
68. See the <u>Acts</u> <u>and</u> <u>Proceedings</u>, <u>supra</u> n. 15.
Proposal of delegation of the Netherlands (Conf.
6/3 Add.2, page 4) p. 102; see also the proposal
of the Hague Conference on Private International
Law (Conf. 6/4, page 3), p. 102.
69. M. Evans, <u>supra</u> n. 44, at 143.
70. Ibid., p. 145.
71. H.A.Stöcker, <u>supra</u> n. 27, at p. 784.
72. <u>Acts</u> <u>and</u> <u>Proceedings</u>, <u>supra</u> n. 15, according
to the Spanish delegate Gondra, p. 388.
73. See G. Conetti's report on pp. 385-399 of
this book.
74. See C. Mouly, "La Convention de Genève sur la
représentation en matière de vente internationale
de marchandises," 1 <u>Rev.int.dr.comp.</u> (1983) p.
829, esp. pp. 833-834.
75. Cf. J. Honnold, <u>supra</u> n. 34, at p. 83.
76. The first analysis prepared by Bonell is not
optimistic at all. See M.J. Bonell, "Is it feasible to elaborate uniform rules governing the
relations between principal and agent?" I <u>Rev.
dr.unif.</u> (1984) pp. 52-70, esp. p. 67. According
to Bonell, "any attempt at global unification
appears to be unrealistic, in view of different
approaches followed by the Common law systems and
the Civil law systems in respect to the internal
relationships."

INDEX

INDEX

Acceptance of offer 115-129
awareness of 122
becoming effective 116,
   121
binding effect 119, 120
dispatch of 116
form of 127
late 128
modification of offer
   111-115, 121, 124-127,
   312
period of 118, 128
revocation of 116
terms of 342

Acquisition of property
407-437
bona fide 414-437
for valuable consideration
   414, 415

Agencies 86

Agency 443-479
in civil law 443
in common law 443
contract of 445, 451
definition 444
external aspects of 445,
   448
indirect 444
internal aspects of 445

Agent 443-479
acts undertaken by 454
advertising 449
authority of 460-463
commission 444
habitual residence 452
literary 449
place of business 451, 452
self-employed commercial
   448
stockbroker 449, 454
travel 449

Agreement
explicit 123
on modification 130
mutual 98
of the parties 102, 408
in rem 410
on termination 130

Alternation
of contract terms 127

Anti-dumping 370

Applicable law (see conflict-of-laws rules, law
applicable, private in-
ternational law)

Arbitration 60-64, 85-92,
102, 240-256
case law 71
clause 340
clause as material alter-
   ation of offer 126
commercial 65, 55-103, 126
   331-361
international 73
and standard forms 337
tribunal 86, 138, 189
as usage 127

**Asian-African Legal Con-
sultative Committee** 9

Assent
to additions 124
indication of 118
to modifications 124
notice of 122

Asser Institute 42

Assists
dutiable 373, 377

Aution sale
excluded 36

Authority
(see also: agent)
abstract nature of 445
apparent 469
termination of 473-475

Authorization
act without 463, 468-477
express 461, 462
implied 461, 462
unilateral 111

Autonomy of the parties
(see: parties)

Avoidance of contract
(see also: breach funda-
mental, notice, remedies,
restitution)
additional period 224-227
after cancellation of
  buyer's order 227
after delivery of goods
  195
anticipatory breach of the
  buyer 228
automatic, not 195
causes 194, 315
conditions for 224, 225
consequences of 195, 221
- notice 195
- received goods returned
  195
contract, of 239-250
declaration, by 195
delay in payment, for 227
deterioration of buyer's
  conditions 227
effects of 239, 255-259,
  315
ex nunc, ex tunc 315
failure of delivery, for
  195
failure to pay price, for
  224, 227

failure to perform, for
  194
fundamental breach, by 194
  227
grounds for 226
installment contract, and
  195
liquidated damages, and
  256
penalty clauses, and 256
prior to performance 221
remedy, as a 180-195
restitution, and
- of goods 157, 258
- of price 257
right to 257
seller, by
- unjustified 228
time of 249, 250

Bankruptcy 337

Battle of the forms 127,
341, 360

Bill of lading 153-199,
215, 242, 277
functions of 271, 272
identifying the goods 290
security for payment, as
  272
transfer of risk, and 292

Breach of contract
anticipatory 188, 220, 239
  240, 243
buyer, by the
- delay in transfer of
  price 213
- taking delivery, in 243
- under UCP 352
causes for 317
early delivery 152
fundamental 190-198, 221-
  244, 347, 358
late delivery 195, 347
non-delivery 347

ordinary 187
partial delivery 152
remedies for 137, 187, 188
  193
responsibility for 318
seller, by 188-203
- defect in packaging 169
strict liability 318

Breach of obligation 172,
220, 221
delay, by 347
pay price, to
- avoidance of contract
  221
- preservation of goods
  221
- remedies 221
- suspension of perfor-
  mance 221
remedies for 338, 339

Business
associations 86
community 93
conditions 142
international 70-93
practices 56, 59, 60-72,
  143
transactions 60-101

Buyer
notice of non-conformity
  of goods
- rights related to 170
- lack of notice 170
offer, of 123
rights of 163

Cancellation
(see also: avoidance)
of promise 112

Carriage of goods
allocation of risk 278
arrangement for insurance
  286

arrangement for insurance
  by
- air 282
- buyer 285, 286
- rail, road 147, 282
- seller 285, 286
- water 147
contract, under 215
costs 374
expenses
- repayment 273
handover of goods
- according to Incoterms
  287
- place of 287
international sale, in 270
obligation
- to arrange carriage 148
  231, 285
- of the parties 278, 294
passing of risk, and 279,
  288
price, and 216
seller's risk up to border
  282
splitting of transit risk
  288

Carrier
delivery against documents
  215
duty to deliver 215
first carrier 145, 146,
  216
- seller's staff as 287
seller as 146
several carriers 145

Case law 57, 91, 99

Certificate
of quality 153
of origin 153

Characterization 387, 430

Chattel morgage 407, 418

Choice of law
(see: private international law, law applicable,
conflict-of-laws rules)

CIF, C & F contracts 126,
147, 150, 275, 335-361

Civil law 90-117, 240-253,
401, 443

Claims
third party 143, 155

Climate
economic and social 102

CMEA (Council of Mutual
Economic Assistance) 9, 64
-75, 91, 139, 307, 382

Code of conduct 72, 74, 86,
87, 100

Codification
characteristics of 65
international 67

Co-existence
of States 143

Commercial
agreement 98, 102
arbitration 55-103, 331,
332-361
dispute 86
law 65-69, 84, 85, 101
- development, of 12
- domestic 89
- international character
69, 89
- organizations 90
- sources of 59
- transactions 55-103
- transnational 71
- usages and practices 55-
103
- practice 135

Common law 92, 113-117, 136
240-253, 269, 443

Communication
of information 75

Comparative law   40, 70,
111, 113, 142

Conduct 102
of parties 96, 118

Conflict-of-laws rules 24
25-29, 42-44, 385-397, 404
426-437

Conformity
of goods 76
non-conformity 339

Consent
defects 314
lack of 432
principles of 407
of transferer and trans-
feree 409

Consumer
protection 460
sales 36, 135, 142

Contract
(see also: avoidance,
breach of, performance)
affreightment, of 271
acceptance 28, 112, 113
adaptation of 142
binding effect 313, 431
buyer and seller 12, 35
change of 199
character of 4
clauses 71
commercial 55-92, 141
completion 266
complex 66
conclusion 25, 121, 213,
266, 312
control over 84, 354

control over-contd
- and national legislation 357
conveyance 405-437
creation of 147
defects of 411
delivery 140
draft text of 4
economic 91
effects of 431
enforceability 111
exclusion of 100
expectation of 116
fine print 126
formation of 4, 32-45, 77-113, 114-131, 240, 312-360
form of 126, 129, 159
forms 71, 127, 339
freedom of 1, 58-61, 92-111, 136, 311
fulfillment of 28, 231-271
gap-filling 40-46, 428
individual types of 102
innominate 59, 64, 453
installment 188, 239, 240-246
international 27, 29, 72, 80, 356, 451
interpretation of 38-55, 100, 136
involving carriage 145, 215, 283
law of the 68-94
meaning of 79
missing terms 120
model 98
modification of 130, 351
- and national legislation 357
nominate 59-64, 94
non-fulfillment 182
non-mandatory 204
obligations
- of the buyer 203-236
- of the seller 133-199
oppressive 359

passing of risk 265-298
period for payment 225
place of business 25
planned 311
power of creation 114, 118
price 370
promise 313
proper law of 65, 95, 97
real 411
remedies 188
requirements of 143
rights and duties 12, 35
sale of goods 55, 56, 94, 231, 453
standard forms of 335-361
suspension of 240
termination of 130, 256, 326-328
- and damages 328
- and insolvency 326
- fundamental breach 327
- procedure of 327
- restitution of goods 328
- under ULIS 326, 327
terms of 125, 341
time of conclusion 146, 159, 249, 266
time of delivery 156, 151
transportation 307
types of sales 34, 59-64
validity of 4, 35, 97, 137, 313, 315, 355, 411, 454
- avoidance 315
- binding effect of promise 313, 431
- defect of consent 313, 411
- general principles 315
- illegality 313
- immorality 313
- without indication of price 210
in writing 35, 129, 209, 430

Contract Act 142

Contracting party
rights and duties 78

Contracting State
implementary legislation
20
requirements 25
rights and duties 20

Conventions, international
(See: Geneva, Hague, New
York, Rome, Vienna Conventions)
classification of 385
compatibility clauses 399,
394
conflicts between 392, 395
consultation procedure 397
coordination of 385, 392,
396
draft 58, 76
international 385
interpretation of 385
in general 1, 21, 56
mandatory rules 392
multilateral 62
overlapping 387, 392
principle of speciality
393
scope of 385
sphere of application 388,
392, 395
uniform substantive law,
on 387, 392

Conveyance 405-437
anticipated 409
contract, and 405, 407
limits of 408
consent to 410

Cooperation
commercial 92
duty of 250
in case of breach 250
international 57, 92
obstacles to 5
State planning, and 141

Costs
distribution of 213
enabling payment 220
increase in 213
packaging, of 213
parties, of 130
preservation of goods, for
229
production, of 378
storage of goods, for 229
transportation, of 216,
374
under Incoterms 374

Counter-offer 124-127

Counter-performance 76, 314

Countries
developing 58, 245
industrial 58

Custom
commercial 71-82
customary rule 85
international 70
law creating 86
proof of 98
of the sea 85
transnational 71

Customs
appraisal 367
cooperation 368
council 368
CUC 366, 371
EEC regulations 366
GATT (see: Gatt)
planning 365
valuation of goods 365
value 378

Damages
abstract, concrete 249
acceptance of early de-
livery, and 199
amount of 229

breach of contract, for
187, 239, 246-250
calculation of 188, 229,
246-250
compensation of loss, and
243
current price, and 250
during transportation 278
exceeding loss 324
failure to perform, for
188, 228
functioning, of 233-326
goods, of 269
justifiable amount of 248
limitation of 188
liquidated 188
liquidation of 247
loss, and 324
mitigation of 188, 228
nominal 324
prevention of 269
recovery of 324
- limited 325
- gains 326
- savings 326
seller, of
- compensation of loss 235
- loss of profit 235
tortious liability 247
under GCD 188

Defective goods 76
apparent, latent defects
159, 160, 172
curing of 158, 159-165
- after date of delivery
163
- before end of delivery
period 163
- costs of 165
- defect in title 165
- missing parts 164
- quality 164
disclosure by seller 175
elimination of right to
- repair 191
- replacement 191

nature of defect 191
repair 165
replacement 165
seller's right to cure 162

Delay 125
in payment 213
in performance 317
of the buyer, seller 206

Delivery
according to Incoterms 343
344-345
at special place 285
carriage of goods, and 343
date of 120, 162
early 152, 162, 164, 198
- acceptance of 198
- additional expenses 198
- buyer's rights 198
- consequences 198
- recovery of loss, and
198
- under GCD
failure to take 232, 233
fulfillment of 144
goods, of 143, 144, 199,
216
- excess in quantity 199
handover 276
in time 145
late 348
meaning under ULIS 276
moment of 277
obligation of 133, 145
partial 152, 164
passing of risk 276
payment of price 276
performance 275
place of 125, 144-147, 342
procedure of 217
refrain from taking 216
requirement to take 232
terms of 148
time of 120, 150-156
under
- Vienna Convention 342

under-contd
- GCD 198
- Incoterms 163, 342

Denunciation
contract under obligation
of 33
Convention, of 31
effect of 33
period of 32

Development
economic 57
industrial 57

Disclosure, public
lack of 409
of rights 409
of security 419, 424
of title 408

Dispatch
of goods 122
of notice 125

Documentary credit
duty to open 352
uniform customs and prac-
tices 84, 336

Documents
controlling delivery 153
controlling disposition
215
for the buyer 150
goods, on 152
handing over of 143, 152
nature of 153
non-conformity of 154
- right to cure 154
shipping 149
title 153
transportation of 243, 271

Duty
Duty and Royalties 372
imposed on importation 375

Duty
of parties 75
to cooperate 86, 240
to inform 86

ECE/UN 68, 83, 91
contract conditions 278,
336, 341
- avoidance 351
- damages 351
- loss of profit 351
- personal injuries 356
- oppressive contracts 359

Economic
competition 63
factors 65
interdependence 90
laws 83
relations 74

Economy
free market 74, 311, 321
planned 61-74, 311, 320,
321

EEC 21, 42, 375

Estoppel 415

Examination of goods
after carriage 168
at the time of passing of
risk 168
circumstances of 167
deferring 169
length of 167
manner 166, 167
place and period of 167
seller, by 175
spot-checks 169

Exemption 252-254
additional period of time
354
- in commodity sales 354
- in machinery sales 354
fraud 337

from
- contractual obligations
  252, 254
- damages 254
- liability 254
- mandatory national rules
  358
fundamental breach 255
impediment 255
international contracts,
  for 375
notice of 256
period of 254, 255
self-made failure 255
standard form contract 353
temporary 255
third party 254
under Vienna Convention
  254
vis major 253, 254, 353,
  354

Export 26

Fair dealing 136

Federal clause 30, 476

Federal State 30

Fees
  commissions, of 373
  license 372

Fidic 84

FOB 147, 149

FORIFOT 149

Foreign
  exchange and price 207
  trade 61
  trade contract 311

Form of contract
  oral 129

telegram, by 130
telex, by 130
written 129, 130

Formation of contract
(see: contract)

Forum 28, 29

Freedom of parties 136, 430

Frustration
(see: exemption)

Gap-filling
  under Vienna Convention
    19-43, 137, 402
  under Geneva Convention
    457-458

Gaps
  avoidance of 205
  standard forms 336

GATT 21, 365-378

GCD/CMEA (General Condi-
  tions of Delivery of Goods
  between the Member States
  of CMEA [Comecon])
  agreement of parties 140
  application by agreement
    140
  character or uniform law
    140, 141
  confidentiality 153
  damages 188
  disclosure of defects 175
  documents on goods 153
  early delivery 152
  examination of goods 175
  history of 140
  mode of carriage, and 145
  non-conformity of goods
    155, 172
  notice of delivery 149,
    151

passing of risk 278
period of notice 173
place of delivery 147
scope 140
trade secrecy 153

General conditions 71, 72,
86-99, 137, 278
CMEA/Finland, of (General
Conditions of Delivery be-
tween the CMEA States and
Finland) 141-153

General principles
contract law, of 305-328
- elaboration of 310
- European sources 370
gap-filling 308
law, of 71-86
lex contractus, as 309

Geneva Convention on Agency
(1983) 386-394, 443-479
scope of 449, 455-456
signatory States 449

**Geneva Convention on bills
of exchange** (1930) **and
checks** (1931) 22, 385-399

Good faith 34, 86, 101, 136
415, 457

Goods
against payment 216
conformity of 76, 143, 155
-161
cure of
- deficient quantity 164
- delivery in parts 164
- end of period of deliv-
ery, before 164
- replacement of goods 164
damaged 267, 277
defect in quantity 177
defective 76, 147, 159,
190

delivery of 143, 147
delivery of substitute 190
dispatch of 242, 243
dispose of, to 147
examination of 146, 163-
166
handing over of 145, 146,
216
identification of 149, 290
imported 375
inspection of 137, 160,
161
in transitu 217, 242
lack of conformity 155-
163, 171-180, 191, 216
- defect in description
170
- defect in title 165
- duty to give notice 169
170
- in quality, quantity
170
- missing parts 164
- notice of seller 176
- remedy 190, 191
- right of reliance 169
- time of discovery 169
- time of knowledge 176
loss of 267
maintenance of 161
models, samples 156, 157
ownership 266
packaging 125, 148, 158
place of destination 146,
147
preservation of 233, 235
purchase 246
- in replacement 248, 249
quality of 137, 155-159,
219
quantity of 136, 147, 148,
209
replacement of 164
resale 246, 248, 249
restitution of 190
retention of 242
retransfer of 425

rights of buyer in event
of non-conformity
- additional period 183
- avoidance of contract
183
- damages 183
- replacement of goods 183
seizure of 406, 409
specific 146
stolen 415
stoppage of 242
taking over of 150
third party rights
- absence of 177
- intellectual property
177-182
- lease 178
- liability of seller 182
- notice by buyer 183
- pledge 178
- possession 178
- rent 178
- reservation of title 178
- title, on 177
transport of 148
unidentified 146
value of 372

Guarantee
additional 240
bank guarantee 243
conformity of goods 161
examination of goods under
173
notice of defects, and 173
payment, for 220
performance, for 220
period of 173
remedies and 173
time of notice 173

Habitual residence 25, 452

Hague Academy 73

Hague Convention (1955) 388
390, 393, 394

Hague Convention (1964) 2-
10, 56-85, 138, 205, 208,
274, 385-401
bank guarantee 243
calculation of damages 247
choice of parties 389
delivery 276
history 3
non-conformity of goods
177
opting out 389-394
reasons for failure 3, 6,
21
sphere of application 391
substantive rules 388

Hague Diplomatic Conference
(1964) 75

Harmonization of law 91

ICC (International Chamber
of Commerce) 10, 68-94,
148, 251-281, 336
ICC arbitration rules 92
ICC conventions 388
ICC standard forms 336

Illegality 316
causes of 316
immorality 316

Import 26, 371, 372

Incoterms 84, 94, 147
handover of documents 158
passing of risk 277, 278,
294, 296
place of delivery 144, 148
standard forms 336, 340
usages, as 280

Inspection
(see: examination)

Insurance
claim of damages 297
claim of loss 297

contract 286
during shipment 150
policy 153
transportation risk, on
297

**Intellectual property
rights** 179-181
as third party rights 180
territorial limits of liability, for 181

Intent of parties 95

Interest
calculation of 251
delay, for 326
payment of 326
period of 252
price, of 252
rate of 229, 252
repayment of price 252
right to 229, 239

Intermediaryship 446

International
agencies 68
commercial law 21, 68
commercial custom 67
community 70

**International Court of Jus-
tice** 71
international practice 67

International trade 55-113,
169, 172, 191, 242, 385

**International sales of
goods** 59-81, 203, 240
carriage of goods 145
contract on 111-131
passing of risk 265, 270
preparatory work 4
security interests 401-437
standard forms 335

Interpretation
contract, of 38, 40, 55,
457, 458
Convention, of 19, 22, 38-
44, 76
elements of 39, 40
functional approach 40
intent of parties 44
rules of 148
standard forms 336
theories of 40
uniform 68, 368
usages of trade 56

Intertemporal law 33

Invoice 365-378

Judicial intervention 102

Jura
novit curia 98
in personam 405
in rem 405

Jurisdiction
over registered ships 421
over security items 421

Justinian Code 406

Law
applicable 33, 55, 127,
243, 256, 385, 402, 432
autonomous 88
commercial 85, 93
contract, of 83, 88, 93
municipal 85
obligations, of 404
private 65
property, of 404
supranational 68
trade, of 93
transnational 68, 69, 85-
88

Law of treaties 20

League of Nations 2

Legal order 100, 101

Legal system 101

Legal title
(see: title)

Letter of credit
(see: payment)

Lex contractus 84, 97

Lex fori 452

Lex mercatoria 12, 59-61,
67-74, 85-93, 95, 102

Lex rei sitae 430-437

Liability 125
breach of contract, for
319
contractual 247
exclusion of 135
exemption from 146, 319
loss, for 240
release, from 253
seller, of 159, 162
- for intellectual property 179, 181
- limits 181
- restriction 179-182
tortious 247
vis major, and 223
- duty to pay 223
- exemption from damages
223
- right to interest 223

Limitation period 11, 243

Lois impératives 89

Loss
avoidance 248
calculation of 249

caused by 248
compensation of 243, 249
difference in price 249
due to non-performance 247
foreseeable 246, 247
goods, of 267, 269
insurance, and 269
liability for 240
mitigation of 250, 325
prevention of 269
profit, of 235-250, 351

Macroeconomic relations 82

Mandate 445

Mandatory rules
conventions as 387, 397
in general 36, 58, 80, 83,
97, 137, 139
provisions 99
standard forms, and 336
under Vienna Convention
(1980) 81, 135

Market economies 61

Microeconomic relations 82

Middle Ages 85-87

Mitigation
(see: damages, loss)

Modification
contract, of 130, 131
material 125
offer, of 125
terms, of 126

Monopoly 61
law-making, of 66
position 103

Movables 401-437
law applicable to 433-437
real rights to 435, 436

Multimodal transport 145

Municipal law 63, 66, 83
non-mandatory 65

National
legislation 60, 88
- conflict with 207
trade terms 280

Nationalism 90

Nationality
irrelevant 1, 24

Negligence
presumption of 269

Negotiable instruments 434

Negotiation
engaged in 119
practices 95
time of 247

New International Economic
Order (NIEO) 61, 81
and lex mercatoria 74

New law merchant 62, 73, 86
(see also: lex mercatoria)

New York Prescription Convention (1974) 9,10, 11,
386, 394, 395

Non-conformity of goods
avoidance of contract, and
349
damages, and 349-351
guarantee, and 349
irremedial defects 350
price reduction 349
remedies for 349
substitute goods 349
under ECE/UN contract conditions 349, 351

Nordic Sales of Goods Act
228

Notary public 85, 430

Notice
avoidance, of 195, 245
consignment, of 149
defects, of
- delayed transmission 174
- failure to arrive 174
- time 171, 173
dispatch of 291, 292
- as identification of
goods 291
- as moment of passing of
risk 291, 292
duty to give 255
effective
- at dispatch 194, 290
- on receipt 194
expiration of offer, on
128, 129
exception to notice re-
quirement 184, 185
failure to give 184-186
guarantee, and 173
handing over, on 149
impediment, of 255
modification of offer, on
125, 126
non-conformity, of
- description 172
- evidence 172
- remedy requested 171
performance, without 122
period of time 172, 184
reasonable time of 171
requirement of 76
seller, to
- of defects 171
- of non-conformity 166
sending of 243
shipment, on 149
specification of rights to
sue 184

Obligation
buyer, of 33, 203-205
- extent of 206
- payment of price 206, 223, 267
- take delivery, to 206, 230
buyer and seller, of 239-261
contractual 241
deliver goods, to 147, 284
exemption from 252-254
fulfillment, of 240
fundamental 244
handover to carrier 284
insurance, of 274
pay the price, to
- arrange for letter of credit 222
- apply for exchange license 222
- comply with statutory requirements 222
payment accommodations 274
place goods at buyer's disposal, to 284
providing information on production, of 230
security, and 404
seller, of 33, 133-199, 203-206
- carriage of goods 284
- change by contract 188
- discharge of 267
transportation 274

Offer
acceptance, and 111, 117, 312
acceptance of 118
addition to 125
assent to 128
catalogue as 119
characteristics of 209
definition of 124, 204
effects of termination 117
effective 121
invitation to make 119

irrevocable 116, 117
modification of 125
notice of 122
oral 118
price 120
rejection of 122-125
revocability 114
revocation of 116
silence to 122
terms of 124, 125
with fixed time 117

Opinio juris 98

Opting out
- under Vienna Convention 26
- under Agency Convention 456, 476-477

Optional rules 80-97, 135

Order 120, 127
receipt of 124

Ordre public 63, 65, 388

Ownership
acquisition of 407, 410
of first purchaser 407

Pacta sunt servanda 64, 86

Parties
autonomy 14, 58, 62, 64-88, 135, 387, 456, 457, 461
third 466-479

Passing of risk
according to trade usages 296
according to type of contract 297
breach of contract, and 295
carriage of goods, and 272

carriage not involved 294
conclusion of contract, at
    267-270
delivery, on 345
effect on breach of con-
    tract 265
goods sold in transit 293,
    346
handover
- documents, of 346
- first carrier, to 278
- place of 289
identification of goods,
    and 290
in international sales 265
    273
international transport
    265
in usages 265
latent defects 172
local transportation, and
    287
moment of 267-273, 289
non-mandatory rules 296
place of delivery 144
remedies of buyer, and 265
retroactive 293
risk of loading 289
rules of interpretation
    296
time of 160, 294
transfer
- of ownership 268
- of possession 268, 269,
    272
under
- CMEA conditions 282
- Vienna Convention 278
- ECE/UN conditions 283
- Incoterms 277, 280, 281,
    345
- ULIS 286

Pawn
possessory 413
non-possessory 422

Payment
against transport docu-
    ments 217
into bank account 213
bank operation, by 219
carriage expenses, of 273
change of place of busi-
    ness 213
claim for the balance 224
control over goods 216
costs to enable 220
currency of 219
date fixed, on 218
delay in 213, 214
delivery, on 295
documentary credit, by 346
early 164
equivalent of 219
exchange for goods, in 214
    216
guarantee of 220
handing over of goods, and
    216
impossibility
- due to currency 219
inspection of goods, and
    217
invoice, on 212
letter of credit, by 220,
    272
method of 219, 220
partial 219
place of 212-214
price, of 121, 122, 203,
    207, 218, 267, 372
recovery of price 224
reimbursement 243
request, without 218
requirement for 232
specific performance, as
    224
terms of 125
time for 214
undertakings for 220

Penalty 188, 318
clauses 323
contractual 322

Performance
assurance of 243
contract, of 25, 28, 98,
  130, 135, 411, 454
date of delivery, after
  194
deficiency in 241
delay in 317
delivery, and 275
difficulty of 245
enforced 319–322
exemption from 188
extent of 190
failure 76, 101, 188, 253,
  254
- self-made 255
impediment to 253–255
impossibility 317, 321
late 206
natura, in 321
non-performance 317
- precontractual 241
- responsibility for 318
notice of 122
part performance 197
real 320
risk of 267
seller, by
- period of 192
specific 190, 223, 240,
  320–329
suspension of 240–245
third party, of 254

Place of business 1, 24–29,
451–452
seller, of 29

Place of delivery 168

Place of destination 168
change of 213
choice of 204

Plain meaning rule 40

Pledge
acquisition of 421

conditions 413
contract 413
expiration of 425
export ban 413
non-possessory 421
registration of 413, 422
secured 421

Practice
established 117, 118
commercial 91, 149, 446
contractual 70
international 95

Prescription 172

Prescription Convention
(see: New York Convention
on Prescription, 1974)

Preservation
costs for 229, 235
goods, of 221–239, 251–261
refused goods, of 199
selling goods 222

Price
as basis for customs val-
  uation 366
awarded by court 223
balance of 235
calculable 120
calculation of 197, 207–
  209
commodities, of 292
costs, and 211
current 249
determinable 211
determination, time of 218
determined by practice 209
elements of 211
excessive 218
fixed by third party 209
fixing 121, 208
for spare parts 210
goods, of 135, 365
implicit agreement on 210

indicated in contract 211
invoice, per 211, 370
list 120
market price 209, 367, 378
method of calculation 208
net weight 208
open price 208
payment of 121, 207
reduction 197, 216, 348
regulation 207
sales price 365-378
terms relating to 125
usually charged 209, 218, 219

Principal 451-479
disclosed 463
named 463
undisclosed 444

Private international law 21-29, 95, 99, 387, 430-437
characteristic performance 29
choice of law by parties 29
conventions on 386
gap-filling, and 39, 409
substantive 387

Product liability 35, 356

Property
acquisition of 404, 411, 433
effect of contract on 137
law of 403
passing of 337, 423, 424
pledged 412
protection of 404
reservation of 402, 403, 420
right to retain 426
transfer of 133, 143, 144, 309, 402

Possession
bona fide 407
goods, of 408, 409
holding for s.o. 409
loss of 414
transfer of 140

Procurist 455

Public
international law 20, 22, 38
policy 77, 88, 129

Publicity
certificate, by 412
pledges, of 411
rights in rem 411
registration, by 412

Purchase 62, 246

Purchaser
bona fide 177, 413

Quality
(see also: goods)
certificate of 218
terms of 125

Quantity
(see: goods)

Ratification 28-31

Reasonability
circumstances 240
notice, of 240
person, of 95, 240
resale 248
replacement purchase 248
time 240, 248, 470
undertakings, of 95

Reciprocity 91

Regulations
exchange, on 129

export/import, on 129

Rejection
duties of buyer 231
goods, of 231
offer, of 122, 125

Remedies
breach of contract, for 134, 206, 347
- by buyer 203-207, 221
- by seller 143, 189, 193
breach of obligation to pay price 221
buyer, of 166, 189, 193
- avoidance 189, 193
- change by contract 188
- damages 189, 193
- performance 189
- price reduction 189
choice of 221
conformity of goods 147, 162
damages 222, 232, 347
delivery, for
- components 230
- defective goods, of 167, 162
- early/partial 152
- failure to take 232
part performance 197
payment not in time 222
price reduction 197
repair 189-192
seller, of 221, 230, 236, 352
- additional period of time 221, 222, 347, 354
- avoidance 221, 222, 232 347
- performance 221, 222, 232, 347
substitute goods 147, 162
third party rights 192
under
- ECE/UN contract conditions 347, 353

under-contd
- Incoterms 347

Repair
conformity 339
reasonable 192
as a remedy 189-192

Replacement of defective goods 165

Reservation
of conflict-of-laws rules 29

Revocation of offer 112, 114, 115

Rights in rem 412

Risk
allocation of 273-275
- handover of documents 277
- handover of goods before contract 292
delivery of goods, and 275, 276
insurance for 269
loss, of 269, 273
payment, of 267
transportation, during 273

Rome Convention on the Law Applicable to Contractual Obligations(1980) 392, 393, 396

Sales
auction, by 36
authority, by 36
character, optional 62
commodities 337
during transit 292
machinery, of 338
price 365-378

Sales contract 1, 26, 27,
82, 140, 143, 204, 453
category of goods 34
character of
– international/domestic
140, 26
characterization, of 453
consumer sales 34
sales excluded 34
time of delivery 292, 385
types of 33, 34, 136, 327

Sales of Goods Act (UK)
407

Secured debt 420

Security
acquisition of 402, 404,
420, 433
characterization, of 418
custody of goods 421
disclosure of 419, 420
expiration/extinction of
402, 404, 419, 420, 423,
425
interests in 401
loss, of 402
public disclosure 424
register 419, 421, 422
transfer of 419
validity of 421

Self-regulation 78

Seller
acceptance of offer 123
obligations of 143, 155–
165
rights and obligations
133–199

Settlement of disputes 125,
126, 340

Shipment
contract 343
of goods 27, 42, 131, 145

Ships
excluded 36
registered 35

Silence
as acceptance 123, 129
to offer 122

Sociological factors 65

Soft law 100

Sovereignty 77, 78, 88

Sphere of application
contracts, of 23
Sales Convention, of 23–38
Agency Convention, of 451–
456

Standard 67
conduct, of 102
contract 99
contract forms 71, 86, 90

Standard clauses
in general 70–72
reasonable person 45

Standard form contracts
arbitration, and 336
contradiction between 341
control of 357
force majeure 353
gaps in 336
interpretation of
– under ECE/UN contract
conditions 336
– under Incoterms 336
– under ULIS 337
mandatory rules 336
preference of 341
Vienna Convention, and the
351–356

Standard terms
control of 355

Takeover of goods 169

Taxes 375

Theory
identity, of 446
law, of 100
separation, of 445
transformation 22, 23

Time limits 137
reasonable 470

Title
acquisition of 407
legal 410
public disclosure of 408
registration of 408

Trade
agreements 140
center 99, 102
definitions
- American/foreign 280
intergovernmental 140
international 60-96, 126
law 88
practice 82, 95, 459
relations 90, 195
terms 94, 148, 280, 296
usages 71-96, 117, 118,
121, 128, 459

Traditio 407-410

Transaction
barter 377
commercial 57-80, 102-126,
372
companies, related 377
excluded 34
exclusive effect 412
international 56-80, 377
legal 410
secured 403, 421-422
standard value 365-378
trade, of 62, 96

Transfer
approval of 409
license 220
money abroad, of 220, 408
ownership, of 409, 419
principles of 408
property, of 401-437
risk of 260
security, of 419
third party, to 419
title, of 402, 403
- applicable law 402
- contractual prerequi-
sites 402
- in accordance with Vienna Convention 402

Translation
of conventions 41

Transportation of goods
arrangement for 151, 271
costs 374
documents 234
instructions for 151
means of 148, 149
multimodal 145, 296
passing of risk 265, 296
place of destination 148
port of shipment 282
seller, by 287
under CMR 388

Treaties
lawmaking 20
self-executing 20-22

Trustee 455

UCC (Uniform Commercial
Code/US) 40, 101, 114, 223
224, 269

UFL (Hague Uniform Law on
the Formation of Contracts
1964) 2-5, 22-45, 74, 81
386, 390, 401

ULIS (Hague Uniform Law on the International Sale of Goods, 1964) 2, 22-44, 74-95, 138-175, 205-276, 307-386

UNCITRAL (United Nations Commssion on International Trade Law) 2, 37-58, 75-91, 136, 141, 205, 208, 315
arbitration rules 92
cure lack of conformity 154
draft on formation 5
intellectual property, and 179
preparatory work 5, 37
working group 4

UNCTAD 81

UN Diplomatic Conference
limitation period, on 75
sale of goods, on   5, 29, 46, 135

UNESCO 62

UNIDROIT 2
agency 386, 443, 447, 448
restitution of goods 258
validity of contract 5, 42, 46, 87, 91, 315

Unification
contract law 307
control 361
deficiencies 308
fragmentary character 308
limited scope 308
private law 93
regional 31

Uniform law 21, 77-96, 138, 385, 393
conflict-of-laws rules, and 389

conventions on 387

Uniform rules 312, 392
conflict of laws 385
substantive 385-387

United Nations Convention on Contracts for the International Sale of Goods (1980) (see: Vienna Convention, also referred to as Sales Convention)

Unjust enrichment 210

Unreasonable expenses 169

Usages of trade 55-101, 204
about costs
- for packaging 212
- for transportation 212
as to packaging 208
as to price 212
as to price fixing 208
commercial 70-78, 296
documents, on 152
ECE/UN conditions 283
existence of 97, 137
formation of contract 126
international 143
interpretation of 56
reservations to 58
validity of 98

Validity
of contract 4
agreed contract terms 207
of provisions on price 207

Valuation 365

Value of goods 365
actual value 365-367
discount 375
market value 377
transaction value 365-367

Vienna Convention on the Law of Treaties (1969) 38, 393

Vienna Convention (= UN Convention on Contracts for the International Sale of Goods, 11 April 1980, also referred to as Sales Convention) 1, 21-27, 43, 56-64, 74-80, 83, 93-95, 111, 112, 115, 385-397, 450
accession to 8-10, 30
and agency 450, 453, 457, 458, 475-476
applicability 29, 31
avoidance 255-259
bank guarantee under 243
binding effect 31, 32
characteristics of 6
conflict-of-laws rules 19-41, 385-394, 426
confidentiality 153
definitions 6
delivery 120
denunciation 31
entry into force 8, 10, 31, 32
exclusion of 35, 95
final clauses 5, 31, 38
formation of contract 111-131, 135
freedom of parties 35, 430
gap-filling 19, 41-44, 430
general provisions 55
history 5, 12, 39, 205
implementory legislation 30
as infrastructure for standard form contracts 360
interpretation of 19, 39-45, 55, 76, 100, 136, 204, 360, 430
jurisdiction 214
law and justice 305
law seminars on 10
legal nature 20
as lex contractus 429
matters outside of scope 33-38, 404
modification 35, 95
non-mandatory 94, 207
rules on offer 111-131
obligations of parties 133-199, 203-236, 239-271
official languages 41
optional character 30-36, 426, 427, 429
passing of risk 265-298
performance 239-271
perspectives 12, 15
price fixing 121, 218
ratification 28, 30, 31, 38, 72
reservation 130, 135
rights and duties 38
- of buyer 203-236
- of seller 133-199
- common to buyer and seller 239-261
scope of application 10, 19, 24, 135, 402
and security interests 401-437
standard form contracts 335-361
third party rights 177
trade secrecy 153
translation of 41
uniform application 430

Vienna Diplomatic Conference 5, 29, 46, 208-253, 342

Warehouse receipt 153, 215, 234, 422

Warrant 422

Warranty
condition of purchase 127

Washington ICSID Conven-tion (1965) 385-399

Way bills
under CIM, CMR 215

Weaker party
protection of 83

Withdrawal
acceptance 112, 116
offer 115

World market 61